The

Tongue and Quill

AFH 33-337
27 MAY 2015
Incorporating Change 1, 19 November 2015
Certified Current 27 July 2016

Air Force Core Values

Integrity First, Service Before Self, and Excellence in All We Do.

Acknowledgement

The Tongue and Quill has been a valued Air Force resource for decades and many Airmen from our Total Force of uniformed and civilian members have contributed their talents to various editions over the years. This revision is built upon the foundation of governing directives and user's inputs from the unit level all the way up to Headquarters Air Force. A small team of Total Force Airmen from the Air University, the United States Air Force Academy, Headquarters Air Education and Training Command (AETC), the Air Force Reserve Command (AFRC), Air National Guard (ANG), and Headquarters Air Force compiled inputs from the field and rebuilt *The Tongue and Quill* to meet the needs of today's Airmen. The team put many hours into this effort over a span of almost two years to improve the content, relevance, and organization of material throughout this handbook. As the final files go to press it is the desire of *The Tongue and Quill* team to say thank you to every Airman who assisted in making this edition better; you have our sincere appreciation!

–*The Tongue and Quill* Team

BY ORDER OF THE

SECRETARY OF THE AIR FORCE

AIR FORCE HANDBOOK 33-337

27 MAY 2015

Incorporating Change 1, 19 November 2015

Communications and Information

THE TONGUE AND QUILL

ACCESSIBILITY: Publications and forms are available for downloading or ordering on the e-Publishing website at **http://www.e-publishing.af.mil**.

RELEASABILITY: There are no releasability restrictions on this publication.

OPR: SAF/CIO A6SS

Certified by: SAF/CIO A6SS
(Col Heather L. McGee)

Supersedes: AFH33-337, 1 August 2004

Pages: 370

The men and women of the United States Air Force must communicate clearly and effectively to carry out our missions. Although we live in an era of rapid personal and mass communication that was barely imagined just a few years ago, our Air Force still requires face-to-face briefings, background papers, and staff packages to keep the mission moving forward. This handbook, together with Air Force Manual (AFMAN) 33-326, *Preparing Official Communications*, provides the information to ensure clear communications—written or spoken.

Send recommended changes or comments using AF Form 847, *Recommendation for Change of Publication*, to the Air Force Cyberspace Strategy & Policy Division (SAF/CIO A6SS) at USAF.pentagon.saf-cio-a6.mbx.a6ss-workflow@mail.mil. Ensure that all records created as a result of processes prescribed in this publication are maintained IAW AFMAN 33-363, *Management of Records*, and disposed of IAW the Air Force Records Disposition Schedule (RDS) in the Air Force Records Information Management System (AFRIMS). The use of the name or mark of any specific manufacturer, commercial product, commodity, or service in this publication does not imply endorsement by the Air Force.

SUMMARY OF CHANGES

This edition has been substantially revised to 1) standardize the format and layout for readability; 2) improve the organization of chapters and content within each chapter; 3) provide additional material on preparing to write and speak, writing with focus, communicating to persuade, research, meetings, briefings and listening; 4) clarify guidance for Air Force written products with formatted examples for each product; and 5) update guidance for electronic communications. A margin bar (|) indicates newly revised material

Table of Contents

PART I: COMMUNICATION BASICS 1
    Plain Language Requirement: It's the Law 2
    Plain Language in the Air Force: Be Clear, Concise and Specific 2

CHAPTER 1: A Basic Philosophy of Communication 3
    What Do We Mean by Communication? 4
    Communication, Teamwork and Leadership 5
    Principles of Effective Communication 5

CHAPTER 2: Seven Steps to Effective Communication (Overview) 8
    Preparing to Write and Speak (Steps 1-4) 9
    Drafting, Editing, and Feedback (Steps 5-7) 11
    Seven Steps to Effective Communication: Quick Reference List 13

PART II: PREPARING TO WRITE AND SPEAK 14

CHAPTER 3: Step 1 (Analyze Purpose and Audience) 15
    Key Questions 16
    What Is My Purpose? 16
    Drafting a Purpose Statement 17
    Analyzing Purpose: Other Issues 18
    Audience Analysis: The Human Factor 18
    Tips for Success 20

CHAPTER 4: Step 2 (Research Your Topic) 23
    Start Smart 24
    Getting Data 25
    Search Engines and Databases 26
    Evaluate Your Sources 30
    Useful Online Resources 31

CHAPTER 5: Step 3 (Support Your Ideas) 41
    The Logic of Arguments: Fundamentals 42
    Evidence: Proving Your Point 44
    Characteristics of Good Supporting Evidence 45
    Logical Errors: Flawed Arguments 46
    Arguments, Truth and Persuasion 52

CHAPTER 6: Step 4 (Organize and Outline) 53
    Organizing: Finalizing Your Purpose Statement and Bottom Line 54
    The Outline: Why Do I Need One? 55
    Outlining the Body: Pick a Pattern 59

PART III: WRITING WITH FOCUS 63

CHAPTER 7: Step 5 (Draft) 65

Drafting: Basic Philosophy 66
Drafting Effective Paragraphs 69
Drafting Effective Sentences 73
Overcoming Writer's Block 90

CHAPTER 8: Step 6 (Edit) 91

Editing vs. Feedback 92
Editing Fundamentals 92
Editing Efficiently: A Three-Step Approach 93
Drafting Basics: Did You Apply Them? 96
Common Grammar Traps 97
Common Writing Errors 101

CHAPTER 9: Step 7 (Fight for Feedback and Get Approval) 103

Fighting For Feedback 104
Getting Approval: Staff Coordination 106

PART IV: SPEAKING AND LISTENING 110

CHAPTER 10: Air Force Speaking 111

Verbal Communication 112
Non-Verbal Communication 113
Overcoming Anxiety: Some Simple Steps 114
Common Nonverbal Quirks 115
Delivery Formats: Impromptu, Prepared and Manuscript 115
Preparing Your Slides 118

CHAPTER 11: Effective Listening Strategies 123

Understanding Hearing and Listening 123
Informative, Critical and Empathic Listening 124
Better Listening 129
Overcoming Barriers to Listening 130

PART V: WORKPLACE CHALLENGES 132

CHAPTER 12: Electronic Communications and Social Media 133

Electronic Mail (E-Mail) 134
Social Media 142
Instant Messaging (IM) and Texting 146
Telephones, Voice Mail and Fax 147
Electronic Communications Glossary 150

CHAPTER 13: Meetings 153
- Planning an Effective Meeting 154
- Running Your Meeting 157
- Group Dynamics and Fun 159

PART VI: DOCUMENT STANDARDS 161

CHAPTER 14: The Official Memorandum 163
- The Heading Section 164
- The Text of the Official Memorandum 169
- The Closing Section 169
- Additional Information 173
- Attachments 174
- The Official Memorandum: Examples 177
- Spelling Checkers: Before You Sign 190

CHAPTER 15 The Personal Letter 191
- The Heading Section 192
- The Text of the Personal Letter 193
- The Closing Section 193
- Forms of Address, Salutation and Complimentary Close 194
- Military Ranks and Abbreviations 211
- The Personal Letter: Examples 213

CHAPTER 16: Air Force "Papers" 219
- Form and Function 219
- Point Paper 222
- Talking Paper 223
- Bullet Background Paper 224
- Background Paper 226
- Position Paper 228

CHAPTER 17: The Staff Study 229
- Purpose 229
- Process: Critical Thinking and Problem Solving 230
- Writing the Report 232
- Complete the Study 235

CHAPTER 18: The Staff Package 237
- SSS Fundamentals 238
- Completing the SSS Form 238
- Assembling the Package 241
- Coordinating the Package 242
- Sample SSS and eSSS 243

CHAPTER 19: Writing Better Bullet Statements 247
Getting Started 248
Drafting Accomplishment-Impact Bullet Statements 248
Polishing Accomplishment-Impact Bullet Statements 253
Bullet Statement Mechanics 256

CHAPTER 20: The Official Biography 257
The Official Biography: Fundamentals 257
Getting Started 258
Associated Press (AP) Style Guidance for Official Biographies 258
Official Biography Elements 259

CHAPTER 21: The Résumé 265
Function and Organization 266
Seven Steps to an Effective Résumé 267
Things to Include 268
Things to Omit 269
The Résumé Cover Letter 269
Examples 269

CHAPTER 22: Envelopes and Mail 275
Envelope Fundamentals 276
Envelope Anatomy 276
Address Format Standards 277
USPS Mail Terminology 281

CHAPTER 23: Air Force Publications/Forms 283
Dual Responsibilities in Developing Publications/Forms 283
Publications/Forms Process Overview 284
Plain Language Challenge 284

PART VII: WRITING MECHANICS 285

CHAPTER 24: Writing Terminology 287
Common Grammatical and Writing Terms 288
Irregular Verbs 294

CHAPTER 25: Punctuation 295
Punctuation: Why Do We Need It? 295
Open and Closed Punctuation 296
Punctuating Terms in a Series 296
Punctuation Usage Guide 297
Summary 330

CHAPTER 26: Abbreviations 331
- Definition and Implications 331
- Types of Abbreviations 332
- General Guidelines 334
- Common Abbreviations.. 335
- Researcher's Guide to Abbreviations 340

CHAPTER 27: Capitalization 341
- General Capitalization Guidelines.. 341
- Specific Capitalization Guidelines 342

CHAPTER 28: Numbers 355
- Three General Rules 355
- Specific Guidance.. 356
- Summing Things Up... 362

PART I:

COMMUNICATION BASICS

Plain Language Requirement: It's the Law

Agencies of the US Government have a long history of trying to improve their ability to communicate with the public they serve. Public Law 111-274, *Plain Writing Act of 2010*, is the most recent mandate to target unclear language in government documents. The *Plain Writing Act* is implemented in the Department of Defense (DoD) by DoD Instruction 5025.13, *DoD Plain Language Program*, which "promotes the use of clear, concise, and well organized language in documents to effectively communicate with intended audiences." **Everything you write in your official Air Force capacity needs to comply with the *Plain Writing Act* as directed by *DoDI 5025.13*.** It should also comply with the specifics of Air Force Instruction (AFI) 33-360, *Publications and Forms Management*, for any Air Force publications. So, when you are preparing to write or speak, and before putting pen to paper for a report or publication, remember to keep it plain.

Plain Language in the Air Force: Be Clear, Concise and Specific

When drafting new publications or revising existing ones, authors will follow the Federal Plain Language Guidelines available at http://www.plainlanguage.gov, as appropriate. Specialized language may be required depending on the intended audience, but language and content organization should be as clear as possible.

–AFI 33-360, para. 6.5.10

The instruction also provides three plain language concepts (be clear, be concise, and be specific) with tips on how to write to achieve each concept. Keep these concepts in mind as you work prepare to write any document. These concepts will help with your briefings, too!

Plain Language Concepts (Adapted from AFI 33-360, Table 6.3)	
Be Clear	• Use plain language whenever possible; avoid jargon • Avoid overuse of acronyms; when used, make certain acronyms are established [written out] upon first use • Use the active voice • Format documents so that they are easy to read and understand • Use tables and figures if that's the best way to show information
Be Concise	• Remove unnecessary words • Focus sentences on a single thought or action; strive to write sentences with no more than 20 words • Focus paragraphs on a single main point; strive to write paragraphs with no more than seven sentences
Be Specific	• Include only information that the reader must know • Use words with precise meaning • Include details that are directly relevant to the main point

CHAPTER 1:

A Basic Philosophy of Communication

This chapter covers:

- What do We Mean by Communication?
- Communication, Teamwork and Leadership
- Principles of Effective Communication

This is an exciting time to be in the United States Air Force! Our mission and our operations tempo reflect the larger world around us—a world of rapidly accelerating technology and nearly unlimited access to information. Airmen successfully accomplish more missions with fewer people than ever before and there is a constant battle to cover the bases with limited resources.

What Do We Mean by Communication?

Communication is defined as the process of sharing ideas, information and messages with others. In the Air Force, most communication involves speaking and writing, but this definition also includes nonverbal communication, such as body language, graphics, electronic messages, etc.

Any communication can be broken into three parts: the **sender**, the **message** and the **audience**. For communication to be successful, the audience must not only get the message, but must interpret the message in the way the sender intended.

> **com·mu·ni·ca·tion** *n*
> 1. an act or instance of transmitting information
> 2. a verbal or written message
> 3. a process by which information is exchanged between individuals through a common system of symbols, signs or behavior

Since communication requires effort, it should always have a purpose. If the purpose isn't clear to the audience, you have a problem! Most Air Force communication is intended to direct, inform (or educate), persuade or inspire. Often the sender has some combination of these motives in mind.

Chapter 3 describes the process of determining your purpose and audience in detail, but here are a few examples of Air Force communication targeted toward a specific objective:

1. The headquarters staff (the sender); writes a new policy on trip report procedures (the message); and sends a copy to all subordinate units (the audience).
   Purpose of this communication: to direct.

2. An aircraft technician (the sender); reports the results of an aircraft engine inspection (the message); to his supervisor (the audience).
   Purpose of this communication: to inform.

3. A branch chief (the sender); requests additional funding for new office furniture (the message); in a meeting with the division chief (the audience).
   Purpose of this communication: to persuade.

Most communication outside the Air Force falls in these categories as well. If you look carefully, you can see the efforts to inform, direct, persuade or inspire in this common conversation. Can you spot the purpose of each of the following sentences?

"You didn't wash the car like you promised."

"But Dad! Everyone else is going to the beach. Why can't I go?"

"Son, I know you're a fine young man and fine young men keep their promises."

"Aw, Dad…"

"Wash the car NOW!"

CHAPTER 1: A Basic Philosophy of Communication

Communication, Teamwork and Leadership

Communication skills are vitally important in any environment where teamwork is important. Simply put, communication enables us to come together to accomplish things better as a group than we can accomplish as individuals. Communication skills are particularly important for leaders. The ability to communicate a vision and direction, to motivate and inspire others and to persuade our superiors are all essential in bringing people together to achieve a common goal.

The military environment is unique and much of its uniqueness requires extraordinary communication skills. We operate highly technical equipment in a lethal environment and we are held to very high standards by the country we serve. Miscommunication can cause expensive mistakes, embarrass our organization and in some cases cause accidents or even death. This handbook is designed to give you tools and ideas that will help you learn to communicate better … and to teach others as well.

The call to arms to improve our communication skills is clear. Both the Air Force and the large culture we live in are drowning in a sea of information. Around-the-clock media coverage, universal electronic mail (e-mail) and the overwhelming amount of data on the Internet make it difficult for us to sift out the valuable information we need to accomplish our mission. Now, more than ever, it's important to communicate with clarity and focus.

The only way to become a better writer and speaker is to work at it—there are no short cuts. The good news is that service in the Air Force will provide plenty of opportunities for you to improve. Your communication skills will become stronger with practice, regardless of your initial ability, and this book is designed to help you on your journey.

Principles of Effective Communication

Once you accept that communication is important, it's important to understand what makes communication succeed and what makes it fail. Most mistakes are caused by forgetting one of five principles of good communication. This section addresses these core principles for strong writing and speaking, which we've organized to spell out the acronym FOCUS.

FOCUS Principles

- **Focused:** Address the issue, the whole issue, and nothing but the issue.
- **Organized:** Systematically present your information and ideas.
- **Clear:** Communicate with clarity and make each word count.
- **Understanding:** Understand your audience and its expectations.
- **Supported:** Use logic and support to make your point.

FOCUSED: Address the Issue, the Whole Issue and Nothing but the Issue

The first hallmark of good communication is that it is focused. In a staff or academic environment, writing and speaking often attempts to answer a question provided by either a boss or an instructor. In such situations, ***answer the question, the whole question and nothing but the question***. Failure to focus comes in three forms:

1. **Answering the wrong question.** This happens when we don't understand the assignment or what the audience really wants. Have you ever written what you thought was an excellent paper, only to be told you answered the wrong question or you missed the point? Have you ever asked someone a question and received a long answer that had nothing to do with what you asked?

2. **Answering only part of the question.** If a problem or question has multiple parts, sometimes we work out the easiest or most interesting part of the solution and forget the unpleasant remainder.

3. **Adding irrelevant information.** Here the communicator answers the question, but mixes in information that is interesting but unnecessary. Though the answer is complete, it's hard to understand—it's like finding that needle in the haystack.

> **fo·cus** *n*
> 1. a state or condition permitting clear perception or understanding: direction;
> 2. a center of activity, attraction, or attention; a point of concentration; directed attention: emphasis.

Failure to focus can really hurt staff communication. Time and time again, our efforts crash and burn because we don't carefully read the words or really listen to the speaker for the real message … for the specific question! Most executive officers will tell you that failing to answer the question is one of the primary reasons staff packages are returned. Chapter 3 provides suggestions on how to be clear in your purpose and avoid these problems.

ORGANIZED: Systematically Present Your Information and Ideas

Good organization means your material is presented in a logical, systematic manner. This helps your audience understand you without reading your words over and over, trying to sort out what you're really trying to say.

When writing or speaking is not well organized, audiences become easily confused or impatient and may stop reading or listening. Even if you're providing useful, relevant information, your audience may underestimate its value and your own credibility.

Chapter 6 is full of suggestions on how to organize well. Problems with organization are relatively easy to fix and the payoffs are enormous. In our limited time and resource environments, a little effort on your part will save your audience a lot of time and pain.

CLEAR: Communicate With Clarity and Make Each Word Count

This principle covers two interrelated ideas. First, to communicate clearly, we need to understand the rules of language—how to spell and pronounce words and how to assemble and punctuate sentences. Second, we should get to the point, not hide our ideas in a jungle of words.

People are quick to judge your credibility through your mastery of language to convey ideas. Acceptable English is part of the job, so commit to improving any problems you may have. Developing strong language skills is a lot like developing strong muscles—steady commitment produces steady improvement. Always remember that progress, not perfection, is the goal.

Grammar scares most of us, but the good news is that many common mistakes can be corrected by understanding a few rules. Start by scanning our section on editing sentences, phrases and words. If you want to dig deeper, then check out some of the books and Internet sites that address grammar and writing—contact your local librarian or our *References* section for some suggestions.

Using language correctly is only half of the battle, though—many Air Force writers and speakers cripple themselves with bureaucratic jargon, big words and lots of passive voice. These bad habits make it hard to understand the message.

UNDERSTANDING: Understand Your Audience and Its Expectations

If you want to share an idea with others, it helps to understand their current knowledge, views and level of interest in the topic. If you've been asked to write a report, it helps to understand the expected format and length of the response, the due date, the level of formality and any staffing requirements. It's easy to see how mistakes in understanding your audience can lead to communication problems, and I'm sure you've watched others make this mistake. Check out Chapter 3 for some helpful hints on audience analysis.

SUPPORTED: Use Logic and Support to Make Your Point

Most writers and speakers try to inform or persuade their audience. Part of the communicator's challenge is to assemble and organize information to help build his or her case. Support and logic are the tools used to build credibility and trust with our audience.

> **sup·port** *n* information that substantiates a position; *v* to furnish evidence for a position.

Nothing cripples a clearly written, properly punctuated paper quicker than a fractured fact or a distorted argument. Avoiding this pitfall is most difficult, even for good writers and speakers. Logic is tough to teach and learn because it challenges the highest levels of human intellect—the ability to think in the abstract. We slip into bad habits at an early age and it takes effort to break them. Chapter 4 provides practical advice on how to use support and logic to enhance your effectiveness as a speaker and how to avoid common mistakes.

SUMMARY: In this chapter, we defined communication as the process of sharing ideas, information and messages with others and described how effective communication enables military personnel to work together. To help writers and speakers stay on target, we introduced five FOCUS principles of effective communication. In the next chapter, we'll describe a systematic approach to help you attain these principles and meet your communication goals.

CHAPTER 2:

Seven Steps to Effective Communication (Overview)

> ***This chapter covers:***
> - Preparing to Write and Speak (Steps 1–4)
> - Drafting, Editing, and Feedback (Steps 5–7)
> - Seven Steps to Effective Communication: Quick Reference List

Chapter 1 introduced the FOCUS principles of effective communication (Focused, Organized, Clear, Understanding and Supported). In this chapter, we'll introduce a seven-step approach to effective communication based on the FOCUS principles. Here you'll get the big picture introduction, but later chapters will describe each of the seven steps in greater detail.

You can tailor the steps to your own style and approach, but completing each of them will increase your chances of speaking and writing success. These steps are not always used in sequence and for long and complicated assignments you may find yourself moving back and forth between steps. That's OK—it's better to deviate from a plan than to have no plan at all.

Preparing to Write and Speak (Steps 1-4)

Like many things, good communication requires preparation and the first four steps lay the groundwork for the drafting process. Though much of this seems like common sense, you'd be surprised at how many people skip the preparation and launch into writing sentences and paragraphs (or speaking "off the cuff"). DON'T DO IT! Good speaking or writing is like building a house—you need a good plan and a firm foundation.

> **Seven Steps For Effective Communication**
> 1. Analyze Purpose and Audience
> 2. Research Your Topic
> 3. Support Your Ideas
> 4. Organize and Outline
> 5. Draft
> 6. Edit
> 7. Fight for Feedback and Get Approval

1. Analyze Purpose and Audience

> *To effectively communicate, we must realize that we are all different in the way we perceive the world and use this understanding as a guide to our communication with others.*
>
> —Anthony Robbins

Too many writers launch into their project without a clear understanding of their purpose or audience. This is a shame—a few minutes spent on this step can save hours of frustration later and help determine whether you end up looking like an eagle or a turkey. You're much more likely to hit the target if you know what and who you're aiming at.

Carefully analyzing your purpose helps with FOCUS Principle #1: "Focused—answer the question, the whole question and nothing but the question." In some cases, if you take a hard look at the purpose, you might find that a formal paper or briefing might not be needed. You'd be startled at how many briefings, paper documents and electronic messages are processed in a typical day in a major command (MAJCOM) or wing. Formal communication takes effort and costs money—make sure you don't unnecessarily add to everybody's workload.

If you take the time to "understand your audience" (FOCUS Principle #4) and think about their current knowledge, interest and motives, you'll be better able to tailor your message so that you'll accomplish your purpose, regardless of what it is. Instructing a hostile audience about changes in medical benefits will be different than inspiring a friendly audience at a Veteran's Day celebration and writing for the general's signature will be different than writing for the base webpage. Chapter 3 has lots of helpful suggestions about analyzing purpose and audience.

2. Research Your Topic

Truth is generally the best vindication against slander.

–Abraham Lincoln

Remember that FOCUS Principle #5 states good communication should be *supported* with information relevant to your point. Step Two—"Research your topic"—gives you the raw material to build your case.

For many of us, "research" sounds intimidating—it brings back memories of painful school projects and hostile librarians who wouldn't let us sneak coffee into the building. Don't let the idea of research scare you. In the context of the seven-step approach, research is the process of digging up information that supports your communication goals. Think of it as "doing your homework" to get smart on your communication topic. Chapter 4 is full of helpful advice on how to approach the challenge. For those of you interested in academic research, Appendix 2 has additional information on the topic.

3. Support Your Ideas

If you wish to converse with me, define your terms.

–Voltaire

Often our communication goal involves persuasion. In such cases, throwing information at our audiences isn't enough—we have to assemble and arrange our facts to support our position. Different kinds of information gathered during the research process can be used to form a *logical argument*. A logical argument is not a disagreement or a fight—it's how we assemble information to make decisions and solve problems.

At the same time we are trying to persuade others, others are trying to persuade us and not all their arguments are airtight. A *logical fallacy* is a weakness or failure in the logic of an argument. Chapter 5 describes logical arguments and several common logical fallacies—allowing you to recognize mistakes in other's arguments and avoid them in your own.

Building logical arguments are part of everyday life. We build arguments when we decide which new car to buy, who to nominate for a quarterly award or how we should spend our training budget. You'll find that many of the ideas described in Chapter 5 are part of the way you think, even if you didn't know the formal terminology.

4. Organize and Outline

Organizing is our core principle. It is our north star.

–Anna Burger

You know your purpose and audience, you've done your homework—it's time to deliver your message, right? Not so fast! Before starting to write sentences and paragraphs (or deliver your speech), you'll save time and frustration by organizing your thoughts and developing an outline of how you are going to present your information.

Successful communicators organize their material logically and in a sequence that leads their audience from one point to the next. Audiences often "tune out" a speaker or writer who rambles on without a logical pattern. Poorly organized essays are a common complaint in both civilian and military schools. Save yourself and your audience a lot of pain—read chapter 6 to learn different patterns and techniques to organize and outline your material.

FOCUS Principle #2 states that good communication should be *organized* so that the audience can efficiently understand your point. You've taken the first steps towards accomplishing this principle when you take the time to organize and outline your work before starting to write ... but how you actually draft and edit paragraphs will take you the rest of the way.

Drafting, Editing, and Feedback (Steps 5-7)

The first four steps are identical for both writing and speaking assignments, but the drafting and editing processes are somewhat different for the two forms of communication. In this section we'll describe the steps from a writing perspective and chapters 9 and 10 will describe how the steps are adapted for Air Force speaking.

5. Draft

> *It is a draft—a draft which should be discussed and improved.*
>
> –Michael Barnier

When we think about the writing process, we immediately think of drafting sentences and paragraphs. If you're uncomfortable with your writing skills, this step usually causes the most anxiety. The good news is that your work on Steps 1-4 will make the drafting process less painful and more efficient.

Once you've completed the preliminaries and are ready to write, there are several practical ways to ensure you connect with your readers.

- First, get to the point quickly—use one or more introductory paragraphs to state your purpose up front. Most Air Force readers don't have the time or patience to read a staff paper written like a mystery novel with a surprise ending.

- Second, organize your paragraphs so the readers know where you're leading them and use transitions to guide them along.

- Third, make sure your sentences are clear and direct. Cut through the jargon and passive voice, use the right word for the job and be as concise as possible. Finally, summarize your message in a concluding paragraph that connects all the dots and completes the message.

Chapter 7 is full of practical advice on drafting and it takes a top-down approach. It begins with preliminaries such as writing tone and formats, transitions to paragraph construction, provides practical tips on writing clear, vigorous sentences, then concludes with advice on overcoming writer's block.

6. Edit

Editing is the same thing as quarreling with writers—same thing exactly.

–Harold Ross

Experienced writers know that editing should be a separate, distinct process from drafting. When you draft, you create something new. When you edit, you shift from creator to critic. This change in roles can be tough, and no one wants to admit that the draft may not be as good as he thought. Remember that criticism and judgment are inevitable in communication. The better you are at critically evaluating and correcting your own writing, the fewer people will be doing it for you.

There are two important aspects of the editing process—WHAT you are editing for and HOW to edit efficiently. What to edit for is simple—remember those FOCUS principles from chapter 1? How to edit is a little more complicated, but we recommend starting with the big picture and working down to details like spelling and punctuation. Ironically, many people do just the opposite; they focus on details first. Some even think that editing is all about the details. Nothing could be farther from the truth. Though details are part of editing, they're only part of the puzzle. Chapter 8 provides information on editing fundamentals and procedures.

7. Fight for Feedback and Get Approval

There is no failure. Only feedback.

–Robert G. Allen

When you've completed the editing process and done what you can to improve your communication, it's time to move outside yourself to get feedback. We are all limited in our ability to criticize our own work, and sometimes an outside opinion can help us see how to improve or strengthen our communication. Your objective is to produce the best possible product; don't let pride of authorship and fear of criticism close your mind to suggestions from other people. Also, what we write or say at work often must be approved by our chain of command through a formal coordination process. Your supervisor needs to see it, the executive officer needs to see it, then the big boss and so on. Chapter 9 provides tips on how to give and receive feedback and how to manage the coordination process.

SUMMARY: In this chapter, we summarized a systematic process—**Seven Steps to Effective Communication**—that will help you achieve the five FOCUS principles. These steps will help you improve your writing and speaking products. Each step is described in greater detail in subsequent chapters. The table on the next page lists the seven steps for effective communication and where you can find more information about each step in this handbook.

Seven Steps to Effective Communication: Quick Reference List

THE BASIC STEPS...	FOR MORE DETAILS, REFER TO:
1. Analyze Purpose and Audience	Chapter 3
2. Research Your Topic	Chapter 4
3. Support Your Ideas	Chapter 5
4. Organize and Outline	Chapter 6
5. Draft	Chapter 7 (Writing); Chapter 11 (Speaking)
6. Edit	Chapter 8 (Writing); Chapter 11 (Speaking)
7. Fight for Feedback and Get Approval	Chapter 9

PART II:

PREPARING TO WRITE AND SPEAK

CHAPTER 3:

Step 1
(Analyze Purpose and Audience)

> *This chapter covers:*
> - Key Questions
> - What Is My Purpose?
> - Drafting a Purpose Statement
> - Analyzing Purpose: Other Issues
> - Audience Analysis: The Human Factor
> - Tips for Success

In Chapter 2, we introduced the Seven Steps for Effective Communication. Now we're going to discuss the first of these steps in further detail. First and most importantly, you can save yourself a lot of work by asking yourself if the briefing slides, memo, e-mail or meeting is going to help get the mission done or a task accomplished. In today's fast-paced work environment, we don't need to create unnecessary work for anyone.

Once you're clear on the need for communication, Step 1 requires you to get clear on your purpose and audience. As you'll see in this chapter, these are not two distinct categories. The characteristics of your audience will influence all parts of your message and your purpose often involves influencing your audience. To begin analyzing purpose and audience you should consider several key questions.

Key Questions

Masters in the art of communication stay focused on their objective and approach audience analysis seriously. The more you know about your audience, the more comfortable you will feel. Where do you start in this? Here are some questions to help you begin to analyze your purpose and audience and get you on the right track. We'll discuss many of them in more detail later in the chapter.

- What is the overall purpose of the communication? Are you trying to make a change in your audience? Are you writing just to inform your audience?

- If you had one sentence or 30 seconds to explain your specific objective, what would you write or say? (What is your "elevator speech" on the subject?)

- What format are you using to communicate? How much time do you have to prepare?

- Is there anything unusual about the time and place your audience will receive your communication (is it 1600 on a Friday before a holiday weekend)? A lengthy informative e-mail sent out late on a Friday afternoon may not be appreciated or even worse—not read!

- Who will read this communication? Your boss? Your subordinates? Civilians? The answers will have a direct bearing on the tone and formality of your message.

- What are the education levels, career fields and areas of expertise of your readers and/or listeners?

- Do you need to supply any background information, explanation of terms, or other information to your audience? Does your audience have experience with the ideas and concepts you are presenting?

- What does the audience think of you? Are you known and trusted?

- Is your audience motivated to hear and/or read your communication?

- Do you need to coordinate your communication?

- Are you making promises your organization will have to keep?

What Is My Purpose?

Most Air Force writing or speaking falls under one of the following purposes: **to direct, inform, persuade or inspire.** Your task is to think about the message you want to send (the "what") and make some sort of determination of what your purpose is (the "why"). Some communication has primary and secondary purposes, so don't kill yourself trying to make sure your message fits neatly in one of these categories. Once you decide the purpose, you'll know where to place the emphasis and what the tone of your communication should be. Here's a quick synopsis of these purposes and how they might work for you.

- **To Direct.** *Directive communication* is generally used to pass on information describing actions you expect to be carried out by your audience. The emphasis in directive communication is clear, concise directions and expectations of your audience.

- **To Inform.** The goal of *informative communication* is to pass on information to the audience. The communication is successful if the audience understands the message exactly the way the speaker or writer intended. The emphasis in informative communication is clear, direct communication with accurate and adequate information tailored to the education and skill levels of the audience. Audience feedback and interaction may be appropriate in some situations to make sure they "got the message."

- **To Persuade.** *Persuasive communication* is typically used when you are trying to "sell" your audience on a new idea, new policy, new product or change in current operations. Though emotions are one tool of persuasion, most persuasive communication in the workplace requires convincing evidence put together in a logical way. Audience analysis is critical because different audiences have different views on what evidence is convincing. Since the purpose is to guide your audience to a specific course of action, you cannot overlook tone and delivery. Chapter 5, *Supporting Your Ideas*, describes how to build your persuasive skills.

- **To Inspire.** One final purpose for writing or speaking that doesn't get much attention but is frequently used in the military is to *inspire*. As you climb the leadership ladder you will increasingly be requested to perform retirements, promotions, commander's calls—opportunities where you will want to inspire the audience with your profound insight on someone's career or possibly your philosophy on leadership. Although protocol drives portions of these events, the opportunity to send a personal message and inspire the audience should not be overlooked. The emphasis in inspirational communication is delivery, a thorough knowledge of your topic and likewise your audience.

Regardless of whether your mission is to direct, inform, persuade or inspire, there are general principles that apply to almost all communication. See "Tips for Success" at the end of this chapter to round out your portfolio for analyzing purpose and audience.

Drafting a Purpose Statement

OK, you have a feel for the general purpose of your communication (to direct, inform, persuade or inspire), but what is your "bottom line" you need to communicate to your audience? If you have difficulty nailing down your objective, your audience will be equally confused.

One way to make sure you're clear on your objective is to write a *purpose statement,* which is one sentence that captures the essence of what you're trying to do—your "bottom line." It's the one sentence you'd keep if you were allowed only one. Developing a clear purpose statement will help you in two ways:

- It will help you *focus* as you develop your communication.
- It will help your audience *focus when* you deliver your message.

Think about it; your audience wants a clear statement of your position and where you are going. This is especially true when your audience consists of higher-ranking individuals with many demands on their time and issues requiring their attention. Now, let's look at some examples of **draft purpose statements**:

- To inform individuals in the Civil Engineering Squadron about new policies on hazardous waste disposal.

- To encourage (inspire) at-risk high school students to work hard, stay in school and have hope in the future.
- To persuade the division chief to buy three laptops for use during official travel.

As we'll mention in chapter 5, you may update your purpose statement after researching your topic. (For example, you might find out you need four laptops, not three.) Even if it isn't locked down, a draft statement will help guide your research and support efforts.

Analyzing Purpose: Other Issues

Knowing your "bottom line" is not the end of analyzing purpose. Here are some questions you want to ask to make sure you look at all parts of the equation. The answers will help refine your purpose and shape your entire project.

- **What format will I use to communicate?** Today's commanders are increasingly more vigilant of the value of their troops' time—and their own. Make sure that the communication is required and that you select the most appropriate format for delivery. Think about how much time you will have to deliver your message before you go any further. Will you have 2 minutes in a staff meeting with the general that starts in 1 hour? One hour at your commander's call next week?

- **How much time do I have to prepare my communication?** The breadth and scope of a report your boss needs the next day will be different than a staff project due by the end of the fiscal year. What's the suspense? How long is it going to take to write the report? Be sure to budget adequate time for all "Seven Steps," especially "Researching your Topic" (Step 2), "Drafting" (Step 5) and "Editing" (Step 6). If coordination is part of the master plan, it will also affect your timelines.

There's more to successful communication than getting clear on purpose. There's always that human factor and in the communication game that translates to *analyzing your audience*.

Audience Analysis: The Human Factor

As stated in chapter 1, all communication involves a sender, a message and an audience. "A" sends the message (either verbally or in writing) with a specific intended meaning to "B." "B" receives the message, processes the message and attaches perceived meaning to the message. This is where it gets interesting. Did the intended message actually get to "B"? Was the perceived meaning what "A" intended? If not, why not?

Know Yourself

Before you look around, look in the mirror. Knowing your strengths and weaknesses will help you meet your communication goals.

- Do you do better with certain communication formats than others? Be aware of your personal strengths. If you know that you'd rather be buried in a pile of fire ants than speak in public, you may choose to send your message in writing—if that's an option. If not, spend some time in chapter 10 and improve your speaking skills!

- Are you an inexperienced briefer that needs notes? If so, make sure they are written in a format that is easy to refer to while the general is listening intently and watching the beads of sweat form on your forehead.

- Do you have expertise in the area? If so ... great! But don't lose your audience with lots of lingo and unfamiliar jargon. You may think it's cool; others may not. On the other hand, if you lack expertise in the area, you will need to focus your research to beef up on unfamiliar territory. Remember, there's always someone in the crowd that knows as much or more, so you want to be as prepared as possible to answer potential questions.

- What is your relationship with the audience? Are you personally familiar with them? You may be able to present a more informal briefing or written document if you know this is acceptable to the audience. See the section on tone for more guidance.

Know Your Organization

Once you've taken a hard look at yourself, take a look at your work environment and your organization. In the military we rarely act or speak in a vacuum. Often we represent our organization, unit or functional area and must understand them and accommodate their views, capabilities or concerns in our communications. The following questions may help bring things into focus.

- Am I promising something my organization can deliver? (You can substitute boss or personnel for organization.) If not, why are you bothering?

- Is what I'm saying consistent with previous policy or operating philosophy? If not, you need to shift to a persuasive tone and explain why your approach warrants a change or breach in policy.

- Who needs to coordinate on this? Who else owns a piece of this action? The coordination game can be a mind maze, but if you leave a key player out, you will undoubtedly hear about it.

Know Your Audience

The receiving audience falls into one of four sub-categories. Depending on the type of communication and coordination needed, you may or may not deal with every one of them.

- **Primary receiver:** The person you directly communicate with either verbally or in writing.

- **Secondary receiver:** People you indirectly communicate with through the primary receivers. Let's say, for example, that you're a wing commander. You send an e-mail to your wing first sergeants (primary receivers) identifying establishments near your base that are now designated "off limits" to troops. The first sergeants forward this e-mail to their unit personnel for "widest dissemination." The secondary receivers would be the troops that read the commander's directive.

- **Key decision makers:** These are the most powerful members of the audience ... the ones that really make the decisions. Knowing who they are will help focus your attention and potentially your delivery in larger briefings and certain written communication.

- **Gatekeepers:** These are people in the chain that typically review the communication before it reaches your intended audience. Knowing who they are and their expectations can save you embarrassment and help ensure your success in the long run. We all know that administrative assistants are keenly aware of their bosses' preferences. Listen to their inputs!

Knowing your audience is nothing new. When you consider warfare as an engagement of strategy and the adversary is your audience (and you are the adversary's audience!), then the importance of knowing your audience is clear.

> *Therefore I say: Know the enemy and know yourself; in a hundred battles you will never be in peril. When you are ignorant of the enemy but know yourself, your chances of winning or losing are equal. If ignorant of your enemy and of yourself, you are certain in every battle to be in peril.*
>
> –Sun Tzu

Sun Tzu was ahead of his time. He knew the importance of audience analysis! We're not recommending you view your audience as "the enemy," but Sun Tzu had the right idea. It is essential that we know the audience being engaged—in communication or in conflict. Read on for some final tips for connecting with your audience.

Tips for Success

- **RANK—don't be afraid of it.** Differences in military rank can be a real barrier to communication. Too many of us become tongue-tied when communicating with those senior in rank and cursory or impatient with those who are junior in rank. We must constantly remind ourselves we are all communicative equals and should strive to be candid, direct and respectful with everyone.

- **JARGON—tailor to your audience.** Don't overestimate the knowledge and/or expertise of your readers, but don't talk down to them either. Be careful with excessive use of career-field specific jargon and acronyms. Yes, they are second nature to most of us in the military, but you can lose your audience with unfamiliar terminology.

- **Be INCLUSIVE—remember our diverse force.** Sometimes we inadvertently exclude members of our audience by falling into communication traps involving references to race, religion, ethnicity or sex. Remember this concept when designing your visual support. Your visual aids should show a range of people who represent our Air Force. Avoid traditional stereotyping of jobs based on sex or race. Inclusiveness also applies to humor. Humor is not universal and joke telling is the biggest area where otherwise sensitive people unknowingly get themselves into trouble. Knowing your audience and adhering to good taste and sensitivity will keep you in check.

- **TONE—more than what you say, it is how you say it.** Closely tied to the purpose of your communication is the tone you take with your audience. Speakers have gestures, voice and movements to help them communicate. Writers only have words on paper. How many times have you seen colleagues get bent out of shape over a misunderstood e-mail? Why? Because the nonverbal signals available during face-to-face communication are absent. Recognize this disadvantage in written communication and pay close attention to it. Words that carry uncomplimentary insinuations (ignorant, opinionated) make negative suggestions (failure, impossible) or call up unpleasant thoughts (liable, unsuccessful) can potentially defeat your purpose.

- **COURTESY—be polite (please!).** The first rule of writing is to be polite. Forego anger, criticism and sarcasm—strive to be reasonable and persuasive. Try not to deliberately embarrass someone if it can be avoided with a more tactful choice of words. Rudeness is a weak person's imitation of strength.

- **Make it PERSONAL—but it's not all about you!** When appropriate, use pronouns to create instant rapport, show concern and keep your reader involved. Using pronouns also keeps your writing from being monotonous, dry and abstract. The pronouns you'll probably use the most are *you*, *yours*, *we*, *us* and *our*. Use *I*, *me,* and *my* sparingly. One rule of business writing is "put your audience first," so when possible, avoid using *I* as the first word of an opening sentence and avoid starting two sentences in a row with *we* or *I* unless you're trying to hammer home a point. These guidelines will help you to avoid sounding self-centered and repetitive.

- **FORMAL ("To be, or not to be") versus INFORMAL ("hey dude").** Different communication situations require different levels of formality. The informal tone is more like a conversation between you and your reader and it is characterized by clear, direct, active language. In today's Air Force, most of your writing will be informal, though ceremonies and awards may require more *elaborate* (formal) language. Whether your tone is formal or informal, you still need to follow the accepted rules of grammar. In any case, the best advice is to keep your writing clear, concise and simple. See chapter 7 for more details.

- **Be POSITIVE.** To cultivate a positive tone, give praise where praise is due; acknowledge acceptance before focusing on additional improvements; and express criticism in the form of helpful questions, suggestions, requests, recommendations, or clear directives rather than accusations. When having to give bad news, lead with a neutral comment before jumping in with the bad news. Save the positive for the closing by offering alternatives, etc. Stay away from using clichés, restating the refusal, hiding bad news in a fog of wordiness and inappropriate apologizing. Your audience always appreciates sincerity and honesty. To get you started thinking "positive," listen for the tone of the following sentences:

  o Commanders *will recommend only qualified* persons for training. [Constructive]

  o Commanders *may not recommend* for training any person who *is not qualified*. [Destructive]

The following list provides additional tone comparisons to help you see the tone you may be setting in your communication. This list is not absolute, but it does show how changing just one word can change the tone of a communication, oral or written, and thereby lead to a different conversation characterized by cooperation rather than conflict.

Positive, Constructive Tone	Negative, Destructive Tone
• reception area	• waiting room
• established policy	• old policy
• change of schedule	• postponement
• confirm meeting	• reminder
• competition is keen	• opportunity is limited
• start writing well	• stop writing badly
• use the big hoist	• don't use the small hoist
• the cup is half full	• the cup is half empty

SUMMARY: This chapter covered the key concepts of analyzing your purpose and audience—the first step towards developing effective communication. Getting clear on your purpose early in the process helps you focus your preparation. Taking the time to understand your audience will help you tailor your message to their knowledge, interests and motives. Once you've determined your purpose, nailed down your purpose statement and carefully analyzed your audience, you need to do some homework on your topic … that's why it's called *research*.

CHAPTER 4:

Step 2 (Research Your Topic)

> ***This chapter covers:***
> - Start Smart
> - Getting Data
> - Search Engines and Databases
> - Evaluate Your Sources
> - Useful Online Resources

Whether your communication goal is to persuade or inform, you'll need more than fancy words to win the day—you'll need substance as well as style. Once you're clear on your purpose and audience (Step 1), you'll need to research your topic to uncover information that will support your communication goals.

In some ways, research has never been easier—electronic databases and the Internet give us access to quantities of information unthinkable 20 years ago. But new opportunities bring new challenges. With so much information, how do we find the data we need to meet our purpose? And how do we know a source should be trusted? This chapter gives some basic suggestions that will be useful in nearly any assignment.

Start Smart

The day will come when you need to research a topic; how do you approach the task? If you do a little early planning, you'll be more focused and effective when searching for data and information. Start smart and do a little preparation before starting your research.

The word "research" is often used to describe a multistep investigation process used to either answer a question or solve a problem. Academic research expands knowledge by finding answers to questions, while nearly all military staff research revolves around identifying and solving problems. This chapter emphasizes information retrieval and evaluation of sources—this chapter does not describe the end-to-end process associated with academic research (see Appendix 2) or details of systematic problem solving (also covered in a separate chapter).

Nonetheless, for simple projects, planning means spending a few quiet moments thinking about your task. For longer projects, you may write out a detailed research plan. Regardless of the scope, think through these issues:

Review the Purpose and Scope of the Overall Project

After completing Step 1, Analyzing Purpose and Audience, you should have a good idea of what you need, but sometimes your purpose and scope may evolve as you learn more about the topic. You may also need to do some preliminary research just to get smart enough to scope out the effort. If you've been handed a vague topic, try to get some feel for how far you should go in your research, what you can realistically do and where you should stop.

Assign Yourself a Deadline for the Research Effort

It's easy to get lost in the research process. Don't do an outstanding job of data retrieval, then a marginal job on the presentation because you ran out of time. For larger projects, assign yourself a timeline for the data gathering process.

Get a Vector from the Boss

Ask the boss if there are unusual sources or knowledgeable individuals you should seek out. Your boss gave you this research problem for a reason—he or she thought that you were capable of finding the answer. Even if you can eventually find the answer on your own, you might save some time by asking for suggestions on where to start. An early vector could be particularly helpful if you're working on a practical problem that's "local," specialized, or requires information that isn't available to the general public.

How Much Do I Know Already; What Are My Biases?

Before you look for answers outside yourself, look in the mirror first. You may have valuable knowledge about an assigned research project, but you need to acknowledge and guard against your own biases in working a research problem. It's tough to keep an unbiased attitude; in fact, it's probably impossible if you know anything about the subject in question. The good news is once you realize you may be biased, you'll be less likely to automatically dismiss data that's not consistent with your personal philosophy.

Getting Data

Three things will probably influence how you approach the data gathering process:

- Your research topic.
- Your experience as a researcher and your expertise in this research area.
- Your experience with Internet and electronic database searches.

If you are seeking information that's publicly available and are comfortable with electronic search tools, you'd probably start with the Internet. If you are dealing with a local problem, a sensitive topic, or feel uncomfortable with the research process or search technology, you'll probably want to start by talking to another person. Regardless of the order you approach them, here are four major categories of information:

Coworkers, Base Personnel

These are colleagues that you can easily meet face to face who may be subject matter experts on your topic. They may also know where you can get valuable information on local projects, even if they are not subject matter experts themselves. The person who gave you the research assignment may also be a resource. Get clear on the big picture and be specific when you ask others for information—you'll save everybody's time.

Your Office Files and References

Data from work, in hard copy and electronic files, may be valuable sources of information. Some older files may still be stored in hard copy records in your office, but in most offices, the majority of current information on policies and procedures is contained on computer networks, the Electronic Records Management (ERM) solution (file plan), or electronic record keeping system Paper files are still used for correspondence, sensitive information and older archives; however, the US Office of Management and Budget Memorandum M-12-18, *Managing Government Records Directive*, requires that to the fullest extent possible, Federal agencies such as the Air Force to create and manage records electronically and not in paper. Each office has its own policies, check them out. In addition to office files, larger units typically produce unit histories that can be very useful for staff research. They tell what happened as well as when it happened, why, and where. A good history also shows how past experiences relate to current plans and how recent experiences relate to future plans.

The Internet

The amount of information available from your computer is nearly limitless. The Internet can be intimidating if you didn't grow up with computers, but set your fears aside—the payoffs are enormous. The two biggest challenges in using the Internet are 1) finding the information you need; and 2) sorting out what you can believe and what you can't. Anyone with an ax to grind can build a website and there's no one out there checking to see if the facts are correct. It's an interesting environment—information ranges from official, credible sources to the lunatic fringe, and websites may appear and disappear without notice. Later in this chapter, we'll give you details on searching the net and evaluating what you find. Be aware that copyright law now protects all materials the instant it is reduced to tangible form.

The Library

Libraries have unique benefits for the researcher:

- Librarians (real, honest-to-goodness humans!) who can help you find information and give basic research advice.
- Free access to books and periodicals—some of which may be available on the Internet.
- Access to the Internet and other electronic databases not always free to the public.
- Interlibrary loans that let you borrow nearly any book in print—even at small libraries

Though the Internet is a convenient source of information, you may eventually run into a point where the information you need is not available on the Internet, but it may still be found in books and periodicals, available for use freely at your local library. Libraries can also be of assistance in evaluating the quality of the information since most content in a library has been reviewed by someone other than the author. The end result is less trash and outright errors than you find out on the Internet. You will find a wealth of resources at your local base, city, or college and university libraries. Even if you can't borrow books, many of them allow nonstudents to visit and read books.

"Virtual libraries" are another important resource—they're websites that give you access to several library resources. Though these can be reached through an Internet browser, the information meets the same quality standards as the material in the physical library.

- **Muir S. Fairchild Research Information Center (MSFRIC) (http://www.au.af.mil/au/aul/lane.htm)** has online research tools and traditional library resources that include access to databases, bibliographies, online library assistance, full-text journal articles, relevant research links and assignment assistance for the Professional Military Education (PME).
- **Internet Public Library (http://www.ipl.org/)** organizes websites, e-texts, online magazines and other journals by subject/topic.
- **WWW Virtual Library (http://vlib.org/)** has topic-based links to sites usually maintained by universities and research centers.
- **The Library of Congress (http://www.loc.gov)** has excellent tools for research, including an Ask the Librarian feature for some topics.
- **The Library of Congress Online Catalog (http://catalog.loc.gov/)** includes online help pages on a variety of different searches–from basic to complex.

Search Engines and Databases

Search engines and database searches were once the realm of only the experienced Internet surfer. Today, finding relevant, quality information is fairly simple. Simply choose a search engine, enter what you are looking for into the search window and select enter. Within a fraction of a second the search engine will typically find scores of resources for you in an instant. From this basic search, you can conduct your preliminary research, find outlying sources and different views, or refine your search criteria with the terms you find from each successive search.

Search engines and Internet browsers are excellent tools to start your research but there are cautions. Search engines look for and find only what you ask of them—they do not evaluate the quality of the source. This is a risky venture for most research that you will be called upon to generate in your career. A better option is to use the academic databases provided by your local university library, if you can get access, or through the MSFRIC for students and faculty enrolled in Air University courses. Academic databases contain thousands of rigorous, peer-reviewed articles that are suitable for substantiating claims with research-based evidence.

Starting Points

There are many starting points on the Internet which may introduce you to your topic and/or point you to important resources. Reputable sources are those with verifiable, researched information, such as found in virtual libraries and library databases. There are also a host of shared content sites, such as wikis, that may also get you started; however, be warned that information from public sites where the content is generated by anyone with access to the internet should be questioned and subjected to verification before becoming that key point in your paper or presentation. Remember, starting points are best for getting to know some basics about your topic so you can refine your search engine terms to find reputable sources.

- **Wikipedia^{TM} (http://www.wikipedia.org/)** is considered by many to not be citable in a formal research paper, due to the anonymous nature of contributors. However, it often proves a very useful introduction to a subject and in the margin or at the bottom of the article there are usually links to usable sources, sometimes primary sources.
- **Yahoo!^{TM} Directory (http://dir.yahoo.com/)** is an example of a directory of topics and subtopics, with links to references, to survey the resources available for a given topic.
- **Open Directory Project (http://www.dmoz.org/)** is another extensive directory of links organized by topic.
- **Congressional Research Service (CRS)** reports, short summaries written by subject matter experts at the Library of Congress, are excellent starting points for becoming familiar with a topic. See the government resources section later for information on finding CRS reports.

Search Engines

If you do *not* know exactly what you want, you'll need to use a search engine to find websites that have useful information. Search engines use key words and phrases to search the Internet. Some allow you to type in questions and most have catalogs that sort a limited number of sites by topic. For whichever search engine you're using, look first for a link to "advanced" search tools on that search engine. You may also want to do a search for hints and tips for using that search engine. Getting to know your search engine may greatly improve your search results as well as speed up your search. One popular search engine is Google^{TM} which can be found by typing "www.Google.com" into your Internet browser. Once you are at the site, type in a few words or phrases that describe the main concepts of a topic. Google^{TM} only returns web pages that contain all the words you type in, making it easy to refine or narrow your search. It will definitely be worth your time to search for hints and tips on doing Google^{TM} searches. Much of what you learn will also carry over to other search engines.

- **The use of the <site:___> operator to restrict searches.** Most search engines have the site: operator, which can be used to search the .mil or other domains, or even specific folders on a site. Just type in the search box the term(s) you wish to search for and then add site:domain [*site then colon then domain, with no space on either side of the colon*]. Below are examples. Here and elsewhere in this chapter < and > enclose the search terms to be typed into the search engines, but the < and > are not themselves typed in.
    - <doctrine site:mil> will search for doctrine on all DoD public web pages.
    - <space doctrine site:af.mil> will search Air Force pages for space doctrine.
    - <future warfare site:au.af.mil/au/awc/awcgate/cst/> will search for future warfare in the research papers written by Air War College students for the Center for Strategy and Technology. Those papers were discovered to be in this folder.
    - <china site:cia.gov> will search the CIA site for information on China.

- **Refining your keyword searches to improve search efficiency.** Once you're comfortable with the Internet, you may want to learn some tricks to improve your search efficiency. Most search engines use the tools below or variations on them. Learn the "advanced" features of whichever search engine you use. Many of the features mentioned for Google™ also apply to other search engines.

- Use **"and"** or the **plus symbol "+"** to make sure that your search engine gives you pages that have all the words you enter. For example, either of these searches will keep you away from sites that describe military aviation, but not military aviation accidents.
    - <Military AND aviation AND accidents>
    - <Military+aviation+accidents>

- Use **"not"** or the **minus symbol "-"** to eliminate sites with unrelated words that clutter your search. For example, if you're looking for Microsoft™ Windows 8 information but keep getting Windows 7 or Windows Vista sites, you can eliminate them by using the following search (Note: The Google™ search engine requires a space before the minus sign, but none between it and the term to be eliminated).
    - <Windows 8 -7 -Vista >
    - <Windows 8 NOT 7 NOT Vista>

- **Using Quotation Marks ("   ")** to get websites that have your search words in the order you specify. For example, <"Operation Desert Storm"> gives a much tighter search than <Operation+Desert+Storm>.

- **Google™ automatically searches for synonyms,** but you can turn that off by putting quotes around a word. For example <Internet searching "tips"> would yield results only for tips–not guides, help, or tutorials–about Internet searching.

- **Other Google™ operators (a sampling):** for more, do a search on Google™ operators.
    - cache: shows Google™ cache of a page, such as cache: cia.gov
    - related: shows pages on related topics, such as related: nasa.gov

CHAPTER 4:
Step 2 (Research Your Topic)

- o define: shows a word's definition, such as define: pecuniary
- o filetype: limits search to only those type files, such as filetype: pdf

- **Combining Operations:** Once you've got the basics down, you can combine operations. For example, <"Operation IRAQI FREEDOM" AND "Air Operations"> gives you relevant sites on Air Operations during Operation IRAQI FREEDOM. If you want to research Operation DESERT STORM, but do *not* want information relating to Gulf War Syndrome, you can use the form below to subtract topics you do *not* want: <"Operation DESERT STORM" + "Air Operations"–"gulf war syndrome">

- **Internet searches require some judgment.** If you don't use enough keywords to narrow your topic, you'll end up spending a lot of time scanning sites and trying to find the ones that are most relevant. On the other hand, a tightly focused search might overlook a relevant citation. There are no easy answers, but through trial and error you'll probably find the balance that works for your particular topic. *In either case, you must evaluate the quality of the information (see below).*

- **Search Engine Options.** If you're having trouble finding material on your topic, you might try more than one search engine. Different search engines may yield different results and some specialize in certain fields of study. To find out more details, do an Internet search for current rankings and recommendations. Here are some of the current search engines at the time of publication: Google™, Yahoo!™, and Bing™.

- **Specialized Military and Government Search Engines.** Several search engines are tailored to search for military and government information. **Search.USA.gov (http://usasearch.gov)** searches over 30 million US government web pages. **Searchmil.com,** Google™ powered, searches the .mil domain. The **Center for Army Lessons Learned (CALL)** has a search function that searches multiple military-related sites, including CALL, Army, Army Field Manuals, Army regulations and other sites. DoD registered log-in is required for full access.

- **Other Specialized Search Engines.** Following searches are examples of how to find search engines that may specialize in your topic, or that may combine results from multiple search engines (these are called meta search engines).

    - o <international relations search engine> will yield results that include search engines or directories that specialize in international relations.
    - o <meta search engine list> will point you to the latest meta search engines.
    - o <international relations meta search engine> will lead to meta search engines that deal with international relations. There may not always be such engines, depending on the topic area.

> **Did you know?** The words AND, OR and NOT, when used between keywords in a database search, are called *Boolean operators*. Boolean operators were developed in the 1800s by George Boole, an English mathematician. Boolean operators are heavily used in the design of electronic circuits.

Evaluate Your Sources

Once you've found websites on your topic, you need to decide which ones to take seriously. Some feel that a positive attitude is the key to success in life, but in the case of the Internet, your attitude should be deep suspicion unless the source is official and you can confirm the site is what it pretends to be. Numerous credible web sources with a known pedigree can be found through the MSFRIC (**http://www.au.af.mil/au/aul/lane.htm**). Domain searches of .mil, .gov, or .edu *may* lead you to some of the more credible sources, but factual errors may be present in any domain and there are many sites that may be factually incorrect or deliberately misleading.

When looking at a website, ask yourself some questions. Who is responsible for the website and can you confirm that? How distant are the authors from the "event" they are writing about? (See the section later in this chapter on primary, secondary and tertiary sources.) What are the authors' motives? Are they part of a group whose goal is to influence public opinion or to sell you something? Are there things about the site that make you question its accuracy, objectivity or currency? Take a look at the checklist on the next page for more specifics to add to your paranoia.

Another way to build confidence in the information you gather is to seek confirmation of the facts from multiple sources. The weaker the source, the more important it is to get a second opinion before believing it. Most of us instinctively do this in the workplace—we have a very short list of people we absolutely believe every time they open their mouths (these folks usually don't talk much!), we have a longer list of people who are right most of the time and then there's usually one or two who have no credibility whatsoever. If the issue is important and you want to be sure, try to get the answer in stereo.

- <evaluating web sources site: edu> searches university sites for criteria and tips on evaluating web resources. There are some excellent such sites.
- <evaluating web sources site: loc.gov> searches the Library of Congress site for help with evaluating online sources.

While the guide on the following page provides an excellent overview of evaluating a web source, you may want to do the searches above to see if any new criteria come into play as the Internet continues to evolve. Social media, blogs and crowd-sourced references may need additional methods for evaluating their accuracy, currency and other criteria.

A note on Wikis, Blogs, e-journals and social media posts. The central goal of the Internet is the sharing of information. However, as access to the electronic archives has improved, so have the posts of less credible sources. This is not to say that the information found from a less credible source is wrong or invalid, but it is to say that the quality and credibility of an argument is only as good as the quality and credibility of the sources used. So how do you use these types of sources in your research? *The Tongue and Quill* recommends that wikis, blogs, e-journals and social media be treated as bread crumbs on the trail to creating basic understanding of a topic and any corollary issues that may be relevant. The fact is just about everyone uses these sources to get started in finding out more on a topic—be it from the news of the day to more challenging staff research. However, these sites are not considered authoritative and should not be sited as the evidence to support any claim in a credible research effort of any kind. **Bottom Line: Wikis can get you intellectually started but there are no shortcuts for obtaining valid, credible, authoritative content to support claims—you must do some digging.**

When evaluating a source, one factor to consider is the distance between the writer and his or her subject. Since people and their research are often misquoted, it's better to refer back to original material than rely on someone else's interpretation of existing work. This is true for research published in books and print journals, as well as Internet sites. The material you find can be classified as either a primary, secondary or tertiary source.

- A **primary source** is a first-hand account of an historical event, a physical artifact or record of that event or a description of research written by the people that actually performed it.

- A **secondary source** is one step removed from the event or research. It documents the findings of someone else who took the time to review primary sources.

- A **tertiary source** summarizes findings published in secondary sources.

Let's look at some examples. If you were doing research on a friendly fire incident, primary sources would include interviews of the parties involved, radio recordings, gun camera footage and black box recordings. The *Summary of Official Findings* published by the investigation board would be a secondary source. A tertiary source might be a magazine article that quoted the *Summary of Official Findings* as part of a larger discussion on the topic.

If you wanted to learn about the foundations of logic and persuasion in Western culture, a primary source would be essays on the subject by the Greek philosopher Aristotle, a secondary source would be an academic textbook that refers back to these writings and a tertiary source would be a lecture given by an instructor that used the academic textbook as a reference.

In general, primary and secondary sources are considered more reliable than tertiary sources. Each level of interpretation can introduce potential errors or bias and ideas can be misquoted or quoted out of context. On the other hand, sometimes a tertiary source might be useful to get a "big picture view" of a topic before you start slogging through primary and secondary sources.

Useful Online Resources

In some situations, you may want to start your research by referring to one authoritative and relevant source instead of searching the library or Internet. This might be particularly useful for situations where you want a quick and official answer to a relatively noncontroversial topic. The lists of sources that follow are either "official" in nature or involve publications that typically include at least one layer of critical review. Those sources that have not been critically reviewed will be fairly obvious. Be aware that online resources and links change quickly; the links below represent a snapshot of what was available as this edition went into publication.

Air Force Sources

- **Air Force Link (http://www.af.mil/).** The official website of the United States Air Force with the latest Air Force news, career information, biographies, images, and a host of information useful to all members of the Department of the Air Force,. There are links to other related sites including the full text of key reports, the online version of *Airman Magazine*, other publications and social media sites.

- **Air Force Portal (https://www.my.af.mil/).** The Air Force portal combines a number of Air Force websites and computer systems into one common interface. Individuals must register and establish an account.

- **Air Force Publications (http://www.e-publishing.af.mil).** The full-text of most standard Air Force publications.

- **Air Force Historical Research Agency (AFHRA) (http://www.afhra.af.mil/).** This agency's holdings consist of over 70,000,000 pages devoted to the history of the United States Air Force. Contact information is listed on the AFHRA home page above.

- **Air University (AU) Press (http://aupress.au.af.mil/).** The AU Press publication program is designed primarily to help war fighters and policy makers understand and apply air, space and cyber power in peacetime and conflict. AU Press publishes books, monographs and research papers by military authors and civilian scholars.

- **Air War College (AWC) Gateway to Internet Resources (http://www.au.af.mil/au/awc/awcgate/awcgate.htm).** This site includes documents and links organized for topics across the breadth of military and national security issues and resources.

- **Internet Searching Tools (http://www.au.af.mil/au/awc/awcgate/awc-srch.htm).** This site includes links helpful for anyone wishing to improve their Internet research skills.

- *Morning Report* **(https://cs.eis.af.mil/afpa/AFStory/default.aspx).** The Morning Report is produced by the Secretary of the Air Force Office of Public Affairs. Access requires a dot.mil connection and secure login. Once logged in, click on the "Links Version" banner for the current Morning Report.

- **Muir S. Fairchild Research Information Center (MSFRIC) (http://www.au.af.mil/au/aul/lane.htm).** The Muir S. Fairchild Research Information Center, founded in 1946 as the Air University Library, is the premier library in DoD. MSFRIC improves Air Force education by providing access to the world of information through quality library services. Resources available on the website include access to databases, bibliographies, online library assistance, full-text journal articles, relevant research links and assignment assistance for students and faculty enrolled in AU courses. Submit research requests at: **http://www.au.af.mil/mailer/index.asp?AUL-Reference.**

Other US Military Services

- **US Army (http://www.army.mil/).** This is the official website of the US Army. It provides the latest news, as well as information about careers, a library (of public websites), an image gallery and social media links.

- **US Army Publications (http://www.apd.army.mil/).** The full text of most standard Army publications.

- **US Army Military History Institute (USAHMI) (http://www.carlisle.army.mil/AHEC/USAMHI/).** USAHMI collects, organizes, preserves and makes available source materials on American military history to the defense community, academic researchers and the public. Research requests can be submitted using the submittal info on the site.

- **US Coast Guard (http://www.uscg.mil/).** The official website of the US Coast Guard. It provides the latest news, as well as information about careers, a library (of public websites) and an image gallery.

- **US Marine Corps (http://www.marines.mil/).** The official website of the US Marine Corps. It provides the latest news, as well as information about careers, a library (of public websites), an image gallery and social media links

- **US Marine Corps Publications (http://www.marines.mil/news/publications/).** The full-text of most standard Marine Corps publications.

- **US Marine Corps History Division (http://www.tecom.usmc.mil/HD/).** The official United States Marine Corps History Division website. This site provides a variety of information about the division and most importantly on the histories and traditions of the United States Marine Corps.

- **US Navy (http://www.navy.mil/).** The official website of the US Navy. It provides the latest news, as well as information about careers, a library (of public websites), an image gallery and social media links.

- **US Navy Issuances, Manuals and Directives (http://doni.daps.dla.mil/).** The full-text of most standard Navy directives.

- **US Naval History & Heritage Command (http://www.history.navy.mil/).** The Naval Historical Center is the official history program of the Department of the Navy. It includes a museum, art gallery, research library, archives and curator as well as research and writing programs.

- **National Guard (http://www.nationalguard.mil/).** The official website of the National Guard. It provides the latest news, as well as information about careers, a library (of public websites), an image gallery and social media links.

- **Reserve Affairs (http://ra.defense.gov/).** The official website for reserve affairs. It provides the latest news, as well as information about careers, a library (of public websites), an image gallery and social media links.

Department of Defense (DoD) Sources

- **Defense.gov (http://www.defense.gov/Defense.gov).** The official website for the Department of Defense and the starting point for finding US military information online. It contains links to publications, statements, social media, etc.

- **Defense Technical Information Center (DTIC) (http://www.dtic.mil/DTIC).** DTIC serves the DoD community as the largest central resource for DoD and government-funded scientific, technical, engineering and business related information available today. The DTIC network provides access to all unclassified, unlimited documents added into DTIC since December 1974. Descriptive summaries and full-text files are available for some documents.

- **Early Bird. This service was discontinued effective 1 Nov 13.** See *Morning Report*, above, under "Air Force Sources."

- **Foreign Military Studies Office (http://fmso.leavenworth.army.mil/).** The Foreign Military Studies Office (FMSO) at Fort Leavenworth, Kansas, is an open source research organization of the US Army. FMSO conducts unclassified research of foreign perspectives of defense and security issues that are understudied or unconsidered but that are important for understanding the environments in which the US military operates.

- **Joint Electronic Library (http://www.dtic.mil/doctrine/index.html).** The Joint Electronic Library (JEL) provides access to full-text copies of Joint Publications, the Department of Defense Dictionary, Service Publications, History Publications, Chairman of the Joint Chiefs of Staff (CJCS) Directives, research papers and other publications.

- **MERLN (http://merln.ndu.edu/).** The Military Education Research Library Network (MERLN) is a comprehensive website devoted to international military education outreach. It represents a consortium of military education research libraries that work together to provide access to a variety of unique electronic resources for the use of researchers and scholars. On the Internet since 1990, MERLN provides indexing to significant articles, news items, editorials and book reviews appearing in military and aeronautical periodicals, many of which are not indexed elsewhere. MERLN also provides access to the major library catalogs of several PME schools.

Military Bibliographies

A bibliography is a great starting point for research. These bibliographies are compiled by librarians who have examined relevant sources from Internet sites, books, documents, magazine articles, and videos. Some of the most useful military bibliographies include

- Muir S. Fairchild Research Information Center (MSFRIC) Bibliographies. **(http://www.au.af.mil/au/aul/bib97.htm).**
- Joint Forces Staff College Library. **(http://www.jfsc.ndu.edu/library/publications/bibliography/).**
- Marine Corps University Research Guides **(http://guides.grc.usmcu.edu/).**
- Naval Postgraduate School **(http://www.nps.edu/Library/).**
- US Army Military History Institute **(http://www.carlisle.army.mil/ahec/USAMHI/).**
- US Army War College Library **(http://www.carlisle.army.mil/library/bibliographies.htm).**

Military Newspaper and Magazine Indexes and Lists

Some indexes listed below require a paid subscription. Contact your local or base library for free availability using their subscription.

- **Air University Library Index to Military Periodicals (AULIMP) (http://aulimp.au.af.mil).** AULIMP is produced by the MSFRIC and contains citations to articles in English language military journals. The MSFRIC (formally AU Library) has been producing AULIMP since 1949 and material after 1987 is available on the web.

- **DoD and Military Electronic Journals (http://www.au.af.mil/au/aul/periodicals/DoDelecj.htm).** An electronic list compiled and maintained by the staff of the MSFRIC.

- **Read Military News (http://www.au.af.mil/au/aul/periodicals/milnews.htm).** A listing of defense and military service news including base newspapers compiled and maintained by MSFRIC.

- **Staff College Automated Military Periodicals Index (SCAMPI) (http://www.dtic.mil/dtic/scampi/).** Developed to support the Armed Forces Staff College; SCAMPI provides selected citations to journal articles and selected documents and reports. Subject, author, and keyword indexing is provided.

Other Government Sources

- **Census Bureau (http://www.census.gov/).** The Census Bureau website has demographic, geographic, business and other data. It also has US population projections, fact books, interactive maps and world statistics.

- **CIA (http://www.cia.gov).** This is the CIA home page. The site has several useful publications, including *The World Fact Book*, *World Leaders* and maps.

- **Congress.** See THOMAS below. You can also search for testimony and committee minutes and other information by searching for <searchterm site:house.gov> or <searchterm site: senate.gov>.

- **Congressional Research Service Reports. (http://www.loc.gov/crsinfo/).** These are short reports created by the Congressional Research Service (CRS) and the Library of Congress subject matter experts to update members of Congress on a wide range of topics. You can search for individual reports on this site or from a search engine. Search for <searchterm "Congressional Research Service"> to find CRS reports containing the searchterm. Add "site: state.gov" to search the wealth of CRS reports continually updated on the State Department website. Add "site: fas.org" to search the FAS library of CRS reports.

- **Copyright Office (http://copyright.gov/).** Copyright Office site includes handouts and research guides on copyright law and practice.

- **Federal Digital System–GPO Access (http://www.gpo.gov/fdsys/).** FDsys is the Government Printing Office's Federal Digital System which provides public access to government publications.

- **FEDSTATS (http://www.fedstats.gov/).** Statistics from more than 100 government agencies.

- **Government Accountability Office (GAO) (http://www.gao.gov/).** The US Government Accountability Office (GAO) is an independent, nonpartisan agency that works for Congress. Often called the "congressional watchdog," GAO investigates how the federal government spends taxpayer dollars. Their unclassified reports on are on this website.

- **Government Printing Office (GPO) (http://www.gpo.gov/).** Includes the GPO bookstore.

- **The National Archives and Records Administration (NARA) (http://www.archives.gov/).** An independent federal agency that preserves our nation's history and defines us as a people by overseeing the management of all federal records. It includes the Federal Register, which has the official text of federal laws, presidential documents, administrative notices and more.

- **National Technical Information Service (NTIS) (http://www.ntis.gov/).** NTIS is the nation's top resource for government reports and information.

- **Office of Scientific & Technical Information (OSTI) (http://www.osti.gov/).** OSTI collects, preserves and disseminates DOE-sponsored research and development (R&D) results that are the outcomes of R&D projects or other funded activities at DOE labs and facilities nationwide and grantees at universities and other institutions. The information is typically in the form of technical documents, conference papers, articles, multimedia and software, collectively referred to as scientific and technical information (STI).

- **Open Source Center (OSC) (https://www.opensource.gov/).** The OSC, formerly known as Foreign Broadcast Information Service (FBIS) is an electronic information service that collects and translates current political, economic, technical and military information from the media worldwide for the US government. Users must register and establish an account.

- **Science.Gov (http://www.science.gov/).** Science.gov searches over 50 databases and over 2,100 selected websites from **12 federal agencies**, offering 200 million pages of authoritative US government science information including research and development results.

- **Department of State (http://www.state.gov/).** The Department of State site includes a wealth of information on countries, regions, treaties, international issues, aid for development, arms control and more.

- **Thomas (http://thomas.loc.gov/).** Library of Congress resource covering the legislative branch, laws, treaties, bills, reports, etc.

- **USA.gov (http://www.usa.gov/).** The US government's official web portal.

- **USA.gov Data and Statistics (http://www.usa.gov/Topics/Reference-Shelf/Data.shtml).** Provides links to wide range of government sources of data and statistics, domestic and international.

- **The White House (http://www.whitehouse.gov/).** Provides the latest official presidential releases.

- **World News Connection (WNC) (http://wnc.fedworld.gov/).** Foreign news service provided by the NTIS using material provided by the OSC. It is a subscription service for use by personnel not eligible for an OSC account. It includes the portion of OSC news/articles for which copyright can be cleared.

Other Magazine and News Indexes

Some indexes listed below require a paid subscription. Contact your local or base library for free availability using their subscription.

- **Access Science™ (http://www.accessscience.com/).** Provides on-line access to the McGraw-Hill Encyclopedia of Science and Technology, including 7,100+ articles, 115,000 dictionary terms and hundreds of Research Updates—in all areas of science and technology—updated daily, plus these great features: Over 2,000 in-depth biographies of leading scientists through history; weekly updates on breakthroughs and discoveries in the world of science and technology; resources to guide your research; and links to websites for further research. Copyrighted material requires a paid subscription.

- **Air Force Times™ and related publications.** Provides full-text access to Army Times, Air Force Times, Navy Times and the Marine Corps Times and includes current issues and archives. Copyrighted material requires a paid subscription.
    - Army Times™ (http://www.armytimes.com/).
    - Air Force Times™ (http://www.airforcetimes.com/).
    - Navy Times™ (http://www.navytimes.com/).
    - Marine Corps Times™ (http://www.marinetimes.com/).

- **Country Watch Country Review™ (http://www.countrywatch.com/).** Provides the political, economic, corporate and environmental trends for each of the approximately 200 countries around the world. Copyrighted material requires a paid subscription.

- **CQ Library, *CQ Weekly*™ (http://library.cqpress.com/cqweekly/).** Congressional Quarterly's magazine on government, commerce and politics.

- **EBSCOhost® (http://search.ebscohost.com/).** A web-based periodical index that provides abstracts and indexing for over 4,800 scholarly journals covering the social sciences, military science, humanities, education and more. Also included is the full text for over 1,000 journals—with many dating back to 1990—and over 1,700 peer-reviewed journals. Copyright requires a paid subscription.

- **Lexis-Nexis Academic® (http://www.lexisnexis.com/).** Provides access to a wide range of full-text news, business info, legal cases, and world news about countries and research about public figures. Copyrighted material requires a paid subscription.

- **NewsBank™ (http://infoweb.newsbank.com/).** Provides news articles covering social, economic, environmental, government, sports, health, science and military issues and events from more than 500 US regional and national newspapers and wire services and 140 full-text general news, subject-specific and military magazines. Copyrighted material requires a paid subscription.

- **ProQuest® (http://search.proquest.com/login).** Magazine articles from 8,000+ publications. Copyrighted material requires a paid subscription.

- **STRATFOR™ (http://www.stratfor.com/).** Combines intelligence analysis and news archives on various countries. Copyrighted material requires a paid subscription.

- **Wiley Interscience® (http://onlinelibrary.wiley.com/advanced/search).** Provides the full text of over 300 leading scientific, technical, medical and professional journals. Copyrighted material requires a paid subscription required.

Graphics, Photos and Maps

Each military service home page has links to photos, videos, graphics, and/or artwork related to that particular service. The DoD home page also has links to photos and videos. Most search engines also have specialized searches for graphics, images and videos. Most special operators work in the image/video searches as well. For instance, <f-16 site: af.mil> in the Google™ image search will give you F-16 images from only Air Force web pages. Similarly, <f-16 filetype: gif> will give you only .gif images, excluding .jpg and other file types. Combining the operators <f-16 site: mil filetype: jpg> will give you only .jpg images from .mil web pages. Look at additional features of specialized search engines. At this time Google™ Image search offers you the choice of face, photo, clip art, or line drawing.

- **AP Multimedia Archive (http://www.apimages.com/).** An electronic library containing the AP's current photos from their 50 million-image print and negative library, as well as charts, graphs, tables and maps from the AP's graphics portfolio. Copyrighted material requires a paid subscription.

- **defenseimagery.mil (http://DoDimagery.afis.osd.mil/).** Contains official US Military images, both still and motion, from around the world. Provides oversight for the Joint Combat Camera Program. Individuals must register and establish an account.

- **University Of Texas Map Database (http://www.lib.utexas.edu/maps/).** The Perry-Castaneda Library Map Collection, at the University of Texas, has more than 250,000 maps. Many are online, organized by region, historical period, theme, or current event.

Other Sources

Some indexes listed below require a paid subscription. Contact your local or base library for free availability using their subscription.

- **Britannica® Online (http://www.britannica.com/).** A full-text encyclopedia that is accessible via the Internet. It provides articles as well as related resources on the Internet. Copyrighted material requires a paid subscription.

- **Columbia International Affairs® Online (CIAO) (http://www.ciaonet.org/).** A web-based database designed to be the most comprehensive source for theory and research in international affairs. It publishes a wide range of scholarship from 1991 on, which includes working papers from university research institutes, occasional papers from NGOs, foundation-funded research projects and proceedings from conferences. Copyrighted material requires a paid subscription.

- **Firstsearch® (http://www.oclc.org/firstsearch/).** An electronic information service that is accessible over the Internet. This service provides access to over 70 databases on a wide variety of local and global subjects. Copyrighted material requires a paid subscription.

- **Infotrac™ (http://infotrac.galegroup.com).** An electronic information service that is accessible over the Internet, providing access to Cengage Learning databases. This education related service may require a paid subscription, depending on your institution.

- **Jane's Online (http://www.janes.com/).** Provides access to select Jane's resources. Copyrighted material requires a paid subscription.

- **ProQuest® Congressional Universe (http://congressional.proquest.com/congressional).** Provides access to a wealth of congressional publications such as hearings, reports, bills, laws, regulations, and CIS Legislative Histories. This site also allows you to locate specific information about members and committees. Copyrighted material requires a paid subscription.

- **PERISCOPE (http://www.militaryperiscope.com/).** Provides open-source intelligence on orders of battle, equipment inventories, and procurement plans and programs for 165 nations. It also provides technical descriptions and characteristics for nearly every major weapon system and platform. Copyrighted material requires a paid subscription.

- **RAND (http://www.rand.org/).** The RAND Corporation is a nonprofit institution that helps improve policy and decision making through research and analysis. Its website includes reports on many military and security issues, as well as other issues of concern to lawmakers and decision makers.

- **REFDESK (http://www.refdesk.com/).** REFDESK is a large compilation of news, almanacs, encyclopedias, magazine articles, commentaries and other daily sampling of US and worldwide information sources.

- **First Things First (http://www.refdesk.com/first.html)** is a list of newspapers, online magazines and specialty news.

Copyrights

Bottom Line Up Front (BLUF): There are many misconceptions about copyrights, especially with the ability to cut and paste or transfer whole files electronically. Remember, copyrights protect the intellectual property of others; violating copyrights and passing the work off as your original work is plagiarism—distributing copyrighted materials without permission is criminal.

Consider the satirical comment by Wilson Mizner, an American playwright from the late 1800s, who once said, "Copy from one, it's plagiarism; copy from many, it's research." Sorry, but Wilson is wrong–it's still plagiarism no matter how many times you copy material or paraphrase it without proper citation or attribution. The Copyright Office **(http://copyright.gov/)** website includes handouts and research guides on copyright law and practice. The following searches give a wealth of tips and handouts on copyright and researching.

"copyright for researchers site:edu" or "copyright for researchers site:gov"

If you search for documents, images and other material using the site: gov or site: mil operators, you'll be most likely to find copyright unencumbered material. But you still need to verify the copyright ownership and rules for usage.

Social Media and Networks

There are many brand name social media sites along with personal or professional blogs and discussion groups or networks that are increasingly the predominant form of information sharing. Many times they offer you the chance to meet online with subject matter experts who have ideas and facts to offer your research. Just remember to verify their identities and qualifications. In addition, many of the social media sites are now searchable using search engines. But before you venture out there too far, or set up your own social network, please do the following searches and read some of the existing guides. Your safety and security could be at risk.

Internet safety site: gov; social networking safety site: gov
social media guidelines site: mil; preventing online identity theft site: gov

Most government and military websites now include links to their social media sites You need to strike a careful balance between risk and communication openness. Many browsers now have "privacy" or "stealth" modes, which allow you to limit your exposure to information mining by sites you visit.

Other Help and Tips

- Web pages or sites vanishing. This frequently happens, which is why we suggest you save web pages you paraphrase, quote from, or use for ideas.

- Google™ cache can be searched using the cache: URL tool, such as "cache: cia.gov"

- The Wayback Machine (**http://www.archive.org/**) has selected web pages after 1996.

- If any of the URLs in this chapter fail to work, just use the name of the site or document as a search term in a search engine. Search engines are continually re-indexing the Internet and therefore can usually find documents and pages when they are moved.

- If you want to be continually updated on a topic, try signing up for topic-specific alerts and RSS feeds and other updating services available from many websites. Notices of updates can be sent directly to your phone, computer, tablet, or other device.

- Search for tools relating to the "invisible web"–the portion of the Internet which search engines can't find. For example, a database that assembles results pages only after you enter a specific search. Regular searches may find the link to the database, but you may be able to examine the contents of the database only through using its interface directly.

SUMMARY: When you're trying to inform or persuade others, you need to do some research—there is no substitute for good research. Use the Internet, library, your office files, and your coworkers to get the best information possible and be sure to critically evaluate your sources. With good research, you will find more than you need. Carefully select what is important to advance your argument and you will find that research is enjoyable and rewarding. Stay focused on your purpose and you can stay on schedule.

CHAPTER 5:

Step 3 (Support Your Ideas)

> **This chapter covers:**
> - The Logic of Arguments: Fundamentals
> - Evidence: Proving Your Point
> - Characteristics of Good Supporting Evidence
> - Logical Errors: Flawed Arguments
> - Arguments, Truth and Persuasion

Once you've researched your topic and collected information, you need to figure out how to use what you've found to meet your communication goals. If you're dealing with a controversial question or problem, throwing facts at your audience won't be enough—you'll need to assemble it into a logical argument that can stand up to critical attack. This chapter will give you some helpful pointers on how to build an argument and support your ideas.

Logical arguments are instruments of power. They're how you make things happen. It's worth the effort to understand some basics, even if some of this chapter makes your head hurt.

> *A moment's thought would have shown him. But a moment is a long time and thought is a painful process.*
>
> –A.E. Housman

The Logic of Arguments: Fundamentals

When you present a solution to a problem or answer a controversial question, persuasion is part of the assignment. There are different approaches to persuade members of your audience—you can appeal to their emotions, their ability to reason or even your own credibility on the topic being discussed. In the Air Force environment, your best approach to support your ideas and persuade others is by building a solid logical argument.

Though the word "argument" is commonly used to describe a quarrel or disagreement, it also has a positive meaning—it's a series of statements intended to persuade others. In this chapter, when we use the term *logical argument,* we're referring to a coherent set of statements that provide a position and support for that position based on information and facts, not just emotions.

This is important for two reasons. First, you build logical arguments every day: when you talk to your team about duties; when you talk to your boss about your workload and schedules; and when you sort out how best to accomplish the mission. If you build strong arguments, things are more likely to work out the way you think they should. Second, others are aiming arguments at you every day and many of these arguments fail logically. If you understand how arguments are constructed and where they go wrong, you're less likely to buy into a failed logic.

Elements of a Logical Argument

Different textbooks have different terms and approaches to describe logical arguments. This chapter uses terminology found in *The Craft of Research,* by Booth, Comb and Williams. Logical arguments contain four elements:

- a claim
- evidence that supports the claim
- warrants linking pieces of evidence to the claim
- qualifications that limit the claim

First we'll describe each of these terms and then we'll illustrate them in a real-life example of an argument in the next section. The example will help clarify each point.

The Claim

Your claim is simply your position on an issue, your answer to a controversial question or your recommendation for resolving a problem. In academic writing, a claim is also called a *thesis*.

Evidence That Supports the Claim

By definition, every argument has *evidence* intended to give reasons for your claim. Another term for evidence is *support* ("support" and "evidence" are used interchangeably in this text). The similarity of these terms is clear in their definitions:

> *Evidence* (a noun) is the data by which proof or probability may be based or may be admissible as testimony in a court of law.

> *Support,* as a noun, is the information that substantiates a position; as a verb, *support* is the act to furnish evidence for a position.

If a piece of evidence is questionable, it may be attacked as a *sub-claim*. Then, you either have to provide additional evidence to prove the sub-claim is true, or eliminate it from your argument.

Warrants That Link Evidence to the Claim

With every piece of evidence, there are often assumptions, either stated or unstated, that link the evidence to the claim and explain why the evidence is relevant to the argument. These linking statements or concepts are called *warrants*. Warrants are important because they can be potential weaknesses in an argument.

Qualifications That Limit the Claim

Sometimes the argument will have *qualifications*—conditions that limit the claim. You can think of a qualification as a statement you attach to the claim with a big IF statement. We often notice these qualifications as we critically look at the evidence we have and realize its limitations.

Elements of a Logical Argument: An Example

Let's use a real life example of a logical argument to show how the different elements work together. Suppose you're responsible for selecting a guest speaker to teach topic XYZ at a PME school. Ms. Jane Doe spoke last year and you've decided to invite her back. Your boss wants to know your recommendation and your rationale. Guess what? You've just been asked to produce a logical argument

CLAIM: We should invite Ms. Jane Doe to teach topic XYZ at this year's class.

EVIDENCE, item #1: Ms. Doe has spent 26 years working with XYZ and is an expert in this field.

WARRANT, item #1: Spending 26 years of working with XYZ makes her an expert. (Another implied warrant is that we want an expert to teach topic XYZ.)

> If someone wanted to attack this bit of evidence, he might ask you to prove the fact that she's spent 26 years in the field—let's see a resume!
>
> If someone wanted to attack the underlying warrant, he may argue that she isn't really an expert—maybe she's been doing an entry-level job for 26 years.
>
> But let's suppose that Ms. Doe is indeed an expert in the field, and this is solid evidence.

EVIDENCE, item #2: Last year's course directors all thought she did an excellent job.

WARRANT, item #2: These people know what they're talking about.

> If someone wanted to challenge this evidence, he might ask you to produce letters of recommendation. How enthusiastic are the directors about the job she did?
>
> If someone wanted to attack the underlying warrant, he might question the course directors' judgment. Maybe they were new to the job and didn't know much about the topic. Maybe they were TDY during the presentation and were basing their recommendation on what they heard from others.
>
> In this case, let's assume that the course directors are both credible and enthusiastic.

EVIDENCE, item #3: Ms. Doe is a very dynamic lecturer.

WARRANT, item #3: It's good to have a dynamic lecturer.

Recall that evidence you provide to support your claim can be attacked as a sub-claim … and this last bit of evidence looks vulnerable. How do we know that Ms. Doe is a dynamic lecturer? To back it up, you'd have to "support your support" on item #3 with something like this:

SUBCLAIM: Ms. Doe is a very dynamic lecturer.

SUBCLAIM EVIDENCE #1: Students provided five times the amount of feedback than is typical for a lecture.

SUBCLAIM WARRANT #1: Student interest is proportional to volume of feedback.

SUBCLAIM EVIDENCE #2: Ninety-two percent of feedback was very favorable and 8 percent was very unfavorable.

SUBCLAIM WARRANT #2: Polarized feedback implies a dynamic lecture.

Well, this additional information really does back up the fact that Ms. Doe is a dynamic lecturer, but it also indicates her views are controversial—8 percent of the student population really didn't like her presentation. You may believe that your school's goal is education and not to make every student happy, but you might qualify your claim with the following "IF" statement:

QUALIFICATION:

Ms. Jane Doe should be invited back to teach topic XYZ
IF
it is acceptable to have a controversial speaker at the school.

Evidence: Proving Your Point

As you see, individual pieces of evidence are used to build your argument. In this section, we identify some common types of evidence as well as approaches to help explain your ideas to your audience.

- A *definition* is a precise meaning or significance of a word or phrase. In an argument, it can be helpful to establish a common frame of reference for important or ambiguous words, so don't underestimate the importance of definitions.

- An *example* is a specific instance chosen to represent a larger fact in order to clarify an abstract idea or support a claim. Good examples must be appropriate, brief and attention arresting. Quite often they are presented in groups of two or three for impact.

- *Testimony* uses the comments of recognized authorities to support your claim. These comments can be direct quotations or paraphrases, but direct quotations tend to carry more weight with listeners or readers. When using testimony as support, make sure the individuals being quoted are both generally credible—no unknown relatives or convicted felons, please—and knowledgeable in the field under discussion.

- *Statistics* provide a summary of data that allows your audience to better interpret quantitative information. Statistics can be very persuasive and provide excellent support if handled competently. Keep them simple and easy to read and understand. Also, remember to round off your statistics whenever possible and document the exact source of your statistics.

The persuasive power of statistics means that you need to be particularly careful to use them properly. Many people will put blind trust in numbers and fall prey to people or papers that spout numbers or statistical proof. (Ironically, people who work with numbers for a living are the most cautious about trusting someone else's statistics!).

Always, always examine the basic assumption(s) on which the analysis rests. Some of the most compelling statistical arguments turn out to be intricate sand castles built on a foundation of shaky assumptions. The math may be technically correct, but the assumptions can't stand up to scrutiny.

In their book *Writing Arguments*, John Ramage, John Bean, and June Johnson define a *fact* as a noncontroversial piece of data that can be confirmed by observation or by talking to communally accepted authorities. The authors distinguish a fact from an *inference*, which is an interpretation or explanation of the facts that may be reasonably doubted. They recommend that writers distinguish facts from inferences and handle inferences as testimony. Definitions, testimony, statistics and facts provide data that you can use to construct an argument. This next category—*explanation*—can also be helpful in supporting your ideas.

- *Explanation* makes a point plain or understandable or gives the cause of some effect. It can be used to clarify your position or provide additional evidence to help make your case. The following three techniques can be used as part of an explanation:
- *Analysis*: The separation of a whole into smaller pieces for further study; clarifying a complex issue by examining one piece at a time.
- *Comparison and Contrast*: *Comparison* and *Contrast* are birds of similar feather. Use comparison to dramatize similarities between two objects or situations and contrast to emphasize differences.
- *Description*: To tell about in detail, to paint a picture with words—typically more personal and subjective than definition.

Characteristics of Good Supporting Evidence

There are two kinds of truth. There are real truths and there are made-up truths.

–Marion Barry
(As Mayor of Washington, D.C., after his arrest for drug use.)

Though different professions and academic fields have their own standards of what is "good" evidence, there are some common characteristics to consider.

Trust

Is the information from an authoritative, trustworthy source? Will your audience trust this source and should you? In the previous chapter we stressed the importance of being cautious with Internet sites, but you should be wary of any source's credibility. Also, remember that it's better to refer back to original material than rely on someone else's interpretation of existing work since people and their research are often misquoted.

Accuracy

Is the information accurate and free from error? Check and recheck your facts—errors can seriously damage your credibility. Critically evaluate your sources and if you're uncertain about your facts, be honest with your audience. You can increase your confidence in the accuracy of your information by using multiple sources to confirm key facts.

Precision

Is your information appropriately precise? When we talk about "precision," we mean the information should be specified within appropriately narrow limits. The level of required precision will vary with the topic being discussed. Describing regulations for uniform wear may require a precision of fractions of an inch and telling someone that his operational specialty badge should be in the middle of their shirt or within a meter of his belt buckle is not adequately precise. On the other hand, when reporting on the designated mean point of impact for munitions, a measurement in meters or feet would be an appropriate level of precision.

When talking about some subset of a group, explain how many or what percentage of the total you're talking about. If you find yourself constantly using qualifiers like "some, most, many, almost, usually, frequently, rarely…" you probably need to find some convincing statistics to help you make your case.

Relevance

Is your evidence relevant? Evidence can be authoritative, accurate and precise, yet still be totally irrelevant. Don't shove in interesting facts that have nothing to do with the claim; help the reader understand the relevance of your material by explaining its significance. Explain charts, graphs and figures and use transitions in your writing to "connect the dots" for the reader.

Sufficiency

Is your evidence sufficient to support your claim and representative of the whole situation or group? If you are trying to form some conclusions about a situation or group, you need data that represents the complete situation. For example, if you were trying to form conclusions about the overall military population, you would want to gather evidence from all services, not just one career field in one service. If you find that your evidence is either not representative or not sufficient, you need to find more evidence, limit the claim to what you can prove or qualify your claim. You may have to let go of evidence that doesn't fit or data that is no longer current.

Logical Errors: Flawed Arguments

Many people would sooner die than think—in fact, they do so.

–Bertrand Russell

Some of you may have studied formal logic in school. These classes used a lot of complex language and theory to describe what makes an argument "good" or "bad." Unfortunately, many real-life arguments outside of math and engineering are more "squishy" ... and sometimes it's hard to draw a diagram or write an equation to explain exactly what's wrong.

Common errors in reasoning are called *informal fallacies.* They are called "informal" fallacies because they're harder to pin down than some of the "formal" errors in logic. Still, you see them around you every day—especially in advertising, talk radio or political debates. Keep them out of your staff work and learn to identify them in others.

The *informal fallacies* below have been grouped into categories that make sense to the editors, but there's no universally accepted approach to categorizing them. Also note that labeling something as a fallacy requires some judgment—after all, many of these are "gray areas."

Asserted Conclusion

An **asserted conclusion** is the practice of slipping in an assertion and passing it off as a fact. There are two variations of asserted conclusions: circular reasoning and loaded questions.

> **Circular reasoning** (also known as **begging the question**) involves rewording your claim and trying to use it as evidence, usually with a lot of other "filler sentences" designed to confuse the other person. This is popular in advertising where different versions of the claim are repeated over and over again. If the advertisers have their way, you may not notice that the "support" merely restates the claim using different words—a textbook case of circular reasoning. After a while, it's easy to forget there's absolutely no support there at all.
>
> **CLAIM**: "Hey guys! Drink Energy Drink X and you'll be great at sports!"
>
> **SUPPORT:**
>
> - "Great athletes are alert and energized—Energy Drink X keeps you alert and gives you energy to perform!"
> - "You'll have many good looking and physically fit friends!"
>
> A **Loaded question** has an assertion embedded in it—it's another form of an asserted conclusion. One example of a loaded question is "Do you think John Smith is going to improve his rude behavior?" The phrasing of the question itself implies that John has behaved poorly in the past—regardless of how you answer the question. "When are we going to stop sinking money on this expensive program?" has an embedded assumption: the money we've spent to date hasn't been effective.

Sometimes an arguer will assert a conclusion and then challenge someone else to disprove it. The best defense is to ask him or her to prove their claim. "How do you know these programs are effective?" puts the listener on the defensive. The proper response would be, "How do you know the programs are not effective?" Those who assert should have the burden of proof.

2. Character Attack

The classic name for a **character attack** is the **ad hominem** fallacy (in Latin, *Ad Hominem* means "to the man"). Character attacks are also sometimes called **poisoning the well**. A character attack involves an assault on your opponent as an individual, instead of his or her position. It's very common in political advertisements, but you see it in the workplace as well. Here are some examples:

- "Mr. Smith is a tax and spend liberal who voted himself a pay raise last year." (Depending on the topic being discussed, this may be irrelevant to the core of the debate).
- "That guy is an egotistical windbag—what would he know about A-76 contract transitions?" (He may know a lot—his personality is irrelevant to the issue).

3. Emotional Appeals

Emotional appeals try to persuade the heart, not the head. Though emotion plays a role in persuasion, when emotion replaces reasoning in an argument, you've committed a foul. Often arguers attempt to appeal to our emotions in an argument through biased language, vivid language and stirring symbols. They may try to persuade us using "character" issues such as glowing testimonials from popular but non-credible sources. Here are some examples of logical fallacies in this area:

Emotional appeal (to force):

These arguments target the audience's fear of punishment. What characterizes these examples as fallacies is that they make no attempt to persuade using anything other than pressure.

- "Keep this quiet, or I'll implicate you in my wrongdoing."
- "Give me your lunch money, or I'll give you a busted lip."

Emotional appeal (to pity):

This is an argument that targets the audience's compassion and concern for others. Though most people would agree that ethics and values should be part of the decision-making process, an appeal solely to emotion, even a positive one, can be dangerous and misguided.

- "You can't give me a D on this paper—I'll lose my tuition assistance!"
- "We've got to stop the warlords—look at the poor, starving people on the news!"

Emotional appeal (to popularity or tradition):

- *Stirring Symbols*: Using a powerful symbol or attractive label to build support.
  - "I stand before our nation's flag to announce my run for President…."
  - "Good management principles demand we take this course of action."
- *Bandwagon Appeal:* Using peer pressure to build support.
  - "It must be right—everybody else thinks so."
  - "Buy the Ford Escort; it's the world's #1 best seller."
  - "Every good fighter pilot knows…."
- *Precedent as sole support*: Using custom as the only justification for a decision.
  - "It must be right—we've always done it that way."
  - "The Royal Air Force has found the procedure very useful and we should try it."
  - "The last three commanders supported this policy and that's good enough for me."

4. False Authority

False authority is a fallacy tied to accepting facts based on the opinion of an unqualified authority. The Air Force is chock-full of people who, because of their position or authority in one field, are quoted on subjects in other fields for which they have limited or no expertise. Don't be swayed (or try to sway someone else).

A false authority variant is called the **primacy-of-print** fallacy, where facts are believed because they are published in a book, periodical or on a website. Be as skeptical and thoughtfully critical of the printed word as you are of the spoken word.

5. False cause

False cause (also known as the **Post Hoc fallacy**) occurs when you assume one event causes a second event merely because it precedes the second event. Many people observe that Event B occurred after Event A and conclude that A caused B. This is not necessarily true—maybe a third factor, Event C, caused both A and B. Consider the following example:

> Event A = At Base X, "Retreat" plays over the intercom at 1635 each day.
>
> Event B = At Base X, outbound traffic increases at the gate at 1640 each day.

There is a statistical *correlation* between these two events: if Event A happens, Event B is more likely to happen and vice versa. Does that mean A causes B? Not necessarily—possibly a third event may "cause" both A and B:

> Event C = At Base X the official duty day ends at 1630 for much of the workforce.

6. Single Cause

A **single cause** fallacy occurs when you assume there is a single cause for an outcome, when in fact multiple causes exist.

Let's consider a real-life example of a single cause fallacy. Suppose you're very physically fit, and in a few months you'll take a fitness test. You can't run due to an injury so you are required to walk a certain distance while having your heart rate measured. You've set a goal to score in the top 10 percent for your age group—an "excellent" rating. You know that a disciplined exercise program will cause you to improve your score, but is it this simple?

> Event A = disciplined, intense exercise program CAUSES
> Event B = excellent score on the fitness test

People who've had trouble with similar fitness tests would be quick to point out that cause and effect may be a little more complicated in this case:

> Event A = disciplined, intense exercise program;
> Event B = genetically low resting heart rate;
> Event C = no caffeine or nervousness about the test; CAUSES
> Event D = excellent score on the fitness test

On the other hand, people who have the genetically low heart rate and nerves of steel may think an excellent rating has a single cause because they've never had to deal with the other ones.

7. Faulty Analogy

The **faulty analogy** is very common. Though we often make analogies to make a point, sometimes they go astray—there's something about the comparison that isn't relevant. A faulty analogy implies that because two things are alike in one way, they are alike in all the ways that matter. It can be thought of as one example of a **non sequitur** fallacy (see item 11) such as in this example:

> "Leading a coalition is just like leading a squadron."

Well, not exactly. Leadership is required in both situations, but leading a coalition requires technical expertise as well as the ability to work with people from other services and countries; it requires great communication skills, tact, and diplomacy. Leading an Air Force squadron requires a high level of technical proficiency but this does not ensure success leading a coalition.

8. Faulty Dilemma

A **faulty dilemma** implies there is no middle ground between two options. Typically one option is what the speaker prefers and the other option is clearly unacceptable, such as in this example:

> "Spend one hour a day reading *The Tongue and Quill* to improve your writing skills … or remain ignorant of writing standards. It's your choice."

Clearly this is a faulty dilemma—it falsely suggests you only have two choices, when you really have many options. Maybe you can read *The Tongue and Quill* once a week or once a month. Maybe you'll find some other way to improve your writing skills—take a class, find a grammar website, get feedback from your boss, etc. Though sometimes life really does give us an "either-or" choice, in most cases we find a considerable range of options between two positions.

9. Hasty Generalization

A **hasty generalization** results when we "jump to conclusions" without enough evidence. A few examples used as proof may not represent the whole.

> "I asked three student pilots what they thought of the program and it's obvious that Undergraduate Pilot Training needs an overhaul."

One of the challenges with this fallacy is it's hard to determine how much evidence is "enough" to form a reasonable conclusion. The rules will vary with the situation; more evidence is needed to form a conclusion if the stakes are high. The Food and Drug Administration may require a great deal of evidence before deciding a drug is safe for human use, while SSgt Snuffy may require very little evidence before forming a generalized conclusion about which candy bars should be sold at the snack bar.

10. Non sequitur

Non sequitur is Latin for "it does not follow" and is the generic term for a conclusion that does not necessarily follow from the facts presented. The facts may not be relevant, or there may be some sort of illogical leap made. Several fallacies, such as hasty generalization and faulty analogy, can be thought of as different types of *non sequitur*. For example, "*John Doe will make a great squadron commander because he is an expert in his career field.*" This is a *non sequitur* error because it implies strong technical skills equate to the skills needed to command. A similar *non sequitur* argument assumes athletic prowess indicates strong leadership skills.

11. Slippery Slope

The **slippery slope** implies that if we take one small step in an unpleasant or dangerous direction, we'll have to go all the way—like slipping down a hill. Here's an example from *Writing Arguments* by Ramage, Bean and Johnson: *"We don't dare send weapons to Country X. If we do so, next we will send in military advisors, then a Special Forces battalion and then large numbers of troops. Finally, we will be in an all-out war."* Though not every slippery slope argument is false, in some cases we can identify lines that we will not cross. In general, it is best to evaluate each argument on its merits using a foundation of agreed-upon principles.

12. Red Herring

Red herring fallacies occur when an arguer deliberately brings up irrelevant information to get the audience off track. The origins of the "red herring" name are debatable, but the central idea is to divert attention from the topic with content that has no bearing on the outcome.

13. Stacked Evidence

Stacked evidence is the tendency to withhold facts or manipulate support so that the evidence points in only one direction. This happens when you gather only the data or opinions that support your position. This may be done deliberately or may occur due to unconscious bias or carelessness. We may not see counterarguments or alternative interpretations of the facts because of our firm belief in our own position, or we just stop gathering information once we we've found enough support to make our case. Even if you decide to push for your favorite interpretation of the data, never stack evidence by misrepresenting or manipulating the basic information. If you decide that you don't want to discuss the opposing viewpoint, you should at least be aware of it, so you can prepare a counterpunch if needed.

14. Straw Man

Straw man is a fallacy where you attack a weaker, grossly simplified version of the opponent's argument rather than directly addressing the argument presented. In effect, you are attacking a "straw man"—the argument that you wished your opponent made, not the one he actually did. The straw man fallacy is popular in political campaigns. For example, suppose a candidate believed that a major goal of prisons should be rehabilitation, not just punishment. An opponent could exploit that with a straw man attack: *"My opponent coddles convicted felons and wants to make life easier behind bars than on the street. Prison should be a deterrent, not a reward for bad behavior!"*

This list of fallacies captures most of the common errors we hear and see daily. Our challenge is to sharpen our professional senses so we can quickly sniff out the rational from the ridiculous and avoid adding to the epidemic of poor reasoning and weak support we encounter around us.

We've all had experience with using logical arguments to persuade someone else. In the middle of such a discussion, you may have asked yourself, "What's my goal—to persuade the other guy and make my case; or to find out the truth and the best answer to the problem?" (This usually comes up when your opponent comes up with a valid point you hadn't considered before.) Ever since the ancient Greeks were walking around in togas, people have struggled with this issue. The next section introduces this tension between truth and persuasion so that you are aware of it in both your arguments and those of others.

Arguments, Truth and Persuasion

We believe that argument is a matter not of fist banging or of win-lose debate but of finding, through a process of rational inquiry, the best solution of a problem.

–John D. Ramage, John C. Bean, and June Johnson

There will always be reasons to use argument as a tool of persuasion—you want your subordinate to win that award, you really need additional funding for your branch and you want your spouse to visit his or her in-laws over the Thanksgiving weekend.

Sometimes in the heat of verbal battle, it's tempting to focus on persuasion and forget about truth. Don't do it. "Integrity First" is one of our Air Force Core Values and you have to look at yourself in the mirror every morning. You don't have to be a doormat, but if you find out about some new information that may change your position, keep an open mind. In most situations, you don't only want your way, you want the best way. Besides, if you pull a fast one and get your way through deception, you've won a battle, but your credibility is shot and you've crippled yourself for future skirmishes.

Other ways to build credibility with your audience include being knowledgeable and fair. Research your topic carefully and take the time to get the facts right. Don't bluff if you don't have an answer, or mislead others about the strength of your support. Consider your audience's values and assumptions when selecting evidence. Make sure you get the easy things right—the spelling of names, significant dates and other details like grammar and punctuation. Demonstrate goodwill in your writing tone—don't be condescending or act superior. If you make a mistake, acknowledge it and move on. Credibility takes a long time to build, but it is invaluable when trying to support your ideas and persuade others.

SUMMARY: In this chapter we covered several topics that should help you support your ideas. We defined a *logical argument* as a set of statements designed to persuade others. Logical arguments have four components:

1. a *claim*—your position on a controversial topic;
2. *evidence* that supports your claim;
3. *warrants* that identify why the evidence is relevant; and
4. *qualifications* that limit the claim.

Your argument is built upon evidence and it should be authoritative, accurate, precise, relevant and adequate to support your claim. As you build or listen to logical arguments, watch out for *logical fallacies*—common mistakes many people make when building an argument. Arguments are everywhere. To write and speak persuasively, it helps to understand how arguments are constructed and where they go wrong. These insights will be helpful as you start to organize and outline your thoughts—the next step of the process.

CHAPTER 6:

Step 4 (Organize and Outline)

> ***This chapter covers:***
> - Organizing: Finalizing Your Purpose Statement and Bottom Line
> - The Outline: Why Do I Need One?
> - Outlining the Body: Pick a Pattern

After completing the first three steps of the Seven Steps to Effective Communication you are well on your way to an outstanding spoken or written product. Now it's time to talk about *organizing* and *outlining*, the final step in prewriting. A detailed outline helps you arrange your material logically, see relationships between ideas, and serves as a reference point to keep you on target as you write your draft. Think of your outline as the blueprint for your communication product, and realize that the time you spend preparing it will pay off when you start writing sentences and paragraphs.

Organizing: Finalizing Your Purpose Statement and Bottom Line

Why are we talking about a purpose statement again? Didn't we already determine our "bottom line" back in Step 1? Or did we? Sometimes information uncovered during the research process (Step 2) may point you in an unexpected direction. So do you tweak the data to match your original purpose? No! Now is the time to adjust the vector of your purpose statement to something you can reasonably support and live with.

> A *thesis statement* is a specialized form of purpose statement used in academic or persuasive writing.
>
> The thesis statement captures the author's point of view on a controversial topic, which he or she defends throughout the paper. A thesis statement is usually finalized after the research process.

You're less likely to go astray during the outlining process if you write down your purpose statement and refer to it often. Every main point and supporting idea in your outline should support that purpose statement—irrelevant facts or opinions should be eliminated. Discipline at this stage will save pain later.

Organizing: get your bottom line up front (most of the time). In nearly every communication situation, you need to state your bottom line early in the message. In a direct or *deductive* approach, state your position, main point or purpose up front, then go into the details that support your main point. When you take a direct approach to communication, your audience is better prepared to digest the details of the message and logically make the connections in its own mind.

> *In the future, authors will take a long time to get to the point. That way the book looks thicker.*
>
> –Scott Adams
> (The Dilbert Future: Thriving on Stupidity in the 21st Century)

There is an exception to every rule, and you might want to be less direct when trying to persuade a hostile audience. In such a situation, if you state your bottom line up front, you risk turning them off before you build your argument—regardless of how well it is supported. In this case you might consider using an indirect or *inductive* approach: you may present your support and end with your bottom line. Sometimes this successfully "softens the blow" and gives your audience time to warm up to your views.

In the inductive approach, you still need an introduction, but it would be less direct. Here's an example of two purpose statements:

Direct: Women should be allowed in combat because….
Indirect: The issue of women in combat has been hotly debated and both sides have valid points….

Use the inductive approach with caution; it's an advanced technique and difficult to execute without confusing your audience. In an academic setting, seek your instructor's advice before applying this method to your assignments.

The Outline: Why Do I Need One?

To some people, preparing an outline looks like a chore. Though an outline does take some effort, it's a time-saver, not a time-waster: an outline organizes your main points and supporting ideas in a logical order. It allows you to see the flow of your ideas on paper without having to write out complete sentences and paragraphs. If the ideas don't fit together or flow naturally, you can rearrange them without a lot of effort. Like the blueprint of a house, an outline makes the "construction process" efficient and effective—and results in a better quality product.

Does all writing require a detailed outline with several layers of detail? No. If you plan to write a short letter, message or report, a list of main points may be all you need. For longer papers, Air Force publications, reports, staff studies, etc., you'll find a detailed outline is usually an indispensable aid. The outline then serves as the framework to write well-organized instructions, reports, background or position papers, letters and memorandums.

Outlining Structure: Three Parts

Chapter 7 describes how most writing and speaking is organized into three parts: an introduction, a body and a conclusion. Most of the work in developing an outline involves organizing the body of your communication, but if you are building a detailed outline on a lengthy written product, you should probably include the introduction and conclusion in the outline. Skilled communicators writing short, informal assignments may just outline the body and work out the introduction and conclusion during the drafting process.

Outlining Formats: Headings and Structure Used in Formal Outlines

Though most outlines you produce will never be seen by anyone else, the logic you develop in an outline will show through in your communications—written an oral. You might also be asked to produce a formal outline for "public consumption" in some cases, such as these scenarios:

- Your boss wants to review what you plan to cover before you start drafting.
- You're organizing the efforts of multiple writers who must work together.

In these situations, it's helpful to have a consistent approach to outlining your project. A recent Internet search for outline formats yielded 3.6 million results; however, this handbook embraces only a few. Be consistent once you pick an approach and do your homework to find out if there is a preferred standard for your project.

✪ **Tip:** Turn off the automatic format function of your word processor. Many format headaches can be stopped before they start by disabling the automatic format function.

Outlining: The Cardinal Rule

The cardinal rule of outlining: *any topic that is divided must have at least two parts.* Every "1" must have a "2" (and so forth) for every level. Some official publications violate this rule but this does not mean the standard has changed, only that the author did not follow the rule, either by direction or in error.

The Classic Outline Format

The first option for an outline format is to use the classic outline format. The classic outline format uses Arabic numerals and the lower-case Latin alphabet characters in an alternating pattern to identify the different levels of the outline.

THE CLASSIC OUTLINE FORMAT

1. Level 1. Classic outline levels are formatted as shown below. Each paragraph is identified with a number or letter element followed by two spaces preceding the content of the paragraph.
    a. Level 2. [5 spaces precede "a." using Times New Roman (TNR) 12 point font]
       (1) Level 3. [10 spaces precede "(1)" using TNR 12]
          (a) Level 4. [16 spaces precede "(a)" using TNR 12]
             1 Level 5. [22 spaces precede "1" using TNR 12]
               a Level 6. [26 spaces precede "a" using TNR 12]
                  [1] Level 7. [30 spaces precede "[1]" using TNR 12]
                  [2] Level 7. Second item required by the cardinal rule of outlining.
               b Level 6. Second item required by the cardinal rule of outlining.
             2 Level 5. Second item required by the cardinal rule of outlining.
          (b) Level 4. Second item required by the cardinal rule of outlining.
       (2) Level 3. Second item required by the cardinal rule of outlining.
    b. Level 2. Second item required by the cardinal rule of outlining.
2. Paragraphs are numbered by alternating Arabic numerals with characters from the Latin alphabet, along with a period, parenthesis, underline or bracket to identify each paragraph.
    a. Each level is indented so that the paragraph number or letter is aligned under the first character in the preceding paragraph. Using Times New Roman 12 point font the spaces preceding each level to create this example are shown in [grey brackets]; however, if the font style or point size changes, the number of spaces will change due to the proportional spacing function of word processing software. ***Regardless of the font style or point size, maintaining the alignment of the paragraph number or letter of subordinate paragraphs with the first character of the preceding level is the key***.
    b. The text wraps all the way to left margin for all levels.
    c. Use bold font for main points or headings, as desired.
3. You can organize and subdivide in any number of ways (see "Outlining the Body: Pick a Pattern" latter in this chapter).
    a. Some sections may be more detailed than others resulting in some levels that will be divided while others will not, but remember, the cardinal rule of outlining applies when you do divide: ***any topic or outline level that is divided must have at least two parts.***.
    b. Most letters and memorandums use no more than three levels and AU-1, the *Air University Style and Author Guide*, recommends no more than three levels for most written work.
    c. Technical works may require more than three levels to maintain clarity and organization.
4. The **Classic Outline Format** is the standard format commonly used by senior Air Force executive staffs (directors of staff, secretaries, executive officers, command chiefs, etc.) and is the format used in official memorandum examples later in this handbook.

The Numbered Outline Format

The **numbered outline** is directed by Air Force Instruction (AFI) 33-360, *Publications and Forms Management*, for use in Air Force instructions. This format numbers every paragraph, indents each level one-quarter inch from the previous level, and wraps the text to align under the paragraph number. See AFI 33-360, paragraph 6.5.10.1, "Paragraph Numbering," for further details. The numbered outline format presented here is the final product format for AFIs; see AFI 33-360 for guidance on the format for drafting instructions.

NUMBERED OUTLINE FORMAT (Reference AFI 33-360, paragraph 6.5.10.1.)

Chapter 1
1.1.   Section 1. [Tip: Each item at a specific level in an outline should begin at the same level of indentation from the left margin (i.e., paragraphs 1.1. and 1.2. have the same indentation.]
    1.1.1.   First subheading to paragraph 1.1 [Tip: For each level of detail the paragraph numbers are indented one-quarter inch.]
    1.1.2.   Second subheading to paragraph 1.1. [Tip: Narrative text at every level should wrap as in this example—indented from the left to be aligned under the paragraph number.]
        1.1.2.1.   First subheading to paragraph 1.1.2. [Tip: Air Force Instructions frequently have levels of detail beyond this level. If possible, avoid too many levels of detail as the paragraph numbers becomes very long and the effectiveness of the system is degraded.]
        1.1.2.2.   Second subheading to paragraph 1.1.2. [Tip: Organize content to follow the cardinal rule of outlining: **any topic that is divided must have at least two parts.** Never create a Part 1 without a Part 2, a Section A without a Section B, a Paragraph 1.1.1 without a Paragraph 1.1.2.
    1.1.3.   Third subheading to paragraph 1.1.
1.2.   Section 2 of Chapter 1. [and so forth, as above.]

Chapter 2
2.1.   Section 1 of Chapter 2.
    2.1.1.   First subheading to paragraph 2.1.
        2.1.1.1.   First subheading to paragraph 2.1.1
        2.1.1.2.   Second subheading to paragraph 2.1.1.
    2.1.2.   Second subheading to paragraph 2.1
2.2.   Section 2 of Chapter 2. [and so forth, as above.]

The Modern Outline Format

The **modern outline** format is commonly used in Air Force PME courses. The modern outline is based on the *The Chicago Manual of Style* (16th Edition, pages 347-348). The modern outline uses upper- and lower-case Roman numerals as well as upper- and lower-case Latin alphabet and Arabic numbers. Remember to turn off the auto format function of your word processor when creating an outline.

MODERN OUTLINE FORMAT (Based on *The Chicago Manual of Style*)

I. Level 1. [1 space precedes "I" using TNR 12 to maintain alignment with paragraph "II." For further information, see paragraph "i)"]
   A. Level 2. [5 spaces precede "A." using Times New Roman (TNR) 12 point font]
      1. Level 3. [11 spaces precede "1." using TNR 12]
         a) Level 4. [16 spaces precede "a)" using TNR 12]
           (1) Level 5. [21 spaces precede "(1)" using TNR 12]
              (a) Level 6. Levels are numbered by alternating Arabic numerals with characters from the Latin alphabet, along with a period, parentheses, or brackets to uniquely identify each level [27 spaces precede "(a)" using TNR 12]
                  i) Level 7. This is the final outline level of detail available. The Roman numerals are right-aligned (the numerals extend to the left). Right-alignment can be difficult to format and maintain paragraph alignment, especially as the numeral increases; hence, lower-case Roman numerals are reserved for the level least likely to be used. (The same difficulty with right alignment of upper-case Roman numerals exists at Level 1. Often, the Level 1 Roman numerals are reserved for sections or chapters and Level 7 is not used. Some outlines omit all Roman numerals, using Levels 2 through 6 as Levels 1 through 5. [34 spaces]
                  ii) Each level is indented so that the paragraph number or letter is aligned under the first character in the preceding paragraph. Using Times New Roman 12 point font the spaces preceding each level to create this example are shown in [grey brackets]; however, if the font style or point size changes, the number of spaces will change due to the proportional spacing function of word processing software (the differences in this example compared to the Classic Outline example are due to differences in paragraph numbers, letters, and the number of parentheses or brackets). *Regardless of the font style or point size, maintaining the alignment of the paragraph number or letter of subordinate paragraphs with the first character of the preceding level is the key.* [33 spaces]
                  iii) Use bold font for main points or headings, as desired. [33 spaces]
                  iv) *The Chicago Manual of Style* suggests that papers not needing seven levels of detail omit Level 1 (upper-case Roman numerals) and Level 2 (upper-case Latin alphabet) and start with the Arabic numerals of Level 3 (1, 2, 3,…). [33 spaces]
                (b) Level 6. Second item required by the cardinal rule of outlining.
           (2) Level 5. Second item required by the cardinal rule of outlining.
         b. Level 4. Second item required by the cardinal rule of outlining.
      2. Level 3. Second item required by the cardinal rule of outlining.
   B. Level 2. Second item required by the cardinal rule of outlining.
II. You can organize and subdivide in any number of ways (see "Outlining the Body: Pick a Pattern" latter in this chapter).
   A. Some sections may be more detailed than others resulting in some levels that will be divided while others will not, but remember, the cardinal rule of outlining applies when you do divide: *Any topic or outline level that is divided must have at least two parts.*
   B. Most Air Force letters and memorandums use three levels and the *Air University Style and Author Guide* recommends no more than three levels for most short documents.
   C. Technical or lengthy documents may require more than three levels to maintain clarity and organization.

✪ **Tip**: Regardless of which outline format you use, remember that the primary purpose of an outline is to arrange your thoughts into main points and subordinate ideas. The bottom line is that outlining will help you organize content for greater clarity and improved communication. Use the format that helps you achieve better communication.

Outlining the Body: Pick a Pattern

Your next step is to select a pattern that enables you and your readers to move systematically and logically through your ideas from a beginning to a conclusion. Some of the most common organizational patterns are listed below. Your purpose, the needs of your audience and the nature of your material will influence your choice of pattern.

1. Topical or Classification Pattern

Use this format to present groups of ideas, objects or events by categories. This is a commonly used pattern to present general statements followed by numbered listings of subtopics to support, explain or expand the statements. A topical pattern usually follows some logical order that reflects the nature of the material and the purpose of the communication. For example, if you are giving a briefing on helicopters, you might separate them into light, medium and heavy lift capabilities and briefly describe the weight limits for each category. You could begin with the lightest capability and move to the heaviest or begin with the heaviest and move to the lightest.

✪ **Tip:** To help your readers absorb complex or unfamiliar material, consider organizing your material to move from the most familiar to the unfamiliar or from the simplest category to the most complex. When using this pattern, experiment to find the arrangement that will be most comfortable for your audience.

2. Comparison and Contrast Pattern

Use this style when you need to discuss similarities and/or differences between topics, concepts or ideas. When you are describing similarities and differences, it often helps the reader to see a point-by-point comparison of the two items. For example, if you were writing a document that compares and contrasts certain characteristics of the F-22 and the F-16, you might go item by item, discussing similarities and differences between the two as you go.

3. Chronological Pattern

When you use this pattern, you discuss events, problems or processes in the sequence of time in which they take place or should take place (past to present or present to future). This pattern is commonly used in writing histories, tracing the evolution of processes, recording problem conditions, and documenting situations that evolve over time. This approach is also used in official biographies, which are written in chronological order because they serve as a history of the member's professional career.

This pattern is simple to use, but judgment is required when deciding what events to leave in and what events to leave out. For example, if you were preparing a short biography to introduce a distinguished guest speaker, you may decide to emphasize experiences that demonstrate his subject matter expertise and leave out other important but less relevant details. When unsure what to include, think back to your purpose and audience.

✪ **Tip:** You may want to consider a chronological approach to your topic when it is known to be controversial. Many writers and speakers will announce, "First let's take a look at the history of the problem." This starts the sender and audience out on neutral ground instead of just launching into the issue at hand. This is a type of inductive approach, and again, should be used with caution.

4. Sequential Pattern

The *sequential* or *step-by-step* approach is similar to the chronological pattern. Use this approach to describe a sequence of steps necessary to complete a technical procedure or process. Usually the timing of steps is not as important as the specific order in which they are performed. The outline on the first page of this chapter ("Seven Steps to Effective Communication") is an example of a sequential approach. The sequential approach is often used in manuals and other instruction books. For example, a Security Forces noncommissioned officer (NCO) in charge of small arms training might use this pattern when rewriting the teaching manual on how to safely inspect, load, fire, disassemble and clean weapons. Since safety is paramount, the process must be written in a precise, stepwise fashion to ensure that nothing is overlooked.

✪ **Tip:** When describing a procedure, explain the importance of *sequence* so your audience is mentally prepared to pay close attention to the order, not just the content, of the information.

5. Spatial or Geographical Pattern

When using this pattern, you'll start at some point in space and proceed in sequence to other points. The pattern is based on a directional strategy—north to south, east to west, clockwise or counterclockwise, bottom to top, above and below, etc. Let's say you are a weather officer briefing pilots about current and anticipated conditions in the geographic region where they will be flying a mission. You would most likely describe conditions in reference to the terrain and describe weather systems that will affect their mission on a map.

✪ **Tip:** Make sure to use appropriate transitions to indicate spatial relationships: to the left, farther to the left, still farthermost to the left; adjacent to, a short distance away, etc. These signal the flow of the communication; if missing, your audience is easily confused.

6. Problem and Solution Pattern

You can use this pattern to identify and describe a problem and one or more possible solutions, or an issue and possible techniques for resolving the issue. Discuss all facets of the problem—its origin, its characteristics and its impact. When describing the proposed solution, include enough support to convince your readers the solution is practical and cost effective. After presenting your solution, you may want to identify immediate actions required to implement the solution.

The problem and solution pattern may be used in several variations:

- One Solution: Discuss the problem and follow with the single, most logical solution.
- Multiple Solutions: Discuss the problem, several possible solutions, the effects of each and your recommendation.
- Multiple Solutions, Pro-Con: This popular format includes a discussion of the advantages ("Pros") and disadvantages ("Cons") of each solution.

Remember that a problem-solution pattern is not a format for a personal attack on an adversary; it's simply a systematic approach to use in persuading people either to accept your ideas or to modify their own ideas. Note that this example uses the same paragraph headings (purpose, background, discussion, views of others and recommendation) as used in the electronic staff summary sheet (eSSS) discussed later in this handbook.

Problem and Solution Example: The Staff Study

The Staff Study format described in chapter 17 is a classic example of a problem and solution pattern. Within this format, you can present several possible solutions or just the one you recommend. A staff study with three options might have an outline that looks like this:

1. PURPOSE: (Problem)

2. BACKGROUND: (Factors bearing on the problem)

   a. Facts

   b. Assumptions

   c. Evaluation criteria for solutions

3. DISCUSSION: (Possible solutions and/or major factors or contentious points)

   a. Option 1: pros and cons

   b. Option 2: pros and cons

   c. Option 3: pros and cons

4. VIEWS OF OTHERS: (Consider the views of others so that the package creates buy-in from stakeholders and presents a complete analysis to the decision maker.)

5. RECOMMENDATION: (Clearly state in a single sentence what action you recommend to the approving official. Though you can list your options in any order, skilled writers often "save the best for last" and put their recommended option last on the list to help readability.)

---

7. Reasoning or Logic Pattern

In this pattern, you state an opinion and then make your case by providing support for your position. This is the classic "logical argument" described in chapter 5. This approach works well when your goal is more than just discussion of problems and possible solutions. Use this pattern when your mission is to present research that will lead your audience down the path to your point of view!

✪ **Tip:** Remember your audience analysis? If members of your audience are hostile to your position, try to look at this issue through their eyes. Start out with the support they are most likely to accept, and then move into the less popular issues that support your main point.

8. Cause and Effect

You can use this pattern to show how one or more ideas, actions or conditions lead to other ideas, actions or conditions. Two variations of this pattern are possible: (1) begin with the effect, then identify the causes; or (2) begin with the causes, then identify the effects. The technique you use depends on the context of your discussion.

Causes, Effects, and Faulty Logic

Be careful to avoid faulty logic traps when writing about cause and effect. You're guilty of a *false cause fallacy* when you assume one event causes a second event merely because it precedes the second event. You're guilty of a *single cause fallacy* when you assume only one factor caused an outcome, when in fact there are multiple causes. For more details on fallacies, refer back to chapter 5.

Sometimes an effect-to-cause approach is used when your purpose is to identify WHY something happened. When might you use this approach? Let's say you are the president of the Safety Investigation Board following a fatal aircraft mishap (*the effect*). Your report might begin by describing the mishap itself, and then explain the factors that led up to the mishap and conclude with your determination of one or more *causes* for the effect.

Sometimes a cause-to-effect pattern is used when your purpose is to explain HOW current actions or conditions (causes) may produce future consequences (effects). For example, someone might use this pattern to present how a series of causes—larger automobiles, reduced financial incentives for energy conservation and reduced research funding for alternative energy technologies—might result in an undesirable effect—a US shortage of fossil fuels.

SUMMARY: A well-planned outline can ease the pain of writing your first draft. Remember, building a house is much easier with a blueprint! This invaluable tool will help you remain focused on your purpose statement and help ensure your support is organized, relevant and tailored to your mission and audience. The outline will also help in the editing process. Take a break after working on your outline and start fresh before you begin your draft. Good luck!

PART III:

WRITING WITH FOCUS

Prewriting Process Summary: Steps 1-4

Before starting your draft, you should know…

Step 1. Analyze Purpose and Audience.

- Your purpose: to direct, inform, persuade or inspire.
- Your purpose statement: one sentence that captures your bottom line.
- Your communication format: Point paper? Staff study? Academic essay?
- Your audience: experience, education, attitudes about topic, etc.
- Your unit's position: Could you create problems for others? Should you coordinate this?
- The appropriate tone will depend on purpose and audience: usually polite, personal, positive and inclusive; often informal and direct.

Step 2. Research Your Topic. Relevant information from boss, coworkers, office files, Internet and the library.

Step 3. Support your Ideas.

- How to use relevant information to support your ideas and meet your purpose.
- How to "build a case" (a logical argument) for your position, if needed.
- How to use facts, definitions, statistics and testimony as evidence for your position.
- How to avoid mistakes in your logic and notice problems with your evidence.

Step 4. Organize and Outline.

- Your chosen organizational pattern (topical, chronological, problem and solution, etc.).
- Your outline, which graphically shows the flow of your main points.

CHAPTER 7:

Step 5 (Draft)

> *This chapter covers:*
> - Drafting: Basic Philosophy
> - Drafting Effective Paragraphs
> - Drafting Effective Sentences
> - Overcoming Writer's Block

After completing the prewriting process, you've got what you need to produce a first-rate communication product. Congratulations! You're ready to write your first draft! In this chapter we'll take a "top-down" approach to writing a draft. We'll start with the big picture: a three-part structure consisting of the introduction, the body and the conclusion. Next, we'll describe how to write effective paragraphs within the body. Finally, we'll dig down deeper into the sentences, phrases and words that make up the paragraphs of your draft.

Drafting: Basic Philosophy

Keep a few things in mind as you start the drafting process. A draft is not the finished product, and each sentence does not have to be polished and perfect. Your focus should be to get your ideas on paper. Don't obsess about grammar, punctuation, spelling and word choice at this point—that comes later. You don't have to fix every mistake as you see it—you can catch these during the editing process.

It's helpful to keep an eye on your outline when drafting your masterpiece, especially when you're writing something longer than a page or two. By periodically checking your outline, you are less likely to lose focus and include irrelevant information.

Have you ever sat down to start your first draft and found yourself just staring at the blank computer screen or paper? If you suffer from writer's block, we'll cover strategies for overcoming this fairly common problem at the end of this chapter.

Three Part Structure: An Introduction, Body and Conclusion

What is your draft going to look like? Is it going to be one huge paragraph? In most cases, you'll organize your draft in a three-part structure—introduction, body and conclusion.

- The **introduction** must capture your audience's attention, establish rapport and announce your purpose.
- The **body** must be an effective sequence of ideas that flows logically in a series of paragraphs.
- The **conclusion** must summarize the main points stated in the body and close smoothly.

Let's take a closer look at this structure. We'll examine these parts out of order—first, the introduction, then the conclusion and lastly the body where we'll spend most of our time.

Drafting the Introduction

The *introduction* sets the stage and tone for your message. Although the content and length of your introduction may vary with the writing template, the introduction should, at a minimum, clearly state your purpose ("bottom line") and the direction you plan to take the audience.

A typical introduction has three components: *stage setting remarks*, a *purpose statement* and an *overview*.

- *Stage-setting remarks* set the tone of the communication, capture the audience's attention and encourage them to read further. Stage-setting remarks are *optional*, so you can omit them in very short messages or in messages where you don't want to waste words.
- The *purpose statement* is the one sentence you'd keep if you had only one. It specifically states your purpose, thesis or main point. For some examples and more details, refer back to chapter 3.
- The *overview* is like a good roadmap—it clearly presents your main points, previews your paragraph sequence and ties your main points to your purpose.

> **Stage-Setting Remarks: Use them properly!**
>
> Stage-setting remarks are optional. Though they add polish to an introduction, your reader has to be able to pick which sentences are "setting the stage" and which sentence is the "bottom line."
>
> If you've received feedback that readers are sometimes confused about the purpose of your writing, get to the point quickly and don't overdo stage-setting remarks. Too many preliminaries can backfire and actually confuse the reader.
>
> Keep the BLUF (bottom line up front) acronym in mind as you write.

Here's an example of a short introduction that contains all three components:

> Communication is essential to mission accomplishment, and all Air Force personnel should be able to write effectively. (*Stage-Setting Remarks*) This handbook provides general guidelines and specific formats for use in both staff environments and Professional Military Education schools. (*Purpose Statement*) It begins with an overarching philosophy on military communication, then describes processes and techniques to improve writing and speaking products, and summarizes the most common formats used in Air Force communication. (*Overview*)

Even though readers read the introduction first, you don't have to write it first. If the introduction doesn't come easily or naturally, you can work on another part of the communication and then return to it. Some writers backpedal and don't want to work on the introduction until the rest of the communication is written. Others insist it guides them in shaping the content or body of their message. Regardless of when you write the introduction, make sure that it captures your purpose and make sure it prepares your audience for what is to come.

Here's the bottom line on your introduction: It must be an appropriate length for your specific communication and it should contain a clear statement of your purpose and direction.

Drafting the Conclusion

The *conclusion* is the last and often neglected part of a well-arranged communication. Sometimes inexperienced writers stop writing as soon as they finish discussing their last main idea. That's not an effective conclusion. The conclusion is your last chance to summarize your communication and give your audience a sense of closure.

An effective conclusion often summarizes the overall theme and main points discussed in the body. If you have a simple, straightforward purpose, you might want to emphasize it by restating it in slightly different words in the conclusion. If you have a complicated purpose or a long, involved communication, you'll probably need to emphasize your main ideas and state your proposals or recommendations.

For effective endings, restate the main ideas or observations or emphasize the main thrusts of arguments. Under no circumstances apologize for real or perceived inadequacies or inject weak afterthoughts. Conclude your communication with positive statements based on your preceding discussion. In general, avoid bringing up new ideas in the conclusion; these belong in the body of your communication.

Your introduction and conclusion should balance each other without being identical. To check this, read your introduction and then immediately read your conclusion to determine if your conclusion flows logically from your introduction and whether it fulfills your purpose. An effective conclusion leaves you with a sense you're justified in ending your communication. You're ready to call it a day only when you assure your audience you've accomplished the purpose stated in your introduction.

Introductions and conclusions: How long?

The length of your introduction and conclusion will be proportional to the length of your overall writing assignment. On a one-page assignment, they may be very short, while lengthy staff studies or publications may contain introductions and conclusions that are several paragraphs long. Introductions and conclusions to books are often an entire chapter!

Remember that introductions and conclusions are designed to help your readers; use good judgment in determining the appropriate length for your assignment.

Recall our sample introduction; here's a short conclusion derived from that introduction and the body (which we don't have right now):

> As Air Force personnel, we can't accomplish our mission without effective communication. Hopefully, this handbook has provided you with some practical tools to improve your communication skills, specifically speaking and writing. Keep it handy and refer to it often as you prepare and review a variety of spoken and written products throughout your career.

Even without the "body" available, you can see how the introduction and conclusion complement each other.

Drafting the Body

The *body* of your communication is the heart of your message. It includes your main ideas about your subject and supporting details under each main idea.

The body typically consists of several paragraphs. The total number of paragraphs (and overall length of the body) will depend on your purpose and subject. As a general rule, write a separate paragraph for each main idea—you might confuse your reader if you have two or more main ideas in a single paragraph. In a longer communication, you may find it necessary to use more than one paragraph to cover one main point or idea.

So much for a quick review of introductions, conclusions and bodies, let's now dig down a little deeper into the paragraphs that make up the body of your communication.

Drafting Effective Paragraphs

Paragraphs Should Contain One Main Point

Paragraphs are the primary vehicles to develop ideas in your writing. They serve three purposes:

1. To group related ideas into single units of thought.
2. To separate one unit of thought from another unit.
3. To alert your readers you're shifting to another phase of your subject.

An effective paragraph is a functional unit with clusters of ideas built around a single main point or idea and linked with other clusters preceding and following it. It's not an arbitrary collection designed for physical convenience. It performs a definite, planned function—it presents a single major idea or point, describes an event, or creates an impression.

Most staff writing depends on relatively short paragraphs of three to seven sentences. If you follow this practice, you'll be more likely to develop clear, easy-to-read paragraphs. The length of each paragraph will vary because some main points need more supporting details than others.

In general, the flow of your paragraphs will follow the organizational pattern or format you selected in Step 4: "Organizing and Outlining" (chapter 6). That is, you build your paragraphs to meet the structural requirements of your overall communication. But you can use analogy, examples, definition, and comparison and contrast to develop single paragraphs within your overall pattern. The guiding principle is to develop one main idea or point in each paragraph.

Topic Sentences: Capturing the Main Point of Each Paragraph

In staff writing, it's helpful to start off each paragraph with a *topic sentence* that captures the subject or controlling idea of the paragraph. The topic sentence prepares the reader for the rest of the paragraph and provides a point of focus for support, details, facts, figures and examples.

If your readers are confused, check your topic sentences!

A *topic sentence* announces your intent for a single paragraph in the same way a *purpose statement* announces your intent for the entire writing assignment. Most readers are better able to understand how ideas relate to each other if they know what's coming.

If you've received feedback that readers have trouble understanding the "flow" of your writing, check your topic sentences. Does one exist for each paragraph? Can you find it? Do they start off the paragraph? Do they tie back to your purpose statement?

In the body, don't make your reader search for the topic sentences of your paragraphs. (As stated earlier, the rules are different for introductions and conclusions.) Since the topic sentence is the subject and main idea of the paragraph, the best place for it is up front—the first sentence. This helps with clarity and makes things convenient for your readers. Many people need only general information about the content of certain letters, reports and directives. Scanning topic sentences at the beginning of paragraphs for the most important ideas saves a lot of time. If your readers need more details, they can always read beyond your topic sentences.

Once you've written a topic sentence, the rest of the paragraph should fall neatly in place. Other sentences between the topic sentence and the last sentence must be closely related to expand, emphasize and support the topic sentence. In some paragraphs, the last sentence is used to summarize key points, clinch the main idea in the reader's mind, or serve as a transition to the next topic sentence. (We'll talk more about transitions in the next section.) Eliminate any "extra" sentences that don't perform one of these functions.

Though most writers will draft an entire paragraph at a time, **an alternate drafting strategy is to first write all the topic sentences in your body**. Once the topic sentences are completed, go back and write the rest of the paragraphs, one at a time. Drafting the topic sentences first requires the writer to stay focused on the "big picture" and can help produce a clear and well-organized draft. This technique can be very useful for longer writing assignments and is recommended for writers who struggle to organize their writing.

Here's the bottom line on body paragraphs: Each paragraph should have one main point or idea captured in a topic sentence, preferably at the beginning of the paragraph. Use supporting ideas to prove, clarify, illustrate and develop your main point. Your objective is to help your readers see your paragraphs as integrated units rather than mere collections of sentences.

Transitions: Bridges between Different Ideas

One way to make sure your paragraphs flow together, both internally and externally, is by using transitions in the form of words, phrases and sentences. *Internal transitions* improve the flow of sentences within a paragraph while *external transitions* link separate paragraphs together within the body of your communication.

Internal Transitions

Internal transitions are one or more related words that show the relationship between ideas *within a paragraph*. Woven skillfully into your writing, internal transitions help your reader follow your line of thought. Some internal transitions show a relationship between two ideas inside a single sentence: "**First** go home, and **then** clean your room."

Other internal transitions show a relationship between two or more sentences within a single paragraph such as this example: "Our plan for Saturday afternoon involves both business and pleasure. **First,** all the kids will come home at noon, and we'll eat lunch. **Next,** we'll get the house cleaned—the whole mess. **Finally,** we'll go out for ice cream and a movie."

Take a look at the next page for a bulletin board of transitional words and phrases that provide the ideal logic links between your key points and the mind of the reader. In most cases, favor the short, spoken ones over the long, bookish ones. For example, use *but* more than *however*, *so* more than *therefore*, and *also* more than *in addition*. Remember, different transitions require different punctuation. If you're uncertain about the rules, check out Appendix 1. For example, you can use "so" in place of "therefore" for a much easier to read sentence, as shown below:

"The movie was too long; therefore, we left after three hours."
"The movie was too long, so we left after three hours."

Transition "Bulletin Board"

To Contrast Ideas	To Show Time	To Relate Thoughts
<ul><li>but</li><li>yet</li><li>nevertheless</li><li>however</li><li>still</li><li>conversely</li><li>on the one hand</li><li>instead of</li><li>neither of these</li><li>(to) (on) the contrary</li><li>rather than</li><li>no matter what</li><li>much less as</li><li>in contrast</li><li>otherwise</li><li>on the other hand</li><li>in the (first) (second) place</li><li>nor</li><li>according to</li></ul>	<ul><li>immediately</li><li>presently</li><li>nearly a ___ later</li><li>meantime</li><li>meanwhile</li><li>afterward</li><li>next</li><li>as of today</li><li>this year, however</li><li>a little later</li><li>then last year</li><li>next week</li><li>tomorrow</li><li>as of now</li><li>finally</li></ul>	<ul><li>indeed</li><li>anyway, anyhow</li><li>elsewhere</li><li>nearby</li><li>above all</li><li>even these</li><li>beyond</li><li>in other words</li><li>for instance</li><li>of course</li><li>in short</li><li>in sum</li><li>yet</li><li>in reality</li><li>that is</li><li>by consequence</li><li>notwithstanding</li><li>nonetheless</li><li>as a general rule</li><li>understandably</li><li>traditionally</li><li>the reason, of course</li><li>the lesson here is</li><li>from all information</li><li>at best</li><li>naturally</li><li>in the broader sense</li><li>to this end</li><li>in fact</li></ul>
To Compare Ideas	**To Show Results**	**To Add Ideas**
<ul><li>like</li><li>just as</li><li>similar</li><li>this</li></ul>	<ul><li>therefore</li><li>as a result</li><li>thus</li><li>consequently</li><li>hence</li></ul>	<ul><li>first, second, next, last, etc.</li><li>in addition</li><li>additionally</li><li>moreover</li><li>furthermore</li><li>another</li><li>besides</li><li>clear, too, is</li><li>the answer does not only lie</li><li>to all that</li><li>more than anything else</li><li>here are some ... facts</li><li>now, of course, there are</li><li>now however</li></ul>

There are many ways to bridge gaps in thought and move the reader from one idea to another. One classic transitional approach involves repetition of key words at the beginning of individual sentences. This is especially popular in formal or ceremonial writing or speaking. Notice how the writer of the following paragraph repeated *simplicity, incisiveness* and *focus* to make points clear:

> The effective presentation of concepts depends on simplicity, incisiveness and focus. Simplicity is necessary under time constraints when there's insufficient time for complicated relationships. Incisiveness fixes an idea in the listener's mind, appeals to common sense and facilitates understanding. Focus limits the subject to essentials, promoting the presenter's objectives.

Internal transitions, in the form of one or more related words, are key to a well-written paragraph because they guide the reader between related ideas. But how do we move from paragraph to paragraph? We need *external transitions* to knit together their main points.

External Transitions

External transitions are typically sentences or paragraphs that guide the reader **between separate paragraphs** and **major sections** of your communication.

Transitional paragraphs are usually reserved for long papers, books and reports that contain major sections or chapters. They are used to summarize one section and lead the reader to the next section, or they introduce the next section and tie it to the preceding section. Transitional paragraphs are not commonly used in staff writing, but are often seen in books and academic essays.

The short paragraph immediately above this section ("Internal transitions, in the form of one or more related words...") is an example of a transitional paragraph. As you can see, it sums up the previous section on internal transitions and then introduces the new section on external transitions.

Let's look closer at transitional sentences, which you'll probably use more frequently than transitional paragraphs. A transitional sentence is often used to bridge main points in two separate paragraphs (though not every new paragraph requires an external transition). There are three options of a transitional sentence bridging paragraph 1 and paragraph 2:

- Option 1: It can be a stand-alone sentence at the end of paragraph 1.

- Option 2: It can be a stand-alone sentence at the beginning of paragraph 2 (In this case, paragraph 2's topic sentence is the second sentence in the paragraph).

- Option 3: It can be merged with the topic sentence of paragraph 2 (In this case, the "transitional" part of the sentence is a separate clause at the beginning of the sentence).

Let's look at a situation where a transitional sentence is appropriate. Suppose we have two paragraphs: Paragraph 1 describes parking problems; paragraph 2 describes potential solutions to the parking problems. Here's an example of a stand-alone transitional sentence for these paragraphs:

> **Fortunately, we can solve these parking problems if we offer our people some incentives to use car pools.** *(transitional sentence)*

If this sentence were at the end of paragraph 1 (option 1), paragraph 2 would start with a topic sentence written something like this:

> **We can offer our personnel three incentives to participate in car pools: preferred parking spaces, guaranteed duty hours and distant parking for nonparticipants.** *(topic sentence)*

If our transitional sentence were at the beginning of paragraph 2 (option 2), then our topic sentence would be the second sentence in paragraph 2, like this:

> **Fortunately, we can solve these parking problems if we offer our people some incentives to use carpools.** *(transitional sentence)* **We can offer them three incentives: preferred parking spaces, guaranteed duty hours, and distant parking for nonparticipants.** *(topic sentence)*

Now let's look at our third option where we merge the transition with the topic sentence of paragraph 2. In this case, we have one sentence instead of two, like this:

> **Fortunately, we can solve these parking problems** *(transitional clause)* **by offering our people three incentives to participate in car pools: preferred parking spaces, guaranteed duty hours and distant parking for nonparticipants** *(topic of paragraph 2)*.

Whether used at the end or beginning of a paragraph, transitional sentences can make your writing smoother and make your reader happier!

Headings as Transitions

Another effective way to transition from one major area to another, especially in a longer report, is to use *headings*. They allow your reader to follow along easily, even at a glance. Headings are also helpful when topics vary widely. Be informative: headings focus readers from broad topics to more detailed topics. Avoid relying on headings that use one or two vague words but do not use more words than are needed. Here are a couple examples.

> For: Procedures; Try: *How to Complete AF Form XXXX*

> For: *Contractors;* Try: *How Much Contractors May Charge*

Now that you have a good idea of how to draft "the big picture" part of your communication—your introduction, conclusion and paragraphs in the body—it's time to dig a little deeper. It's time to look at building effective sentences within your paragraphs.

Drafting Effective Sentences

To draft clear and concise sentences, choose clear and concise words and phrases to make up your sentences. In this section, we'll cover some of the most important considerations when writing effective sentences: active voice, smothered verbs, parallel construction, misplaced modifiers, using the right word for the job and avoiding wordy words and phrases. Let's get started with probably the most common pitfall to clear and concise sentences—not writing actively.

Write Actively: Doers Before Verbs

Is your active voice all bottled up? Active voice shows the subject as the actor. For example: *The girl sang a song.* By using mostly active voice, your writing is clear, concise and alive—it reaches out to the reader and gets to the point quickly with fewer words. Unfortunately, many writers overuse passive voice. Passive voice shows the subject as receiver of the action. For example: *A song was sung by her.* Besides lengthening and twisting sentences, passive verbs often muddy them. Whereas active sentences must have doers, passive ones are complete without them. When you overuse passive voice and reverse the natural subject-verb-object pattern, your writing becomes lifeless.

- Your support is appreciated ...
- Requisitions should be submitted ...
- The IG team will be appointed ...
- It is requested that you submit ...

The actor (or doer) in the sentence is either obscure, absent altogether or just lying there. Who appreciates? Who should requisition? Who appoints? Why not write ...

- I appreciate your support ...
- Submit your requisitions ...
- Colonel Hall will appoint the IG team ...
- Please submit ...

The Symptoms of Passive Voice and Three Cures

How can you diagnose passive voice? You don't have to be a grammarian to recognize passive voice. First, find the verb by asking yourself, "What's happening in this sentence?" Then find the actor by asking, "Who's doing it?" If the actor comes after the verb, it's passive voice. Also, watch for these forms of the verb *to be* (*am, is, are, was, were, be, being, been*) *and* a main verb usually ending in *-ed* or *-en*. Let's look at a few examples and then try the cures, below.

> **Passive:** The mouse *was* eat*en* by the cat.
> **Active:** The *cat ate* the mouse.
>
> **Passive:** Livelier sentences will be written by you.
> **Active:** You will write livelier sentences.
>
> **Passive:** Water is drunk by everybody.
> **Active:** Everybody drinks water.

1. Put the Actor (Doer) Before the Verb.

> **This:** The *handlers* must have broken the part.
> **Not:** The part must have been broken by the *handlers*.

2. Drop Part of the Verb.

> **This:** The results *are* in the attachment.
> **Not:** The results *are listed* in the attachment.

3. Change the Verb.

> **This:** The replacement has not *arrived* yet.
> **Not:** The replacement has not *been received* yet.

Though most writers overuse passive voice, sometimes it's appropriate. Clear and forceful language may be inappropriate in diplomacy or in political negotiations. Passive voice is also used to soften bad news, or when the doer or actor of the action is unknown, unimportant, obvious or better left unnamed. Here are a few examples:

> The part was shipped on 1 June. (The *doer* is unimportant.)
> Presidents are elected every four years. (The *doer* is obvious.)
> Christmas has been scheduled as a workday. (The *doer* is better left unnamed.)

The bottom line: Passive voice is wordy, indirect, unclear and reverses the natural order of English. Active voice is clear and concise. Using verbs correctly—actively—is key to writing clear, concise and interesting sentences. Activate your writing!

Smothered Verbs

Make your verbs do the work for you. Weak writing relies on general verbs that take extra words to complete their meaning. Don't use a general verb (make) plus extra words (a choice) when you can use one specific verb (choose).

> **Wordy**: The IG team held a meeting to give consideration to the printing issue.
> **Better**: The IG team met to consider the printing issue.

> **Wordy**: They made the decision to give their approval.
> **Better**: They decided to approve it.

Here's another tip on verbs—watch out for words ending in *-ion* and *-ment*—these are verbs turned into nouns. Change these nouns to verbs: your sentences will be shorter and livelier.

> **Wordy**: Use that format *for the preparation of* your command history.
> **Better**: Use that format *to prepare* your command history.

> **Wordy**: *The settlement of* travel claims involves *the examination of* orders.
> **Better**: *Settling* travel claims involves *examining* orders.

We've spent a lot of time looking at verbs because they're the most important words in your sentences. **The bottom line:** keep verbs active, lively, specific, concise and out in front, not hidden. Another potential stumbling block for readers is "unparallelism."

Parallel Construction (Parallelism)

Use a consistent pattern when making a list. If your sentence contains a series of items separated by commas, keep the grammatical construction similar—if two of three items start with a verb, make the third item start with a verb. Violations occur when writers mix things and actions, statements and questions, and active and passive instructions. The trick is to be consistent. Make ideas of equal importance look equal.

> **Needs work:** The functions of a military staff are to *advise* the commander, *transmit* instructions and *implementation* of decisions. [Advise and transmit are verbs, while implementation is a noun.]
> **Acceptable:** The functions of a military staff are to *advise* the commander, *transmit* instructions and *implement* decisions. [Parallel ideas are now written in the same grammatical form.]

Needs work: The security policeman told us *to observe the speed limit* and *we should dim our lights*. [Parallel ideas are not written in the same grammatical form.]
Acceptable: The security policeman told us *to observe the speed limit* and *to dim our lights*.

Needs work: Universal military values include that we should act with integrity, dedication to duty, the belief that freedom is worth dying for and service before self.
Acceptable: Universal military values include commitment to integrity, dedication to duty, service before self, and the belief that freedom is worth dying for.

If one of the items in a list can't be written in the same grammatical structure, place it at the end of the sentence. In the previous example, "the belief that freedom is worth dying for" does not match the three-word construction of the other items, but its placement helps the sentence's readability. Active voice, strong verbs and parallelism can help make your sentences clear and concise. Now, let's look at some more things you can do to write effective sentences—using the right word for the job.

Use the Right Word for the Job

Without generalizations and abstractions, and lots of them, we would drown in detail. We sum up vast amounts of experience when we speak of dedication, programs, hardware and lines of authority. But such abstract language isn't likely to evoke the same experiences in each reader's mind. Lazy writing overuses vague terms such as *immense dedication, enhanced programs, viable hardware* and *responsive lines of authority*. It especially weakens job descriptions and performance evaluations, etc.

Be Concrete

Do not write "The commander will give guidance," or "The equipment must meet specs." Your reader might wonder what kind of guidance or what kind of specs? Neither you nor your readers can tackle the problem until you are specific. Be as definite as the situation permits. Include only the ideas your reader needs and then give those ideas no more words than they deserve.

Use the Right Word for the Job			
For	**Try**	**For**	**Try**
commanders	MAJCOM commanders	Ford	Focus
headache	migraine	emotion	love
car, vehicle	Ford	plane	F-22
smartphone	iPhone 4	socialize	mingle, meet

Know Various Shades of Meaning.

Use different words to express various shades of meaning. The writer with an adequate vocabulary writes about the *aroma* of a cigar, the *fragrance* of a flower, the *scent* of perfume or the *odor* of gas instead of the *smell* of all these things.

CHAPTER 7:
Step 5 (Draft)

Judge the Jargon

The aim of all communication is to make a personal contact in the simplest possible way, and the simplest way is to use familiar, everyday words. Above all, it must be adapted to specific circumstances with a minimum of jargon. Jargon consists of "shorthand" words, phrases or abbreviations that are peculiar to a relatively small group of people. *DEROS* (Date Eligible to Return from Overseas) and *AWOL* (Absent Without Leave) are examples of military jargon. Every profession has it. *NPO* which means Nil Per Os (nothing by mouth) and contusion (bruise) are examples of medical jargon. Writers often use jargon in their sentences to fill space and impress the naive. Unfortunately, overuse of jargon can backfire on you by actually confusing your reader. **CAUTION!** Before you use jargon, make sure you have carefully assessed the audience and use terms that will be familiar to them. Keep it simple with everyday words and phrases, or at least explain any jargon you must use. If you use an abbreviation, spell it out the first time it appears. If it appears only twice or infrequently, spell out the term every time and avoid the abbreviation entirely. For more on abbreviations see Appendix 1.

Clichés

Clichés are expressions that have lost their impact because they have been overused. Strive for originality in your choice of words and phrases. The list of clichés below is not exhaustive. You just may not find your favorite here.

Clichés		
acid test	add insult to injury	armed to the teeth
as a matter of fact	at a loss for words	banker's hours
battle royal	beat a hasty retreat	beauty and the beast
benefit of the doubt	better late than never	bewildering variety
beyond the shadow of a doubt	bite the dust	blazing inferno
blessed event	blessing in disguise	blissful ignorance
brave as a lion	break of day	bright and early
bull in a china shop	burn one's bridges	burn the midnight oil
burning issue	bury the hatchet	busy as a bee
by the same token	calm before the storm	cherished belief
clear the decks	club-wielding police	colorful scene
conspicuous by its absence	cool as a cucumber	coveted award
crack of dawn	crack troops	cutting edge
dramatic new move	dread disease	dream come true
drop in the bucket	easier said than done	fame and fortune
feast or famine	fickle fortune	food for thought
from the face of the earth	gentle hint	glaring omission
glutton for punishment	gory details	grief stricken
grim reaper	hammer out (an agreement)	hand in glove
happy couple	hard as a rock	head over heels in love
heart of gold	heavily armed troops	honest as the day is long
hook, line and sinker	hungry as wolves	in short supply
in this day and age	intensive investigation	iron out (problems)
irony of fate	it goes without saying	Lady Luck
lash out	last but not least	last-ditch stand
leaps and bounds	leave no stone unturned	lend a helping hand

Clichés		
light at the end of the tunnel	lightning speed	limp into port
lock, stock and barrel	long arm of the law	man in the street
marvels of science	matrimonial bliss (knot)	meager pension
miraculous escape	moment of truth	more than meets the eye
Mother Nature	move into high gear	never a dull moment
Old Man Winter	on more than one occasion	paint a grim picture
pay the supreme penalty	picture of health	pillar of (the church, society)
pinpoint the cause	police dragnet	pool of blood
posh resort	powder keg	predawn darkness
prestigious law firm	proud heritage	proud parents
pursuit of excellence	quick as a flash	radiant bride
red faces, red-faced	reign supreme	reins of government
round of applause	rushed to the scene	sadder but wiser
scantily clad	scintilla of evidence	scurried to shelter
selling like hotcakes	sharp as a razor	sings like a bird
spearheading the campaign	spirited debate	spotlessly clean
sprawling base, facility	spreading like wildfire	steaming jungle
stick out like a sore thumb	storm of protest	stranger than fiction
supreme sacrifice	surprise move	sweep under the rug
sweet harmony	sweetness and light	tempest in a teapot
tender mercies	terror stricken	tip of the iceberg
to no avail	too numerous to mention	tower of strength
tragic death	trail of death and destruction	true colors
vanish in thin air	walking encyclopedia	wave of the future
wealth of information	whirlwind campaign	wouldn't touch that with a 10-foot pole

Easily Confused Words

Many writers and speakers frequently confuse the meaning of some words. Here's a small list of some easily confused words. Be on the lookout for others.

Easily Confused Words	
• accept: verb, receive • except: verb or preposition, omitting or leaving out	• exceptional: out of the ordinary • exceptionable: objectionable
• advice: noun, counsel given, an opinion • advise: verb, to give counsel or advice	• farther: expresses distance • further: expresses degree
• affect: verb, to influence or feign • effect: noun, result; verb, to bring about	• fewer: refers to numbers; countable items • less: refers to mass; items can't be counted
• aggravate: make worse or intensify • annoy: disturb or irritate	• formally: in a formal manner • formerly: in the past
• all ready: everyone is prepared • already: adverb, by specific time	• hanged: to execute; criminals are hanged • hung: suspended or nailed up; pictures are hung

Easily Confused Words

• all together: collectively or in a group • altogether: wholly or entirely	• healthy: possessing health • healthful: conducive to health • wholesome: healthful as applied to food or climate
• alright: not acceptable spelling • all right: satisfactory	• imply: to hint at or suggest • infer: to draw a conclusion based on evidence
• allusion: indirect reference • delusion: false belief • illusion: a false impression	• incredible: unbelievable, improbable • incredulous: skeptical, doubting
• alumni: men graduates or group of men and women graduates • alumnae: women graduates	• instance: example • instant: moment of time • incident: event or an occurrence
• among: used when more than two alternatives • between: used when only two alternatives	• ingenious: clever or resourceful • ingenuous: innocently frank or candid
• amount: quantity that can't be counted or measured in units • number: quantity counted and measured in units	• later: after the usual time • latter: to designate the second of two things mentioned
• anxious: worry or fearfulness • eager: keen desire	• lay: to place • lie: to recline; to stretch out
• apt: suitable, quick to learn, natural tendency • liable: legally responsible • likely: refers to the probable, probability	• likely: a favorable probability • liable: legally responsible • apt: a natural fitness or tendency
• as: a subordinate conjunction • like: a preposition	• lose: a verb • loose: primarily an adjective
• avocation: hobby • vocation: customary employment	• luxuriant: abundant growth • luxurious: pertains to luxury
• beside: preposition, next to or near • besides: adverb, in addition; preposition, addition to	• may be: a modal verb • maybe: perhaps
• bi-: occurring every two (units of time) • semi-: occurring twice (during the time period)	• moneys: currency • monies: amount of money
• bring: action toward the speaker • take: action away from the speaker	• morale: refers to a spirit or a mood • moral: refers to right conduct
• can: ability • may: permission	• persecute: to afflict or harass • prosecute: to pursue until finished or to bring legal action against a defendant

Easily Confused Words

• capital: city or money • capitol: a building	• practical: useful, sensible • practicable: feasible; a person cannot be practicable
• censor: examine in order to forbid if objectionable • censure: condemn or to reprimand	• principal: adjective, foremost; noun, main person • principle: noun, precept or idea
• compliment: praise • complement: supplies a lack; it completes	• raise: to lift or cause to be lifted • rise: to move to a higher position
• compose: to constitute • comprise: to include or consist of	• respectively: in the order given • respectfully: full of respect
• consul: foreign representative • council: a group • counsel: advice, to give advice	• set: to put or to place • sit: to occupy a seat
• contemptible: base, worthless, despicable • contemptuous: expressing contempt or disdain	• shape: condition of being • condition: state, situation
• continually: closely recurrent intervals • continuously: without pause or break	• sometime: at some unspecified time • some time: a period of time • sometimes: now and then
• credible: believable • creditable: deserving credit or honor • credulous: ready to believe anything	• specie: coin • species: a kind or variety
• disinterested: impartial or objective • uninterested: indifferent	• stationary: in a fixed place • stationery: writing paper, envelopes
• eligible: qualified to be chosen • illegible: unable to read	• than: conjunction of comparison • then: adverb, at that time
• emigrate: to leave a country to settle in another • immigrate: to enter a country to settle there	• their: third person plural pronoun, possessive • there: adverb or interjection • they're: contraction of they are
• eminent: noted or renowned • imminent: impending	• verbal: applies to that which is communicated in words, spoken or written • oral: applies only to that which is spoken
• enervating: weakening • invigorating: stimulating	• who: refers to people • which: refers to things
• ensure: guarantee • insure: obtain insurance for	

CHAPTER 7:
Step 5 (Draft)

Doubleheaders

The Word by Rene J. Cappon details how to avoid writing a project's *importance and significance* when importance will do. Even a person's *success and achievement* is okay with just success. Pairs of words with similar meanings add bulk. Although *test and evaluate* are different, the differences may not be important for all audiences. When you're tempted to use two words, try one to say it all. Thomas Jefferson said: "The most valuable of all talents is that of never using *two* words when *one* will do."

Doubleheaders		
aid and abet	each and every	ready and willing
beck and call	fair and just	right and proper
betwixt and between	few and far between	safe and sound
bits and pieces	irrelevant and immaterial	shy and withdrawn
blunt and brutal	nervous and distraught	smooth and silky
bound and determined	nook and cranny	success and achievement
clear and simple	null and void	sum and substance
confused and bewildered	part and parcel	test and evaluate
disgraced and dishonored	pick and choose	various and sundry

Repetitive Redundancy

Not every noun needs an adjective. Not every adjective needs an adverb. Not every writer has gotten the message. Keep your pencil from adding modifiers to those nouns that need no additional voltage. *Serious* danger, *stern* warning, *deadly* poison, *grave* crisis are examples; the nouns operate better without the modifiers.

Repetitive Redundancy		
absolutely conclusive	advance planning	agricultural crops
anthracite coal	ascend upward	assemble together
awkward dilemma	basic fundamental	big in size
bisect in two	blend together	both alike
capitol building	chief protagonist; leading protagonist; or main protagonist	close proximity
coalesce together	collaborate together or jointly	complete monopoly
completely full	completely unanimous	congregate together
connect together	consensus of opinion	continue to persist
courthouse building	current or present incumbent	descend downward
divisive quarrel	doctorate degree	end result
exact counterpart	entirely absent	erupt violently
first beginning	fellow colleague	few in number
from whence	founder and sink	free gift
gather together	fuse together	future plan
habitual custom	general public	grateful thanks
individual person	hired mercenary	hoist up
join together	invited guest	irreducible minimum

Repetitive Redundancy		
lonely hermit	knots per hour	large in size
mutual cooperation	meaningless gibberish	merge together
new record	necessary need	new innovation
old antique	new recruit	old adage
original founder	opening gambit	organic life
past history	original prototype	passing fad
personal opinion	patently obvious	personal friend
protrude out	pointed barb	present incumbent
recoil back	real fact	recall back
shuttle back and forth	recur again or repeatedly	short in length or height
small in size	single unit	skirt around
temporary reprieve	tall in height	two twins
universal panacea	true facts	ultimate outcome
vitally necessary	violent explosion	visible to the eye

Wordy Words and Phrases vs. Simpler Words and Phrases

Many people use certain wordy words and needless phrases, such as phrases introduced by prepositions like *at, on, for, in, to* and *by*. They don't add substance; they weaken the message by cluttering the words that carry meaning. So prune the deadwood. The longer it takes to say something, the weaker you come across.

The use of simpler words and phrases in your communications may help convey your meaning; however, there are times when more formal or complex words and phrases convey the intended meaning best and are appropriate. For example, contractions are generally not used in formal policy letters or directions intended for a wide audience, such as an entire squadron, group, wing, or higher, or in academic work. This ensures clarity over simplicity. Your situation will dictate which is best to use; when appropriate, use simpler words and phrases.

INSTEAD OF	TRY	INSTEAD OF	TRY
a great deal of	much	activate	start, drive, put into action, turn on
a minimum of	at least	active consideration	consider
a number of	some, many, few	activities	actions
a period of (2 days)	for	actual	real, true
abandon	give up	actual emergency	emergency
abet	help, assist, aid	actual facts	facts
abeyance (hold in)	delay, postpone, wait	actuate	induce, move, drive, impel
abridge	shorten, condense	additional	added, more, other, further
abrogate	do away with, abolish, cancel, revoke	address	speech, speak of, speak to, deal with
accelerate	speed up, hasten	adequate	enough, plenty
accept	take, receive	adjacent to	next to
accommodate	make fit, make room for, allow for	advanced plans	plans
accompany	go with	advantageous	helpful, useful, beneficial, good
accomplish	carry out, do, complete	adverse to	against, opposed to
accomplish (a form)	fill out, complete, fill in, prepare	advise	recommend, tell, inform
according to	per	advised (keep me)	informed (or "inform me")
accordingly	so, then, therefore	affirmative	agree, assent to, say "yes"
accrue	add, gain	affix	put, stick, attach, place, add
accumulate	gather, amass, collect	affix a signature	sign
accurate	correct, exact, right	afford an opportunity	allow, let, permit
achieve	do, make	after the conclusion of	after
achieve the maximum	get the most from, excel	agency	office
acquire	get, gain, earn, win	aggregate	all, total, sum, combined, whole, entire

CHAPTER 7:
Step 5 (Draft)

INSTEAD OF	TRY
aircraft	military plane
all of	all
allegation	charge, claim, assertion
alleviate	ease, relieve, lessen
allotment	share, portion
along the lines of	like, similar to
alter, alteration	change
alternative	choice, option, substitute
amalgamate	merge, combine, unite, mix
ambient	surrounding
ameliorate	better, improve
annually	yearly
antedate	precede
anticipate	expect, foresee
antipathy	dislike, distaste
antithesis	opposite, contrast
anxiety	fear
apparent	clear, plain, visible
apparently	seemingly, clearly
appear	seem
appellation	name
append	add, attach
applicable	which applies, proper, correct, suitable
application	use (noun)
appreciable	many
appreciate	value
apprise	tell, inform
appropriate	proper, right, apt, pertinent, fit
approximately	about, nearly, almost
are desirous of	want to
are in receipt of	received
as a matter of fact	in fact
as a means of	to
as a result of	because
as against	against
as and when	as, when (not both)
as at present advised	as advised
as of (this date)	by (today), today
as prescribed by	under, per
as to whether	whether, if
ascertain	find out, learn, make sure
assert	claim, declare
assimilate	absorb, digest, join, include
assist, assistance	aid, help
at a later date	later
at a much greater rate	faster, more quickly
at all times	always
at an early date	soon
at present	now, currently, presently
at such time	when
at the present time	currently, at present, now
at the time of	when
at this juncture (time)	now
at your earliest convenience (formal)	as soon as you can (informal, more direct)
attached herewith is	here is
attached please find	here is, attached is, enclosed is
attain	reach, gain, achieve
attempt	try
attempts to	tries
attention is invited to	note, see
attired	dressed
augment	add, increase, extend, enlarge, raise
authored	wrote
authoritative	valid, official

INSTEAD OF	TRY
authority	sanction, control, guidance
authorize	allow, let, permit, empower, prescribe
autonomous	independent
avail yourself of	use
availability	presence, use
based on the fact that	because
be acquainted with	know
be cognizant of	know
be of assistance to	assist, help, aid
befall	happen, occur
behest	request, order
behoove	(avoid) proper, helpful, beneficial
benefit	help
bestow	give
betterment	improvement
biannual	twice a year
biennial	once in 2 years
bilateral	two sided
bona fide	real, genuine, sincere
brief (duration)	short, quick
brook (tolerate)	allow
burgeoning	increasing, growing
by means of	by, with
by virtue of	because, by, under
came to an end	ended
capability	ability
capable	able
care should be taken	be careful, take care
category	class, group
characteristic	trait (noun), typical of (adjective)
characterize	describe, portray
circuitous	roundabout
classify	arrange
close proximity	close, near
cognizant of	aware of, know, understand, comprehend
coincidentally	at the same time
collaboration	(see "cooperation")
colloquy	discussion, talk
combine	join
combined	joint
comes into conflict	conflicts
commence	begin, start
commensurate	equal to, to agree with
commensurate with	corresponding, according, equal to
communicate verbally	talk, discuss, say, tell
compensate, compensation	pay
comply (with)	follow, carry out, meet, satisfy
component	part
comprehend	grasp, take in, understand
comprehensive	all-inclusive, thorough
comprise	form, include, make up, contain
comprised of	made up of, consists of
concerning	about, on
conclude	close, end, think, figure, decide
conclusion	end
concur	agree, approve
condition	state, event, facts
conduct (verb)	carry out, manage, direct, lead
confront	face, meet, oppose
conjecture	guess
connection	link, tie
connotation	meaning
consensus of opinion	agreement, verdict, general, view

INSTEAD OF	TRY	INSTEAD OF	TRY
consequently	so, therefore	due to the fact that	because of, hence, since, due to
consider	look at, think about, regard	duplicate	copy
considerable (amount)	large, great	duration	time, period
consolidate	combine, join, merge	during such time	while
constitutes	is, forms, makes up	during the periods when	when
construct	build, make	echelon	level, grade, rank
consult	ask	edifice	building
consummate	finish, complete	educator	teacher, trainer
contained in	in	effect (verb)	make, cause, bring about
containing	has, that have, etc.	effect an improvement	improve
contains	has	effectuate	carry out, put into effect
contemporaneously	at the same time	elaborate (on)	expand on, develop
contiguous	next to, near, touching	elapsed (time has)	passed
continue	keep on	elect	choose, pick
contractual agreement	agreement, contract	elementary	simple, basic
contribute	give	elevated	height, altitude
cooperate together	cooperate, help	elicit	draw out, bring out, prompt, cause
cooperation	jointly, with	eliminate	cut, drop, end, remove, omit, delete
coordination	staff action, relate, agree, conform	elimination	removal, discarding, omission
couched	phrased, worded	elucidate	explain, clarify
course of time	time	emanates	emits, comes from, gives out
criteria (plural)	standards, rules, yardsticks	emphasize	stress, point out
criterion (singular)	standard, norm	employ	use
currently	now (or leave out)	enable	let
de-emphasize	play down	encompass in	include, enclose
decelerate	slow down, reduce speed	encounter	meet, find, meeting
deem	think, judge, hold, believe	encourage	urge, promote, favor, persuade
deficiency	defect, shortage, lack	end product	result, product, outcome
definitely	final	end result	end, result, outcome
delegate authority	empower, assign	endeavor	try, effort, action
delineate	draw, describe, portray, outline	enhance	increase, raise, heighten, improve
delinquent	late	ensue	follow, result
demeanor	manner, conduct	ensure	make sure, see that
demise	death	enumerate	count, list
demonstrate	prove, show, explain	envisage	picture, view, have in mind, regard
depart	leave	equally as	as
depict	describe, show	equanimity	poise, balance
deprivation	loss	equitable	fair, just
deprive	take away, remove, withhold	equivalent	equal
derive	receive, take	eradicate	wipe out, remove, destroy, erase
derogatory	damaging, slighting	erroneous	wrong, mistaken
descend	go down	especially	chiefly
designate	appoint, name, pick, assign, select	essential	basic, necessary, vital, important
desire	wish, want	establish	set up, prove, show, make, set, fix
detailed	more, full	estimate	conclude, appraise, judge
deteriorate	run down, grow worse	evaluate	check, rate, test, measure, analyze, price
determination	ruling	evaluation	rating
determine	decide, figure, find	eventuate	result
detrimental	harmful	every effort will be made	(I/you/we/they) will try
develop	grow, make, take place	everybody, everyone	each, all
dialogue, dialog	talk, discussion	evidence	fact
dichotomy	split, separation	evidenced	showed
difficult	hard	evident	clear, plain, obvious
dimension	size	evince	show, display, express
diminish	drop, lessen, reduce, decrease	evolution	change, growth
disadvantage	drawback, handicap	exacerbate	to make more severe, worse, or bitter
disallow	reject, deny, refuse	examination	checkup, test, check, search, questioning
disclose	show, reveal, make known	examine	check, look at or into, test, study, inspect
discontinue	drop, stop, end	exceed	go beyond, surpass
disseminate	issue, send, pass out, spread, announce	exceedingly	notable, extremely, very
distribute	spread, share, allot	excessive	too much, too many
divulge	make known, reveal		
donate	give		
downward adjustment	decrease		
due in large measure	because, due to		

CHAPTER 7: Step 5 (Draft)

INSTEAD OF	TRY
execute	sign, perform, do act
exercise (authority)	use
exhaustive	thorough, complete
exhibit	show, display
exigency	urgent demand, urgent need, emergency
exorbitant	too much, abnormal
expedite	hurry, rush, speed up, fast, quick, hasten
expeditious	fast, quick, prompt, speedy; exercise care, watch out, take care, use care
expend	pay out, spend, use
expendable	used up, consumed, replaceable
expenditure	(see "expense")
expense	cost, fee, price, loss, charges
experience indicates	experience shows, learned
experiment	test, try, trial
expertise	expert opinion, skill, knowledge
explain	show, tell
expostulate	demand, discuss, object
extant	existing, current
extend	spread, stretch
extensive	large, wide
extenuating	qualifying, justifying
external	outer
extinguish	quench, put out
fabricate	construct, make, build, invent
facilitate	ease, help along, make easy, further, aid
factor	reason, cause
failed to	did not
familiarity	knowledge
familiarize	inform, learn, teach
fatuous numskull	jerk
feasible	possible, can be done, workable, practical
females	women
final	last
finalize	complete, finish, conclude, end
firstly	first
foe	enemy
for example	such as
for the purpose of	for, to
for the reason that	because, since
for this reason	so
for your information	(usually not needed)
forfeit	give up, lose
formulate	make, devise, repair
forthcoming	coming, future, approaching
forthwith	at once, right away
fortuitous	by chance, lucky, fortunate
forward	send
fragment	piece, part
frequently	often
fullest possible extent	as much as possible, fully
function	act, role, work
fundamental	basic, main, primary
furnish	give, send, provide, supply
furthermore	besides, also
future date	sometime, later
gained from	obtained, learned, source
gainsay	deny, dispute, contradict
generate	produce
germane	relevant, fitting, related
give consideration to	consider
give encouragement to	encourage, urge (see "encourage")
give feedback	respond
give instructions to	instruct, direct

INSTEAD OF	TRY
give rise to	raise, cause, bring about
goes without saying	(unnecessary)
govern	rule
habituate	accustom, make use to, adapt, adjust
has the ability	can
has the capability	can
has the capability of	is capable of, can, is able to
have the need for	need
have to	must, need to
held a meeting	met
henceforth	until now
hereby	by this
herein	here (often unnecessary)
heretofore	until now
hiatus	gap, lapse
higher degree of	more
hitherto	up to now, until now
hold in abeyance	suspend, delay, wait
homogeneity	unity, agreement, consensus
hopefully	I hope
however	but
identical	same
identification	name, designation
identify	find, name, show, point out, recognize
if and when	if, when (not both)
ilk	sort, kind
illustrate	show, make clear
immediately	at once, now, promptly, quickly
imminent	near
impact	affect (verb), effect (noun)
impacted	affected, changed, hit
impediment	block, barrier
imperative	urgent
impetus	drive, power, force
implement	carry out, do, follow, complete, fulfill
implication	impact meaning, effect
important	major, greater, main
impugn	assail, attack, criticize
impulse	drive, push, thrust
in a manner similar to	like, in the same way, as
in a number of cases	some, often, at times
in a position to	can
in a satisfactory manner	satisfactorily
in a situation in which	when
in accordance with	by, under, per, according to (AFI XX-XXX, commander's order, law)
in addition to	also, besides, too, plus
in an effort to	to, so that, so
in case of	if
in close proximity	near, nearby, close
in compliance with the	as directed, as requested, request
in conjunction with	with, together
in connection with	in, with, on, about
in favor of	for
in its entirety	all of it
in lieu of	instead of, in place of
in order that	for, so, so that
in order to	to
in process of preparation	being prepared
in recent past	lately
in reference to	regarding, about, on, concerning
in regard to	about, concerning, on
in relation to	about, concerning, on
in respect to	regarding, about, concerning, on

- 85 -

INSTEAD OF	TRY
in sufficient time	early or soon enough, ahead of time
in the amount of	for, of
in the course of	during, in, when
in the event of	if
in the event that	if, in case
in the immediate future	soon
in the majority of instances	most cases or most times
in the matter of	in, on
in the nature of	like
in the near future	soon
in the negative	no, denied, disapproved
in the neighborhood	about, around
in the time of	during
in the vicinity of	near, around
in view of	since
in view of the above	so, since, therefore
in view of the fact	because, as
in this day and age	today, nowadays
in this instance	here (often necessary)
in-depth	(avoid if possible) thorough, complete
inaccurate	wrong, incorrect
inadvertently	accidentally, mistakenly
inasmuch as	since, because
inaugurate	start, begin, open
inception	start, beginning
incident to	pertaining, connected with
incidental	related, by chance
incombustible	fireproof, (it) will not burn
incorporate	blend, join, merge, include, combine, add
increase	rise, grow, enlarge, add to
increment	increase, gain, amount
incumbent upon	must
indebtedness	debt
indefinite	vague, uncertain
indeterminate	vague, uncertain
indicate	show, write down, call for, point out
indication	sign, evidence
individual (noun)	person, member
individually	each, one at a time, singly
ineffectual	futile, useless, ineffective
inexpensive	cheap, low-priced
infinite	endless
inflammable	(it) burns, flammable, burnable
inherent	basic, natural
inimical	hostile, unfriendly, opposed
initial (adjective)	first
initially	first, at first
initiate	start, begin, act
innate	basic, native, inborn
innuendo	hint
input (provide)	data, thoughts, advise, respond
insignificant	slight, trivial, unimportant
insofar as	since, for, because
insomuch as	since
instance	case, example
instantaneously	instantly, at once, suddenly
institute (verb)	set up, start
integrate	combine
interface	connect, talk, coordinate, join, work together, merge, joint, point of contact, frontier, junction, common boundary
interpose no objection	do not object
interpose objections to	disapprove, disagree, object, non-concur

INSTEAD OF	TRY
interpret	grasp, explain, understand
interrogate	question
investigate	examine, study
irrespective	regardless
is dependent upon	depends on
is in receipt of	receives, got
is responsible for obtaining	obtains
is responsible for selection	selects
is symptomatic of	shows
it is	(leave out)
it is essential	must
it is important to note	note
it is obvious that	clearly, obviously
it is possible that	may, possibly
it is recommended	I, we recommend
it is requested	please, request
jeopardize	endanger
jurisdictional authority	control
justification	grounds, reasons
justify	prove
juxtaposition (in)	alongside, next to
knowledge	experienced, well-trained
legislation	law
limitations	limits
limited number	few
locate	find
location	place, scene, site
magnitude	size, extent
maintain (maintenance)	keep, support (upkeep)
majority	greatest, longest, most
make a decision	decide
make a reply	reply
make a request	request, ask for
make a statement	state
make an adjustment	adjust, resolve
make every effort	try
make provisions for	provide, do
mandatory	must, required
manifest (to be)	clear, plain
manufacture	make, build
materialize	appear, take form
materially	greatly
maximal	highest, greatest
maximize	increase
maximum	most, greatest
meets with approval	is approved
mention	refer to
metamorphosis	change
minimal	least, lowest, smallest
minimize	decrease, lessen, reduce
minimum	least, lowest, small
mitigate	lessen, ease
mode	way, style
modify	change, moderate, qualify
monitor	check, watch, oversee, regulate
multitudinous	populous, large (crowd)
more specifically	for example
most unique	unique
negligible	small, trifling
neophyte	new, novice
nevertheless	however, even so, but
nebulous	vague
necessitate	cause, need, make, require, cause to be

CHAPTER 7:
Step 5 (Draft)

INSTEAD OF	TRY
not infrequently	often
not later than	by, before
not often	seldom
notwithstanding the fact	although, nonetheless, nevertheless
notification	announcement, report, warning
notify	let know, tell
numerous	many, most
objective	aim, goal
obligate, obligatory	bind, compel
observe	see
obtain	get
obviate	prevent, remove, rule out
obvious	plain, clear
of great importance	important
of large dimensions	large, big, enormous
of late	lately
of no avail	useless, no use
of the opinion (to be)	to believe, think
often times	often
on account of	because
on behalf of	by, for, representing
on the basis of	based on
on the grounds that	because
on the part of	for
operate	run, work
operation	action, performance
operational	working
optimize	improve, strengthen
optimum	greatest, most favorable, best
option	choice, way
opus	work
organization	makeup, work site
orifice	hole, vent, mouth
originate	start, create, begin
outlook	view
outstanding (debt)	unpaid, unresolved
over the signature of	signed by
overlook	view, sight
parameters	limits, factors, boundaries
paramount	superior, supreme, principal, chief
partake	share, take part in
participate	take part
particularize	(avoid using) details, specifies, itemize
patently	evidently
peculiar to	unusual
penitentiary	prison
per annum	each year, a year
perform	do, act, produce, complete, finish
period of time	period, time
periodic	cyclic, recurring
periphery	confines, limits, perimeter
permit	let
pernicious	deadly, harmful
personnel	people, staff
pertaining to	about, of, on
pertinent	to the point
peruse	read, study
phenomenon	fact, event
pictured	shown, imagined
place	put
plaudits	praise, applause, approval
plethora	excess, too much
point in time	time, now, then
point of view	(usually unnecessary)

INSTEAD OF	TRY
portend	predict, mean
portent	sign, omen
portion	part, share, lot
position	place
positively	(often unnecessary)
possess	have, own
posterior	end, rear
postpone	put off, delay
postulate (verb)	claim, assert, suggest
posture (on an issue)	view, position, attitude
potential (adjective)	possible
practicable	possible, workable
practically (done)	almost, nearly
precept	order, command, principle, rule of action
precipitate (adjective)	rash, sudden, hasty, abrupt
preclude	prevent, shut out
predicament	fix, dilemma
predicated on	based on
predominant	dominant, main, chief
predominantly	mainly, chiefly, mostly
preeminent	chief, outstanding, foremost, first
preliminary to	before
premier	first, leading
preparatory to	before
prepared	ready
preponderantly	mainly, chiefly
presently	now, soon
preserve	keep
prevail upon	persuade
prevalent	widespread
primary	first, chief
prime	best
prior to	before
previous to	before
previously	before
probability	chance, likelihood
problematical	doubtful
procedures	rules, ways
prioritize	rank, order, organized
preventative	preventive
previous	earlier, past
proceed	do, go on, try
procure	get, gain
proficiency	skill, ability
profound	deep
programmed	planned
prohibit	prevent, forbid
project (ed) (verb)	planned
promulgate	announce, issue, set forth
proportion	share, part, size, amount
proposal	plan, offer
prototype	first or original, model, pattern
provide	give, say, supply, furnish
provide for	care for
provided that	if
provides guidance for	guides
provisions (of a law)	terms
proximity	nearness, distance
purchase	buy
purport	claim, mean
pursuant to	comply with, in, under, per, according to
purvey	supply, provide, sell
purview	range, scope

The Tongue and Quill
AFH 337, 27 MAY 2015

INSTEAD OF	TRY
quantify	count, measure, state the amount
rationale	reason
reach a decision	decide
reason for	why
reason is because	because
recapitulate	sum up, summarize, report
recipient	receiver
recommend	propose, suggest, advance
recommendation	advice, thought, counsel, opinion
reduce	cut
referred to as	called, named
reflect	show, say
regarding	about, of, on
regardless	in spite of, no matter
reimbursement	payment, repayment
reiterate	repeat
related with	on, about
relating to	about, on
relative to	on, about, for
relocation	move
remain	stay
remainder	the rest, what remains
remedy	cure
remittance	payment
remove	take away, take off, move
remuneration	pay, payment
render	give, make, report
repeat again	repeat, do again
replete	full, filled
represent	stand for, depict
reproduce, reproduction	copy
request	ask, please
require	must, need, call for
requirement	need
requisite	needed
reside	live
retain	keep
return	go back
review	check, go over
rudiments	first steps, basics
salient	main, important
salutary	good, healthy
sans	without
satisfactory	fine, good, good enough
saturate	soak, fill
scant	little, only
scrupulous	careful
scrutinize	study carefully, look into
segment	part
seldom ever	seldom
selection	choice
serves to	acts, helps, works
significance	meaning, point, importance
significant	main, great, major, marked,
signify	mean, show (verb)
similar to	like
sine qua non	essential
situated	placed, located, work assignment, state
small in size	small
so as to	to
solicit	ask for
solitary	lone, single
somewhat	(usually padding)
specifications	terms, details, conditions

INSTEAD OF	TRY
specify	list
square in shape	square
state (verb)	say
statutory	legal
still remains	remains
stimulate	stir, arouse
stipend	salary, payment, fee
strict accuracy	accuracy
subordinate (verb)	to lower, subdue
subordinate commands	their commands
subsequent to	after, later, next
submit	offer, give, send
substantial	large, real, strong, much, solid
substantiate	prove, support
substitute (verb)	replace
succor	help, aid
succumb	die, yield
such	similar, like
such as	like, that is
sufficient	enough, ample
subsequently	after, later, then, next
stringent	tight, strict
subject	the, this, your
subject to examination	check, examine, verify
sufficiently in advance	early enough
sum total	sum, total
superfluous	extra, too much, useless
supervise	manage
supposition	belief, thought, idea
surmise	think, guess, suppose
susceptible to	open to, subject to
symptom	sign
synthesis	merging, combining
synthesize	put together, group, assemble
tabulation	table
take action	act
take appropriate action	please
take necessary action	act
take necessary steps	do
technicality	detail, fine point
technique	way, method
tender (verb)	offer, give
tentative	uncertain
terminate	end, stop
terrible disaster	disaster
that	(leave out)
that aforesaid	(usually unnecessary) given or said above
the fact that	(usually unnecessary) that
the following	this, these
the foregoing	these, those, (something) above
the fullest degree possible	fully, as much as possible
the provisions of	(leave out)
the question as to whether	whether
the undersigned desires	I want
the use of	(leave out)
thence	from there
therapy	treatment
there are	(leave out)
there is	(leave out)
thereafter	after that, afterwards, then
thereby	by that, by it
therefore	so
therein	in (usually unnecessary)

INSTEAD OF	TRY
thereof	of, its, their
thereon	on (usually unnecessary)
thereto	to that, to it
thereupon	at once
thirdly	third
this office	us, we
this point in time	now
thither	there
through the use of	by, with
thus	so
thwart	frustrate, block, stop, hinder
time period or time frame	time, period, span
timely basis	promptly, fast, quickly
to be aware of	know
to effectively direct	to direct
to the extent that	as far as, so much that
transcend	go beyond
transformation	change
transmit	send
transparent	clear
transpire	happen, occur
transport	carry, move
transverse	crosswise
trauma	shock
true facts	facts
type	(leave out)
ultimate	final, end
ultimately	in the end, finally
under advisement	(avoid) being considered
under separate cover	(usually necessary)
underprivileged	poor, deprived
understand	know
unintentionally	by mistake, mistakenly, accidentally
until such time as	until, when
upgrade	improve
upon	on
upward adjustment	raise, increase
usage	use
utilize, utilization	use, employ
validate	confirm
value	cost, worth
variation	change
velocity	speed
vend	sell
verbatim	word for word, exact
veritable	(padding—usually unnecessary)

INSTEAD OF	TRY
very	(usually unnecessary)
very far	distant, remote
very hot	torrid, scorching, fiery
very large	enormous, immense, huge, spacious, vast
very last	last
very least	least
very near	adjacent, close
very pretty	gorgeous, beautiful
very quiet	still, silent
very small	tiny, puny
very strong	powerful, potent, forceful
very stupid	dense, moronic, idiotic, stupid
very weak	exhausted, frail, flimsy, inadequate
via	in, on, though, by way of
viable	workable, capable of growing
vicinity of	close, near
vicissitudes	ups and downs, changes, difficulties
vie	compete
virtually	almost
visualize	see, imagine, picture
vitiate	weaken, spoil, impair, debase
voluminous	bulky, large
warrant	call for, permit
whence	from where
whenever	when, each time
whereas	since, while
whereby	by which
wherein	in which, where
wherever	where
wherewithal	means
whether or not	whether, if
will be effected	will be done
will make use of	will use
with a view to	to, for
with due regard for, or to	for, to
with reference to	on, about
with regard to	about, on, regarding, concerning
with the exception of	except, except for, but
with the purpose of	to
with the result that	so
within the purview of	under
withstand	stand, resist
witnessed	saw

We've been looking a lot at how to use the right word for the job to write clear and concise sentences. Before we leave this section on effective sentence writing, there are two more areas we need to cover that have an impact on readability—sentence length and using questions.

Sentence Length

The purpose of words on paper is to transfer thoughts in the simplest manner with the greatest clarity. You should avoid long, complicated sentences over 20 words (average is 17 words). Break up long, stuffy sentences by making short sentences of dependent clauses or by using lists. Short sentences increase the pace; long ones usually retard it. The key is to vary your pattern since constant use of either form can be monotonous.

Using Questions

Use questions now and then to call attention to what you want. You're actually reaching out to your reader when a sentence ends with a question mark. In a longer communication, a question can definitely be a welcome change.

Overcoming Writer's Block

Earlier we mentioned writer's block. If you occasionally suffer from writer's block, you're not alone—writer's block can affect even experienced writers. First, a definition: writer's block is a temporary inability to get words on paper (or on the computer). Like many other problems, it has a life cycle—denial, despair, acceptance and recovery. Recognizing this cycle and the causes of writer's block (fear of failure, fear of rejection, fear of success, fear of offending and fear of running out of ideas) are the first steps to overcoming it.

In most cases we just need a gentle nudge to get us back on track. In her book *The Complete Idiot's Guide to Creative Writing*, Laurie E. Rozakis provides several suggestions on how to overcome writer's block. Here are some of her ideas, as well as some of our own:

- Brainstorm or "free write" to get your creative juices flowing. Spill your brains and don't worry about punctuation—just get it down. Stay close to your outline; don't revise or polish. If your outline is comprehensive, you may only need to string the ideas together with brief transitions. If your outline is a series of key words in a logical pattern, you'll have to fill in the larger blanks.

- Start wherever you want. Write the introduction last as many writers do. The key here is to just start writing. Try starting with the part that's easiest to write.

- On a similar note, try writing just the topic sentences for each paragraph. Once you do this, the other support sentences will start really flowing.

- Avoid procrastination. Waiting until the last minute just increases your "blockage"!

- Forget about page length, word count or other constraint. Work these when you edit.

- Tell your ideas to a friend.

- Briefly do some mindless activity—but only briefly!

- Try changing your writing mode (computer to hand-written and vice versa).

- Use visual aids. This can help ignite your ideas and thoughts. Then, you can write them.

- Develop rituals or routines to get in the mood for writing.

- If you work in a noisy area, try using earplugs to cut down on noise and distractions.

SUMMARY: Congratulations! The most difficult task is over—you've successfully written the first draft. Take a break and step back from your draft. When you come back, you'll be ready to revise and edit it. Perhaps more significantly, you've overcome writer's block if you have a draft. Writer's block is temporary and curable: there are lots of ways to overcome it. Hopefully, the tips here will help you. Always remember—writing should be fun, not frightening!

CHAPTER 8:

Step 6 (Edit)

> *This chapter covers:*
> - Editing vs. Feedback
> - Editing Fundamentals
> - Editing Efficiently: A Three-Step Approach
> - Drafting Basics: Do You Apply Them?
> - Common Grammar Traps
> - Common Writing Errors

Spotting problems in our own writing is not easy. Many of us take great pride in what we write. Once our words are on paper, we resent the suggestion that something could be wrong. We don't like to check and change the words, the organization, the limits of the subject, the spelling, the punctuation or anything else, and we often have trouble taking the time to edit properly.

Yet editing is critical. Take the time to make sure you have a cohesive, clear, error-free product that the audience can relate to. Here's the good news: if you completed the steps described in chapters 3-7, the editing will be a lot easier ... and at this point, you're almost home free.

> *When you revise from the top down, from global structure to paragraphs to sentences to words, you are more likely to discover useful revisions than if you start at the bottom with words and sentences and work up.*
>
> –The Craft of Research

Editing vs. Feedback

First, it is important to understand the difference between editing (step 6) versus feedback (step 7). The "Seven Steps for Effective Communication," recommends that you edit your own writing before asking for feedback from someone else. There are many reasons to do this. For one, it develops your own editing skills—you'll be better prepared for those times when you don't have access to a second opinion. Second, it shows respect for the people you're seeking feedback from. Why should someone else invest time and effort to improve your writing if you aren't willing to do so yourself? Finally, you'll catch the worst mistakes and avoid embarrassing yourself in front of your coworkers. It never hurts to put the most professional product you can out for review, even if the review is an informal one. In this chapter, we'll assume it's just you and your draft. In chapter 9, we'll talk more about seeking feedback from others.

FOCUS Principles for Strong Writing and Speaking

Focused: Address the issue, the whole issue, and nothing but the issue.

Organized: Systematically present your information and ideas.

Clear: Communicate with clarity and make each word count.

Understanding: Understand your audience and its expectations.

Supported: Use logic and support to make your point.

Knowing the difference between editing and feedback is the easy part. The hard part is determining your editing goal. Remember the FOCUS principles from chapter 1? Good editing all relates to those principles and will tell you how well you followed the steps for effective writing. As you read through this chapter on editing, keep FOCUS in mind.

Editing Fundamentals

When you edit, there are a few key rules to remember:

1. Edit With Fresh Eyes.

Give yourself time between drafting and editing. By that we mean put the draft on a shelf, in a desk drawer or under a paperweight and let it sit a spell, preferably for several hours for shorter projects and at least a day for longer ones. After this down time you'll come back fresh and will be more likely to catch errors.

2. Review the Basics.

Take the time to review earlier sections on writing tone, drafting clear and concise sentences, common grammatical errors, and any other material that represents a problem area for you. Editing is your last chance to apply the guidelines you've read about in earlier chapters. If the concepts are fresh in your mind when you start editing, you'll be better able to spot problems in your draft.

3. Slow Down and Take Your Time.

You aren't in a race. If you read at your normal pace, you're more likely to miss errors. Try different approaches to slow yourself down, including reading aloud and reading one line at a time using a "cover" to hide the rest of the page. If you're checking for misspelled words, move backwards through a sentence.

4. Remember Your Readers.

Try to put yourself in the role of your audience as you edit. You may catch some areas that may need revision if you read it from their perspective and knowledge base. Also consider your secondary audience—even if you've got your primary audience targeted correctly, are you unnecessarily insulting others that may end up reading this?

5. Start With the Big Picture

Start large and then work down to the details. When you begin to edit, don't focus in on the nitty-gritty—*look at the big picture first*. Misuse of "there" and "their" is really not that important if your paper lacks cohesion, is poorly organized or fails to include a clear purpose statement. Again, anyone can use spellchecker, but a well-edited paper requires much more and begins with *The Big Picture*.

Editing Efficiently: A Three-Step Approach

One way to make sure you edit efficiently is to read your document *at least three times* to allow yourself to really look hard at the problem areas that could botch your product. In the first pass, look at the big picture; in the second pass, look at paragraph construction; and in the third pass look at sentences, phrases and words.

First Pass: The Big Picture

In this first "go around" you should pay attention to the arrangement and flow of ideas. Here are some areas to think about:

> **Review: Elements of an Introduction**
>
> In chapter 7 we described how an introduction often begins with optional **stage-setting remarks** that grab the reader's attention. The introduction should include your **purpose statement**, which informs the reader where you are going and why you are going there. The introduction often contains an **overview** of the main point(s) covered in the body. These are just guidelines: the composition of an introduction should be tailored to the assignment.

Check Your Tasking and Purpose.

- What was my original task? Check the wording one more time.
- What is my purpose statement? For short drafts, underline it in your draft. For longer projects, write it on a separate sheet of paper and refer to it frequently while editing.
- Does the purpose statement "answer the task," or does it miss the point?

Check Your Introduction.

- Does it exist and does it contain my purpose statement?
- Is it an appropriate length? (typically one paragraph long for assignments)
- Does my purpose statement and introduction give the readers a good idea of what they are about to read?

Compare Your Introduction and Conclusion.

- First read your introduction and then read your conclusion.
- Do they sound like they go together without being identical? Does the introduction declare your purpose and does your conclusion show your readers you've accomplished your purpose?
- Do you let your readers down gradually? Or do you stop with a jerk?
- Does the conclusion sum up your point? Don't introduce any new ideas here—you'll leave your readers hanging in limbo!

Check Overall Page Count and Length.

- What are my audience's expectations regarding page count? Am I on target? Will I have to make this draft significantly longer or shorter?
- Check the scope and flow of paragraphs in your body.

Check for Relevance and Completeness.

- Do the paragraphs clearly relate to the thesis statement?
- Are some paragraphs irrelevant or unnecessary?
- Am I missing any main points in this written communication?
- Are paragraphs arranged in a consistent order?

Second Pass: Paragraph Structure and Clarity

After your first pass, you know the paper contains what it needs to do the job. In the second pass, check that the main points and supporting ideas are appropriately organized in paragraphs.

Let's take a close look at individual paragraphs in the body of your writing. For each paragraph, ask the following questions:

Unity of Focus

- Is there one, and only one, main point of the paragraph?
- Is all the information in the paragraph related enough to be in the same paragraph?
- Can you identify the central idea of each paragraph?

Topic Sentence

- Does the paragraph have a topic sentence—one sentence that captures the central idea of the paragraph?
- Is the topic sentence the first sentence of the paragraph? (Or, if you're starting with a transitional sentence, the second sentence?)

Supporting Ideas

- Do sentences expand, clarify, illustrate and explain points mentioned or suggested in each main idea? Your goal is to smoothly lead the reader, step-by-step, to each main idea.
- Are there enough details in the paragraph to support the central idea?
- Are there any "extra sentences" that seem to be irrelevant to the main point?
- Do all transitional words, phrases, and clauses improve the flow and show proper relationships?
- Do most paragraphs contain three to seven sentences?

If you did a lot of rearranging of paragraphs in this step, try the organizational editing check on the previous page—just to make sure you're on track.

- How does your draft compare with your original outline?

Organizational Editing Check

Some writers can write powerful and clear sentences but have trouble keeping "on target" throughout the document. Their editing challenge isn't grammar; it's the big picture. If this sounds like you, try this simple editing check.

This editing check assumes you followed the paragraph construction guidelines previously covered and placed the topic sentence at the beginning of each paragraph.

Read out loud. Read these sections out loud: 1) Your complete introduction; 2) The first sentence of each paragraph in the body, in order of appearance; and 3) Your complete conclusion.

Does it answer the question?
Does it stay on message?
Does it flow well?

Third Pass: Sentences, Phrases, and Words

Now you're ready to look at the details. Though you've probably corrected some minor errors in the first two passes, now is the time to really concentrate on the "small stuff" that can sabotage your communication: passive voice, unclear language, excessive wordiness, grammatical errors and spelling mistakes. Some of these concepts were covered in the chapter on drafting, while others will be introduced in this section.

Let's start with some general advice. **Read the paper out loud.** Reading the paper out loud will increase your chances of catching errors because it requires you to slow down and use two senses—seeing and hearing. What one sense misses, the other may pick up.

Listen to the sound of words, phrases and sentences. Remember, the quicker your audience can read and understand it, the better. If you have to read a sentence two or three times, chances are they will too. Not good! Re-write the sentence to enhance its clarity.

Another helpful piece of advice is to read one line at a time using a "cover" to hide the rest of the page. This procedure helps provide the focus you need to check your sentence structure and individual word usage: subject-verb agreements and identifying homonyms (for example, "their" and "there.") Moving backwards through a sentence can also identify other misspelled words.

Drafting Basics: Did You Apply Them?

As part of your editing step, you need to check some of the same concepts discussed in the previous chapter on drafting. Remember these guidelines, and refer back to the referenced pages if you need more details or additional examples.

1. Write in Active Voice.

In active voice, the subject comes first in the sentence. In passive voice, the "doer" or subject of the sentence shows up late in the sentence or is missing entirely. Avoid overusing passive voice; it often creates lengthy and confusing sentences.

> **Passive**: Captain Smith was given a choice assignment by his career field monitor.
> **Active**: The career field monitor gave Captain Smith a choice assignment.

2. Avoid Smothered Verbs.

Use one specific verb instead of a general verb and extra words.

> **Smothered:** This directive *is applicable* to everyone who *makes use of* the system.
> **Better:** This directive *applies* to everyone who *uses* the system.

3. Check for misspelled or commonly misused words. In today's computer age, your software's spell checker is your first line of defense against misspelled words. Still, you can get into trouble by misusing synonyms or easily confused words like "there" and "their" and "accept" and "except." Spell check will not flag these words because they are spelled correctly, but used in the wrong context. When in doubt, check the dictionary.

4. Use parallel construction (parallelism) in lists and series. Use a similar grammatical construction within a list or series. Make items of equal importance look equal. If one starts with a verb, start the other with a verb. If three items in a list are commands, make the fourth a command. Parallelism helps make sentences clear.

> **Needs work:** Remember the following when editing: *write in active voice, parallelism, smothered verbs should be avoided,* and *spelling.*
> **Better:** Remember the following when editing: *write in active voice, use parallel construction in lists, avoid smothered verbs,* and *check for misspelled words.*

5. Avoid unnecessary redundancy and word doublings.

Don't use one word to modify another unless both add value.

> **Needs work**: *Repetitive redundancy* hurts readability.
> **Better**: *Redundancy* hurts readability.

Don't use two nearly identical words unless both add value.

> **Needs work**: We must comply with the *standards and criteria* for *controlling and reducing* environmental pollution."
> **Better**: We must comply with the *standards* for *reducing* environmental pollution."

Common Grammar Traps

Grammatical errors can confuse your readers and undermine the credibility of your communication. We've listed some of the most common mistakes below—look out for them when editing your work.

1. Misplaced Modifiers

A modifier is a group of words that describes another group of words within the sentence. Modifiers should be placed near the words they describe. Improperly placed modifiers can create ambiguity or imply an illogical relationship. There are two kinds of misplaced modifiers: dangling and ambiguous.

> **a. Dangling modifiers** literally hang illogically on sentences, usually at the beginning. They are placed so they seem to modify the wrong word and, thus, show an illogical relationship. To correct a dangling modifier, either place the modifier next to the word it modifies or change the subject of the sentence to clarify your intent.
>
> > **Confusing:** Approaching the flight line from the east side, the operations building can be easily spotted by a pilot. [The operations building does not approach the flight line—the pilot does!]
> > **Better:** A pilot approaching the flight line from the east side can easily spot the operations building.
> >
> > **Confusing:** To make a climbing turn, the throttle is opened wider. [The throttle doesn't make a climbing turn.]
> > **Better:** To make a climbing turn, open the throttle wider. [The subject "you" is understood.]
>
> **b. Ambiguous modifiers** seem to modify two different parts of a sentence. Readers can't tell whether they modify words that come before or after them. To correct an ambiguous modifier, place the word so its relationship can't be misinterpreted.
>
> > **Confusing:** People who drive to work *occasionally* can expect to find a parking space.
> > **Better:** People who *occasionally* drive to work can expect to find a parking space.
> >
> > **Confusing:** Although working conditions improved *slowly* employees grew dissatisfied.
> > **Better:** Although working conditions *slowly* improved, employees grew dissatisfied. [Case #1: the conditions improved slowly]

Better: Although working conditions improved, employees *slowly* grew dissatisfied.
[Case #2: employee morale dropped slowly]

2. Errors in Subject-Verb Agreement

Plural subjects take plural verbs and singular subjects take singular verbs. Another way to state this rule using grammatical terms is "Subjects and verbs must agree in number."

The key to avoiding most problems in subject-verb agreement is to identify the subject of a sentence, determine whether it's singular or plural, and then choose a verb in the same number and keep it near its subject.

Generally subjects that end in *s* are plural, while verbs that end in *s* are singular. (There are exceptions to this rule—for example, the word *ballistics* is singular.)

   a. **Phrases between the subject and verb** do not change the requirement that the verb must agree in number with its subject.

   An inspection team consisting of 36 people is investigating that problem.
   A general, accompanied by 3 colonels and 15 majors, is attending the conference.

   b. A **linking verb** agrees with its subject, not with its complement.

   The commander's main problem is untrained Airmen.
   Untrained airmen are the commander's main problem.

   c. A **compound subject** consists of two or more nouns or pronouns joined by one of these conjunctions: *and, but, or, for* or *nor*. Some compound subjects are plural; others are not. Here are guidelines for subject-verb agreement when dealing with compound subjects:

   If two nouns are joined by *and*, they typically take a plural verb.
   The *Air Force* and the *Army are* two components of the nation's defense forces.

   If two nouns are joined by *or*, *nor*, or *but*, the verb should agree in number with the subject nearest it.
   Either the *President* or his *cabinet members are* planning to attend.
   Either the *cabinet* members or the *President is* planning to attend.

   Use a singular verb for a compound subject that is preceded by *each* or *every*.
   Every fighter pilot and his aircraft *is* ready for the mission.
   Each boy and girl *brings* a snack to school.

   Use a singular verb for a compound subject whose parts are considered a single unit.
   The *Stars and Stripes was* flown at half-mast at the Headquarters building.
   Ham and *eggs is* a delicious breakfast.

   d. Use a singular verb with **collective nouns** (and noun phrases showing quantity) **treated as a unit**, but a plural verb when treated as individuals.

   The *thousand wounded is* expected to arrive soon. [A quantity or unit]
   A *thousand wounded were* evacuated by air. [Individuals]

- 98 -

e. Use singular verbs with **most indefinite pronouns**: *another, anybody, anything, each, everyone, everybody, everything, neither, nobody, nothing, one, no one, someone, somebody* and *something*.

> *Everyone eats* at the cafeteria.
> The *President* said *everybody was* welcome to join.
> *Everyone* in the squadron *takes* a turn leading a service project.

f. With ***all, any, none*** and ***some***, use a singular or plural verb, depending on the content.

> *All* of the money *is reserved* for emergencies.
> [singular—equivalent to "The money is reserved for emergencies."]
> When the men arrive, all *go* straight to work.
> [plural—equivalent to "The men go straight to work"]
> *All are* expected to have a tour of duty overseas.

Grammar Review: Pronouns

Pronouns are words that replace nouns and refer to a specific noun. The noun being referred to or replaced by the pronoun is called the **antecedent**. Some examples:

- SSgt Smith is our nominee for the award and he has a good chance of winning. [*SSgt Smith* is the antecedent; *he* is a pronoun replacing the noun later in the sentence.]
- Three lieutenants arrived late to the meeting. Their boss was not happy with them. [*Three lieutenants* is the antecedent; *Their* and *them* are pronouns replacing the antecedent in the next sentence.]

---

3. Errors in Pronoun Reference ("Pronoun-Antecedent Agreement")

A common error in pronoun use involves agreement in number. If the noun is singular, the pronoun is singular. If the noun is plural, the pronoun should be plural, too.

Let's look at an example of an incorrect pronoun reference:

> **Incorrect:** *Everyone* should bring *their* books to class.
> [*Everyone* is singular, while *their* is plural.]

When correcting such a sentence, **try for gender inclusive language**. Often the best approach is to make the subject plural and keep the pronoun unchanged:

> **Correct:** *All students* should bring *their* books to class.

Of course, using *his or her* is also acceptable, but it gets cumbersome when overused:

> **Also correct:** *Everyone* should bring *his or her* books to class.

With a compound subject joined by *and*, use a plural pronoun:

> My *advisor and I* can't coordinate *our* schedules. [*our* is a plural pronoun]

When parts of an antecedent are joined by "or" or "nor," make the pronoun agree with the nearest part:

John *or* Steve should have raised *his* hand.

Neither the student *nor* his roommates will have *their* deposit returned.

Avoid awkward phrasing by placing the plural part second if one part of the antecedent is singular and one part is plural.

Awkward: Neither my parents *nor* my sister has stayed on *her* diet.

Better: Neither my sister *nor* my parents have stayed on *their* diet.

Remember that embedded descriptive phrases can be tricky:

Incorrect: He is one of those ambitious ***people*** who ***values*** promotion over personal ethics. [***Values*** should be ***value*** because the pronoun ***who*** refers to ***people,*** not ***one***. Clarification: he is one, but not the only one, of many ambitious people.]

Here are some other examples of *incorrect* pronoun reference:

The Air Force maintains different *types* of numbered forces, but the organization of *its* headquarters is similar. [*Its* should be *their* to refer correctly to *types*.]

The *committee* plans to submit *their* report by the end of the month. [*Their* should be *its* because *committee* functions as a single unit in this sentence.]

4. Comma Placement around Parenthetical Expressions

There are many rules about using commas to punctuate sentences, and we recommend you check out Appendix 1 for the complete list. One class of common mistakes is nearly universal and worth covering in this chapter—placement of commas around groups of words that interrupt the sentence's flow. Here's the basic rule:

Enclose nonrestrictive or parenthetical expressions with commas.

What does this mean? If an expression (a group of words) can be removed from the sentence without changing its meaning, then enclose the expression with commas.

Though the rule is simple, applying the rule requires some judgment. Advocates of open punctuation would argue that if the group of words does not "significantly" interrupt the sentence, you don't need commas. Another judgment area is deciding which expressions are restrictive and which are nonrestrictive. A *restrictive expression* limits or restricts the meaning of the words it applies to, so it can't be removed from the sentence without changing the meaning. A *nonrestrictive* expression merely adds additional information. **Here's the bottom line:** If you can remove the expression from the sentence without changing the meaning, it is a nonrestrictive expression that should be enclosed by commas.

Which punctuation is correct?

1. People who live in glass houses shouldn't throw stones.

2. People, who live in glass houses, shouldn't throw stones.

Answer #1 is correct. The expression *who live in glass houses* is restrictive. If you eliminate it, the sentence changes meaning: *People shouldn't throw stones.*

Which punctuation is correct?

1. My friend the architect who lives in a glass house has a party every year.
2. My friend the architect, who lives in a glass house, has a party every year.

The correct answer depends on your situation. If you are in the Air Force and have one friend who is an architect, then answer #2 is correct. The expression *who lives in a glass house* is nonrestrictive—it provides information that is not essential to the sentence's meaning, and it can be removed without impact. On the other hand, if you work in an architecture firm and all your friends are architects, then answer #1 is correct. In this case the expression identifies which one of your architect friends has a party every year—it's the one who lives in a glass house.

Though there's some judgment involved in deciding if something is nonrestrictive, **once you decide to enclose an expression, don't forget one of the commas.**

Incorrect: The new faculty, including the civilians must show up at 0600 tomorrow for physical training.
Correct: The new faculty, including the civilians, must show up at 0600 tomorrow for physical training.

Incorrect: Grammar errors including misplaced commas, inhibit writing clarity.
Correct: Grammar errors, including misplaced commas, inhibit writing clarity.

Grammar can be challenging, but the fixes can be easy, as shown by the examples in the preceding section. Grammar and writing style can also be humorous (or embarrassing!). Consider the common writing errors in the next section on as you examine your own writing.

Common Writing Errors

These tips are presented as a humorous means to convey some common errors seen in official publications/forms and they represent some serious violations of the English language. The errors are noted in ALL CAPS while comments to think about are in parentheses.

- Verbs HAS to agree with their subjects.
- Prepositions are not words to end sentences WITH.
- AND don't start a sentence with a conjunction.
- It is wrong to EVER SPLIT an infinitive. (Not all style guides agree: where would the crew of the USS Enterprise go without its famous split infinitive "to boldly go…"?
- Avoid clichés like the plague—they're old hat. (Double clichés are worse than one.)
- Also, always avoid annoying alliteration. (Alliteration, and other rhetorical devices, have purpose and add style—what would William Shakespeare's works be without them?)
- Be more or less specific. (Choose one and stay focused.)
- Parenthetical remarks (however relevant) are (usually) unnecessary. (But not always.)
- Also too, never, ever use repetitive redundancies. (Remember, be concise!)

- No sentence fragments. (Sentence fragments make poor bullets, too.)
- Foreign words and phrases are not APROPOS. (Perhaps, but they might be appropriate.)
- Do not be redundant; do not use more words than necessary; it's highly superfluous.
- One should NEVER generalize.
- DON'T use NO double negatives.
- Eschew ampersands & abbreviations, etc. (Better not read your last EPR/OPR.)
- One-word sentences? Eliminate. (Unless you need space on that SSS/eSSS!)
- Analogies in writing are like feathers on a snake.
- Eliminate commas, that are, not necessary. Parenthetical words however should be enclosed in commas.
- Never use a big word when substituting a diminutive one would suffice.
- Kill all multiple exclamation points!!!
- Use words correctly, IRREGARDLESS of how others use them. ("irregardless" is not a word; it is a double negative. The prefix "ir" and the suffix "less" are both negative resulting in a meaning of "regard" which is the opposite of the intent.)
- Understatement is always the absolute best way to put forth earth-shaking ideas.
- Use the apostrophe in IT'S proper place and omit it when ITS not needed.
- Resist hyperbole; not one writer in a million can use it correctly.

A note on proofreader marks. All of the suggestions in this chapter, and more, can be conveyed back to you on your draft by proofreader marks. The technical skills of a professional proofreader are beyond the scope of *The Tongue and Quill*; however, if you should have a need to use proofreader marks, either as a writer who sought professional feedback or if you want to begin using them to provide feedback to others, see *The Air University Style and Author Guide* (published as an Air University number text as AU-1) for current standard proofreader marks.

SUMMARY: Always edit! Editing is crucial to producing professional communication. Without solid editing your writing can be disjointed, your reader becomes confused, and your message may be lost. Does it take time? Absolutely! Budget time for editing—especially for time-critical assignments—and with practice the whole process will seem second nature. Editing isn't the final step, however. Yes, someone else needs to look at your work of art. Get ready to put on your thick skin, as this is not for the meek and timid. Read on to the final step to better communication … how to *fight for feedback*.

CHAPTER 9:

Step 7 (Fight for Feedback and Get Approval)

This chapter covers:

- Fighting for Feedback
- Getting Approval: Staff Coordination

Fighting for feedback and getting approval for your communication are both activities that are part of life in the Air Force. When you fight for feedback, you voluntarily seek out someone else's views on your speaking or writing product. Feedback can be very informal and it doesn't have to be from people with impressive job titles. When you get staff approval, you're going through a more formal process that allows individuals to review and comment on your communication product. Feedback and coordination are closely linked: if you do a good job at fighting for feedback, you'll find that the coordination process becomes much smoother.

Fighting For Feedback

Why Fight For Feedback?

So, why should you fight for feedback? Perhaps the biggest benefit is getting a second set of eyes to review your work. Even the best writers and speakers can become so close to their projects that they can't see where they can be made stronger. They may omit vital information, fail to see a weakness in their argument or just overlook the need for a transition between two main points. Their closeness to the material and pride of authorship can distort or obscure their viewpoint. Smart communicators realize this tendency and seek objective feedback from a fresh set of eyes. If you seek out and listen to feedback, you are much more likely to produce accurate, understandable communication that "answers the mail" and resonates with your audience.

Another reason to fight for feedback is that it often saves time during the coordination process. Whether it's the staff package you've been working hard on for 3 weeks or the briefing you have to present Friday, getting feedback from someone else's point of view will help smooth things out later as your package makes its way up the chain of command. In some cases having someone review and provide feedback can also be a smart political move—if individuals "buy in" early in the process, they may be a source of support later if it becomes necessary to defend the material.

Where Can I Get Feedback?

Meaningful feedback can come from many different sources. Coworkers or fellow staffers may be a good choice because of their familiarity with the issue and its jargon. They may have also briefed or written for the same people on similar issues; if so, they can give you some tips or lessons learned. You may also choose to go to different people for different aspects of your work. For example, you may find it helpful to solicit suggestions for improving grammar, organization and content from three different "trusted agents" who are strong in those particular areas. You may even want to use a trusted agent who's totally outside your organization to see if your message makes sense to someone with no clue about the material.

What Kind Of Feedback Should I Ask For?

Once you've picked out your feedback sources, you should let them know what kind of feedback you're looking for. (We're not suggesting you say, "Tell me how wonderful this is—I've worked so hard on it!") Unless you give them clear guidance, reviewers may focus on details like spelling, grammar and margins. Though these are important, make it clear that you want feedback on the big picture, too. Here are some examples of items you should ask them to address:

Is my purpose clear and am I properly targeting my audience? For starters, you want to give your reviewers a sense of your audience and your purpose. Will the audience positively receive the message you intend to convey? Ask them to tell you the bottom line they walked away with after reviewing your material. Was it what you intended?

Did I address the issue at the right level of detail? Too many details can obscure your message while too few details can lead to confusion, questions and delays. Ask your reviewers if you've addressed the issue(s) without going too far into the weeds. You could also have them ask you questions on the material. Have you anticipated possible questions? If you don't feel comfortable answering their questions, you may need to go back and do more research. Along the same lines, reviewers may help you pinpoint inconsistencies or unclear material that your final audience might find as well.

Are there other viewpoints I need to consider? Finally, your reviewer may offer differing viewpoints on the material. If that's the case, ask for clarification on their viewpoint if necessary, but don't argue with them. Instead, ask yourself if their ideas may come up again later. If so, you probably need to address them in your material.

The bottom line to getting feedback is having an open mind and being able to accept criticism. Don't take comments personally, even if they seem like attacks to your project. Accept feedback willingly and use it constructively—it's part of the process of developing a quality product.

How To Give Feedback

There are certain things to keep in mind when giving feedback. First, effective feedback is consistent, objective and sensitive to the stated purpose. If someone asks you to review a package, make sure you understand what the person wants from your review and stick to it. Second, distinguish between necessary, desirable, and unnecessary changes. A page full of red marks is hard to interpret. Instead, give the author a sense of what really needs to be changed versus the "happy to glad" kinds of suggestions. Next, helpful suggestions pinpoint specific problems, such as awkward sentences, grammar, etc. A general statement like "you need to work on your sentence structure" isn't as helpful as underlining specific sentences that need help. Finally, you should concentrate on improving the message's content, not the style or personal preferences of the author (unless the author has asked you specifically to comment on writing style).

Feedback Philosophy

Feedback should describe rather than judge. Authors are more likely to listen and incorporate feedback if it's phrased constructively. Avoid judgmental language—it places people on the defensive. Remember, feedback should be directed at a person's work or behavior, not at the person.

Feedback is both positive and negative. A balanced description of other people's work takes both strong and weak points into account. Both types of feedback give useful information to those people who want to change and improve their work.

Feedback should be specific rather than general. General statements about other people's work do not indicate the performance elements they may need to change and the elements that may serve as models. Highlight or underline specific items you want to bring to the author's attention, and make annotations or comments in the margins.

Feedback should consider the needs of both the receiver and the giver of the feedback. Feedback often reflects the state of mind of the reviewer, not just the quality of the work. If you're seeking feedback from someone else, try to pick an appropriate time to make the request and be realistic about the time required for the review. Similarly, reviewers should make sure they are in the right frame of mind before analyzing the material and offering feedback.

Feedback should be directed at behavior the receiver can control. Only frustration results when people are reminded of shortcomings they cannot control. A suggestion to improve the briefing room's temperature, for example, is probably beyond the individual's control. However, briefing skills and mannerisms *are* within the person's ability to control.

Feedback should be analyzed to ensure clear communication. Discuss or clarify any feedback you're not sure of to clear up any misinterpretations. The sender's intended message is not always what the receiver hears.

Feedback should be solicited rather than imposed (except for the supervisor-subordinate situation). Feedback is most useful when the receiver asks for it. The receiver is more likely to be receptive to your inputs in that case, as opposed to responding with an attitude of "Who asked *you*?"

A Word on Supervisor-Subordinate Feedback

As a supervisor, you need to be tactful and patient, especially when approving and disapproving the communications of subordinates. As a supervisor, you are obligated to help your people improve their work. This obligation may mean helping them to revise or rewrite their communication, especially if they are inexperienced. Whatever your role, tact and patience come more easily to people once they understand feedback in its broadest context.

Getting Approval: Staff Coordination

A formal coordination process gives interested individuals an opportunity to contribute to and comment on a communication product. Though most staff coordination involves written products (i.e., "the staff package"), important briefings can also be subjected to a formal review process. Formal coordination gives affected individuals a chance to comment, and helps ensure the best course of action is presented to the decision maker. Coordination also lets the decision maker know who supported or disagreed with the position stated in the paper and who agreed to take subsequent actions within their areas of responsibility.

Getting a staff package fully coordinated takes a lot of time, diligence, and hard work. The coordination process has to be closely monitored by the package's OPR to make sure the package gets seen by everyone who needs to see it and doesn't get forgotten in someone's in-box. Here are several considerations that may reduce headaches as you work your package up to the decision maker.

The "Who" of Coordination

One of the first things you need to decide as you get ready to put your package through the approval process is who needs to see the package.

Check your organization's policies on coordination. In many organizations, policies exist on coordination requirements for routine packages: find out if your product falls in this category. Your boss may have a list of people who need to see your package. Also check to see what guidance is available electronically—many units have an Action Officer's Guide posted on their website.

Check with key contacts in the organization. Contacts throughout the organization can be very helpful during the staffing process. Fellow staffers, executive officers and secretaries can provide advice on who needs to coordinate on your package, including individuals or agencies that you hadn't thought of. Also, they can give you perspectives on what the bosses will and won't accept. As you build and get to know this "underground of expertise," use it to your advantage.

Realize that the coordination list may grow with time. Don't be surprised if other offices are added as the coordination process occurs. Depending on the material and which level of staff you're dealing with (wing staff versus Air Staff), you may be unaware of all the offices that need to see your package.

Is there a person on your coordination list who carries a lot of clout? When planning your coordination strategy, you should probably determine who the approval Authority is. Who is the one person that can make or break your package during coordination? Who is the one person who could kill your project with a nonconcur? These people often have strong feelings about how and when they are approached. Some of them may hate a "surprise package" and always want to be the first to be consulted on an issue. In this case you may want to get early buy-in—which can help ensure that others fall into line. Others may want to see what others have to say about the issue before it ever reaches their desk. Use your contacts to find out who these influential people are, what their preferences are and how they like to be approached.

The "How" of Coordination

Aside from deciding who needs to coordinate on your package, you have other things to consider prior to releasing your package for coordination.

Do you want to send out a preview copy? You may want to send a draft package out early to potential coordinators, especially for issues that are complex or for offices whose inputs are crucial to your package's success. Doing so allows them time to study the issue and also saves time later during formal coordination. Also, you may want to coordinate by telephone for small packages, for people who are extremely familiar with the issue or with off-base agencies.

How are you going to route your package to the various coordinating offices? You need to consider how you're going to send your package around. Many organizations now utilize automated tools to assist with the coordination process, such as the Task Management Tool, or TMT. This method allows for multiple offices to see what others are saying about the product. Will you have only one copy that is routed to all affected offices? This may work for high-level packages that don't have a lot of offices to go through, but the more offices you add to the coordination list, the longer this process will take. You may want to "shotgun" out a number of copies of the package so a number of offices can coordinate on the package at the same time. This will speed up the process, but you will have more copies of the package to keep track of and the various offices won't get to see what each other are saying about the material. You will have to figure out which way will work better for your particular case. Also, don't forget to determine when the certifying and approval authority will coordinate on your package.

Consider the boss and the schedule. You're not done yet. There are some more things you want to do while preparing to go for coordination. For one, get your boss's blessing before going out-of-office. You want to make sure the boss agrees with what you are saying. You probably want to establish a tentative schedule, based on any deadlines you are up against. If you have a deadline for completion, build a schedule backwards from that point to allow for reviews, changes and recoordination. As part of your schedule planning, check to see if any key personnel coordinating on your package are going to be TDY or on leave for extended periods.

If you're using e-mail to send your package around, consider the following. Specify who is coordinating, who is getting an informational copy, and who will be approving the package. Use "COORD," "INFO," "APPROVE," or other keywords in the Subject line. Use clear instructions (i.e., how do you want comments documented and what do you want the offices to do with the package when they're finished with it?) and finally, attach all attachments. Chapter 12 provides specific guidance for e-mail communication.

WAIT! One final check. *Before* you hit the SEND button or *before* you go to make all of those copies to send out, get someone else to review the package to make sure you haven't forgotten something obvious. Do one last check for spelling and grammar errors.

Following Your Staff Packages

Know where your staff packages are at all times. Use secretaries, contacts or automated tracking systems to track your package(s) and follow up, follow up, follow up. Keep the packages moving according to your schedule. You want to avoid suspensing higher offices, but at the same time you want to let them know what the situation is so they can help push your package along. As you get the packages back, keep all correspondence and comments and make sure you retrieve all coordination copies before going for signature. Make sure you've incorporated any appropriate suggestions into the final product. You may want to summarize the comments and inputs for the approving authority.

Nonconcurrences

How do you handle a nonconcur? Generally, you only want to send up packages that have received concurrence from all offices. So, do you change the package or do you just include the nonconcurrence in the final package? That may depend on where the nonconcur is coming from. You probably would concede the point to someone with a lot of clout; otherwise your package is as good as dead. Short of that, what can you do? You may be able to persuade the other party to see your point of view. If that doesn't work, do you give in by making small concessions or make a stand? Before you decide to make a stand, you probably want to think about a couple of things. For one, is the issue *that* important, or can you make a concession? Remember also that with the give and take of staff work, a compromise now may help you later. Choose your battles carefully; however, there comes a time to stand firm when you know you're right. Finally, do you have the full support of your boss? Any unresolved disputes at your level may need to be highlighted for resolution at a higher level.

Starting Over

Too many substantial changes may require you to start the coordination process all over. You'll have to decide if you've crossed this threshold once you see what kind of inputs you're getting on the package. If you decide to start over, recirculate both the original and changed packages to illustrate the changes you've made and why you've made them.

Finishing Up

Don't give up. You'll eventually work your way up the chain until you reach the final audience. Remember what we said at the beginning: getting that staff package fully coordinated takes a lot of time, diligence and hard work. Don't get frustrated. Along the way, you will receive lots of suggested improvements to your package, but remember why you are coordinating this material in the first place—to present the boss with the best course of action and to tell him or her who agreed with it and had inputs to it. So don't be surprised by inputs that keep your message consistent with previous decisions by the boss and the other supervisors in your chain of command.

Coordinating On Others' Packages

When asked to coordinate on someone else's package, don't put it off. Review it, make your inputs to it and keep it moving. It helps keep your desk clear and the other person may remember your efficiency when he or she gets *your* package. This will also keep you from busting the suspense. If you need more time to review the material, ask for an extension. But don't wait until the suspense to ask for an extension—be proactive. Finally, ask if there are any nonconcurrences on the package so you can take that into consideration.

SUMMARY: As a staffer, you have to remember the big picture. Your job is to get the corporate stamp on the package. You do this by first getting feedback from a few key individuals to make sure your message is loud and clear. Then, you get other offices to approve what you are proposing through the coordination process. Only after the package is fully coordinated can you provide the boss with the best course of action and tell him who is supporting that action.

Proper coordination is the oil that lubricates complex organizations and enables efficient operations. How you view the process and your critical role is crucial. Is coordination just a bureaucratic hassle that you have to endure, or will you meet the challenge head-on by doing a professional, proper job? Your attitude is key to success.

PART IV:

SPEAKING AND LISTENING

CHAPTER 10:

Air Force Speaking

This chapter covers:
- Verbal Communication
- Non-Verbal Communication
- Overcoming Anxiety: Some Simple Steps
- Common Non-Verbal Quirks
- Delivery Formats: Impromptu, Prepared and Manuscript
- Preparing Your Slides

Sooner or later, you will have to speak in public. It comes with being in the military, there's little you can do to avoid it, and the requirements will increase as you climb the ranks. If the thought makes you nervous, you're not alone! Research shows that most people place fear of public speaking second only to fear of dying. If you are inexperienced, the fundamentals and tips for polished speaking in this chapter will help you solve these problems.

One goal should be to improve your self-concept as a speaker. Think positively, and focus on improvement, not perfection. Like writing and listening, speaking is a skill; once you grasp the basics, the rest is practice, polish and style. You may be embarrassed by your initial mistakes, but keep practicing and you'll see improvement with time. Few of us will become guest speakers, but all of us can become more effective if we practice the basics. Learn all you can from your contemporaries; some of them are accomplished speakers. If you are already a speaker extraordinaire, share your views, tips and personal hang-ups about speaking with others. Everyone improves when they receive timely and objective feedback.

Practice doesn't make perfect; perfect practice makes perfect.

–Joan Ballard and Steve Sifers

Before you consider the fundamentals unique to speaking, you may want to review the chapter 2 summary of the Seven Steps to Effective Communication; the Seven Steps are just as necessary for good speaking as they are for good writing. Although there are subtle differences in the drafting and editing sections, the general concepts apply. Indeed, these basic principles are a good place to start when preparing an oral presentation, but we all know there's more to it than that. Let's talk about delivery techniques by discussing the verbal and non-verbal components of delivery separately.

> **SEVEN STEPS FOR EFFECTIVE COMMUNICATION**
> 1. Analyze Purpose and Audience
> 2. Research Your Topic
> 3. Support Your Ideas
> 4. Organize and Outline
> 5. Draft
> 6. Edit
> 7. Fight for Feedback and Get Approval

Verbal Communication

How effectively do you use your voice to drive home your ideas or information? You have control over rate, volume, pitch, pause and other aspects of your speech. So, use your voice to create interest in your presentation.

Rate

There is no correct rate of speed for every speech. However, you might consider this: People can listen 4 to 5 times faster than the normal spoken rate of 120 words a minute. So, if you speak too slowly, you will lose the interest of an audience who is processing information much faster than you are delivering it! On the other hand, you don't want to use the same rate of speech all the time. Use the rate of speech that you need to add emphasis to what you want during your presentation. Consider speaking at a faster rate to indicate excitement or sudden action or a slower rate to hint at calm or a more serious tone.

Volume

Volume is another verbal technique that can give emphasis to your speech. If possible, check out the room to know how loudly you must talk, remembering you will need to talk louder with a crowd since the sound is absorbed. Ask someone in the back of the room if you can be heard. Remember your voice will carry further when the room is empty versus full. If the audience must strain to hear you, they will eventually tune you out from utter exhaustion. A portable microphone may be a good idea if you know you tend to speak quietly, and one is often required in large auditoriums. Speak louder or softer to emphasize a point—a softer level or lower volume is often the more effective way to achieve emphasis.

Pitch

To use pitch effectively, you need to practice the talents of a singer. Pitch is really the use of notes (higher or lower) in voice range. Start by speaking in a voice range that is comfortable for you and then move up or down your scale for emphasis, using pitch changes in vowels, words or entire sentences. You can use a downward (high to low) inflection in a sentence for an air of certainty and an upward (low to high) inflection for an air of uncertainty. Variety in speech pitch helps to avoid monotone and capture the listener's attention.

Pause

The pause gives you time to catch your breath and the audience time to collect your ideas. Never hurry a speech; pause occasionally so your audience can digest your comments. The important question is this: Where? Pauses serve the same function as punctuation in writing. Short pauses usually divide points within a sentence, and longer pauses note the ends of sentences. You can also use longer pauses for breaks from one main point to another, from the body to the conclusion of your speech, or to set off an important point worthy of short reflection. A pause may seem long to you, but it's usually much shorter than you think ... and your audience will appreciate it. However, don't get pause-happy and make your speech sound choppy.

Articulation and Pronunciation

Your articulation and pronunciation reflect your mastery of the spoken English language. Articulation is the art of expressing words *distinctly*. Pronunciation is the ability to say words *correctly*. Of course, you may be able to articulate your thoughts and still mispronounce words while doing so. Unfortunately (and unfairly), many people consider word pronunciation or mispronunciation a direct reflection on your intelligence. Listen to yourself and make your words distinct, understandable and appropriate to your audience. If you are not sure of your pronunciation, consult a current dictionary.

Length

In our military environment, you must be able to relay your thoughts and ideas succinctly. A key rule in verbal communication is to *keep it short and sweet*. There are few people who will tolerate a briefer or speaker who wastes the audience's time. Know what you want to say and then say it with your purpose and the audience in mind.

Non-Verbal Communication

You never get a second chance to make a first impression.

–Anonymous

Numerous studies have shown that people remember less than 10 percent of what is verbally presented, but first impressions are largely based on nonverbal communication such as how you dress, carry yourself, and use gestures and other body language. Your biggest nonverbal challenge to conquer might be your nervousness, so you must be prepared to overcome (or at least diminish) stage fright. Stage fright is often nothing more than misdirected energy, meaning the excitement and/or anxiety you feel is displayed in some form or fashion for all to see. You probably have witnessed a great presentation "gone bad" solely due to nerves that have gone unchecked. Here's a checklist on how to overcome stage fright and put your best foot forward. Remember, it may be impossible to be entirely free from nervousness—that's OK! But you don't want the nervousness to disable you from sending your message.

Overcoming Anxiety: Some Simple Steps

- **Analyze your audience**: listening traits, needs, desires, behaviors and educational background. This will reduce your fear of the unknown and the resulting nervousness.

- **Check out the place where you're speaking**. Is it large enough to accommodate the number of people? Does it have a video screen, projector, white board, microphone, tables, chairs, ventilation, lighting, pencils, paper, telephones, etc.

- **Practice, practice, practice**. Using a recording device, video camera, full-length mirror or even your peers can be really helpful. Try doing a "dry run" in the room you'll be in.

- **Memorize your introduction and transition into the main point**. It'll help you through the first and most difficult minute.

- **Smile and be positive!** Your audience wants you to succeed! Keep your nervousness to yourself; chances are your audience won't even notice if you don't mention it.

- **Take a short walk** right before you "go on stage" to help release some energy.

- **Deliver your message**. Focus your attention where it belongs, not on yourself.

- **Make eye contact and look for feedback**. Let them know you are looking at and talking to them. It holds their attention. If you look only at your notes, you may lose your listeners

- **Use simple, everyday language appropriate for your audience**. Use contractions and keep sentences short. Use personal pronouns, if appropriate. Repeat key words and follow with specific examples if you get into abstract or complicated reasoning

- **Involve members of your audience** by soliciting their answers and information.

- **Enhance your presentation** through creative use of multi-media examples to get a point across.

- **Use your excess energy naturally**: facial expressions, pertinent gestures, walking, or pressing fingertips or thumbs against lectern or chair. Use your facial expressions, hands and arms to reinforce your speech and your points of emphasis—just don't overdo them. Leaning on the lectern, rocking back and forth or side to side or slouching on one leg and then the other is never a positive way to use your excess energy. Read on for more tips on those dreaded nervous habits.

- **Looking good builds confidence and builds your credibility with the audience**. Do you need a haircut? Is your uniform pressed? Are your ribbons, nametag and insignia attached correctly? Your buttons buttoned? Your shoes shined? Are you standing erect and feeling alert, but relaxed? Remember, in your audience's mind, a frumpy uniform and sloppy bearing equals an equally frumpy presenter. Fair or not, that's the way your audience's mind works. We're all critics!

Common Nonverbal Quirks

Most of us have quirks and our quirks are magnified when we are put in the limelight. The key is to be aware of your quirks and keep them under control by seeking feedback from someone you trust who will be critical and honest. Do any of these common quirks describe you?

- **Life raft.** A speaker who seeks the safety and security of the podium as though his or life depended upon holding the podium. For them, walking about the room is incomprehensible.

- **Awkward hands.** This speaker is venturing out in front of the audience but is still not quite sure what to do with his or her hands. The speaker may want to run back to the safety of the life raft, but instead may place his or her hands awkwardly over certain parts of the body.

- **Hand washer**. A speaker who wrings his or her hands nervously while speaking.

- **Caged tiger.** The speaker paces from one side of the stage to the other without stopping.

- **Rocker.** Rockers are caged tigers on the road to recovery. They have conquered the worst phases of stage fright but retain a fear of standing still and simply talking. There are two style variations: 1) the fore-and-aft rocker and 2) the side-to-side rocker.

- **Pocket maniacs.** These speakers should consider sewing their pants pockets shut. When pocket maniacs speak they jam their hands into their pockets in an effort to avoid the other quirks of the hands. Sadly, this only creates another quirk that is just as distracting.

- **Pen clickers.** These speakers are related to the pocket maniacs but they have substituted the clicking of a pen for other annoying quirks of the hands.

- **Gadgeteers.** These speakers may play with the slide clicker, act as though they have never seen a slide clicker or needlessly employ countless high-tech devices into the presentation in an effort to mask nervousness.

- **Too Cool.** These speakers are overcompensating for a fear of speaking by trying to look extremely comfortable.

By themselves, these quirks won't make you fail as a speaker, but they can create problems if they are severe—the audience begins to focus on the quirk instead of your message. Again, most of us have done some of these things at one time or another. Try to be aware of your own mannerisms, keep them in check and make sure they are not detracting from your message.

Delivery Formats: Impromptu, Prepared and Manuscript

Your approach to delivery of the spoken message may be affected by several factors, including the time you have to prepare and the nature of the message. Three common delivery formats are listed below.

Impromptu speaking is when we respond during a meeting or "take the floor" at a conference. It's what we do when we speak publicly without warning or on a few moments' notice. To do it well requires a great amount of self-confidence, mastery of the subject and the ability to "think on your feet." A superb impromptu speaker has achieved the highest level in verbal communications.

> Both students and instructors have had trouble differentiating impromptu and extemporaneous speaking in the PME classroom. Why? Because dictionaries vary in how they define these terms. Some, including *The Cambridge Dictionary of American English*, define extemporaneous as "done or said without preparation" (synonymous with impromptu). The *Merriam-Webster Dictionary*, on the other hand, states that extemporaneous speech "*is* prepared in advance but delivered without notes." To confuse matters further, extemporaneous briefers in the Air Force frequently use notes or an outline (but not a script) when speaking. So, for ease of discussion in this edition of *The Tongue and Quill*, the term "prepared speaking" will replace extemporaneous speaking.

Prepared (formerly *extemporaneous* speaking or briefing) refers to those times when we have ample opportunity to prepare. Most military briefings are done in this format. This doesn't mean we write a script and memorize it, but it does require a thorough outline with careful planning and practicing. The specific words and phrases used at the time of delivery, however, are basically spontaneous and sound very natural.

A **manuscript** briefing is used in situations that require every word to be absolutely perfect. To do this, you prepare a manuscript, a word-for-word script of what you are going to say. Such a script ensures you get it right every time. Manuscripts are often used at higher management levels for complex or controversial issues (policy briefings, press conferences, source selection briefings to unsuccessful bidders, etc.). They're also used for routine briefings that must be repeated several times a year (base orientation, etc.), or at formal ceremonies (retirements, medal presentations, etc.) that must adhere to established customs and courtesies. Manuscript-style briefings provide several advantages:

- Ensures key information won't be omitted.
- Avoids repercussions caused by a briefer's inadvertent ad-libbing.
- Imparts exact definitions and precise phrasing, if these are important.
- Allows anyone to present a "canned briefing" without extensive preparation and rehearsal time—including less knowledgeable personnel.

CAUTION! Manuscripts do *not* make a briefing easier. Reading aloud often sounds dull, especially when the reader is more focused on saying the right words rather than saying the words right. Manuscript briefings tend to lack spontaneity, eye contact, and speaker engagement with the audience. This results in a loss of credibility, both professional and intellectual. Why should they attend a reading if they can read it themselves? When you can deliver a manuscript briefing without error that engages the audience, you have mastered "speak-reading."

Here are some key points in preparing and presenting a manuscript briefing.

- **Prepare the briefing:**
    - Use a large, easy-to-read font (at least size 12) in all capital letters
    - Write as if you were speaking

- o Fill only the top two-thirds of page so that your eyes won't drop and you won't lose eye contact with your audience
- o Double-space or triple-space the manuscript; never break words at the end of a line or sentences at the end of a page
- o Number pages with bold figures
- o Underscore or highlight words you wish to emphasize; insert double slashes (//) where you plan a major pause
- o Use a loose-leaf binder or stack pages loosely to turn pages
- o Mark script with red dots to show visual aid changes

- **Practice, practice, practice:**
  - o Read and reread until you've practically memorized it
  - o Add the ingredients of volume, inflection and eye contact
  - o Avoid combinations of words that are difficult to say
  - o Look at your audience when uttering emphatic words and during the closing words of a sentence
  - o Practice using gestures—strive for enthusiasm
  - o Dry run your visual aids

- **Close with confidence:**
  - o Never explain why you choose to read (it won't be apparent if you've prepared!)
  - o Be flexible; if necessary (and appropriate), know where you can shorten the speech
  - o Avoid being lengthy after saying "In conclusion."
  - o Don't add new information at the end

Individuals who can strongly present briefings in all three types of delivery formats are the envy of everyone. They appear knowledgeable and comfortable in their roles as speakers because they have done their homework. They may be experts on their subject and know how to present their views with clarity on a moment's notice (impromptu speaking). They have researched and rehearsed their presentations (prepared and manuscript briefings). They think carefully before they speak, outline their main ideas, say what has to be said, and then conclude. Remember, there is no substitution for preparation. If you have the time to prepare—do it!

Enough with the bells and whistles—just get to the point.

–General Hugh Shelton

As always, check with your organization for local policies on formats. These are only general guidelines.

We've spent the majority of the chapter on how to speak and how to get over your nervousness. But there's more you can do to make an oral presentation more professional and useful for your audience. Visual aids can enhance your oral presentation by helping the audience remember and understand the content of your message. Comprehension rises dramatically when we *see* something rather than when we just hear about it. The average person retains 5 percent of what is heard and 65 percent of what is seen. More dramatically, the human brain processes visuals 400,000 times faster than text! In other words, "show and tell" is better than just "tell" alone.

Slides are the most common visual aid used for briefings in today's Air Force. They help the briefer to remember key points and help to keep the presentation brief. The presenter makes the slide simple and fills in the "white space" with concise spoken words.

Before we launch into Slides 101, let's take a second to stress one point—*you* are also a visual aid. If you are well groomed, professional and well prepared, you'll be the most effective visual aid in your presentation. If you look like a slob and appear insecure and awkward, the audience most likely won't take you or your message seriously. Take the time to put on a freshly pressed uniform and look sharp!

Preparing Your Slides

Slides are the most common visual aids used today but each organization is different when it comes down to how your slides should look. However, *most* organizations in today's Air Force agree that the information we present shouldn't be too complex. Custom animation, if used, must serve a substantive purpose—not just looks. Keep these tips in mind as you build your slides or any other visual aid media.

COLOR. Color is a very important communication tool. Good designers limit their color palettes even if 256 different colors may be available.

- Use colors in a standard manner throughout your presentation.
- Limit your choices to 4 or 5 colors.
- Use light colors on a dark background and vice versa.
- Use colors to emphasize key elements, but try to avoid red lettering.
- Use the same background color on all images.
- Avoid red-green and blue-red color combinations.
- Use bright colors (yellow, orange, etc.) sparingly.
- Maintain good contrast between important information and background.
- Check your slide colors in the room you will be briefing in. Projectors do not always show the same level of contrast as your monitor.

Most organizations have standard slide show requirements, so check with your organization's front office to ensure you're using the correct presentation design (font, color, background, etc.).

TEXT. The first rule here is "less is more." Less experienced briefers are often tempted to pack presentations with every detail they can think of for fear they might leave something out during the real thing. Slides should have minimal content and lots of "white space." Slides aim at the visual portion of the brain and will only confuse the audience if they are jam-packed with data. The slides should *not* be self-explanatory. If they are, you probably have too much stuff on them. Remember, you should add value to the presentation and should supplement the slides with your eloquent speaking abilities.

- Keep it simple. Use the "7 x 7 rule:"
    - No more than 7 words per line
    - No more than 7 lines per slide
- Spelling is important!
- Don't read slides—it's insulting.
- If you have more than one slide per main point, add "Continued" on subsequent slides.
- Have only one thought per slide—it gives the audience time to refocus on you.
- Avoid hyphenation at end of lines.
- Use upper and lower case for three reasons:
    - Helps identify acronyms, which we love in the military!
    - More comfortable for audience, because this is how we read.
    - Makes your presentation look more professional.
- Emphasize key words with boldface, italicized, underlined or colored text.
- Left-justify your text.
- Font size: Use the same type font throughout the presentation.
    - Title: 40 point
    - Subtitle: 30 point
    - Text: 20-26 point
- Most importantly, you fill in the information. So, you should always know and be ready to present one level of detail below a piece of information. If you don't, you will end up reading slides or the audience will have many questions left unanswered.

GRAPHICS. Whether designed for a briefing or written report, no graphic should be so elaborate it becomes an end in itself and obscures your intended message. However, when used wisely, graphics can certainly add to your presentation. Although text is important, audiences remember more when content is graphically presented. A 60-minute briefing can be pretty boring if it is all done in text. On the flip side, interesting graphics do not guarantee an effective briefing. Read below for some tips to keep you in check when using graphics.

- Use only artwork suitable for your presentation. Know your audience!
- Use graphs (bar charts, pie charts, etc.) to convey statistics.
- Be careful with graphs: too many can be confusing.
- Line graphs show trends over time.

- Bar graphs compare values.
- Pie charts compare values against a whole.
- Tables: Don't use if you can convey information verbally or in a graph—they usually appear overly "busy" on a slide.
    - Limit to 4 rows and 7 columns.
    - Use footnotes to remove distracting data from tables.
    - Round off numbers if possible.
    - Don't put decimal points in numbers like 10 or 100. The audience may interpret "100.00" as "10,000."
- Place your graphics off-center—use them to lead your audience to important text information.
- Be careful with animation:
    - Sound: Use sound effects sparingly and make sure they add impact.
    - Slide transitions: Most briefers overuse slide transitions. If you decide to use transitions, use the same type throughout your entire briefing, and make sure they add, not detract from your presentation.
- Video can be quite effective, but again, use sparingly.

BOTTOM LINE: *Make it Big, keep it Simple, make it Clear, and be Consistent!*

SUMMARY: We've covered a lot of ground in this section but it all boils down to a few simple ideas.

- Use vocal characteristics such as rate, volume, pitch and pause to enhance the impact of your message.
- Be aware of any nonverbal quirks; reduce nervousness through solid preparation.
- Select an appropriate delivery format: impromptu, prepared or manuscript.
- Visual aids can enhance oral presentations, but don't lose sight of the big picture.
- Stay focused: do your homework on the topic and the delivery.

The more often you speak in front of or with a group, the more self-confident you become. High confidence and thorough knowledge of your subject are important prerequisites for speaking. In the end, if you have the time to prepare—do it! There is no substitute for being prepared and practice. The following lists of "Do's" and "Don'ts" summarize many of the key ideas of this chapter as a quick reference. Keep these lists handy to check yourself (or your friends) before that big presentation to the boss.

CHAPTER 10: Air Force Speaking

Do's (For Air Force Speaking)

1. Stand beside your visual aid. Better yet, get away from slides and walk around.
2. This may depend on your purpose and audience, and location of your briefing.
3. Start out with well-prepared opening statement and try to elicit audience involvement by asking a relevant question or two. Use a personal story or experience (if appropriate) to bridge to your topic.
4. If referring to screen, stand aside, use a pointer, and put it down when done.
5. Give the audience time to read slides.
6. Read the slide silently or watch to see if audience has finished reading. If slide contains a long quote, paraphrase or underline important parts.
7. Speak naturally and use gestures.
8. Make the slide simple and fill it out with concise spoken words.
9. Show only necessary slides.
10. Turn off projector or use a cover slide.
11. Check for spelling and punctuation ... more than once!
12. Practice handling slides and gauging time needed to read them. Use an assistant to advance slides if available.
13. Anticipate likely questions and rehearse possible answers. Keep answers short and simple. Listen carefully to questioner and clarify question if needed.
14. *Know your purpose, audience* and any time constraints.
15. Practice, practice, practice! And test visual aids prior to your briefing.

Don'ts (For Air Force Speaking)

1. Stand between the audience and visual aid and block the audience's view.
2. Jump right into slides.
3. Talk at the screen with back to your audience.
4. Change slides too quickly.
5. Read the slide to the audience.
6. Give a memorized briefing.
7. Show a complicated slide *and* give a complicated explanation of it.
8. Use slides as gimmicks or crutches.
9. Leave projector on with blank screen.
10. Forget to check spelling and punctuation.
11. Disrupt presentation to handle slides.
12. Be caught off-guard by questions from the audience. Don't give quick replies. Don't direct questions to specific members of audience.
13. If time is limited (5-15 minutes), you may want to consider NOT using slides. In these cases, it's more important to establish connection with your audience than it is to show a few slides.
14. **Wing it,** and never apologize because you didn't prepare. This makes you look irresponsible and ruins your credibility before you even start.

CHAPTER 11:

Effective Listening Strategies

> *This chapter covers:*
> - Understanding Hearing and Listening
> - Informative, Critical and Empathic Listening
> - Better Listening
> - Overcoming Barriers to Listening

Listening is a valuable communication skill, but one that gets little respect and attention. Some of us spend hours preparing and practicing our briefings; how much time and effort do we spend on preparing and practicing to listen? Because listening is so undervalued, we'll first make the case for why it's so important and then describe ways to improve your listening skills.

Understanding Hearing and Listening

To better understand the listening process, let's begin by distinguishing between hearing and listening. Hearing occurs when your ears pick up sound waves transmitted by a speaker or some other source. Hearing requires a source of sound and an ear capable of perceiving it. It does not require the conscious decoding of information. Each day, you hear many sounds—background music in an elevator, the hum of the computer, cars passing by outside—sounds you may not even be aware of unless someone draws your attention to them.

Listening, on the other hand, involves making sense out of what is transmitted. Listening involves not only hearing; it involves attending to and considering what is heard. As you listen, you receive sounds and you consciously and actively decode them. Effective listening is an active process and active listening involves exerting energy and responding appropriately in order to hear, comprehend, evaluate and remember the message.

Listening is critical to good oral communications. Though listening is usually ignored in formal education, it is the most common form of communication. According to Dr. John Kline, an authority on Air Force communication and the author of *Listening Effectively*, studies have shown that we spend 70 percent of our waking hours in some form of communication.

When speakers and listeners fail to communicate, the outcomes can be disastrous. Planes can crash, unit morale can deteriorate, "routine" surgeries can have horrendous outcomes and families can self-destruct. Though we often focus on the speaker's role in communication, good listening skills can often make the difference between success and failure.

Both Air Force and civilian managers put a premium on good listening. In a recent study, 282 members of the Academy of Certified Administrative Managers identified listening as the most crucial management skill. In another study published in *Communication Quarterly*, business people were polled on the most important communication skills they used at work and the one they wished they had studied in college: Listening was the #1 answer to both questions.

Listening is especially important in the Air Force and actually in any military unit. Success is a matter of life and death and we routinely maintain and operate equipment valued in the millions. Receiving, comprehending and remembering spoken information is critical and any miscommunication is potentially catastrophic. Effective listening helps to build the trust and mutual respect needed to do our job. Military personnel must understand their team members and the situation, and leaders with good listening skills often make better decisions and have a stronger bond with their troops.

To summarize, listening allows us to learn the facts, evaluate situations, understand our team members and build trust with others. These are all really important, so why do so few people listen well—why is it so hard—and how do we get better at it?

Everybody wants to talk, few want to think and nobody wants to listen.

–Anonymous

Informative, Critical and Empathic Listening

There are different situations where listening is important and different reasons to listen. It's important to acknowledge and identify these differences because appropriate listening behaviors in one situation might be inappropriate in another situation. Part of the challenge of listening is sorting out what situation you're in and what response is appropriate. One way to approach this sorting process is to look at three major reasons why we listen in the workplace. We'll talk more about each of these three categories in later sections, but here's a summary:

Informative Listening: We listen to collect information from others.

- Receiving radio instructions in an aircraft cockpit.
- Listening to an instructor lecture on good writing technique.
- Receiving a briefing on a change to the assignment process.
- Obtaining medical instructions from a doctor.
- Learning your boss's expectations during an initial feedback session.

Critical Listening: We listen to judge—to evaluate a situation and make decisions.

- Investigating causes of a fatal mishap.
- Determining which Airman to nominate for a quarterly award.
- Helping the user formally specify requirements for a new weapon system.
- Deciding which disciplinary action to administer.

Empathic Listening: We listen to understand and help others in situations where emotions are involved and the speaker, not just the message, is important.

- A subordinate is seeking advice on whether to reenlist.
- Your spouse is worried about your next deployment.
- A coworker is unsure how to deal with subtle discrimination.
- Your teenager doesn't want to move during senior year; you've got orders.
- You're trying to mend fences with a coworker after a major conflict.

Informative, Critical and Empathic listening categories can be used in two different ways. First, they can be used to characterize listening situations—that is, *why* we should be listening in this situation. Second, they can be used to describe listening approaches—the behaviors we use in a given situation and *how* we are listening.

Using an incorrect listening category for a certain listening situation may be problematic. For example, using an informative listening approach (taking notes, asking focused questions) in an empathic listening situation (an angry spouse who feels you're neglecting the family) could cause the communicative act to fail. Keep reading to uncover how to match listening categories to particular acts of communication.

Informative Listening

In informative listening, the listener's primary concern is to understand information exactly as transmitted. A successful listening outcome occurs when the listener understands the message exactly as the sender intended. Informative listening is important when receiving information from an established authority or receiving information that is not open for debate.

For example, if you're receiving a briefing on changes to the assignment system, your goal should be to understand exactly what the rules are, not to sort out the reasons why you think the rules are off track. If you're receiving formal training that will be followed by a test, your primary goal should be to understand the material, not to evaluate whether the material should be taught at this level.

Improving informative listening: There are several steps you can take to improve your informative listening skills.

1. **Keep an open mind.** If your primary goal is to understand the message, set aside your preconceptions about the topic and just listen.
2. **Listen as if you had to teach it.** Many education and training specialists suggest this technique. Typically we expend more effort to understand a subject when we know that we have to teach it to someone else. By taking this approach, we have the mental

fortitude to focus longer, ask questions when we don't understand and think more deeply on a topic.

3. **Take notes.** Focus on main points and don't attempt to capture everything. This classic technique is used in situations where you are trying to capture objective information, such as in classes, staff meetings, etc. Note that if the listener and speaker are in a less formal, emotionally-charged situation, note taking might be misconstrued as hostile behavior (i.e., being put "on the record," or being documented for future adverse action) so use your judgment on whether it is appropriate to the situation.

4. **Exploit time gap between thinking and speaking speeds.** The average speaking rate is 180 words per minute while most listeners can process 500 words per minute. Use this extra time to mentally repeat, forecast, summarize and paraphrase the speaker's remarks.

5. **Respond and ask appropriate questions.** Good informative questions help you clarify and confirm you understand the message. Remember that you are trying to absorb as much information as possible and you are less focused on making value judgments on the material. Here are some examples of appropriate questions or responses:

    a. **Repeat exact content back to the speaker**: "You said we need toner, copy paper and a three-hole punch. I'll go get them now."

    b. **Paraphrase the speaker** in your own words: "So if I understand you, then…."

    c. **Ask for more specifics or details**: "When you say a draft is due on 15 April, is that before or after the internal coordination process?" or
    "How does the situation change if you're married to another military member?"

    d. **Request an example for clarity**: "If asking good questions can help listening performance, can you provide some examples?"

Critical Listening

Critical listening can be thought of as the sum of informative listening and *critical thinking*. In this case, the listener actively analyzes and evaluates the message and listening success requires understanding the message and assessing its merit. The listener is evaluating the support offered by the speaker—as well as the speaker's credentials and logic—and may either agree or disagree with the message. Critical listening may be appropriate when seeking input to a decision, evaluating the quality of staff work or a subordinate's capabilities, or conducting research. Also, critical listening is related to critical thinking—they should occur simultaneously for the best critical thinkers.

Critical Thinking

Critical thinking is the act of exercising careful judgment in forming opinions or conclusions. In chapter 4, we described how intellectual standards like accuracy, precision, relevance and clarity can be used to evaluate the quality of information sources. Critical thinking attempts to improve the quality of thought by using these same standards. It is self-directed, self-disciplined and self-corrective thinking applied to an important problem.

Improving critical listening: Several of the suggestions made for improving informative listening are equally important for critical listening: after all, you need to understand the message before you can critically analyze it.

1. **Take notes.** See "Improving Informational Listening" on the previous page.

2. **Listen as if you had to grade it.** Teaching a topic is tough, but grading another's presentation of a topic is even tougher. Is the message clear and precise? Is the supporting material relevant and convincing? Does this make sense? Your attempt to mentally answer questions like these may help you stay focused on the speaker.

3. **Exploit time gap between thinking and speaking speeds.** Use the time gap described on the message. Remember to try to understand first and then evaluate second. Even when you are listening critically, don't mentally argue with the speaker until the message is finished.

4. **Ask appropriate questions.** Good critical listening questions will be probing in nature so you can better evaluate the intellectual content of the speaker's message. Some examples of good critical listening questions can be found in *The Miniature Guide to Critical Thinking* by Richard Paul and Linda Elder.

    a. **Accuracy:** How could we verify or test that? Are others reporting the same results?
    b. **Relevance:** How does that fact relate to the problem?
    c. **Breadth:** Do we need to consider another point of view?
    d. **Logic:** Do our conclusions flow from our evidence?
    e. **Significance:** Is this the central idea? The most important problem?
    f. **Fairness:** Do we have any vested interests? How would opponents view this issue?

Empathic Listening

In empathic listening, we listen with the primary intent to understand the speaker and his or her frame of reference. Empathic listening is often useful when communication is emotional, or when the relationship between speaker and listener is just as important as the message. It is often used as a first step in the listening process, a prerequisite to informational or critical listening. Empathic listening is often appropriate during mentoring and non-punitive counseling sessions and can be very helpful when communicating with family members. Depending on the situation, it may also be useful in negotiation and teambuilding activities.

Empathic Listening: Not just emotional

Though most people quickly see that empathic listening skills are useful in dealing with a spouse or a child, some might think this listening approach is too "sensitive" for the military environment.

Realize that the same reasons these skills are relevant within a family make them relevant within the workplace. Empathic listening builds trust and encourages cooperation and may help small group cohesion—a critical factor in team performance in combat and crisis situations. Though you may not see many empathic listening behaviors when the bullets are flying, it lays the groundwork for success in that environment.

In the book, *The 7 Habits of Highly Effective People,* Dr. Stephen Covey suggests that listening be used to "diagnose before you prescribe" when dealing with others, a concept captured by the phrase: "Seek First to Understand, then to be Understood." Empathic listening is described as a powerful tool to understand others and to build relationships. If you allow yourself to fully listen for both content and feeling and then reflect that back, there are several productive outcomes: 1) The listener truly understands how the speaker feels; 2) The speaker feels understood; 3) The listener can give better advice; and 4) The speaker will be more open to it.

Improving empathic listening: For empathic listening to be successful, the listener must understand the content of the message and the speaker must feel understood. It's this second half—making the speaker feel understood—which requires some specialized skills.

Don't you hate it when others want to "one-up" your story or when they jump in and give advice before they understand? If you'd like to improve your emphatic listening skills, try to avoid the following invasive responses that may prevent you from seeking to understand.

- **AUTOBIOGRAPHICAL STORIES**: "Your situation is just like something that happened to me…" "When I was your age…"
- **ADVISING**: Immediately providing counsel based on our own experience—whether or not it was requested.
- **PROBING**: Asking questions solely from our own frame of reference.
- **EVALUATING**: Immediately agreeing or disagreeing.

These types of responses are discouraged because they distract the speaker from the critical part of the message, and they allow the listener to derail the conversation. Extroverts have more difficulty avoiding autobiographical responses than introverts do. Parents often use these responses with their children—the trick is to decide how much is too much. These responses are appropriate *after* the speaker feels understood and is looking for advice or help; it's just important to wait until that point. The listener should return to empathic listening if emotions rise again.

The skills involved in empathic listening are easy to describe, but difficult to practice. To help you remember them, think about the acronym "HEAR."

H = HEART: Commit to listening sincerely, avoid manipulation; remember the importance of the person, as well as the issue.

E = EMOTIONS: Look and listen for speaker's emotions as much as their words.

A = AVOID: Avoid advice, autobiographies, evaluation; don't interrupt or change the subject.

R = REFLECT: Reflect back meaning and feeling until the speaker feels understood.

Better Listening

Listening takes a lot of effort. Our willingness to exert that effort is linked to our motivation to listen. Techniques to improve listening skills are worthless without cultivating the motivation to use them. To evaluate your own listening motivation, ask yourself the following questions:

- Do I pretend to listen?
- Do I seek distractions?
- Do I criticize the speakers?
- Do I stereotype topics as uninteresting?
- Do I prejudge the meaning and intent of speakers' messages?
- Do I avoid difficult and complex topics?
- Do I get emotionally charged up about minor points a speaker has made?
- In a conversation, do I tune out the speaker because I'm preparing my response?
- Do I interrupt others? Has anyone told me I sometimes interrupt others?
- Do I spend a disproportionate amount of time talking in meetings or social events?
- Does everything a speaker describes remind me of something that happened to me?

Though we've all been guilty of these once in a while, if you answered "yes" to three or more questions, then you might benefit from some of the suggestions to improve your listening skills later in the chapter.

Sometimes we have blind spots and overestimate our success as listeners. In his book, *Listening Effectively*, Dr. Kline describes how most individuals in groups will rate their own listening skills as 7.5 out of 10 while rating the rest of the group as 4.1 out of 10. These data indicate that most people see listening as a problem in others but not in themselves.

Here's another set of "workplace climate" questions to consider. If you have "yes" answers to several of these questions, you might want to take a closer look at how you listen and interact with others.

- Do employees go around you to talk to others about work issues?
- Do you often learn about important events after the fact?
- Do you frequently find yourself putting out organizational fires?
- Are you rarely tasked with complicated responsibilities?
- Do you receive lots of information in writing ... including some items that would normally be handled face to face?

Sometimes it takes a deliberate effort to cultivate our motivation to listen. In today's culture, a "good communicator" is often defined in terms of one's speaking ability, yet many would argue that listening is just as important, if not more so. Today's effective listeners command respect and admiration because listening is crucial to solving problems and making decisions.

Overcoming Barriers to Listening

Think about the times you did a good job of listening. Why did you do well? One of the reasons was probably your level of motivation. Here are four suggestions on how to enhance your motivation to listen in future situations.

1. Recall why this listening situation is important. Listeners should try to remember why this particular situation is important. Speakers should try to remind their audience why it's important to listen, too.

  a. **Informative and listening situations:**

  1) Is it critical to mission success; will this help me do my job better?

  2) Will this information help me make a better decision?

  3) Is it on the test; is it a prerequisite for other material that is on the test?

  4) Can someone get hurt if we mess this up?

  5) Will our unit look bad if I don't "get" it; will I look bad?

  6) Will we be discussing this later; will I have to teach this to someone else?

  7) Is understanding this presentation important to my personal or family goals?

  b. **Critical listening situations:**

  1) Do I have to decide which position to take?

  2) Is the evidence strong and the logic sound?

  3) What unanswered questions surround this issue; what things are being left unsaid?

  c. **Empathic situations:**

  1) Is this speaker having trouble communicating the facts because of strong emotions?

  2) Do I need to mend fences with this coworker?

  3) In this negotiation, am I really sure I know what is most important to the other party?

  4) Does this family member count on me for emotional support?

  5) Do I have a personal commitment to this person as well as this issue?

2. Identify and correct barriers to listening motivation. Both listeners and speaker can benefit from a hard look at factors that may inhibit listening. What factors can you control? What factors do you just have to live with? Fix what you can and acknowledge what you can't.

  a. **Physical barriers** may block listening—noisy equipment, visual distractions, etc. Avoid distractions when possible: If you can, sit up front. This puts less noise and visual distraction between you and the speaker and allows you to more clearly see any visual aids. Sitting next to quiet people also helps you to focus on the speaker.

  b. **Personal barriers** such as physical fatigue, illness and discomfort, as well as psychological distractions like work, family or financial problems, can also affect listening.

c. **Semantic barriers** may create obstacles: the speaker's intent may not be understood by the audience when using words or phrases with more than one meaning; ideas, objects or actions with more than one word image; or slang, jargon or organizational acronyms. For example, the word "crusade" may have one connotation with an audience in Ohio, but have a different connotation when used in a press conference in the Middle East.

3. Look for common ground. Our listening motivation is crippled when we adversely stereotype speakers or topics. Are you carrying around biases that **might** be triggered by a speaker's age, race, religion, gender, ethnicity or personal appearance? Have you already decided that this topic is uninteresting, irrelevant or taught at a level that is below you? This kind of thinking can be lethal to listening motivation.

To break the pattern, ask yourself some more empowering questions. What are the underlying commonalities and interesting interrelationships between your interests and those of the speaker? Relate the topic at hand to your own interests. Sometimes this small, simple exercise creates an interesting challenge and bridges the gaps that exist.

4. Treat listening as a learning opportunity and an intellectual challenge. So, how do you become motivated to listen to a topic that may, at first glance, seem boring, unrelated or irrelevant?

a. If you're listening to an informational briefing on a topic you're already an expert on, listen to improve your ability to teach the topic to someone else. How did the speaker organize the talk? What terms were defined? What terms were not defined? Did the speaker use interesting examples that you could "borrow" when you try to explain to someone else?

b. If you're listening to a speaker who's failing miserably, ask yourself how could he or she do better? Make some notes and offer tactful but constructive feedback later.

c. Translate the problem to a personal, intellectual challenge. Effective and active listening is an exercise in critical thinking and can serve to sharpen your concentration skills. Develop a "remember game" and make listening a learning activity.

SUMMARY: In our eagerness to make our point or make our mark, we often forget there's more to the story than what we know. Listening is a critical communication skill that doesn't get the attention it deserves. Misunderstandings and mistakes in communication can be lethal in the military environment, and listening helps build trust between members of the Air Force team.

In this chapter we have talked about three approaches to listening—informative, critical and empathic listening. Different situations call for different approaches and the listening skills used should be tailored to the situation.

PART V:

WORKPLACE CHALLENGES

CHAPTER 12:

Electronic Communications and Social Media

This chapter covers:
- Electronic Mail (E-mail)
- Social Media
- Instant Messaging (IM) and Texting
- Telephones, Voice Mail and FAX
- Electronic Communications Glossary

Innovation in the 21st century is at your fingertips—literally. The changes in electronic communication technologies, software, and applications are rapid with new methods to stay connected being developed and deployed daily. They are also subsequently disappearing at an alarming rate, as the new next big thing is introduced. *The Tongue and Quill* would be presumptuous to address the specifics of all electronic communication technologies. Such content would fill volumes of books and many large organizations have written guidance on electronic communications. Your unit may fall under the purview of such higher-headquarters guidance. But we would also be remiss if we did not address some fundamental principles applicable to all electronic communications. For these reasons, we'll hit the basics here and suggest you check with your local experts for more details on policies applicable to your electronic communications and social media.

To keep this chapter both simple and relevant, we focus on electronic mail (e-mail), social media, voice mail and FAX since these are the official means of many or most electronic communications in the Air Force; however, the principles here can be applied to other electronic communications and "the next big thing" that is just around the corner. At the end of the day, electronic communications are just forms for communicating with each other and we need to treat all communications with the same attitude as if we were face to face.

Electronic Mail (E-Mail)

The Air Force has learned a great deal about e-mail since it was adopted into the fabric of our Service and these lessons remain valid today. We have learned that there are both advantages and disadvantages; that we must differentiate between personal or official communications; that all communications are more effective when they are well organized; and that there are special considerations and protocols for e-mail.

Advantages and Disadvantages

Though some communication guidelines are universal (FOCUS principles, the Seven Steps to Effective Communication, etc.), e-mail is a unique medium—it's advantages can easily become disadvantages, especially when you consider the ability to reach numerous people at once and the longevity of electronic communications.

- Three common e-mail advantages
    - It's fast.
    - It can get to more people.
    - It's paperless.
- Three common e-mail disadvantages
    - It's fast … but a quickly written e-mail can fan as many fires as it extinguishes.
    - It can get to more people … but too many copies can clog the network and can be forwarded into the wrong hands.
    - It's paperless … but leaves a permanent electronic trail; can disappear permanently with power fluctuations; and too many times we print our e-mail (on recycled paper).

E-mail: Personal and Official

E-mail may have started as an informal communication technique, but today it covers the spectrum from personal to professional. **Professional** or **official e-mail** is different from personal e-mail—it's more like a business memo. It *does* affect the Air Force and the rules you follow should conform to military courtesy. The same care and attention to detail should be taken with professional e-mail as with "paper copy" correspondence. The following pages provide guidelines to help keep you on track with your e-mail correspondence.

Chapter 3 of AFMAN 33-152, *User Responsibilities and Guidance for Information Systems,* provides guidance on what constitutes "effective use of Internet-based capabilities," especially as applied to personal and official use of e-mail. "Government-provided hardware and software are for official use and limited authorized personal use only. Limited personal use must be of reasonable duration and frequency that have been approved by the supervisors and do not adversely affect performance of official duties, overburden systems or reflect adversely on the Air Force or the DOD."

The responsible use of Internet-based capabilities from AFMAN 33-152, chapter 3, specifically addresses or prohibits certain actions on government communication systems. The following actions are prohibited on government communication systems:

- Unauthorized personal use.
- Uses that adversely reflects on the DoD or the Air Force.
- Unauthorized storing, processing, displaying or transmitting prohibited content.
- Storing or processing classified information on any system not approved for classified processing.
- Using copyrighted material in violation of the rights of the owner of the copyrights.
- Unauthorized use of the account or identity of another person or organization.
- Unauthorized viewing, changing, damaging, deleting or blocking of another user's files.
- Attempting to circumvent, modify or defeat security systems.
- Obtaining, installing, copying, storing or using software in violation of the appropriate vendor's license agreement.
- Permitting an unauthorized individual access to a government-owned or government-operated system.
- Unauthorized modification of the network operating system or configuration.
- Copying and posting of FOUO, controlled unclassified information (CUI), Critical Information (CI) and/or personally identifiable information (PII) on DoD–owned, –operated, or –controlled publically accessible sites or on commercial Internet-based capabilities.
- Unauthorized downloading and installing freeware, shareware or any other software.

The network, like the phone, is subject to monitoring. Your e-mail is saved on back-up files and servers. Once written and sent, an e-mail is a permanent part of the electronic record.

Personal E-Mail

Personal e-mail sometimes contains shorthand and slang that would be unacceptable in a professional communication. Emoticons (facial expressions) or abbreviations are sometimes used with humor or satire in an attempt to make sure the audience doesn't "take things the wrong way." They are a resource, but use them sparingly. Some of them are more clever than clear, and much of your audience may only know the smiling face.

Official E-Mail

Official e-mail consumes a large part of the day for many Airmen. We can accomplish a great deal by e-mail, especially with those who are at a distance. E-mail can be particularly useful for electronically staffing official documents, ideas and initiatives. If properly managed, e-mail coordination and staffing can increase efficiency. If not managed well, e-mail staffing is just as problematic as paper folders and distribution envelopes lost in the system. To maximize the efficiency of e-mail coordination and staffing, use organizational accounts when sending correspondence to offices for coordination or action. Each MAJCOM typically issues their own guidance on the details of how electronic staffing should be implemented, and local commanders may provide additional guidelines that take into account the local conditions and unit operating procedures. Check your local guidance for electronic staffing implementation details.

Official E-Mail: An Example

A professional e-mail has three distinct qualities: FOCUS, FOCUS, and FOCUS (focused, organized, clear, understandable and supported). Experience amongst the authors of *The Tongue and Quill* tells us that shorter e-mails tend to communicate better than longer e-mails. This suggests that while you must address the issue, the whole issue, and nothing but the issue you cannot write *War and Peace* levels of detail into every e-mail and expect any action quickly. Balance what you present in an e-mail with the audience and action you need. Focus their attention on the issue and what needs to be done—nothing more, and nothing less.

From: [system-generated user information]
To: [appropriate organizational account, individuals, or distribution list for ACTION]
Cc: [as required for INFORMATION]
Subject: INFO: Air Force Doctrine Update
Date: [system-generated date-time group]

[Greeting],

BLUF: Effective 29 Oct 13, all Air Force Doctrine Documents (AFDDs) have been rescinded and replaced by core doctrine volumes and doctrine annexes.
- Core doctrine is categorized into five volumes: Volume I, Basic Doctrine; Volume II, Leadership; Volume III, Command; Volume IV, Operations; and Volume V, Support
- Each core doctrine volume is supported by one or more annexes.
- For further information, go to https://doctrine.af.mil/.

//SIGNED//
WILLIAM B. MITCHELL, Colonel, USAF
Director, Doctrine Development
LeMay Center for Doctrine Development and Education
Voice: DSN 493-0000 / Comm (334) 953-0000
FAX: DSN 493-0001 / Comm (334) 953-0001
william.mitchell.1947@us.af.mil

This example e-mail focuses readers on a major change in the way Air Force doctrine is organized. You will notice that this e-mail maintains FOCUS by addressing only the issue (F); being organized (O); using clear language (C); understands its audience of all Airmen (U); and is logical with support information used sparingly (S).

Content Organization

A typical official or professional e-mail is brief and provides information or direction clearly. Some e-mails may be lengthy but should be clearly organized so that the reader has a rapid means to find out the facts and any action that may be required. As discussed in chapter 2, the BLIND and BLUF organization techniques work well to convey a message clearly in a limited space. Recent experience suggests that the headings for the electronic staff summary sheet (eSSS) also work very well for all types of messages—not just those requiring coordination. These three methods are outlined, below:

The "BLIND" Organization Method

When your space is limited by a form or process, the BLIND method of organization places emphasis on the bottom line followed by additional key elements. The BLIND method of organization is especially useful in e-mail communications where the content is brief and needs to be seen by "the boss" for action.

- BL = Bottom Line
- I = Impact on the organization
- N = Next steps to be taken
- D = Details to support the bottom line and any significant discussion points

While there are no set limits on how long a BLIND message can be, the point of the format is brevity. It is not unlike the content for the eSSS that includes Purpose, Background, Discussion, Views of Others and Recommendation; however, the BLIND organization technique is more readily used for quick messages in the field or office to a commander, leader or decision maker that provides enough substance to act without providing everything you know.

The "BLUF" Organization Method

The BLUF organization technique is even less structured than the BLIND organization technique. BLUF simply translates to "bottom line up front" with no set format for what follows. The official e-mail example, above, uses the BLUF organization method. With the BLUF method, the elements of the eSSS may be used to follow the BLUF to provide essential information. Use the technique preferred by the level of command for the intended audience of your e-mail. The point of the BLUF organization method is to maintain a focus on the action needed by leaders and decision makers while also providing key background information.

The eSSS Organization Method

By clearly stating your purpose, followed by pertinent background information, you can then present the discussion and views of others followed by a recommendation or bottom line. If used to organize an e-mail the e-SSS headings can be set to the left in all caps followed by the brief, but appropriate, content for each heading. The common eSSS headings, in order, are PURPOSE; BACKGROUND; DISCUSSION; VIEWS OF OTHERS and RECOMMENDATION. They are typically all capitals and numbered as the primary paragraphs (level 1) in an eSSS.

Special Considerations and E-mail Protocol

There are both special considerations and e-mail protocol, or network etiquette ("netiquette"), for proper behavior while communicating electronically on-line and on smart phones, tablets or other mobile devices. In short, there are many ways to make embarrassing social blunders and offend people when communicating electronically. To make matters worse, there is something about cyberspace that causes a "brain burp" and erases the reality that we deal with real, live humans and not just the text on a screen. Respect the netiquette and remember that the network is multicultural: personal and cultural nuances get lost in transmission. Note, some aspects of the e-mail system itself (e.g. software, gateways and hardware) dictate some practices.

Special Considerations

The discussion so far has been fairly general with concepts and procedures that are applicable to any e-mail, but there are special considerations to employ when using e-mail in your official capacity. These considerations will help you decide if e-mail is the correct method to staff your package, get a response from the appropriate office, and avoid misunderstandings at the other end of the electronic trail.

- **Consider whether e-mail is the best choice**. Face-to-face conversations, phone calls, personal letters, or posted documents to a collaborative site may be more appropriate.

- **Use appropriate greetings.** Address people with their rank/title when appropriate.

- **Use appropriate closings.** Official e-mail should close with "//SIGNED//" above the signature block to signify official Air Force information. Restrict the signature block to name, rank, service affiliation, duty title, organization name, phone numbers (DSN and/or commercial as appropriate) and social media contact information. Do not add slogans, quotes or other personalization to an official e-mail/social media signature block.

- **Follow the chain of command.** Comply with standard procedures to correspond with superiors. Be professional and watch what you say since e-mail is easily forwarded.

- **Think of the e-mail address as the recipient's personal phone number.** If the topic is important enough that you'd call the general without talking with the colonel, then send the message to the general. (Don't quibble—sending the colonel an info copy of the message doesn't count as following the chain of command.)

- **Get approval before sending to large groups or the public.** Check local policies for the proper permission you must obtain before using large e-mail distribution lists. Excessive e-mail sent to large distribution lists can waste a great deal of time. E-mail sent to the general public must still be cleared through proper Air Force channels.

- **Classified material.** Classified material should never be stored or transmitted on an unclassified computer network or system.

Rules for the Electronic Communications Network: Netiquette

The special considerations, above, incorporated into a general set of rules for electronic communications on the network, sometimes called network etiquette or "netiquette."

CHAPTER 12:
Electronic Communications and Social Media

Rule #1: Be Clear and Concise

- Filter information to provide what is necessary, not necessarily everything you know. Whether the sender is initiating, replying to, or forwarding an e-mail, it is the sender's responsibility to delete extraneous information and summarize necessary information near the beginning of the e-mail prior to submission.

- The "Subject" line must communicate your purpose succinctly and be specific. A specific, clear, and succinct subject line will help others locate your message later.

- Lead with your most important info. If your goal is to answer a question, then paste the question on top for clearer understanding.

- Use topic sentences if the e-mail has multiple paragraphs. Consider using the e-SSS organization method. Shorter e-mails are likely to benefit from the BLUF or BLIND organization methods.

- Be brief and stick to the point. Follow all the basic rules for drafting clear and concise messages. Clear messages are even more important in e-mail because we get so many every day. Address the issue, the whole issue, and nothing but the issue. Try to get your message into 24 lines or less—the typically viewing area on many computers.

- Use bold, italics or color to emphasize key sentences. If your e-mail doesn't allow these, a common method uses asterisks to provide emphasis of the *key points.*

- Choose readable fonts. Times New Roman and Arial fonts in 12 points or larger are easily readable. Save the script fonts for your signature.

- Spell check. Always spell check the e-mail before sending.

Rule #2: Watch Your Tone

- Be polite. Treat others as you want to be treated. Use tact; then use more tact. Then, for good measure, use more tact. Think of the message as a personal conversation. If you were face to face, would you say the same words and be as abrupt? If not—rewrite the message with a more positive tone.

- Be careful with humor, irony and sarcasm. Electronic postings can be perceived much more harshly than they are intended, mainly because you cannot see body language, tone of voice and other nonverbal signals that make up 90 percent of interpersonal communications. Positive enthusiasm can be easily mistaken for angry defiance when you use capital letters, exclamation points, and strong adjectives and adverbs.

- DON'T SHOUT. Do not write in ALL CAPITAL LETTERS—it's the e-mail version of shouting and it's considered very rude.

- Keep it clean and professional: E-mail is easily forwarded. Harassing, intimidating, abusive or offensive material is obviously unacceptable, but aim for a higher standard. If you wouldn't want it posted on the office bulletin board, it doesn't belong in an e-mail.

- Don't send in haste and repent at leisure. E-mail can get you into trouble—its informality encourages impulsive responses, but your words can be printed out and forwarded. If you're really mad about an issue, go ahead and draft an e-mail, but don't send it until you calm down and read it over. Never flame! If you do, be prepared to apologize.

Rule #3: Be Selective About What Messages You Send

- Don't discuss controversial, sensitive, official use only, classified, personal, privacy act or unclassified information requiring special handling of documents over e-mail. You just may one day see yourself on CNN or America's Most Wanted.

- Remember Operational Security (OPSEC). OPSEC is a continuous analytical process which involves identifying sensitive information, recognizing that information could be valuable to an adversary, and making changes in the way we do things to reduce our risk that the information will be compromised. Even unclassified information, when brought together with other information, can create problems in the wrong hands. The rash of hacking events in the news emphasizes the need for good OPSEC and COMPUSEC.

- Don't create or forward junk mail or chain letters.

- Don't use e-mail for personal ads.

- Don't fire or promote by e-mail. Some messages should be delivered face to face.

- Pick up the phone and call to acknowledge receipt of important or time-sensitive e-mail instead of replying to the sender via e-mail. Face-to-face communication is sometimes still the best means to communicate.

Rule #4: Be Selective About Who Gets the Message

- Target e-mail messages to only those individuals or organizations that need the information. Consciously choose recipients of original messages, forwards or replies.

- Use "reply all" sparingly.

- Get appropriate permission before using large e-mail distribution lists.

- Double-check the address(es) before mailing, especially when selecting from a global list where many people have similar names.

- Send official e-mail to an organizational e-mail account (instead of an individual) when an organization's answer or coordination is required.

Rule #5: Check Your Attachments and Support Material

- Ensure all information is provided the first time—attachments, support, key information.

- Check your attachments to ensure they are correct and you are able to open them.

- Cite all quotes, references and sources. Respect copyright and license agreements … it's the law! The failure to cite sources is, perhaps, the most common omission. Knowing "who says so" is an important factor in weighing the evidence where a decision is needed. Cite your sources.

- If the attachment is a large file, must go to a number of e-mail accounts, or will require frequent viewing, consider posting to a collaborative site such as the Air Force Portal or SharePoint®. This makes the attachments easily available for future search and retrieval and keeps e-mail inboxes from bogging down.

CHAPTER 12:
Electronic Communications and Social Media

Rule #6: Keep Your E-Mail Under Control

- Lock your computer when you leave your workstation to prevent anyone from reading your e-mail or sending unauthorized messages from your account.

- Create mailing lists to save time.

- Read and trash personal e-mails daily. Create a .pst file on your local hard drive to keep e-mails stored on the e-mail server at a minimum.

- Consider using Microsoft Outlook's "Out-of-Office Assistant" if you will be unable to respond to e-mails for an extended period of time. However, OPSEC considerations should take precedence when setting up out-of-office rules.

Rule #7: Use Proper Format for Official E-mail

- Subject lines should follow the format: [Classification/FOUO Marking][KEYWORD] [suspense DD MMM YY][Subject].
    - Classification/FOUO marking are only included if required.
    - Air Force classification marking instructions are found in the following instructions:
        - AFI 33-332, *Air Force Privacy and Civil Liberties Program*
        - AFI 31-401, *Information Security Program Management*
        - DoD 5200.1-R, *Information Security Program*

- Keywords, such as those below, help the recipient prioritize the e-mail.
    - ACTION-Necessary to take action (other than SIGN or COORD)
    - SIGN-Signature required
    - COORD-Coordination required
    - INFO-For information purposes only
    - URGENT-Time-critical information included

- The word "Suspense" or "Tasker" and suspense date are optional; use only when a suspense is required.

- "Subject" should be a short description of the e-mail (5-7 words is optimal) and should be updated with each send, forward or reply to accurately describe the e-mail's contents. Remove the "FW: " and "RE: " on forwards and replies when it does not add value.

- Sample subject lines with Keywords, Suspense Dates and Subjects.
    - ACTION: Suspense: 14 Dec 10; Deliver E-mail Policy to DS for Signature
    - INFO: Plans and Programs Meeting Minutes
    - SIGN: Suspense 14 Dec 10; Congratulatory Letter for Capt LaJonah

- Consider using the Bottom Line Up Front (BLUF) format as the first paragraph.

- E-mail body should:
    - Succinctly capture critical information and describe the issue
    - Describe the current status and actions taken
    - Clearly state expected and requested actions when appropriate

- o For forwards and replies: if the string of previous e-mail forwards or replies does not add value, remove them from the message

Rule #8: Use Organizational E-Mail Accounts

- Organizational Mailboxes (OMs) are shared e-mail accounts specific to an organization. Personnel associated with organizational units should be provided access to the respective OMs. OMs should exist at each level of the organization (e.g., directorate, division, branch, flight or element).

- Distribution Lists (DLs) are specific groups of e-mail addresses and/or other distribution lists aggregated into one named list. When sending e-mail to a DL, every individual in the list, or sub-list, receives a copy of the e-mail. Send e-mail to DLs sparingly.

- When communicating information to an organization, OMs are preferred to DLs. Each organization is then responsible for determining how to manage the e-mails in its mailbox and notifying its personnel accordingly.

- E-mail sent on behalf of an office or organization is official correspondence and should be filed and maintained in an approved file structure. Consult AFMAN 33-363, *Management of Records*, or your organization's Functional Area Records Manager for records management procedures.

Social Media

People of all ages use social media daily. According to December 2012 Pew Internet Project data, 67percentof adults who are online participate in social networking. It's an efficient way to keep in touch with friends and family, and it is how many people get their entertainment, connect with people over common interests and receive news.

You are encouraged to use social media to share your experiences as an Airman. You can contact your local public affairs office to see if they can share your story, or you can publish information on your social media accounts. Whether you're sharing information with just your close friends and family, or sharing it with the world in an online video or a blog, you're informing people on what it's like to be a part of the world's greatest Air Force.

- Your stories might inspire someone to join the Air Force, support the Air Force, comfort a parent or spouse, improve morale or correct inaccurate information.

- Air Force families may want to use social media to keep in touch with deployed Airmen, network with other military families and share stories on social media.

People can feel comfortable about using social media and letting their Airmen use social media. It's one of the many tools available to communicate information, and it has a value-added capability of promoting interaction.

Using Social Media

Social media applications have evolved to become the primary communication methods used by today's Airmen, families and leaders. The dynamic nature of social media lets people interact with diverse audiences in an informal and transparent environment. It's an avenue for leaders to help shape conversations about their units and missions and connect with people on a personal level. However, all Airmen should remember that social media is not intended to push information; it's for sharing interesting content and building relationships with online followers. Social media channels help bridge the information gap for people who know very little about the military in general. Air Force Instruction 1-1, *Air Force Standards*, outlines how Airmen can use social networking sites.

All Airmen are reminded to maintain appropriate respect in their communications and conduct with other Airmen whether they are face to face or connected via social media. Showing respect does not squelch your voice—it enhances the impact of what you share and reflects the high standards of conduct and discipline that are part of the military culture. Respect is reflected in everything you post to social media: your photos, videos, posts, and comments you post to blogs. What you reflect online says a great deal about your values and beliefs and cumulatively creates a public portrait of the Air Force. *The Tongue and Quill* suggests that Airmen paint a portrait of the Air Force they are proud to show to the public; Airmen are encouraged to tell their unique Air Force stories.

Things to Consider when using Social Media:

1. Airmen are encouraged to tell their unique Air Force stories.
    a. You are personally responsible for what you say and post—in all media at all times.
    b. Be honest about your unit and mission (without violating OPSEC).
    c. Consider how a post can be interpreted by the public.
2. Be cautious with the line between "funny" and "distasteful."
    a. Your "funny" may be "distasteful" or offensive to others—see 1.a., above.
    b. When in doubt, err on the side of caution and leave it out.
3. Respect yourself, other Airmen, and your Air Force with what you post: the spoken word can never be taken back; social media magnifies this fact.

Emerging Social Media Trends

More social sharing options: Blogs, status updates, tweets, pins, videos, photos and pod casts are used to share thoughts and ideas with global social media users. The emergence of social sharing brings together all of these communication products to provide Airmen and the general public with multiple avenues for discussing trending topics.

Visual content reigns supreme: Social media conversations have morphed from text-based posts to status updates using photos, graphic illustrations and videos. Social networking websites are optimizing their designs to focus more on photos and video to allow users to tell their stories visually.

Mobile platforms and applications are booming: Telephones have evolved into modern multi-functional smartphones capable of taking photos and videos that can be uploaded to many social networking websites. Social apps are helping mobile and tablet users connect with friends and family members so they can share real-time information from any location.

Emoticons. Social media and e-mail messages frequently include emotional icon or emoticons within the text of the message to convey a sense of emotion that would be evident if the message were delivered face to face. Emoticons can be very useful; but their use should be restricted to personal messages—they have no place in official communications.

Common Social Media Platforms and Terms

Platforms:

- **Blogs:** Websites with regular entries of commentary, descriptions of events or other material such as graphics or video (e.g., WordPress, TypePad).

- **Microblogs:** People share content in a limited message format using status updates, links, photos and video.

- **Location-based social networks:** Allows users to check-in and connect with people as they explore a particular place (e.g., Foursquare).

- **Photo sharing:** Use a website to host and share images (e.g., Flickr, Instagram).

- **Video sharing:** Provides a location where users upload, share, and view videos.

- **Social networking:** Promotes social interaction among users through posts, commentaries, links, photos and videos.

- **Social news and bookmarking:** A forum where users share social news trends. It's common to see social news feeds combine social bookmarking on news-related items. This allows users to manage content by preferences.

- **Visual bookmarking:** A unique platform that uses a "visual" bookmark to allow users to share Web links to information through imagery.

Terms:

- **Circles:** Groups and organizes friends, colleagues and acquaintances on Google™+.

- **Hangout:** Video service on Google™+ that allows you to video chat with up to 10 Google™+ users at a time.

- **Internet Meme:** An idea or concept that is shared be-tween people online.

- **Pin:** An image or video added to a Pinterest® board and shared with other users.

- **Board:** Organizes pins on Pinterest® by topic.

- **Timeline:** Area on your personal Face book account that allows you to display photos, videos and posts by event date.

- **Twitter® chat:** Discussion that occurs on Twitter® around a specific hashtag at a specified date and time.

CHAPTER 12:
Electronic Communications and Social Media

Social Media Tips

The following tips are not exhaustive, but they are a good starting point for Airmen to consider when using social media. Most of these tips are merely extensions of what we have learned through years of good staff work and the emergence of e-mail. The principles of obeying the law, being you, respect and personal security still apply in today's social media environment.

1. **Obey applicable laws.** You are an Airman 24 hours a day, 365 days a year. As such, you must obey federal law, DoD directives, Air Force instructions, and the Uniform Code of Military Justice when using social media. This applies when using social media in either official or unofficial capacities.

    a. **Classified information.** *Do not* post classified, sensitive or For Official Use Only information. If in doubt talk to your supervisor or security manager.

    b. **Copyrights and Trademarks.** *Do not* post any information or other material protected by *copyright* without the permission of the copyright owner. Likewise, do not use any words, logos or other marks that would infringe upon the *trademark*, service mark, certification mark or other intellectual property rights of the owners of such marks without owner permission.

    c. **Air Force symbol.** The Air Force symbol visually represents our service's brand identity. To use the Air Force symbol on a social media platform, you must follow display guidelines found at http://www.trademark.af.mil.

    d. **Terms of service.** Comply with each social media site's terms of service.

2. **Be you.** Represent yourself and only yourself in your social media use.

    a. **Stay in your lane.** Discussing issues related to your career field or personal experiences are acceptable and encouraged. Stay in your lane and do not discuss areas where you have no expertise through direct experience, education or knowledge.

    b. **Endorsements.** Represent only yourself and do not use the Air Force name to endorse or promote products, political positions or religious ideologies.

    c. **Impersonations.** *Do not* manipulate social media identifiers or post content in an attempt to disguise, impersonate or otherwise misrepresent your identity with any other person or entity.

    d. **Promotion for personal or financial gain.** *Do not* use your Air Force affiliation, official title or position to promote, endorse or benefit yourself or any profit-making group or agency. See the *Joint Ethics Regulation* for more details on the ethics and law regarding the "Use of Public Office for Private Gain."

3. **Respect, respect, respect.** *Do not* post anything hateful, offensive or illegal. This includes any defamatory, libelous, vulgar, obscene, abusive, profane, threatening, racially or ethnically hateful, or otherwise offensive or illegal information or material.

    a. **Words have meaning and consequences.** Once you post something on social media it is impossible to "get it back." Even deleting the post doesn't mean it's truly gone. Ultimately, you bear sole responsibility for what you post.

    b. **Replace error with fact.** When you see misrepresentations in social media, identify and correct the error with facts and respect.

    c. **Image.** Any time you use social media, you're presenting an image of yourself and the Air Force. Don't discredit yourself or our service

    d. **Opinion versus official information.** Yes, tell them what you think, just make sure you state that this is your opinion and not that of the organization.

    e. **Privacy.** Do not post any information that would infringe upon the proprietary, privacy or personal rights of others. Respect their privacy and expect the same.

4. **Personal security.** Maintain privacy settings on your social media accounts, change your passwords regularly and don't give out personally identifiable information. Be cautious about the personal details you share with others—live or in social media.

Official Air Force Social Media Sites

The Air Force Social Media Program includes key social networking websites where the Air Force engages with Airmen, families and the general public. Here are a few links to official Air Force social media pages:

- **Social Media Directory.** http://www.af.mil/socialmedia.asp
- **Air Force Live Blog.** http://airforcelive.dodlive.mil
- **Facebook®.** http://facebook.com/usairforce
- **Flickr®.** http://www.flickr.com/airforce
- **Twitter®.** http://www.twitter.com/airforce
- **YouTube™.** http://www.youtube.com/afbluetube
- **Vine®** (for mobile iOS & Android devices). @usairforce
- **Instagram®.** http://instagram.com/officialusairforce

Instant Messaging (IM) and Texting

Instant Messaging (IM) and Texting, once leisure communications activities, have obtained a foothold in the Air Force workplace. When utilized appropriately, IM and Texting can lead to great efficiencies—they can offer advantages over both e-mail and voice conversations and they allow individuals to multitask. Simple questions between co-workers, previously requiring telephone conversations or in-person meetings, can be completed with a single IM or text exchange. On the flip side, they can quickly become a distraction in the workplace with individuals using IM and Texting it outside of their original purpose. The following tips will help you be a responsible user of IM and Texting in the workplace and should sound very familiar when compared to the advantages and disadvantages of electronic communications discussed in the opening of this chapter.

- **IM and Texting do not replace staff work.** While IM can be used for official Air Force business, it does not replace official staff work. If your work requires an official record to be maintained, use e-mail or another means to accomplish your duties.

- **IM and Texting are typically not enduring.** While you can save your IM history, if your work requires an official record to be maintained, another method, such as e-mail, may be more appropriate.

- **IM and Texting can be a distracter.** Users should be careful to not use IM as a leisure activity. Doing so will lead to decreased productivity in the workplace.

- **IM and Texting are quick and easy.** E-mails can get buried and lost. If you need an immediate quick answer to a question, IM is a better choice than e-mail. IM can replace some phone conversations which can save you time.

- **IM and Texting are best utilized for one-on-one discussion.** If you have a large audience, e-mail is better suited to meet those needs than IM or Texting (in general).

Telephones, Voice Mail and Fax

Telephones, voice mail, and fax are key tools for staff communication, so we'll review some of the common courtesies associated with using this equipment. Different systems have different features, so check out your manual for all the bells and whistles. Here are some basic guidelines.

Telephone Protocol: Answering the Phone (Do ...)

- answer the phone on the first ring and in the way you would like to be called after identifying the organization.
- be pleasant and professional—you are representing your organization, as well as yourself, when you answer the phone.
- introduce everyone in the room if you are on a speakerphone—callers may object to the lack of privacy.
- put the radio and TV on hold until you're off.
- speak clearly, keeping your lips about 1 inch from the mouthpiece. Good posture or standing while speaking) will also improve your vocal quality.
- have a pencil, a memo pad, and your directories within easy reach.
- adjust your speaking tempo to match the other person's to establish instant rapport.
- ask if someone else can help if the person isn't there.
- take a number and call back instead of putting them on hold if you are finding something.
- give the caller the phone number before you transfer the call.
- allow the person initiating the call to bring it to a close.
- record important conversations, especially those that result in a decision, in a memo for record and place it in a file.

Telephone Protocol: Answering the Phone (Do NOT …)

- transfer an angry caller. Listen carefully, never interrupt, and ask questions that require more than a "yes" or "no." Take notes and let the caller know; this shows you're interested and are willing to help.
- put the phone over your chest to put someone on hold—your voice goes over the wires loud and clear—use the "hold" button.

Telephone Protocol: Making the Call (Do …)

- have your act together. Organize your thoughts and make notes before you place a call—especially if you're representing your organization, seeking help or information, calling long distance or talking to someone more senior in rank.
- call during core hours (0900-1100 and 1300-1500) to reduce phone tag. What's their time zone? When will they return?
- identify yourself and your organization before asking to speak to _____.
- be pleasant and professional.
- ask if the person has time to talk, but you need to keep it as brief as possible.
- record important conversations in a memo for record and place it in a file.

Telephone Protocol: Making the Call (Do NOT …)

- put the phone over your chest to put someone on hold—your voice goes over the wires loud and clear—use the "hold" button.
- be the source of someone else's problem; courtesy works wonders in both directions.

Voice-mail Protocol (Do…)

- record the message in your own voice.
- identify yourself and your organization.
- check your system regularly.
- return all messages as quickly as possible.

Voice-mail Protocol (Do NOT …)

- leave amusing messages on an official system.
- leave personally identifiable information (PII) on voice-mail.
- assume your voice-mail is a substitute for answering your phone.

Voice-mail Protocol: Out of Office

If you will be unavailable for an extended period, set up your voice mail to be mindful of co-workers by going to voice mail on the first ring and being helpful to callers by identifying whom they can contact for assistance in your absence: *"This is SSgt_____. I am away from my desk. If you need immediate assistance on [topic], please call MSgt _____ at DSN 555-1234."*

FAX Protocol (Do ...)

- make it readable: use Times New Roman and 12 points or larger font
- number your pages.
- protect your document by ensuring correct receiver information is entered.
- use black and white.
- use a fax when you cannot get someone to return your call, including a short explanation, deadline to return your call, and a "Thanks for your time."
- send a return cover sheet with complete return address to encourage a quick reply.

FAX Protocol (Do NOT ...)

- send a legal-sized document unless you know it can be received.
- send personal, confidential or financial info unless you know it will be protected.
- use italic and thin-faced font types. It looks ragged and makes it difficult to read.

This brings us to the end of the general rules and principles for using electronic communications. The following glossary may be of use to those who are new to electronic communications or those wishing to look back on these terms in the future.

SUMMARY: To summarize this chapter in a single sentence, good face-to-face manners extend into the electronic media realm and these manners are captured by the Computer Ethics Institute's "Ten Commandments for Computer Ethics," below.

The Ten Commandments for Computer Ethics

1. Thou shalt not use a computer to harm other people.
2. Thou shalt not interfere with other people's computer work.
3. Thou shalt not snoop around in other people's files.
4. Thou shalt not use a computer to steal.
5. Thou shalt not use a computer to bear false witness.
6. Thou shalt not use or copy software for which you have not paid.
7. Thou shalt not use other people's computer resources without authorization.
8. Thou shalt not appropriate other people's intellectual output.
9. Thou shalt think about the social consequences of the program you write.
10. Thou shalt use a computer in ways that show consideration and respect.

SOURCE: http://computerethicsinstitute.org/publications/tencommandments.html.

Used in accordance with guidance from the Computer Ethics Institute.

Electronic Communications Glossary

American Standard Code for Information Interchange (ASCII /ˈæski/ *ASS-kee*)—The most common international standard for representing alphanumeric text on a computer.

bandwidth—The number of bits that can be passed along a communications channel in a given period of time. Usually expressed as bits per second (bps). Each military installation has a limited amount of bandwidth—don't waste it with frivolous e-mail.

bulletin-board system (BBS)—An electronic system allowing individuals with similar interests to post and view messages in a public electronic form.

binary file—A digital file format used to store non-text data. The information stored includes executable programs, sounds, images and videos.

binary digit (bit)—The smallest unit of storage in a digital computer. All programs and data in a digital computer are composed of bits.

browser—A software program that allows users to interact with World Wide Websites. Example includes Microsoft Internet Explorer, Mozilla and Opera.

client—A computer or program that can download, run or request services from a server.

compact disc (CD, CD-ROM, CD-RW)—A disk that stores digital information using a pattern of microscopic pits and lands to represent ones and zeros. One CD-ROM holds from 650 to 700 megabytes of data or the equivalent of approximately 250,000 pages of text.

data compression—A procedure used to reduce the size of a file to reduce the disk space required to store the file or the bandwidth required to transmit the file. Many different compression formats are available and each requires a program to compress and expand the file—zip format is one of the most common.

digital video disk (DVD, DVD-R, DVD-RW)—A disk that stores digital information using a pattern of pits and lands to represent ones and zeros. A specially formatted DVD is used to store movies. One DVD-ROM holds approximately 4.7 gigabytes of information or the equivalent of approximately 1.8 million pages of text.

Electronic mail (E-mail)—A message sent electronically over a computer network, such as a LAN or the Internet.

emoticon—Facial expressions originally drawn using ASCII characters and more recently drawn using an extended character set.

encryption—Changing the contents of a message in a manner to obscure the contents while still allowing the intended audience to read the message.

executable—A file containing a set of instructions to perform some process on a computer. A word processor and Internet browser are examples of an executable.

facsimile (fax)—A method of transmitting images of printed matter that predates digital computer networks. This method traditionally used phone lines but can now be implemented using computer networks.

flame mail—An e-mail message critical of some person or position taken by a person, usually more derogatory than constructive.

frequently asked questions (FAQ)—A list of questions and corresponding answers focusing on a specific topic. The FAQ is typically provided to members of a community to avoid the repetitious answering of questions asked by new users.

home page—The web page providing the entry point for a website (see web page and website).

hyperlink—A way to link access to information of various sources together within a web document. A way to connect two Internet resources via a simple word or phrase on which a user can click to start a connection.

hypertext—A method for storing, retrieving, and presenting information based on the processing power of computers. Allows computerized linking and almost instantaneous retrieval of information based on a dynamic index.

Hypertext Markup Language (HTML)—The native language of the WWW.

Instant Messaging (IM)—A type of communications service that enables you to create a kind of private chat room with another individual in order to communicate in real time over the Internet, analogous to a telephone conversation but using text-based, not voice-based, communication. Typically, the instant messaging system alerts you whenever somebody on your private list is online. You can then initiate a chat session with that particular individual.

Internet—The overarching global computer network connecting computers, servers and local area networks across the globe.

intranet—A network with restricted availability. An intranet may provide web pages, printing and e-mail services similar to those available using the Internet, but only for a restricted set of users. Most military bases run an intranet that is only available to personnel on that base.

Internet Relay Chat (IRC)—A communications program that allows real-time text-based conversations along multiple users.

list server—A computer running an electronic mailing list subscribed to by individuals with some common area of interest. Individuals typically subscribe by sending an e-mail asking to be placed on the list. Once added to the list, subscribers automatically receive messages sent to the list by other subscribers and may send their own messages to the list which are then relayed to all other subscribers.

local area network (LAN)—A system occupying a relatively small geographic area providing digital communications between automated data processing equipment, such as computers and printers.

modem—A device allowing a computer to send and receive data over telephone lines.

netiquette—Commonly accepted etiquette used when communicating over a computer network—network etiquette. Specific forms of communications might include e-mail, list server or IRC.

newbie—An individual new to using computers or new to a specific group.

newsgroup—A network service allowing individuals to post, read messages, and respond to messages posted by other users. Newsgroups may be moderated or un-moderated. If the newsgroup is moderated, messages may be removed by the moderator and user posting privileges controlled by the moderator.

organizational e-mail account—An e-mail account used to receive and send messages on behalf of an organization. This type of account allows an organization to maintain a single address for correspondence despite changing responsibilities within that organization.

server—A computer that responds to requests for information from client computers—see client.

web browser—See browser.

web page—An electronic document available on the Internet or an intranet that is viewable using a web browser (see browser, Internet and intranet).

website—A collection of related web pages.

World Wide Web (WWW)—The entire web pages on all of the websites available through the Internet.

CHAPTER 13:

Meetings

This chapter covers:
- Planning an Effective Meeting
- Running Your Meeting
- Group Dynamics and Fun

All of us attend meetings. Some of us feel we attend too many of them. Others may be conducting more business electronically and attending fewer meetings than in the past. But, in today's world of trying to do things "faster and smarter," technology is not always all it's cracked up to be. How many times have you e-mailed someone who works 20 feet or one office away? Have you ever spent 20 minutes to write an e-mail to four people to discuss a topic that would take 2 minutes of a meeting? Despite the surge in electronic staffing, there is no substitute for the human element found in meetings; thus it is unlikely they will ever be completely replaced.

So why does the mere word "meeting" strike a nerve in so many of us? Perhaps because we've all attended so many that were so inefficient. But meetings don't have to be that way; there are ways to make them better! If they are done right, they can go a long way in helping your organization run more efficiently. Simply put, meetings are used to share information, solve problems, plan, brainstorm or motivate. Whatever the purpose, it's good to know some basics about conducting an effective meeting. That's what this chapter is all about.

Planning an Effective Meeting

At some time or another, you may be the one calling the meeting. A meeting doesn't always have to be a major production, but there are some key points to consider during planning, execution and follow-up. Here are some tips on making the most of everyone's time—including your own!

Success or failure in a meeting can usually be traced to the planning phase. Do your homework and you're well on your way to success. If you don't do your homework, you'll pay a heavy price during the execution and follow-up phases.

Listed below are the key issues associated with planning a meeting. As you step through these items, remember to check on what is standard operating procedure in your organization. Meetings vary from totally spontaneous to highly structured and ceremonial. Most are in the middle. If this group has been meeting regularly for a while, try to find out how they've done business in the past.

1. Decide If a Meeting Is Appropriate

In the book *How to Make Meetings Work*, Michael Doyle and David Strauss identify seven situations when having a meeting might be a good idea:

- You want information or advice from the group.
- You want to involve a group in solving a problem or making a decision.
- An issue needs to be clarified.
- You want to address concerns with the entire group.
- The group itself wants a meeting.
- There is a problem that involves people from different groups.
- There is a problem, but it's not clear what it is or who is responsible for dealing with it.

In these situations, face-to-face discussion can help speed up the process. If your goal is just to pass on information, ask yourself if e-mail is a viable and *appropriate* substitute for the meeting. The purpose of many meetings is simply to share information and keep people up to date on a project. In these cases, try to substitute the meeting with an e-mail. This saves everyone's time and still keeps everyone in the loop and you're still meeting the goal for the meeting you just avoided! Local policy may dictate that some groups meet weekly, monthly, or quarterly, but if you're not directed to meet and don't need to … don't!

2. Define Your Purpose

Most Air Force professionals want to feel like they've accomplished something in a meeting. A clear purpose for the meeting is the first step towards success. If the meeting has no purpose, you shouldn't meet. When you think about your purpose, try to define it in terms of a product that you want at the end of the meeting. "Talking about Issue X" is not an ideal purpose statement for the meeting because it describes a process, not a product—try these alternatives:

- To identify why Issue X is a problem.
  [The product is a clearer understanding of the problem.]

- To brainstorm ways to resolve Issue X.
  [The product is a list of ideas about potential solutions.]

- To discuss different options for resolving Issue X.
  [The product is list of pros and cons … the decision will happen later.]

- To decide how the unit will handle Issue X.
  [The product is discussion of pros and cons and a decision. Make sure attendees know who makes the decision. Is it the team, or is it the boss?]

3. Decide Who Should Be Invited

Have you gone to a meeting and after 5 or 10 minutes asked yourself, "Why am I here?" Remember that when you are holding a meeting! Invite only those directly involved in the issues being discussed. Meetings can be a time waster if too many or too few participants attend. Too many people equals chaos; too few means decisions have to be put on hold. If you're trying to solve a problem or make a decision on a controversial issue, make sure you have adequate representation from all groups who have a voice in the decision. If you only invite people with one point of view, your meeting will run smoothly, but your decision may not stand up later.

4. Decide Where and When the Meeting Should Occur

Check the schedules of key personnel. Often the scheduling of your meetings will be determined by the schedule of any key personnel that will be attending. If you're briefing a three-star, odds are that his secretary will be telling you when the meeting can occur, not the other way around.

If possible, pick the time of day to meet your purpose. If you've got flexibility, you might select the time of day for your meeting to help you meet your objectives. If you want your meeting attendees fired up and eager to contribute, you may want to schedule a meeting in the morning, the time when most people have more energy. If you want them inpatient and anxious to get done, try just before lunch. If you want them agreeable, try right after lunch. If you want them asleep, try midafternoon. Finally, you might try the just-before-quitting time tactic. If you're lucky, you might have any opposition collapse just so they can catch the car pool.

Try to avoid meetings the first thing Monday morning. Give folks some time to read e-mail and prioritize the days and week ahead. If your organization is a service organization, don't schedule meetings during customer service hours. The "Closed for Training" sign on the door does not fare well in the customer satisfaction department!

Keep it under an hour, or plan for breaks. Keep in mind that after 20 minutes or so, our minds tend to get lazy and wander. Try to keep the flow of the meeting going so that no agenda item goes longer than 20 minutes. Watch the clock (a timekeeper comes in handy). Try to keep the meeting to 90 minutes or less and plan for breaks if the meeting goes over an hour.

Reserve the room. Follow established procedures to reserve a conference room that can handle the attendee list.

5. Plan for Capturing Meeting Information

If this is not a routine meeting with an appointed recorder, take a moment to think about how you will capture the meeting information, both during the meeting and afterwards. Capturing the information is critical, but how best to do it will depend on the nature of the meeting. For example, during the meeting there may be tools and activities that can help you capture information, such as white boards, interactive whiteboards, recording devices, , photographs of notes, poster boards and flip charts, etc. Also, consider having someone dedicated to capturing notes. Just ask a team member or coworker to act as the recorder and take notes.

Meeting minutes capture the process and outcome of the meeting. They "close the loop" on the meeting and let the attendees know what was decided. If you have administrative personnel that can prepare minutes, consider having them attend the meeting to act as the recorder. If not, appoint someone to capture the minutes or prepare them yourself.

6. Send Out an Agenda

Create an agenda and send it to attendees no later than 1 or 2 days prior to the meeting. If this is not a time critical issue, if the attendees don't work for you, or if you are asking people to present material or review long documents prior to the meeting, try to give at least a week's notice. Also tell presenters to bring a copy of their material to leave with the recorder.

The agenda should include the date, time, location and purpose of the meeting. This advance notice gives everyone an opportunity to prepare their thoughts and know where the meeting is going ahead of time. If you are asking people to present material or prepare their thoughts, make sure they know how much time they have been allocated and when they will present.

Presenting material at a meeting

At some time or another, you may be asked to *present* information at a meeting, possibly in a briefing format. Whether or not you have time to prepare, it's always important to remember the "Seven Steps for Effective Communication" introduced in chapter 2.

A meeting is just another communication platform and it's still important to analyze your purpose and audience, research your topic, support your ideas, organize, draft, edit and seek feedback. If you don't, you may fail to hit the target, lead the audience to an unproductive place, or worst case scenario, waste everyone's time.

You may also want to use a detailed agenda on the day of the meeting to keep the group on track and stay focused. If you have trouble coming up with a solid agenda, chances are you really don't have a reason to meet in the first place (see tip 1)!

7. Meetings Can Be Cancelled

Before you take people away from productive work time, ask yourself these questions:
- Is there a real need for this meeting? Perhaps the business can be accomplished by other means. Consider sending an e-mail or a memo to disseminate information.

- Will the decision makers and the majority of the group be present? If decision makers can't be there, why bother? Likewise, if the majority of the group cannot attend, why hold the meeting? You will spend precious time updating those who missed the meeting before you can come to consensus on the issue. It's better to put the meeting on hold.

Running Your Meeting

You won't peg out anyone's fun meter by dragging a meeting out unnecessarily. It's your job to keep it focused and separate "the wheat from the chaff."

A word about Robert's Rules of Order

Formal meetings sometimes follow the sequence, procedures and terminology documented in *Robert's Rules of Order,* a set of rules used in Parliamentary procedure. General Henry M. Robert first published the rules in 1876 and there are several updated versions and summaries available in print or on the web. (For example, the complete 1915 version is available on line at http://www.bartleby.com/176/).

Most Air Force meetings do not use *Robert's Rules of Order* and we won't go into them here. The terminology is somewhat formal and the structure seems overly constraining to some. Even so, you should be aware that they exist as agreed-upon set of guidelines on how to organize a potentially chaotic situation.

Also, some day you may find yourself in a meeting where there are a lot of rules, where people read out the minutes of the previous meeting and where parts of the meeting seem scripted ("With a quorum present, the meeting is called to order..."). If this happens to you, don't panic. They're probably following some form of *Robert's Rules of Order*. Ask about them, or look them up yourself. Everything will become clear.

Start on Time; Stay on Time

Start on time with an upbeat note and don't wait for tardy attendees. Spend meeting time wisely to accomplish the goal for the meeting. Experienced meeting organizers suggest the following time allocation for meetings:

- 1/4 of meeting—past agenda items and follow-up (old business)
- 1/2 of meeting—current agenda items
- 1/4 of meeting—future agenda items

Follow Your Agenda

One of the worst things you can do is to ignore your own agenda. It drives people nuts! Consider a review of the detailed agenda in the opening minutes of the meeting to remind people of the goals and plan for the meeting. Regular meetings usually follow a fixed order of business. Below is a typical example:

1. Introduction and call to order.
2. Attendance or roll call of members present.

3. Acknowledgment or correction of previous meeting minutes.

4. Reports from committees [these items were previously identified in the Agenda].

5. Old Business from previous minutes and Action Items.

6. New Business previously designated for consideration at this meeting [per Agenda].

7. Round table or New Business not previously identified for consideration at this meeting.

8. Appointments and Assignments [new committees or personnel changes].

9. Establish the date, time and location of the next meeting, if needed and if ready.

10. Evaluate the meeting before adjourning. Are there things that need to be improved?

Understand Group Dynamics and Look for Ways to Make Meetings Fun

If you're in charge of a group that will be meeting over a period of time, it pays to learn the basics about group dynamics. Also, if you dare, you might want to try to inject some fun into your meetings. As always—know your audience.

Following Up: Preparing Meeting Minutes

If you did your homework, following up is a snap—it involves sending out meeting minutes and starting the whole cycle over again. Prepare meeting minutes in the official memo format. Minutes are a clear summary of the agenda items, decisions made and participants' comments. The meeting minutes document planned or completed actions and information regarding any future meeting is in the last paragraph. When a person signs a paper as a member of a board or committee, the signature element indicates that person's status on that board or committee, not any other position the person may hold. Type "Approved as written" two lines below the recorder's signature block, followed by the approving authority's signature block.

Formatting Meeting Minutes. All formatting should be neat and orderly, paying particular attention to uniformity of margins and text. Minutes usually show that a meeting was scheduled for a specific date, time, location, the members present and absent, the order of the agenda, actions taken or decisions made, and any pending tasks. It should be clear to readers the name of the body (The Executive Steering Committed), the kind of meeting held (regular or special), and the word "Minutes" should appear in the subject line. The opening paragraph usually contains a simple statement that includes many of these identifying details, such as "The Executive Steering Committee held a regular meeting on (day, date, time, and place).

Meeting minutes are formatted either single or double-spaced, with additional space between items of business and paragraphs. All names should be spelled correctly. Acceptable grammar should be used; sentences should be well constructed and correctly punctuated; and all verbs should be in the past tense. The narrative should include key points, conclusions or decisions regarding any committee reports, old business carry-over items, current business and new business. The last item of the minutes should state when the meeting was adjourned.

CHAPTER 13:
Meetings

Group Dynamics and Fun

All meetings, teams or groups move through predictable stages. You will save yourself a lot of frustration if you are familiar with these stages. Let's look at a snapshot of these stages of group dynamics first then discuss them in more detail.

Group Dynamics

Because the forming, storming and norming stages result in minimal output, it is tempting to try to rush through or short circuit these stages and hope the team can thereby achieve peak productivity. You may want to stand up and say, "Can't we just all be friends?" Although seductive, this idea is dysfunctional. Just as individuals go through predictable stages of growth (depending on age, experience, maturity and other factors), teams go through predictable stages. The duration of these stages depends on factors such as individual and team maturity, task complexity, leadership, organizational climate and external climate. Teams can fixate at various stages. Some teams (like some people) are never fully functioning. How can you reduce the nonproductive time commonly spent in the forming and storming stages? Given that these stages are inevitable, try sharing rumors, concerns and expectations of the team to minimize their tensions, fears or anxiety. Also, encourage the team members to contact one another so that there will be no "surprises." Therefore, an atmosphere of trust will be achieved early on (norming stage), allowing for interpersonal issues to be put aside in favor of task issues and for the team to move on to the performing stage. Read on for more detailed descriptions of these stages from *The Team Handbook* written by Peter R. Scholtes.

Group Dynamics

FORMING → STORMING → NORMING → PERFORMING

Forming: a period of uncertainty in which members try to determine their place in the team and the procedures and rules of the team. When a team is forming, members cautiously explore the boundaries of acceptable group behavior. This is a stage of transition from individual to member status and of testing the leader's guidance both formally and informally. Because there is so much going on to distract the members' attention in the beginning, the team accomplishes little, if anything, that concerns its project goals. Don't despair and flush your project down the toilet! This is perfectly normal!

Storming: conflicts begin to arise as members resist the influence of the team and rebel against accomplishing the task. Storming is probably the most difficult stage for the team. You may ask yourself, "What was I thinking?" The team members begin to realize the task is different and more difficult than they imagined, becoming testy, blameful, or overzealous. Impatient about the lack of progress, but still too inexperienced to know much about decision making or the scientific approach, members argue about just what actions the team should take. They try to rely solely on their experience, resisting any need for collaborating with other team members. Their behavior means team members have little energy to spend on progressing towards the team's goal. Still, they are beginning to understand one another.

Norming: the team establishes cohesiveness and commitment, discovering new ways to work together and setting norms for appropriate behavior. During this stage, members reconcile competing loyalties and responsibilities. They accept the team, team ground rules (or "norms"), their roles in the team and the individuality of fellow members. Emotional conflict is reduced as previously competitive relationships become more cooperative. As team members begin to work out their differences, they now have more time and energy to spend on the project. Thus, they are able to at last start making significant strides.

Performing: the team develops proficiency in achieving its goals and becomes more flexible in its patterns of working together. By this stage, the team has settled its relationships and expectations. They can begin performing—diagnosing and solving problems and choosing and implementing changes. At last team members have discovered and accepted each other's strengths and weaknesses and learned what their roles are. The team is now an effective, cohesive unit. You can tell when your team has reached this stage: you get a lot of work done!

Fun

Have you ever wondered why cell phones miraculously ring during meetings or "scheduling conflicts" come up at the last minute? It's because many people avoid meetings like the plague. Does that mean you should hold meetings like a standup comedian to draw people to the meeting? No! But you can interject some fun into meetings to encourage participation and creativity. Here are just a few ideas to get you going.

Hold your meeting off-site. Military members are creatures of habit, and this does not change at meetings. Folks usually sit in the same seat and bring the same coffee mug. Sometimes a change of scenery will rejuvenate a stagnant group. **Bonus:** Change the meeting time to coincide with lunch. This gives the group a chance to talk about "non-meeting issues" and connect in a more nonthreatening environment over a meal.

Have a contest to generate ideas for projects. A little friendly competition can be a boost for all and bring great results.

Tone down the conversation dominators with "fees." Attendees are required to pay each time they interject and they are limited to inputs. Be careful with this one … you don't want to shut folks down either.

Appoint a "Director of Creativity" for each meeting to come up with ideas like these! Appoint the next meeting's director at the conclusion of the current meeting to give them time to plan. Have the group vote on the favorite idea at the end of the year and give out a humorous award.

SUMMARY: Meetings are a fact of life and service in the Air Force. They serve a purpose in our mission and how we get things done. This chapter gave you the basics for holding more productive meetings. The "Seven Steps for Effective Communication" and the tips introduced in this chapter will serve you well alongside any local guidelines your command has for conducting meetings.

PART VI:

DOCUMENT STANDARDS

Document Standards: Part VI expands upon the functions of written communications and their formats within the United States Air Force as outlined in AFMAN 33-326, *Preparing Official Communications*. We have included examples of Air Force documents to demonstrate the Air Force standards presented in this publication. However, ***if your command publishes a supplement to AFMAN 33-326, an operating instruction (OI) on document standards, or has its own administrative style guide or preferences, check those sources for guidance on preparing documents before you begin.***

Writing for the Boss: Preparing a staff package, memorandum or personal letter for a senior official's signature demands the product be ready to sign. Write as though every letter were being signed or read well up the chain of command. Consider these tips to improve your written work:

- **Check for preferences.** Contact the senior official's office staff before you start to see if the official has preferences—and get some pointers! For example, the choice of words in the salutation and closing may be different depending on the rank of the recipient.

- **Analyze purpose and Audience (Step 1 of Seven Steps to Effective Communication).** What is the desired purpose? What are the issues (core and peripheral)? Who is the audience? What tone, organizational pattern and correspondence style are most appropriate? Also, use critical thinking skills as you draft. What is the relationship of the sender to the receiver? What are the first, second and third order effects of the package?

- **Keep it simple.** Get to the point, make it and move on. Your first draft will probably be twice as long as needed. If you must include details, use attachments.

- **Go easy on the modifiers.** A senior official doesn't need to be *very* interested in something—being interested is sufficient. Avoid emotional tones.

- **Quality control.** Logic, grammar, facts, figures and format must all be checked, re-checked then checked again. Your credibility is on the line: make it count.

- **Addresses.** Use the correct and current address; avoid embarrassment and delays!

- **Go one step further.** Look efficient when doing a personal letter and, if appropriate, provide the general with the "go-by" name of the addressee on a yellow sticky. Remember to exercise sensitivity in the case of a condolence letter to a spouse or family member.

- **Be realistic.** Don't expect your product to fly the first time; set pride aside and welcome the feedback so you can get it right the next time.

Why should we write differently for senior officials? We shouldn't—we should write right all the time. Write high-quality products for all your written communications, and we will all be better communicators for the effort—and it will make that staff tour less daunting as well.

CHAPTER 14:

The Official Memorandum

This chapter covers:
- The Heading Section
- The Text of the Official Memorandum
- The Closing Section
- Additional Information
- Attachments
- The Official Memorandum: Examples
- Spelling Checkers: Before You Sign

Memorandums are used to communicate throughout the DoD and with other Federal agencies as well as to conduct official business outside the Government with vendors or contractors when a personal letter is inappropriate. Official memorandums may be addressed to specific officials, single offices, multiple offices, multiple offices IN TURN or to DISTRIBUTION lists. *Follow the guidance of this chapter when preparing any official memorandum*, beginning with these basic format requirements:

1. Use printed letterhead, computer-generated letterhead, or plain bond paper.
2. Type or print using black ink.
3. Follow AFI 31-401, *Information Security Program Management*, applicable executive orders and DoD guidance for the necessary markings on classified correspondence.
4. Use 1-inch margins on the left, right and bottom for most memorandums. For shorter communications, you may adjust the margins.
    a. 20 lines or more → 1 inch margins
    b. 10-19 lines → 1 to 1 1/2 inch margins
    c. 1-9 lines → 1 1/2 to 2 inch margins

5. Use 12 point Times New Roman font for text. Smaller sizes, no smaller than 10 point, may be used when required to control page breaks. For example, shrink the font of all text in the memorandum to prevent a page break between the body and closing elements (signature block). The signature block is never on a page by itself.

For most documents, the guidance for the specific elements on the following pages needs no adjustments; however, for short communications, you may adjust the top margin in order to balance the content toward the vertical center of the document by moving all elements from the date to the last line of the closing to achieve visual balance and avoid a top-heavy appearance.

The Heading Section

The heading section is composed of these elements: date, MEMORANDUM FOR, ATTENTION, FROM, SUBJECT and References. Each element is described in detail, below.

Date

Placement and Format: Place the date **1 inch from the right edge, 1.75 inches from the top** of the page. Use the "Day Month Year" or "DD Mmm YY" format for documents addressed to a military organization. In the "DD Mmm YY" format, the month and year are both abbreviated for consistency. For civilian addressees, use the "Month Day, Year" format. Finally, unless the date of signature has legal significance, date the original and all copies of the correspondence at the time of dispatch.

Examples:

Military Addressees–Day Month Year	15 October 2014
Military Addressees–DD Mmm YY	15 Oct 14
Civilian Addressees–Month Day, Year	October 15, 2014

"MEMORANDUM FOR"

Placement: Place "MEMORANDUM FOR" on the **second line below** the date. **Leave two spaces between "MEMORANDUM FOR" and the recipient's organization abbreviation and office symbol (ORG/SYMBOL).** If there are multiple recipients, two or three office symbols may be placed on each line with the second and following lines aligned under the first recipient. If there are numerous recipients, use the "DISTRIBUTION" element.

- **When addressing one office**, enter the organization/office symbol in uppercase letters. To indicate the memorandum is for a specific person, enter the organization/office symbol followed by the person's rank and name in parentheses—all in uppercase. Another option is to use the "ATTENTION" element—see guidance below.

- **When addressing several offices**, align subsequent addressees under the first address. If the office symbols are fairly short and you have several for the memorandum, you may include two or three on a single line by aligning each additional line of recipients under the recipients in the first line in like fashion. Be consistent with your format: write out all organization names or use all organization/office symbols.

CHAPTER 14
The Official Memorandum

- **When addressing several offices IN TURN,** use the "IN TURN" format to distribute the official memorandum to several individuals or offices in sequence. The only difference is the format of the "MEMORANDUM FOR" element, as shown below.
  - "IN TURN" Originators: Prepare an "IN TURN" memorandum when the final addressee or OPR must see the coordination or action of all addressees. Use the official memorandum format. Type "IN TURN" in uppercase, one line below the last address of the "MEMORANDUM FOR" element aligned with the addresses.
  - "IN TURN" Recipients: When you receive an "IN TURN" memorandum, strike through your organization abbreviation and office symbol, then type, sign or initial, and date. Type "Concur," "Nonconcur," "Comments attached" or "Comments sent by separate correspondence to" next to the date. Prepare a separate memorandum for a lengthy comment. Attach comments to the "IN TURN" memorandum if the remaining addressees need them; otherwise, forward comments directly to the final addressee. Forward the "IN TURN" memorandum to the next address and "cc" the OPR for tracking purposes.
- **Using a distribution element or list.** When the address list is too long to include in the "MEMORANDUM FOR" element, use the distribution element or list. Simply leave two spaces after "MEMORANDUM FOR" and add "DISTRIBUTION" in uppercase letters. Include the addressees in the "DISTRIBUTION" element or on a separate page attached to the memorandum.

Headquarters or HQ: The term "Headquarters" and "HQ" are a part of the official title of units at the group level and above. Use HQ as part of the organization abbreviation and office symbol when corresponding with staff elements at MAJCOM and HQ USAF organizations. ***Do not use the term "Headquarters" or "HQ" when corresponding with the office of MAJCOM commanders and vice commanders.***

Examples:

MEMORANDUM FOR	79 FS/DO (LT COL JORGE TORRES)
MEMORANDUM FOR	CHIEF OF STAFF DIRECTOR, INSTALLATIONS AND LOGISTICS GENERAL COUNSEL
MEMORANDUM FOR	42 ABW/JA 42 ABW/SE 42 ABW/XP [SECOND LINE] [SECOND LINE] [SECOND LINE] [THIRD LINE] [THIRD LINE] [THIRD LINE]
MEMORANDUM FOR	HQ USAF/A4 [This format applies to all field units when sending HQ USAF/A3 memorandums to HQ USAF. Air Staff and HQ USAF/A1 Secretary of the Air Force staff offices follow IN TURN Headquarters Operating Instruction 33-3.]
MEMORANDUM FOR	DISTRIBUTION

"ATTENTION:"

Placement: The attention element is **aligned under the address or office symbol** in the "MEMORANDUM FOR" line. The attention element is used when a memorandum is intended for both an office and the attention of a specific person in that office. The format of the attention element is to place "ATTENTION:" or "ATTN:" or "THROUGH:" with the abbreviated rank and last name **in uppercase** on the line immediately below the "MEMORANDUM FOR" line.

Example:

MEMORANDUM FOR 36 FS/DO 　　　　　　　　　　　　ATTENTION: MAJ JONES

"FROM:"

Placement: Place "FROM:" in uppercase, flush with the left margin, on the **second line below** the last line of the MEMORANDUM FOR element (or the ATTENTION element, if used). After the "FROM:" element, leave two spaces followed by the organization abbreviation and office symbol (ORG/SYMBOL) of the originator.

Contents: If the complete mailing address is printed on the letterhead or if all recipients are located on the same installation as the originator, then only a single line FROM element consisting of the organization abbreviation and office symbol is used.

If the complete mailing address is not printed on the letterhead or if the recipients are on another installation, then the FROM element contains the full mailing address of the originator. This enables recipients to easily prepare and address return correspondence.

- The *first* line of the FROM element includes the organization abbreviation and office symbol separated by a virgule and typed in uppercase.
- The *second* line of the FROM element is the delivery address of the originator in upper and lower case.
- The *third* line of the FROM element includes the city, state and ZIP+4 code (without a comma between the city and state). For some installations, the city or installation name may be used interchangeably, as shown in the examples, below. Consult your local United States Post Office for details. The standard format for spacing between the state abbreviation and the ZIP code is two spaces.

Examples:

FROM: 20 FW/CC	[Sender and receiver on same installation]
FROM: HQ SOC/CC 　　　　　125 Chennault Circle 　　　　　Montgomery AL 36112-6430	[Sender and receiver on different installations] [City State option]
FROM: HQ SOC/CC 　　　　　125 Chennault Circle 　　　　　Maxwell AFB AL 36112-6430	[Sender and receiver on different installations] [Installation State option]

"SUBJECT:"

Placement: In all uppercase letters place "SUBJECT:", flush with the left margin, on the **second line below** the last line of the FROM element. After "SUBJECT:", type two spaces followed by the title; capitalize the first letter of each word except articles, prepositions and conjunctions. *Be brief and clear to focus readers*; if you need a second line, align it under the first word of the subject.

- When writing about an individual/employee who is not the addressee, include rank/grade and full name in the subject line. If you refer to the person again in the text of the memorandum, use only the rank/grade and surname.

- Do not include names in the subject line when writing about two or more individuals.

- When writing about several people, state their full names with rank/grade in the text of the memorandum the first time the names appear.

- SUSPENSE items: Include the suspense date in the subject line by typing "SUSPENSE:" or "SUSP:" with the date in parentheses after the title. If additional information for the suspense is necessary, include it in a separate paragraph—not in the SUBJECT line.

Examples:

SUBJECT: Official Memorandum Format Standards
SUBJECT: Letter of Appreciation (SSgt Angela Harkins)
SUBJECT: Self-Inspection Checklist Completion (SUSPENSE: 23 September 2014)
SUBJECT: The Format for a Subject Line That is Too Long for a Single Line Must Wrap and be Aligned Under the First Word of the Subject in the Subject Line

"References"

Placement: There are two options for placement of the references element—within the subject line or below the subject line. Cite a single reference to a communication or a directive in parentheses immediately after the subject title. For two or more references, type "References:" on the **second line below the last line of the SUBJECT element**. Capitalize the first letter of every word except articles, prepositions and conjunctions.

Citation Format: In general, identify references within the DoD by organization, type of communication, date and title. The organization and type of document within the DoD are included in the document's identification (e.g., an AFMAN is an Air Force Manual; a DoDD is a DoD Directive) and need not be written out in the "References" section. For referencing commercial publications, use the notes entry format from AU-1 *Style and Author Guide* or use *The Chicago Manual of Style* (AU-1 is based on *The Chicago Manual of Style*). AU-1 is available online from the Defense Technical Information Center (DTIC). In general, the notes entries include the author's name, publication title, publisher, date, and the paragraph or page number.

Examples:

SUBJECT: PACAF Work Center Standard (PACAF Memo, Same Subject, 6 June 2012)

SUBJECT: Preparation of Memorandums
 	
References: (a) AFMAN 33-326, 25 November 2011, *Preparing Official Communications*.
     (b) SAF/CIO A6 Memo, 12 October 2011, Air Force Guidance Memorandum to AFI 33-360, *Publications and Forms Management*.
     (c) DoDM 5110.04-M-V2, October 26, 2010, *DoD Manual for Written Material*.
     (d) William Strunk, Jr. and E. B. White, *The Elements of Style* (NY: MacMillan Publishing Co, 1989), 70.

Additional Information for References: When completing the reference list, consider the questions the recipients might have based on the memorandum you sent to them. For example, if it can be assumed that the recipient is unfamiliar with the publication or form cited, write out the title the first time you reference it. Also, you may want to attach a copy of the reference, or instructions on how to obtain it, if the reader does not have it. Finally, if the reference was not sent to all addressees previously, type not to all "(NOTAL)" after the citation for the referenced item. The table below summarizes these tips and several other specifics for citing referenced materials.

When you refer to:	*Show it in this format:*
Unfamiliar references	Write out the title the first time you reference
Familiar references	Attached or instructions on how to obtain
References sent to some, but not to all	[Reference citation] (NOTAL)
Other correspondence	AF/A1 Memo, 23 March 2012, Military Training Program
A publication when the communication is addressed within the Department of Defense	AFI 33-360, *Publications and Forms Management*, paragraphs 2.1 through 2.35
A publication when the communication is addressed outside the Department of Defense	Air Force Handbook 33-337, *The Tongue and Quill*
A Government form	AF Form 74, *Communications Status Notice/Request*
A commercial publication	Strunk and White, The Elements of Style (NY: MacMillan Publishing Co, 1989), 70
An item in a magazine, newspaper, or book	"New Optimism About Aging," *The Washington Post,* 9 September 1993, p.1.

The Text of the Official Memorandum

Begin the text of the memorandum on the **second line below the subject** or references (if used).

1. **Spacing paragraphs and subparagraphs.** Single-space the text, but double-space between paragraphs and subparagraphs (one blank line between all paragraphs and subparagraphs). *You may double-space the text of a one-paragraph memorandum less than eight lines.*

2. **Numbering paragraphs.** Number and letter each paragraph and subparagraph. A single paragraph is not numbered. If your organization is a part of Headquarters Air Force (the Air Staff and the Secretariat), follow the guidance in HQ Operating Instruction 33-3, *Correspondence Preparation, Control, and Tracking.*

3. **Formatting short subparagraphs.** Use a run-in method of listing subparagraphs when the subparagraphs consist of short sentences or phrases. The run-in method has several advantages: (a) it's compact, (b) it highlights ideas, and (c) it saves space.

4. **First Line of Text.** The first paragraph is never indented; it is numbered and flush left, two line spaces below the last line of the SUBJECT element (or the References element, if used). Indent the first line of sub-paragraphs to align the number or letter with the first character of its parent level paragraph. Each sub-level is likewise indented to align its paragraph number or letter with the first character of its parent level paragraph.

5. **Subsequent lines of text.** All second and subsequent lines of text for all paragraphs at all levels begin flush with the left margin; *do not indent*.

6. **Punctuation.** Use conventional rules of English grammar for punctuation in the body.

7. **Word Division.** When dividing a word, separate between syllables.

8. **Quotations.** When quoting numbered paragraphs from another document, cite the source and paragraph numbers in your text.

9. **Suspense Dates.** If you include a Suspense date in the text of the memorandum and not in the Subject Element, emphasize it by placing it in a separate paragraph.

10. **Contact information.** Place contact names, e-mail addresses, fax numbers, and telephone numbers in the last paragraph of the memorandum text.

11. **Continuation Pages.** Use plain bond paper. Begin typing the text of the continuation page four lines below the page number. Type at least two lines of the text on each page. Avoid dividing a paragraph of less than four lines between two pages.

12. **Page numbering.** The first page of a memorandum is never numbered. You may omit page numbers on a one- or two-page memorandum; however, memorandums longer than two pages must have page numbers. Number the succeeding pages starting with page 2. Place page numbers 0.5-inch from the top of the page, flush with the right margin. Number the continuation pages of each attachment as a separate sequence.

The Closing Section

The closing section of the document includes these elements: authority line, signature block, signature, attachments, courtesy copy and distribution.

Authority Line

Placement and Use: The authority line informs readers that the person who signed the document acted for the commander, the command section, or the headquarters. If an authority line is used, add "FOR THE COMMANDER" (or appropriate title) in uppercase on the second line below the last line of the text and 4.5 inches from the left edge of the page or three spaces to the right of the page center.

Use the authority line when any of these are true:	*Do **not** use the authority line in any of these conditions:*
1. A commander's designated representative signs for a specific action. 2. A document represents the commander's position or the coordinated position of the headquarters staff. 3. Staff members sign documents that direct action or announce policy within their areas of responsibility.	1. The commander (or head of the organization) signs. 2. The deputy or vice commander signs when the commander is temporarily away from the place of duty unless command action is directed by law and requires an indication of delegation. 3. The correspondence expresses opinions of units, directorates, divisions, offices, or branches. 4. The correspondence is addressed outside the DoD.

Signature Block

Placement: Start the signature block on the **fifth line below the last line of text** and 4.5 inches from the left edge of the page or three spaces to the right of page center. If the authority line is used, type the signature element five lines below the authority line. *If dual signatures are required, type the junior ranking official's signature block at the left margin; type the senior ranking official's signature block 4.5 inches from the left edge of the page or three spaces to the right of page center.* Do not place the signature element on a continuation page by itself. Consider correspondence received via e-mail, copied, or stamped //SIGNED// as authoritative as long as the signed copy is kept on file at the originating office.

1. **First Line.** Type the name in uppercase the way the person signs it (normally as it appears in the member's official records). Include grade and service for military members or grade and "DAF" (Department of the Air Force) for civilians. In general, avoid using legal, educational, or ecclesiastical degrees or titles. *As a rule, the rank for colonels and general officers should not be abbreviated.*

2. **Second Line.** Type the duty title as identified in the "FROM" element. "Acting" may be added before the duty title of a *staff* position if the incumbent is absent or the position is vacant. In addition, *do not* sign "for" or "in the absence of." *Do not* use "Acting" for any command capacity or where prohibited by law or statute (see AFI 33-321, *Authentication of Air Force Records*; and AFI 51-604, *Appointment to and Assumption of Command*).

3. **Third Line.** Type the name of the office or organization level if it is not included on the letterhead or the heading. Limit the signature element to three lines if possible; however, if a line of the signature element is too long, indent the next line to begin under the third character of the line above.

CHAPTER 14
The Official Memorandum

Examples (First two lines of signature blocks):

Standard placement (4.5 inches from left edge):	MARGARETTE S. LEWIS, Colonel, USAF Commander
	RAYMOND L. KENNEDY, MSgt, USAF NCOIC Ground Safety
	ELLEN C. CAMPANA, GS-15, DAF Chief, Quality Assurance Branch
Standard placement with long duty title: (Overflow duty title line is indented to align under the third character of the line above)	JOSE V. MUNEZ, CMSgt, USAF Chief, Computer Systems and Information Technology Customer Service
Long name: (Signature block adjusted to the left)	MARTEL R. WESTHALLER III, Col, USAF, DC Base Dental Surgeon
("Colonel" is usually spelled out. Also, this official may elect to use only initials for his first and middle names with abbreviated rank; if so, the signature block fits in the standard location.)	
Signature block with credentials:	JANICE L. CROWE, Lt Col, USAF, MSC Chief, Family Practice
Air National Guard (Title 10 status)	SCOTT A. BROWN, Lt Col, USAF Operations Officer
Air National Guard (Title 32 status)	SCOTT A. BROWN, Lt Col, ANG Operations Officer
Air Force Reserve (IAW command guidance on using "USAFR")	ELLA M. NEAL, Lt Col, USAFR Commander
Air Force Reserve (IAW command guidance on using "USAF")	ELLA M. NEAL, Lt Col, USAF Commander

Signature

Placement: Sign correspondence with permanent black ink. Use black typewriter ribbons, black printer toner, or black ink for rubber stamps or signature facsimile equipment. See AFI 33-321, *Authentication of Air Force Records*, for authentication of Air Force documents and how to use seals instead of signatures.

Attachment or Attachments

Placement: Place "Attachment:" (for a single attachment) or "# Attachments:" (for two or more attachments) at the left margin, on the **third line below** the signature element. When there are two or more attachments, list each by number and in the order mentioned in the memorandum. Beneath "Attachment" briefly describe each attachment, but do not use general terms or abbreviations such as "as stated," "as described above," or "a/s." Cite the office of origin, type of communication, date, and number of copies (in parentheses) if more than one. Include the subject of the attachment if the receiver will not get copies of attachments or if the subject is not already referenced in text. For classified attachments, show the assigned classification symbol in parentheses. Send a copy of the memorandum when you send the attachment (first example, below). If sending an attachment separately, type "(sep cover)" after the attachment label (see example, below). Do not divide attachment listings between two pages. If the listing is too long, type "Attachments: (listed on next page)," and list the attachments on a separate page.

Examples:

Attachment: ACC/CC Leave Policy Memo, 30 Jun 14	[Memorandum with a single attachment]
3 Attachments: 1. SAF CIO/A6 Memo, 30 Jun 12 (U)(2) 2. 380 FMS/CC Msg, 232300Z May 12 (NOTAL) 3. SAF/CIO Memo, 3 Aug 12 (S)	[Memorandum with 2 or more attachments]
2 Attachments: 1. AFI XX-XXXX, 26 Sep 12 2. AFI XX-XXXX, 14 May 12 (sep cover)	[Memorandum with attachments under separate cover]
12 Attachments (listed on next page)	[Memorandum with attachments listed on next page]

Courtesy Copy Element ("cc:")

Placement: When sending courtesy copies to activities other than to addressee, place "cc:" flush with the left margin, on the **second line below** the attachment element. <u>If the attachment element is not used, place "cc:" on the third line below the signature element</u>. List the organization abbreviation and office symbol of the offices to receive copies. When the copy is intended for a specific person in the office, include the person's Rank and Name in parentheses after the office symbol. If a courtesy copy is sent without including the attachments, type "wo/Atch" after the office. For paper copies, circle, underline, or highlight the office to indicate the recipient.

Examples:

cc: HQ AETC/A1 wo/Atch HQ USAFE/A1 Atch 2 only HQ PACAF/A1 (Atch under sep cover)	[Courtesy copies with attachment variations]
cc: 1 FW/CCP	[Courtesy copy to an office]
cc: 12 FS/DO (Capt Thomas Moore)	[Courtesy copy to a specific individual in an office]

If courtesy copies of a memorandum are not signed, write or stamp "signed" with black or dark blue ink above the signature block. Also, do not show internal distribution of courtesy copies on the original (or courtesy copy) for correspondence addressed outside your activity. However, you may show the distribution if one addressee needs to know who received a courtesy copy, or if correspondence is multiple-addressed and reproduced.

Distribution Element

Placement: If "MEMORANDUM FOR DISTRIBUTION" is used, place "DISTRIBUTION:" flush with the left margin, on the **second line below** the attachment element or the courtesy copy element, if used. If neither the attachment element nor the courtesy copy elements are used, place "DISTRIBUTION" on the third line below the signature element. Do not divide distribution lists between two pages. If the list is too long, type "DISTRIBUTION (listed on next page)," and list the organizations on a separate page.

Additional Information

The automated file designator element is optional and it is frequently beneficial to show if a document is a record or coordination copy. If there are several documents in a package, they should be arranged for action and clarity. See below for further details on these items.

Optional Automated File Designator (AFD) Element

The AFD element documents the storage location for data stored electronically. Type the AFD two line spaces below the courtesy copy distribution element. You may include the AFD in the identification line of talking, position, and bullet background papers. Contents of the AFD are based on the user's needs and the system being used. For example, the element may include the file name, typist's initials, and the uniform resource locator (URL) if stored on a website.

Typeset Correspondence

You may typeset correspondence for a large audience (such as a memorandum to ALMAJCOM-FOA). Use an appropriate letterhead as with other official correspondence. You can use the full range of typesetting capabilities, including, but not limited to, two columns, italics, bold type, variable spacing, boxed inserts, and screened backgrounds.

Record or Coordination Copy

This is the official record for your office files, so make sure it is fully legible. Type or write additional information of value only to the office of record on the record or coordination copy.

- **Showing Coordination.** Type or write the organization abbreviation and office symbol of each office that should coordinate across the bottom or right side of the record copy. The coordinating officials enter their last name and date.

- **Showing Internal Courtesy Copy Distribution.** List all internal courtesy distribution on the record copy unless it is listed on the original.

- **Identifying the Writer.** If identifying the writer is of value to the office of record, place the writer's organization abbreviation and office symbol, name, telephone number, typist's initials, the date the correspondence is typed, and, if desired, the document name/number at the top or bottom margin of the page. Do not repeat the writer's name if the writer signed the correspondence. Use a new identification line, if desired, each time the correspondence is rewritten or retyped. Place the name of the person who rewrote it on the next line followed by the date it was retyped.

- **Annotating for Magnetic Storage Media.** Use the writer identification line to show document name, storage location, or file identification for reference and possible revision or reprinting.

- **Preparing a Memorandum for Record (MR).** When preparing a MR, whether it is for another office or when using it as your primary record, write or type on the record copy any information needed for the record. Continue on the back or a separate sheet if you need more space. The writer then signs the MR. ("MR" is the technical abbreviation for a memorandum for record; however, "MFR" is more widely recognized by Airmen.)

Attachments

Many times you will need to attach supporting documents to your correspondence and the order of these documents has meaning for your correspondence. Placing supporting documents in the right order conveys levels of significance and relationships between documents to convey the context or background related to the issue in the correspondence. Understanding the context and background can be key information for decision makers to understand the issue and make good decisions.

Arranging and Marking Attachments

Attachment, appendix, annex, and exhibit all mean additional or supplementary material and indicate relative position within a correspondence package. The first addition to the document is an **attachment**; an addition to an attachment is an **appendix**; an addition to an appendix is an **annex**; and additions to an annex are **exhibits**. Indicate on the attachment, appendix, annex, or exhibit if there are appendices, annexes, or exhibits to it.

Type or write attachment markings in the same position as on the basic correspondence. Use pencil to allow renumbering and reuse with other documents. Mark attachments as follows:

- Attachments are marked in the lower right corner as Atch 1, Atch 2, Atch 3, etc.

- Appendices to attachments are marked as Appendix A, Appendix B, Appendix C, etc.

- Annexes to appendices are marked as Annex 1, Annex 2, Annex 3, etc.

- Exhibits to annexes are marked as Exhibit A, Exhibit B, Exhibit C, etc.

- For multiple-page attachments, number the pages of each attachment in a separate sequence. For example Atch 1 (1 of 3), Atch 1 (2 of 3), Atch 1 (3 of 3), etc.

- When sending more than one copy of an attachment, place the copy number (typed or handwritten) to the right and slightly above the attachment number to indicate the copy is the first, second, third, etc. For example Atch 1^1, Atch 1^2, Atch 1^3, etc.

Arranging and Marking Attachments (Graphic)

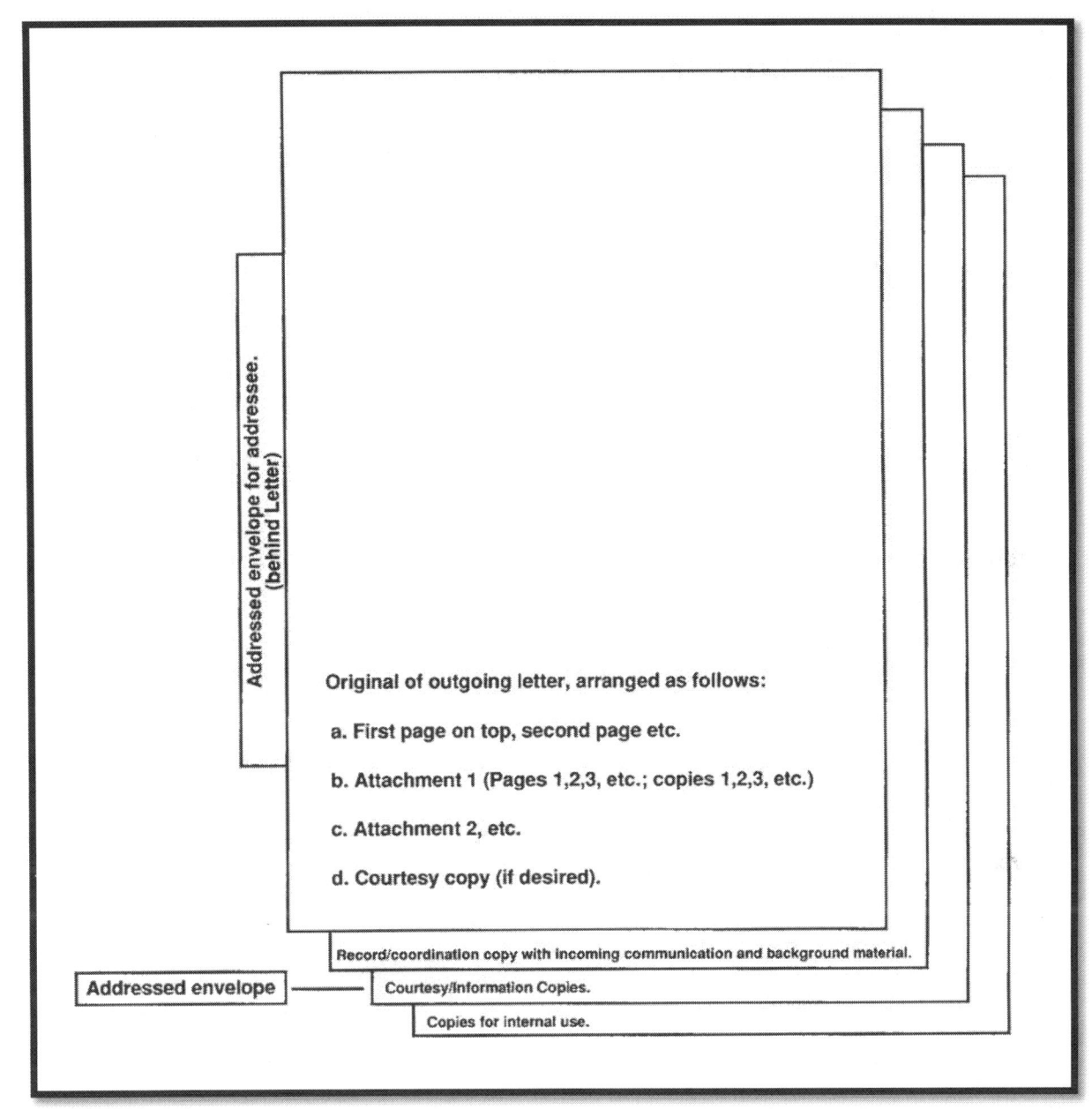

Diagram showing stacked pages with labels:

- Addressed envelope for addressee. (behind Letter)
- Original of outgoing letter, arranged as follows:
  a. First page on top, second page etc.
  b. Attachment 1 (Pages 1,2,3, etc.; copies 1,2,3, etc.)
  c. Attachment 2, etc.
  d. Courtesy copy (if desired).
- Record/coordination copy with incoming communication and background material.
- Courtesy/Information Copies.
- Copies for internal use.
- Addressed envelope

Keep the Package Together

Staple a memorandum of more than one page, or with attachments, in the upper left corner before dispatch. If possible, arrange pages so that the reader can read information without removing the staples or paper clips; for example, turn landscape pages with top to the left. If required, prepare envelopes or facsimile cover sheets, and place them at the left side behind the copies for dispatch. Use a paper or binder clip to hold the packet together before dispatch. Organizations may specify alternate methods to suit their needs.

When using tabs, the first tab is located near the lower right corner and each successive tab is located slightly higher. Keep the spacing between three or more tabs equal for a professional look. The graphic for tab placement, below, depicts proper tab placement.

Tab Placement (Graphic)

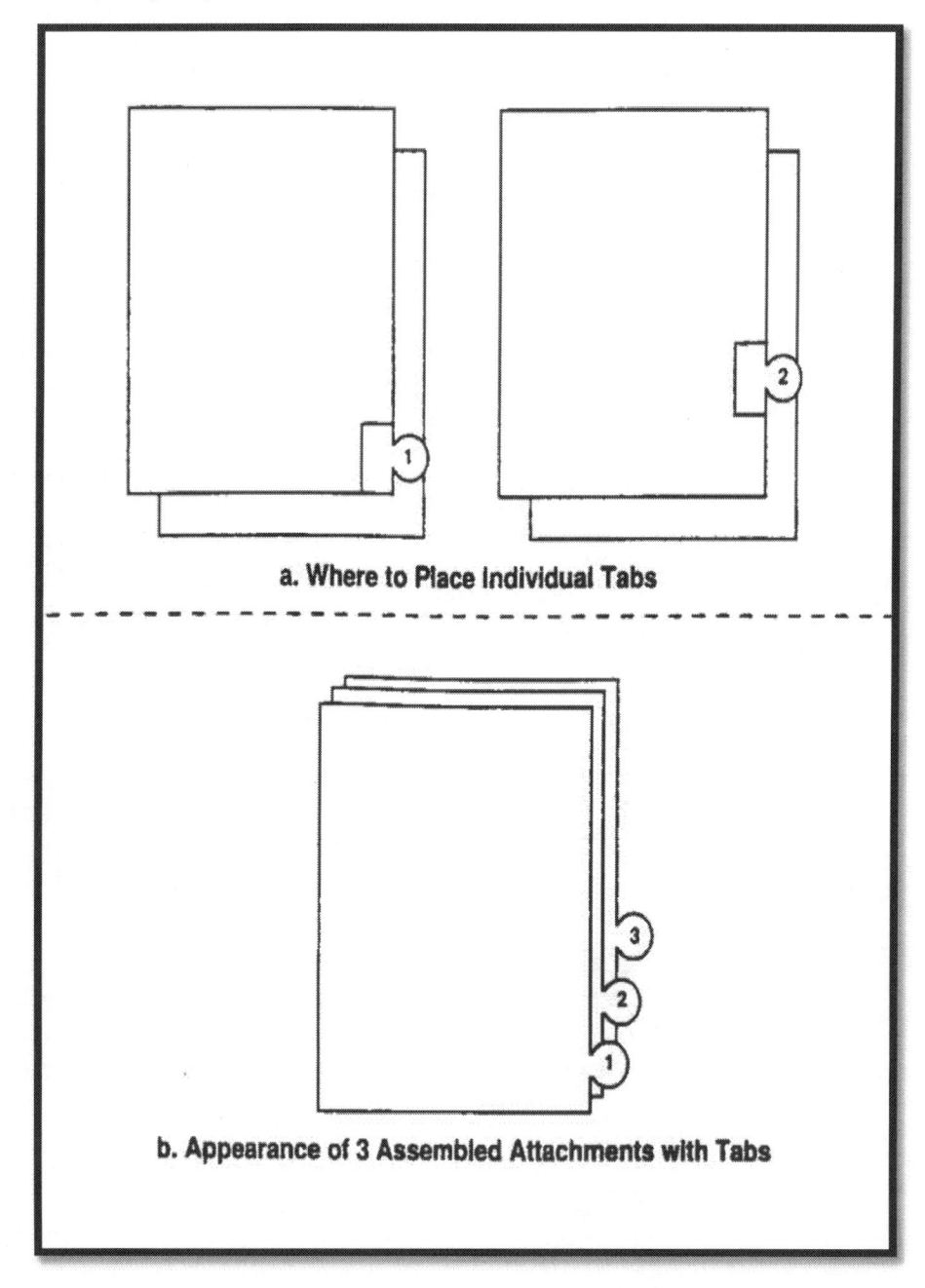

a. Where to Place Individual Tabs

b. Appearance of 3 Assembled Attachments with Tabs

The Official Memorandum: Examples

The official memorandum is a powerful tool that can be used in many ways to accomplish many tasks. The official memorandum informs single and multiple receivers; personnel within and between organizations; leaders up and down the chain of command; and documents actions. The following official memorandums examples are based on many of the typical situations where Airmen need to make an official, written record of an event, decision or action.

- **Format:** The format guidance for an official memorandum written as an official memorandum with visual cues for placement and spacing of the elements described in this chapter shown in grey.

- **Subdividing Paragraphs:** The rules for subdividing paragraphs in the official memorandum are presented in an official memorandum.

- **Indorsement:** When the official memorandum must be signed to acknowledge receipt or action, the indorsement format should be used. The indorsement format has many uses, such as staff coordination, requests for training or disciplinary actions.

- **Letter of Reprimand:** The letter of reprimand (LOR) is a specialized indorsement memorandum. Refer to *The Military Commander and the Law* and your local legal office for more guidance on disciplinary letters.

- **IN TURN:** When the official memorandum needs a record of review without the formality of the indorsement format, the IN TURN format provides reviewer tracking.

- **After-Action Report:** When an action has been completed, the official memorandum can inform others about the results of the action, operation or mission.

- **Trip Report:** The trip report is another form of an after-action report that is commonly used in the Air Force. The trip report concisely conveys information about the trip's purpose, travelers, and itinerary after the trip is concluded. A more detailed discussion of relevant information from the trip is presented followed by any recommendations and/or conclusions. In short, the trip report should answer the who, what, when, where, why and how questions in a concise, orderly format. The trip report should convey everything the addressees need to know about the trip, especially as it relates to the unit's mission and any recommendations or costs.

- **Short Note Reply:** Reply to an official memorandum by adding your short note reply directly to the original memorandum. The short note reply is less formal than other response formats but is entirely appropriate when used correctly.

- **Memorandum for Record (MFR or MR):** The MFR is less formal than the official memorandum but records important information, questions or actions quickly. There are several formats for the MFR depending on the time and space available.

The Tongue and Quill recommends users follow the guidance of this chapter when preparing any official memorandum. This guidance includes checking for command supplements or commander preferences in preparing official memorandums. The examples that follow are just a few of the possible uses for the official memorandum. The goal is to standardize the format so Airmen can focus on the substance to communicate clearly and inform others.

Format of the Official Memorandum

DEPARTMENT OF THE AIR FORCE
[APPROVED ORGANIZATIONAL LETTERHEAD]

[1.75 inches from top of page; flush with the right margin] 15 January 2014

MEMORANDUM FOR ORG/SYMBOL ¶ [Second line below date]

FROM: ORG/SYMBOL ¶ [Second line below MEMORANDUM FOR]
         Organization
         Street address (see paragraph 4)
         City ST 12345-6789 (see paragraph 4)

SUBJECT: Format for the Official Memorandum ¶ [Second line below FROM]

References: (a) AFM 33-326, 25 November 2011, *Preparing Official Communications*. ¶
              (b) DoDM 5110.04-M-V2, October 26, 2010, *DoD Manual for Written Material*. ¶

1. Use only approved organizational letterhead for all correspondence. This applies to all letterhead, both pre-printed and computer generated. Reference (a) details for the format and style of official letterhead such as centering the first line of the header 5/8ths of an inch from the top of the page in 12 point Copperplate Gothic Bold font. The second header line is centered 3 points below the first line in 10.5 point Copperplate Gothic Bold font. ¶

2. The standard location for the date element is 1.75 inches from the top of the page and flush with the right margin whether it is placed by word processor, typewriter, or date stamp. ¶

3. Place "MEMORANDUM FOR" on the second line below the date. Leave two spaces between "MEMORANDUM FOR" and the recipient's office symbol. If there are multiple recipients, two or three office symbols may be placed on each line aligned under the entries on the first line. If there are numerous recipients, use a "DISTRIBUTION" element. ¶

4. Place "FROM:" on the second line below the "MEMORANDUM FOR" line. Leave two spaces between the colon in "FROM:" and the originator's office symbol. The "FROM:" element contains the full mailing address of the originator's office unless the mailing address is in the header or if all the recipients are located on the same installation as the originator. ¶

5. Place "SUBJECT:" in uppercase on the second line below the last line of the FROM element. Leave two spaces between the colon in "SUBJECT:" and the subject. Capitalize the first letter of each word except articles, prepositions, and conjunctions (this is sometimes referred to as "title case"). Be clear and concise. If the subject is long, try to revise and shorten the subject; if shortening is not feasible, align the second line under the first word of the subject. ¶

6. Body text begins on the second line below the last line in the subject element and is flush with the left margin. If the Reference element is used, then the body text begins on the second line below the last line of the Reference element. ¶

[Page numbers are placed 0.5 inches from the top and flush with the right margin] 2

    a. When a paragraph is split between pages, there must be at least two lines from the paragraph on both pages. Similarly, avoid single-sentence paragraphs by revising or reorganizing the content. ¶
¶
    b. Number or letter each body text paragraph and subparagraph according to the format for subdividing paragraphs in official memorandums presented in the *Tongue and Quill*. When a memorandum is subdivided, the number of levels used should be relative to the length of the memorandum. Shorter products typically use three or fewer levels. Longer products may use more levels—but use only the number of levels needed. ¶
¶
7. If the memorandum is three pages or longer, place the page number 0.5 inches from the top of the page at the right margin for page 2 onwards. The first page is never numbered. The second page of a two-page memorandum may be numbered at the discretion of the originator. ¶
¶
8. Follow the spacing guidance for between the text, signature block, attachment element, courtesy copy element, and distribution lists, if used carefully. Never separate the text from the signature block: the signature page must include body text above the signature block. Also, the first element below the signature block begins on the third line below the last line of the duty title: this applies to attachments, courtesy copies, and distribution lists, whichever is used first. ¶
¶
9. The example of this memorandum applies to many official memorandums that Airmen may be tasked to prepare; however, there are additional elements for special uses of the official memorandum. Refer to the *Tongue and Quill* discussion on the official memorandum for more details, or consult published guidance applicable to your duties. ¶
¶
¶
¶
¶
¶
First M. Last
¶ [Fifth line below text; 4.5 inches from left edge]   FIRST M. LAST, Rank, USAF
¶   Director, Information Management and
¶ [Indent to align under third character above]   Publications Policy
¶
¶
¶
2 Attachments: ¶ [Third line below last line of duty title] [If none, delete entire element]
1. [Attachment description, date] ¶
2. [Attachment description, date] ¶
¶
cc: ¶ [Second line below last line of attachment element or third line below signature block]
[Rank and name, ORG/SYMBOL, or both] [If none, delete entire element] ¶
¶
DISTRIBUTION: [* If none, delete entire element] ¶
[Organization name or ORG/SYMBOL] ¶
[Organization name or ORG/SYMBOL] ¶

> *If used, the DISTRIBUTION element begins on the second line below the attachments or courtesy copy; however, it begins on the third line below last line of signature block if the attachment and courtesy copy elements are *not* used.

¶
¶
¶   [Use 1-inch left, right, top, and bottom margins for page 2 onwards]

Format for Subdividing Paragraphs in Official Memorandums

DEPARTMENT OF THE AIR FORCE
[APPROVED ORGANIZATIONAL LETTERHEAD]

12 June 2014

MEMORANDUM FOR ADMINISTRATORS

FROM: ORG/SYMBOL

SUBJECT: Format for Subdividing Paragraphs in Official Memorandums

1. Introductory paragraph with purpose, statement, and overview. Single-space within paragraphs; double-space between paragraphs. Indent only the first line of subparagraphs: all paragraphs wrap to the left margin at all levels.

2. First main idea. [The first line of a first level paragraph is not indented.]

   a. Fact and reasoning supporting this idea. [The first line of all sub-paragraphs is indented. The sub-paragraph letter or number is aligned under the first character of the first word in the first line of its superior paragraph. All other lines for all paragraphs are flush with the left margin. In this example, the "a." is aligned under the "F" of "First main idea."]

      (1) Fact and reasoning to support a. [First line aligned under "F" in "Fact…"]

      (2) Additional fact and reasoning to support a.

         (a) Support for (2). [First line aligned under "A" in "Additional fact…"]

         (b) Additional support for (2).

            1 Support for (b). [First line aligned under "A" in "Additional support…"]

               a Support for 1. [First line aligned under "S" in "Support for (b)"]

               b Additional support for 1.

                  [1] Support for b. [First line aligned under "A" in "Additional…"]

                  [2] Additional support for b.

            2 Additional support for (b).

   b. Additional fact or reasoning to support 2 (first main idea).

      (1) Support for b.

      (2) Additional support for b.

3. Second main idea. Your narrative should flow smoothly from one idea to another with each idea being clearly supported.

    a. Fact and reasoning supporting this idea.

    b. Additional fact and reasoning supporting this idea.

4. The cardinal rule of subdivision.

    a. Subdivision, by its name and nature, requires there be at least two subordinate elements if an idea or support for an idea is subdivided

    b. When subdividing paragraphs, never use a "1" without a "2" or an "a" without a "b."

    c. The cardinal rule of subdivision applies to all correspondence, reports, background papers, outlines, briefings, or presentations: it is fundamental to outlining and content organization.

5. Optional closure and point of contact information. If contact information is used, provide the digital switched network (DSN) and commercial telephone numbers and an email address.

                                    First M. Last
                                    FIRST M. LAST, Rank, USAF
                                    Director, Information Management and
                                    Publications Policy

The Indorsement Format

DEPARTMENT OF THE AIR FORCE
[APPROVED ORGANIZATIONAL LETTERHEAD]

2 April 2014

MEMORANDUM FOR 374 OG/CCE [Office symbol for 1st Indorsement official]
                       ATTENTION: CAPT CATCH [1st Indorsement official, if required]

FROM: 374 AW/CCE [Originator]

SUBJECT: Indorsement Memorandum Format

1. The indorsement memorandum is useful when documented history of action is required, such as when gathering formal comments for a document or in handling legal and disciplinary actions. As such, indorse official memorandums only, not personal letters.

    a. Use the indorsement format within or between US military organizations or between US Military organizations and civilian organizations under contract with the Air Force. When space allows, place indorsements on the original memorandum or a previous indorsement page.

    b. Number each indorsement in sequence (1st Ind, 2d Ind, 3d Ind, …). Begin the first indorsement on the second line below the last element of the original memorandum. Begin subsequent indorsements on the second line below the last element of the previous indorsement. Follow the indorsement number with your office symbol.

2. Please pass this sample to the 374 OSS/CCE. If you have any questions, you can reach me at DSN 888-9999, commercial (555) 888-9999, or by e-mail at noman.hauler@us.af.mil.

[Originator's signature block]
NORMAN B. HAULER, Major, USAF
Executive Officer, 374th Airlift Wing

1st Ind, 374 OG/CCE [Office symbol for 1st Indorsement official]   4 Apr 14

MEMORANDUM FOR 374 OSS/CCE [Office symbol for 2d Indorsement official]

Please review. If you have questions, please contact me first.

[1st Indorsement official's signature block]
MACON D. CATCH, Captain, USAF
Executive Officer, 374th Operations Group

CHAPTER 14
The Official Memorandum

2d Ind to 374 AW/CCE, 2 Apr 14, Indorsement Memorandum Format

374 OSS/CCE [Office symbol for 2d Indorsement official]   8 Apr 14

MEMORANDUM FOR 374 AW/CCE [Originator]

Reviewed. I have posted the sample on the 374 OSS shared drive.

                                                        Justine L. Master
[2d Indorsement official's signature block]   JUSTINE L. MASTER, 1Lt, USAF
                                                        Executive Officer, 374th Operations Support
                                                             Squadron

> Use a separate-page indorsement when there isn't space remaining on the original memorandum or previous indorsement page. The separate-page indorsement is basically the same as the one for the same page except the top line always cites the indorsement number with the originator's office, date, and subject of the original communication; the second line reflects the functional address symbol of the indorsing office with the date. An example is at the top of this page.

The "IN TURN" Format

DEPARTMENT OF THE AIR FORCE
[APPROVED ORGANIZATIONAL LETTERHEAD]

[1.75 inches from top of page; 1 inch from right edge of page]   2 Jan 14

MEMORANDUM FOR   18 OG/~~CC~~ *Concur, ABC, 3 Jan*   [Second line below date]
                 18 MSG/~~CC~~ *Comments attached, DAC, 4 Jan*
                 18 MXG/~~CC~~ *JVK, 5 Jan*
                 IN TURN

FROM: 18 WG/CC   [Second line below MEMORANDUM FOR]

SUBJECT: The IN TURN Memorandum   [Second line below FROM]

1. The IN TURN memorandum is one application of the official memorandum and is used when the final addressee or office of primary responsibility (OPR) must see the coordination or action of all addressees. In this example, the message is being sent to several group commanders in the same wing to coordinate action among all three groups.

2. The format for the IN TURN memorandum is the same as the official memorandum except for the MEMORANDUM FOR element. Simply add "IN TURN" below the last addressee in the "MEMORANDUM FOR" element and aligned with the addresses.

3. When you receive an IN TURN memorandum, strike through your office symbol and put your initials and the date next to the right. Also, indicate concurrence (concur, non-concur) or if there are comments. Then forward the memo to the next addressee. If you have comments, attach them to the package or send them in a separate letter directly to the final addressee.

[Fifth line below text; 4.5 inches from left edge]   *Brian M. Books*
                                                      BRIAN M. BOOKS, Colonel, USAF
                                                      Commander

[1-inch left, right, and bottom margins]

The After-Action Report

DEPARTMENT OF THE AIR FORCE
AIR UNIVERSITY (AETC)

25 March 2014

MEMORANDUM FOR SOC/DE

FROM: SOC/DER

SUBJECT: After-Action Report, Squadron Officer School (SOS) Class 14B

1. Overview. This memorandum documents the end-of-term review (EOTR) for Squadron Officer School (SOS) Class 14B. This review considers student performance, feedback on the curriculum, guidance affecting the curriculum, and course director analysis.

2. Student performance. ...

3. Feedback on the curriculum. ...

   a. Feedback from students. ...

      (1) "What were the most beneficial aspects of the course?"

      (2) "How could we improve the course?"

   b. Feedback from instructors. ...

4. Guidance Affecting Curriculum. ...

5. Course Director Analysis. ...

Vicki C. Williams
VICTORIA C. WILLIAMS, Major, USAF
Course Director, Squadron Officer School

Attachment:
Spaatz ESS/XA Feedback Report, 15 March 2014

> Style Note: If the date format used in the attachment element matches the date format of the memorandum, as is done in this example, the document presents a consistent, professional look.

The Trip Report

DEPARTMENT OF THE AIR FORCE
AIR UNIVERSITY (AETC)

14 July 2014

MEMORANDUM FOR AIR FORCE SENIOR NCO ACADEMY STAFF

FROM: AFSNCOA/CO

SUBJECT: Trip Report Format

1. PURPOSE: Briefly state the reason for the trip (answer the *why* question). [The remaining paragraphs of the trip report should answer the *what*, *when*, *where*, and *how* questions.]

2. TRAVELER(S): Include rank, first name or initial, and surname. Provide position titles if travelers are from different offices or organizations. You may list names of members present in two columns to save space.

3. ITINERARY: List location(s) visited, inclusive dates, and key personnel contacted. This content may be presented as narrative text, columns, or another format that best communicates the information clearly and concisely.

4. DISCUSSION: Base the amount of detailed information you include here on the knowledge level of your intended readers. Always include the trip objective, problems encountered, findings, future commitments made and your contribution to the event. This paragraph may need several sub-paragraphs to cover all the pertinent information. Attach meeting minutes or other background documents that provide more detailed information, if needed.

5. CONCLUSIONS/RECOMMENDATIONS: Summarize your findings and/or recommended actions. If there are several findings and/or recommendations, use sub-paragraphs numbered and/or lettered in accordance with the format for sub-paragraphs in an official memorandum.

Laurence M. Patrick
LAURENCE, M. PATRICK, CMSgt, USAF
Commandant, AF Senior NCO Academy

Attachment:
Professional Military Education Conference Minutes, 8 July 2014

The Short Note Reply

DEPARTMENT OF THE AIR FORCE
AIR EDUCATION AND TRAINING COMMAND

16 June 2014

MEMORANDUM FOR HQ 2 AF/CCS

FROM: HQ AETC/CCS
   1 F Street, Suite 1
   JBSA-Randolph TX 78150-4324

SUBJECT: Use of the Short Note Reply

1. Official memorandums and staff packages sometimes generate additional questions during the staffing process. Some of these questions require additional staff research or a revised staff package to answer while others may be answered directly with a short note reply. The short note reply is a time-saving method to respond to questions directly on the official memorandum and to keep a staff package moving towards a decision.

2. The format for a short note reply is simple. Just write or type the short note reply flush with the left margin on the original memorandum if space allows; if not, put it on a separate page, attach it to the original memorandum, and keep a copy for your files.

3. If you have any questions, please feel free to call at DSN 888-9999, Comm (333) 555-9999, or via email at margaret.wick@us.af.mil.

Margaret C. Wick
MARGARET C. WICK, GS-11, DAF
Executive Assistant to AETC Commander

Memorandum For HQ AETC/CCS [Use upper- and lower-case "Memorandum For"]

Please let the command know the key element of the short note reply is brevity. Following the "Memorandum For" of the reply is a short note of one or two sentences and an abbreviated signature block (name and short duty title or office symbol).

ANDREA NAYFA [USE ALL CAPS FOR NAME]
2 AF/CCS

The Memorandum for Record

DEPARTMENT OF THE AIR FORCE
[APPROVED ORGANIZATIONAL LETTERHEAD]

17 February 2014

MEMORANDUM FOR RECORD

SUBJECT: The Memorandum for Record

1. The memorandum for record, commonly known as a memo for record, MR, or MFR, has three forms: (a) the separate-page memorandum, (b) the explanatory note, and (c) the compact note. The form used is determined by the purpose for the MR and the needs of the writer.

2. The formats for each of the three types of MR are simple. This is the **separate page MR**. It is based on the official memorandum but omits the "FROM:" element since the writer is both the sender and the receiver. The separate page MR also uses a modified signature block by using the organization abbreviation and office symbol rather than the duty title. The formats for the explanatory note MR and compact note MR, shown below, have even fewer required elements to accommodate specific purposes, limited space, or both.

Bestin D. Blue
BESTIN D. BLUE
ACSC/CCS

MEMO FOR RECORD   18 Feb 14

This is an **explanatory note MR**. It omits the subject when it is added to the record copy (as shown in this example). If space permits, type "MEMO FOR RECORD" and the date on the second line below the signature block. If the explanatory note will not fit on the bottom of the record copy, simply type "MR ATTACHED" or "MR ON REVERSE" on the bottom of the record copy and put the MR on a separate sheet or on the back of the record copy. Number the paragraphs as you would in an official memorandum when there is more than one paragraph. No signature block is required; merely sign your last name after the last word of the MR.
                                                                Blue

MR: The **compact note MR** is the shortest format for a memorandum for record and is useful when space is limited. Sign your last name and put the date following the last word.
                                                                Blue
                                                                19 Feb

MR ATTACHED

The Memorandum for Record: Separate Page Attachment

DEPARTMENT OF THE AIR FORCE
[APPROVED ORGANIZATIONAL LETTERHEAD]

20 February 2014

MEMORANDUM FOR RECORD

SUBJECT: Additional Information on the Memorandum for Record

Reference: MFR, The Memorandum for Record, 17 Feb 14

1. Summary: People working together every day frequently pass information back and forth verbally—even in the social media world of today—but sometimes the information needs to be documented in a memorandum for record (MR or MFR).

2. Format: Follow the format for the official memorandum. If there are multiple paragraphs, they are numbered or lettered, and indented, according to the format for subdividing paragraphs in the official memorandum. The margins are the same (1.75 inches on the top and one (1) inch on the left, right, and bottom) as is the font style (Times New Roman) font size (12 points). The reference line must clearly identify the document (a previous MFR in this case) being referenced.

    a. The separate page MFR documents information that is usually first presented orally, such as telephone calls or verbal tasks from leaders, as a record of the event for later reference or to informally pass the information to others. The separate page MFR also serves as "a note to self" to document tasks, disciplinary, or other legal actions.

    b. The explanatory note MFR adds a "MEMO FOR RECORD" line to any correspondence and can be used to target a specific addressee. The explanatory MFR gives the reader a synopsis of the purpose of the original memorandum, tells who got involved and provides additional background information not included in the original memorandum. By reading the original memorandum and the MFR, readers should understand enough about the subject to coordinate or sign the memorandum without having to ask for more information.

    c. The compact note MFR is the most compact version of the MFR. When there is very little space at the bottom of the correspondence and you need to make a recorded note, use the compact note format.

3. MFRs are flexible and important tools for today's Airmen to document and record events. They are simple to create and adaptable.

Deborah A. Woodson
DEBORAH A. WOODSON
SOC/CCS

Spelling Checkers: Before You Sign

Before you—or your boss—signs an official memorandum (or a personal letter)—run your spell checking software and READ the document again. The extreme examples below may never happen to you; however, there are some very embarrassing spelling checker suggestions for some military terms not recognized by the software.

READ the document; avoid embarrassment.

Spell Chequer

Eye halve a spelling chequer
It came with my pea sea
It plainly marques four my revue
Miss Steaks eye kin knot sea.

Eye strike a key and type a word
And weight four it two say
Weather eye am wrong oar write
It shows me strait a weigh.
As soon as a mist ache is maid
It nose bee fore two long
And eye can put the error rite
Its rarely ever wrong.

Eye have run this poem threw it
I am shore your pleased two no.
Its letter perfect in it's weigh
My chequer tolled me sew.

—Sauce Unknown

CHAPTER 15

The Personal Letter

This chapter covers:
- The Heading Section
- The Text of the Personal Letter
- The Closing Section
- Forms of Address, Salutation and Complimentary Close
- Military Ranks and Abbreviations
- The Personal Letter: Examples

Use a personalized letter when your communication needs a personal touch or when warmth or sincerity is essential. You may use it to write to an individual on a private matter for praise, condolence, sponsorship, etc. Keep it brief, preferably no longer than one page, and avoid using acronyms. For envelopes, always use United States Postal Service (USPS) abbreviations for addresses. For further information, see USPS Publication 28, *Postal Addressing Standards*.

The Heading Section

The heading section of the personal letter includes these elements: date, return address, address of the individual being sent the letter and the salutation elements.

Date

Placement and Format: Place the date **1 inch from the right edge, 1.75 inches from the top** of the page. Use the "Day Month Year" or "DD Mmm YY" format for letters addressed to a military/government organization. In the "DD Mmm YY" format, the month and year are both abbreviated for consistency. For civilian addressees, use the "Month Day, Year" format. Finally, unless the date of signature has legal significance, date the original and all copies of the correspondence at the time of dispatch.

Examples:

Military Addressees–Day Month Year	15 October 2014
Military Addressees–DD Mmm YY	15 Oct 14
Civilian Addressees–Month Day, Year	October 15, 2014

Return Address

Place the sender's return address flush with the left margin on the **second line below** the date. Include the sender's rank, full name, duty title, organization and complete mailing address using single spacing between lines.. Use a period after abbreviations such as "Mr.," "Ms.," "Mrs." and "Dr." *Do not use punctuation in the last line of the address* except for the dash in the ZIP+4 code. The standard format for spacing between the state abbreviation and the ZIP code is two spaces. For examples, refer to the "Forms of Address, Salutation and Complimentary Close" section of this chapter.

Example:

Chief Master Sergeant David L. Jones Duty Title Organization Street Address City ST 12345-6789

Receiver's Address

Place the address of the individual the letter is being sent to on the **third line below** the return address. Include the receiver's title or rank, full name and complete mailing address using single spacing between lines. Use a period after abbreviations such as "Mr.," "Ms.," "Mrs." and "Dr." *Do not use punctuation in the last line of the address* except for the dash in the ZIP+4 code. The standard format for spacing between the state abbreviation and the ZIP code is two spaces. For examples, refer to the "Forms of Address, Salutation and Complimentary Close" section of this chapter.

Example:

```
Lieutenant Colonel Getty A. Letter
Duty Title
Organization
Street Address
City ST  12345-6789
```

Salutation

Place the salutation on the **second line below** the receiver's address. The salutation begins with "Dear" followed by the title (or rank) and last name of the receiver. ***Do not* use punctuation in the salutation.** For examples, refer to the "Forms of Address, Salutation and Complimentary Close" section of this chapter.

The Text of the Personal Letter

Start the text of a letter on the **second line below** the salutation. *Do not* number the paragraphs. Indent the first line of text for all major paragraphs 0.5 inches; if there are sub-paragraphs, follow the same guidance for sub-paragraph numbering and indentation as in the official memorandum. All second and subsequent lines of text for all paragraphs are flush with the left margin. You may double-space text of a one-paragraph letter with less than eight lines. Include any relevant references in the first paragraph rather than using a references element.

The Closing Section

Complimentary Close.

Place "Sincerely" on the **second line below** the text and 4.5 inches from the left edge of the page or three spaces to the right of page center. ***Do not* punctuate the complimentary close.**

Authority Line Element: The authority line is *not* used for Personal Letters.

Signature Element.

Place the signature element on the **fifth line below** and aligned with the complimentary close (4.5 inches from the left edge of the page). Use the sender's full signature block.

Attachment Element.

Place "Attachment:" (single attachment) or "# Attachments:" (two or more attachments) flush with the left margin, on the **third line below** the signature element.

Courtesy Copy Element ("cc:")

Placement: For courtesy copies to activities other than the addressee, place "cc:" flush with the left margin, on the **second line below** the attachment element. If the attachment element is not used, place "cc:" on the third line below the signature element. List the names or unit designators of the recipients. If a courtesy copy is sent without including the attachments, type "wo/Atch" after the office. Circle, underline or highlight the office to indicate the recipient.

Forms of Address, Salutation and Complimentary Close

The *DoD Manual for Written Material* provides "Forms of Address, Salutation, and Complimentary Close" tables as references for composing the address, salutation and complimentary closing elements of a personal letter. The tables provide examples for every branch of government, as well as many departments, agencies or groups of people from the White House to private citizens. These tables have long been staples of *The Tongue and Quill* and continue to be an important reference for all Airmen: using the proper address, salutation and complimentary close for correspondence makes a good first impression.

For this edition of *The Tongue and Quill*, The "Forms of Address, Salutation, and Complimentary Close" tables from the DoD manual were extracted, combined into a single table, and edited to conform to Air Force standards: the Air Force uses the open punctuation style and spells out the ranks of all military members in the addresses on personal letters (for the address on the envelope, refer to the Envelope section of this publication). Also, the standard to abbreviate "U.S." and "U.N." is to write them without the periods (i.e. "US" and "UN"). The tips below and the entries in the table are the standards useful to most Airmen in their daily work; however, always check to see if your command has additional or supplementary guidance.

- **Name or Gender Unknown:** Use professional or organizational title when the name or the gender of the receiver (or both) are not known (e.g., Dear Resource Manager).

- **Responding to Jointly Written Letters:** Respond to letters written jointly by more than three people by preparing single replies, or reply to the person signing the original letter and mentioning the others early in the letter.

- **Titles:** In the salutation for letters addressed to persons in formal positions such as "President," "Vice President," "Chairman," "Secretary," "Ambassador" or "Minister" that may be held by men or women, use the title "Mr." or "Madam." For example, use "Dear Mr. President" or "Dear Madam Secretary" if using the formal position in the salutation.
    - The title "Ms.," "Miss" or "Mrs." is used when the last name rather than a formal title follows. (e.g., Ms. Smith, Miss Rice, Mrs. Gartner)
    - "Ms." may be used when an incumbent or correspondent has indicated this preference or when a woman's marital status is unknown.
    - Spell out titles (except Dr., Mr. and Mrs.) but do not duplicate titles (Dr. Charles Norris or Charles Norris, MD; *not* Dr. Charles Norris, MD).

- **Punctuation:** The Air Force uses open punctuation in the salutation and complimentary close (no punctuation after the salutation or close). A period is used after "Mr.," "Mrs." or "Dr." and similar titles and a dash is used in the ZIP+4 code (e.g., 12345-6789).

- **Spacing:** Single space between lines.

- **Readability:** Readability of the addresses is essential. Use single spacing between lines. *On the envelope, do not include punctuation except for the dash in the ZIP+4 to facilitate the optical character recognition (OCR) processing of correspondence.*

CHAPTER 15
The Personal Letter

Addressee	Address on Letter	Salutation / Complimentary Close
The White House		
The President	The President (Full Name) The White House 1600 Pennsylvania Avenue NW Washington DC 20500	Dear Mr./Madam President Respectfully yours
Spouse of the President	Mr./Mrs. (full name) The White House 1600 Pennsylvania Avenue NW Washington DC 20500	Dear Mr./Mrs. (last name) Sincerely
Assistant or Special Assistant to the President	The Honorable (full name) Assistant (Special Assistant) to the President for (title) The White House 1600 Pennsylvania Avenue NW Washington DC 20500	Dear Mr./Ms. (last name) Sincerely
The Vice President	The Vice President 276 Eisenhower Executive Office Building Washington DC 20501	Dear Mr./Madam Vice President Sincerely
The Vice President As President of the Senate	The Honorable (full name) President of the Senate United States Senate S-212 Capitol Building Washington DC 20510	Dear Mr. President Sincerely
Director, Office of Management and Budget	The Honorable (full name) Director, Office of Management and Budget Washington DC 20503	Dear Mr./Ms. (last name) Sincerely
The Federal Judiciary		
The Chief Justice	The Chief Justice The Supreme Court Washington DC 20543	Dear Chief Justice Sincerely
Associate Justice	The Honorable (full name) The Supreme Court Washington DC 20543	Dear Justice (last name) Sincerely
Retired Justice	The Honorable (full name) (address)	Dear Justice (last name) Sincerely
Judge of a Federal, State, or Local Court	The Honorable (full name) Judge of the (name of court) (address)	Dear Judge (last name) Sincerely
Clerk of a Court	Mr. (full name) Clerk of the (name of court) (address)	Dear Mr./Ms. (last name) Sincerely

The Tongue and Quill
AFH 33-337, 27 MAY 2015

Addressee	Address on Letter	Salutation / Complimentary Close
The Congress Use "+4" codes if available. For Congressional Member individual ZIP+4 Codes, see the *Congressional Staff Directory*. Also see US Senate and US House websites at http://www.senate.gov and http://www.house.gov.		
President pro tempore of the Senate	The Honorable (full name) President pro tempore United States Senate Washington DC 20510-(+4 Code)	Dear Senator (last name) Sincerely
Majority Leader, Senate	The Honorable (full name) Majority Leader United States Senate Washington DC 20510-(+4 Code)	Dear Mr./Madam Majority Leader Sincerely
Committee Chairman, Senate	The Honorable (full name) Chairman Committee on (name of committee) United States Senate Washington DC 20510-(+4 Code)	Dear Mr./Madam Chairman Sincerely
Committee Ranking Member, Senate	The Honorable (full name) Ranking Member Committee on (name of committee) United States Senate Washington DC 20510-(+4 Code)	Dear Senator (last name) Sincerely
Subcommittee Chairman, Senate	The Honorable (full name) Chairman Subcommittee on (name of committee) Committee on (name of full committee) United States Senate Washington DC 20510-(+4 Code)	Dear Mr./Madam Chairman Sincerely
Senator (Washington office)	The Honorable (full name) United States Senate Washington DC 20510-(+4 Code)	Dear Senator (last name) Sincerely
Senator (home state office)	The Honorable (full name) United States Senator (address)	Dear Senator (last name) Sincerely
Senator-elect	Senator-elect (full name) ---or if applicable*--- The Honorable (full name) Senator-elect (address)	Dear Senator-elect (last name) Sincerely
*A Senator-elect may be referred to as "The Honorable" if applicable to the individual's prior or current position.		
Office of a deceased senator	Office of Senator (full name) United States Senate Washington DC 20510-(+4 Code)	Sirs or Dear Mr./Ms. (name of contact) Sincerely

CHAPTER 15
The Personal Letter

Addressee	Address on Letter	Salutation / Complimentary Close
Speaker of the House of Representatives	The Honorable (full name) Speaker of the House US House of Representatives Washington DC 20515-(+4 Code)	Dear Mr./Madam Speaker Sincerely
Majority Leader, House	The Honorable (full name) Majority Leader US House of Representatives Washington DC 20515-(+4 Code)	Dear Mr./Madam Majority Leader Sincerely
Committee Chairman, House of Representatives	The Honorable (full name) Chairman Committee on (name of committee) US House of Representatives Washington DC 20515-(+4 Code)	Dear Mr./Madam Chairman Sincerely
Committee Ranking Member, House of Representatives	The Honorable (full name) Ranking Member Committee on (name of committee) US House of Representatives Washington DC 20515-(+4 Code)	Dear Representative (last name) Sincerely
Subcommittee Chairman, House of Representatives	The Honorable (full name) Chairman Subcommittee on (name of committee) Committee on (name of full committee) US House of Representatives Washington DC 20515-(+4 Code)	Dear Mr./Madam Chairman Sincerely
Representative (Washington office)	The Honorable (full name) US House of Representatives Washington DC 20515-(+4 Code)	Dear Representative (last name) Sincerely
Representative (home state office)	The Honorable (full name) US Representative (address)	Dear Representative (last name) Sincerely
Representative-elect	Representative-elect (full name) ---or if applicable*--- The Honorable (full name) Representative-elect (address)	Dear Representative-elect (last name) Sincerely

*A Representative-elect may be referred to as "The Honorable" if applicable to the individual's prior or current position.

| Office of a deceased representative | Office of the late Honorable (full name)
---or---
Office of the (number of) District of (State)
US House of Representatives
Washington DC 20515-(+4 Code) | Dear Mr./Ms. (name of contact)
Sincerely |

Addressee	Address on Letter	Salutation / Complimentary Close
Resident Commissioner	The Honorable (full name) Resident Commissioner from Puerto Rico US House of Representatives Washington DC 20515-(+4 Code)	Dear Mr./Ms. (last name) Sincerely
Delegate	The Honorable (full name) Delegate from (location) US House of Representatives Washington DC 20515-(+4 Code)	Dear Mr./Ms. (last name) Sincerely

Legislative Agencies

Addressee	Address on Letter	Salutation / Complimentary Close
Comptroller General	The Honorable (full name) Comptroller General of the United States Washington DC 20548	Dear Mr./Ms. (last name) Sincerely
Public Printer	The Honorable (full name) Public Printer US Government Printing Office Washington DC 20401	Dear Mr./Ms. (last name) Sincerely
Librarian of Congress	The Honorable (full name) Librarian of Congress Washington DC 20540	Dear Mr./Ms. (last name) Sincerely

The Executive Departments

For Executive Department Zip+4 Codes, see the *Federal Yellow Book*.

The titles for Cabinet Secretaries are Secretary of Agriculture, Secretary of Commerce, Secretary of Defense, Secretary of Education, Secretary of Energy, Secretary of Health and Human Services, Secretary of Homeland Security, Secretary of Housing and Urban Development, Secretary of the Interior, Attorney General (Department of Justice), Secretary of Labor, Secretary of State, Secretary of Transportation, Secretary of the Treasury, and Secretary of Veteran Affairs.

Addressee	Address on Letter	Salutation / Complimentary Close
Members of the Cabinet addressed as Secretary	The Honorable (full name) Secretary of (Department) Washington DC (ZIP+4 Code)	Dear Mr./Madam Secretary Sincerely
Attorney General	The Honorable (full name) Attorney General Washington DC 20530	Dear Mr./Madam Attorney General Sincerely
Deputy Secretary of a Department	The Honorable (full name) Deputy Secretary of (Department) Washington DC (ZIP+4 Code)	Dear Mr./Ms. (last name) Sincerely
Under Secretary of a Department	The Honorable (full name) Under Secretary of (Department) Washington DC (ZIP+4 Code)	Dear Mr./Ms. (last name) Sincerely
Assistant Secretary of a Department	The Honorable (full name) Assistant Secretary of (Department) Washington DC (ZIP+4 Code)	Dear Mr./Ms. (last name) Sincerely

CHAPTER 15
The Personal Letter

Addressee	Address on Letter	Salutation / Complimentary Close
Deputy Under Secretary of a Department who is Senate-confirmed	The Honorable (full name) Deputy Under Secretary of (Department) Washington DC (ZIP+4 Code)	Dear Mr./Ms. (last name) Sincerely

The Military Departments

Addressee	Address on Letter	Salutation / Complimentary Close
The Secretaries of the Military Departments	The Honorable (full name) Secretary of (Department) Washington DC (ZIP+4 Code)	Dear Mr./Madam Secretary Sincerely
Under Secretary of the Military Department	The Honorable (full name) Under Secretary of (Department) Washington DC (ZIP+4 Code)	Dear Mr./Ms. (last name) Sincerely

Army, Air Force, and Marine Corps Officers

Addressee	Address on Letter	Salutation / Complimentary Close
General, Lieutenant General, Major General, Brigadier General	(full rank) (full name), (Service abbreviation) (address)	Dear General (last name) Sincerely
Colonel, Lieutenant Colonel	(same as above)	Dear Colonel (last name) Sincerely
Major	(same as above)	Dear Major (last name) Sincerely
Captain	(same as above)	Dear Captain (last name) Sincerely
First Lieutenant, Second Lieutenant	(same as above)	Dear Lieutenant (last name) Sincerely
Chief Warrant Officer	(same as above)	Dear Mr./Miss/ Ms./Mrs. (last name) Sincerely

Navy Officers

Addressee	Address on Letter	Salutation / Complimentary Close
Admiral; Vice Admiral; Rear Admiral; Rear Admiral (lower half)	(full rank) (full name), (Service abbreviation) (address)	Dear Admiral (last name) Sincerely
Captain	(same as above)	Dear Captain (last name) Sincerely
Commander, Lieutenant Commander	(same as above)	Dear Commander (last name) Sincerely
Lieutenant, Lieutenant (Junior Grade)	(same as above)	Dear Lieutenant (last name) Sincerely

Addressee	Address on Letter	Salutation / Complimentary Close
Ensign	(same as above)	Dear Ensign (last name) Sincerely
Chief Warrant Officer (Number)	(same as above)	Dear Chief Warrant Officer (last name) Sincerely
Warrant Officer	(same as above)	Dear Warrant Officer (last name) Sincerely

Army Enlisted Personnel

Addressee	Address on Letter	Salutation / Complimentary Close
Sergeant Major of the Army	Sergeant Major of the Army (full name), USA (address)	Dear Sergeant Major (last name) Sincerely
Command Sergeant Major	Command Sergeant Major (full name), USA (address)	Dear Sergeant Major (last name) Sincerely
Sergeant Major	Sergeant Major (full name), USA (address)	Dear Sergeant Major (last name) Sincerely
First Sergeant	First Sergeant (full name), USA (address)	Dear First Sergeant (last name) Sincerely
Master Sergeant	Master Sergeant (full name), USA (address)	Dear Sergeant (last name) Sincerely
Sergeant First Class	Sergeant First Class (full name), USA (address)	Dear Sergeant (last name) Sincerely
Staff Sergeant	Staff Sergeant (full name), USA (address)	Dear Sergeant (last name) Sincerely
Sergeant	Sergeant (full name), USA (address)	Dear Sergeant (last name) Sincerely
Corporal	Corporal (full name), USA (address)	Dear Corporal (last name) Sincerely
Specialists (all grades)	Specialist (full name), USA (address)	Dear Specialist (last name) Sincerely
Private First Class	Private First Class (full name), USA (address)	Dear Private (last name) Sincerely
Private	Private (full name), USA (address)	Dear Private (last name) Sincerely

Navy Enlisted Personnel

Addressee	Address on Letter	Salutation / Complimentary Close
Master Chief Petty Officer of the Navy	Master Chief Petty Officer of the Navy (full name), USN (address)	Dear Master Chief (last name) Sincerely

Addressee	Address on Letter	Salutation / Complimentary Close
Master Chief Petty Officer	Master Chief Petty Officer (full name), USN (address)	Dear Master Chief (last name) Sincerely
Senior Chief Petty Officer	Senior Chief Petty Officer (full name), USN (address)	Dear Senior Chief (last name) Sincerely
Chief Petty Officer	Chief Petty Officer (full name), USN (address)	Dear Chief (last name) Sincerely
Petty Officer First Class	Petty Officer First Class (full name), USN (address)	Dear Petty Officer (last name) Sincerely
Petty Officer Second Class	Petty Officer Second Class (full name), USN (address)	Dear Petty Officer (last name) Sincerely
Petty Officer Third Class	Petty Officer Third Class (full name), USN (address)	Dear Petty Officer (last name) Sincerely
Airman (includes Apprentice and Recruit)	Airman (full name), USN (address)	Dear Airman (last name) Sincerely
Constructionman (includes Apprentice and Recruit)	Constructionman (full name), USN (address)	Dear Constructionman (last name) Sincerely
Dentalman (includes Apprentice and Recruit)	Dentalman (full name), USN (address)	Dear Dentalman (last name) Sincerely
Fireman (includes Apprentice and Recruit)	Fireman (full name), USN (address)	Dear Fireman (last name) Sincerely
Hospital Corpsman (includes Apprentice and Recruit)	Hospital Corpsman (full name), USN (address)	Dear Hospital Corpsman (last name) Sincerely
Seaman (includes Apprentice and Recruit)	Seaman (full name), USN (address)	Dear Seaman (last name) Sincerely

Marine Corps Enlisted Personnel

Addressee	Address on Letter	Salutation / Complimentary Close
Sergeant Major of the Marine Corps	Sergeant Major of the Marine Corps (full name), USMC (address)	Dear Sergeant Major (last name) Sincerely
Sergeant Major	Sergeant Major (full name), USMC (address)	Dear Sergeant Major (last name) Sincerely
Master Gunnery Sergeant	Master Gunnery Sergeant (full name), USMC (address)	Dear Master Gunnery Sergeant (last name) Sincerely
First Sergeant	First Sergeant (full name), USMC (address)	Dear First Sergeant (last name) Sincerely
Master Sergeant	Master Sergeant (full name), USMC (address)	Dear Master Sergeant (last name) Sincerely

Addressee	Address on Letter	Salutation / Complimentary Close
Gunnery Sergeant	Gunnery Sergeant (full name), USMC (address)	Dear Gunnery Sergeant (last name) Sincerely
Staff Sergeant	Staff Sergeant (full name), USMC (address)	Dear Staff Sergeant (last name) Sincerely
Sergeant	Sergeant (full name), USMC (address)	Dear Sergeant (last name) Sincerely
Corporal	Corporal (full name), USMC (address)	Dear Corporal (last name) Sincerely
Lance Corporal	Lance Corporal (full name), USMC (address)	Dear Corporal (last name) Sincerely
Private First Class	Private First Class (full name), USMC (address)	Dear Private First Class (last name) Sincerely
Private	Private (full name), USMC (address)	Dear Private (last name) Sincerely

Air Force Enlisted Personnel

Addressee	Address on Letter	Salutation / Complimentary Close
Chief Master Sergeant of the Air Force	Chief Master Sergeant of the Air Force (full name), USAF (address)	Dear Chief (last name) Sincerely
Chief Master Sergeant	Chief Master Sergeant (full name), USAF (address)	Dear Chief (last name) Sincerely
Senior Master Sergeant	Senior Master Sergeant (full name), USAF (address)	Dear Sergeant (last name) Sincerely
Master Sergeant	Master Sergeant (full name), USAF (address)	Dear Sergeant (last name) Sincerely
Technical Sergeant	Technical Sergeant (full name), USAF (address)	Dear Sergeant (last name) Sincerely
Staff Sergeant	Staff Sergeant (full name), USAF (address)	Dear Sergeant (last name) Sincerely
Senior Airman	Senior Airman (full name), USAF (address)	Dear Airman (last name) Sincerely
Airman First Class	Airman First Class (full name), USAF (address)	Dear Airman (last name) Sincerely
Airman	Airman (full name), USAF (address)	Dear Airman (last name) Sincerely
Airman Basic	Airman Basic (full name), USAF (address)	Dear Airman (last name) Sincerely

CHAPTER 15
The Personal Letter

Addressee	Address on Letter	Salutation / Complimentary Close
Other Military Personnel		
All retired military personnel	(rank) (full name), (Service abbreviation) (Ret) (address)	Dear (rank) (last name) Sincerely
Cadet	Cadet (full name) (address)	Dear Cadet (last name) Sincerely
Midshipman	Midshipman (full name) (address)	Dear Midshipman (last name) Sincerely
Air Cadet	Air Cadet (full name) (address)	Dear Air Cadet (last name) Sincerely

Independent Agencies

A Military head of a Federal agency, authority, or board shall be addressed by military rank.

Addressee	Address on Letter	Salutation / Complimentary Close
Head of a Federal Agency, Authority, or Board	The Honorable (full name) (title) (agency) Washington DC (ZIP+4 Code)	Dear Mr./Ms. (last name) Sincerely
President of a Commission or Board	The Honorable (full name) President, (name of commission) Washington DC (ZIP+4 Code)	Dear Mr./Ms. (last name) Sincerely
Chairman of a Commission or Board	The Honorable (full name) Chairman, (name of commission) Washington DC (ZIP+4 Code)	Dear Mr./Madam Chairman Sincerely
Postmaster General	The Honorable (full name) Postmaster General 475 L'Enfant Plaza West SW Washington DC 20260	Dear Mr./Madam Postmaster General Sincerely

American Missions

Addressee	Address on Letter	Salutation / Complimentary Close
American Ambassador	The Honorable (full name) American Ambassador (city), (country) (address)	Dear Mr./Madam Ambassador Sincerely
American Ambassador (with military rank)	(Full rank) (full name) American Ambassador (city), (country) (address)	Dear (rank) (last name) Sincerely
Personal/Special Representative of the President	The Honorable (full name) Personal Representative of the President of the United States of America to (country) (address)	Dear Mr./Ms. (last name) Sincerely

Addressee	Address on Letter	Salutation / Complimentary Close
American Foreign Service Officer with personal rank of Minister	The Honorable (full name) (rank: Minister Counselor or Counselor) American Embassy (address)	Dear Mr./Ms. (last name) Sincerely
American Minister (with military rank)	(full rank) (full name) (title) American Embassy (address)	Dear (rank) (last name) Sincerely
American Consul General, Consul, or Vice Consul	Mr./Ms. (full name) American Consul General (or Consul or Vice Consul) (address)	Dear Mr./Ms. (last name) Sincerely
US Political Advisor	The Honorable (full name) United States Political Advisor for (country) (address)	Dear Mr./Ms. (last name) Sincerely

Foreign Diplomatic Missions to the United States

Addressee	Address on Letter	Salutation / Complimentary Close
Foreign Ambassador in the United States	His/Her Excellency (full name) Ambassador of (country) Washington DC (ZIP+4 Code)	Dear Mr./Madam Ambassador Sincerely
Foreign Minister in the United States (head of a delegation)	The Honorable (full name) Minister of (country) Washington DC (ZIP +4 Code)	Dear Mr./Madam Minister Sincerely
Foreign Minister Counselor in the United States	The Honorable (full name) Minister Counselor Embassy of (country) Washington DC (ZIP +4 Code)	Dear Mr./Madam Minister Sincerely
Foreign Chargé d'Affaires in the United States	Mr./Madam (full name) Chargé d'Affaires of (country) (address)	Dear Mr./Madam Chargé d'Affaires Sincerely

International Organizations

Addressee	Address on Letter	Salutation / Complimentary Close
Organization with no US Representative*	The (title of officer) of the (organization name) (address)	Dear Sir/Madam Sincerely

*Address communications to the ranking officer of an international organization that has no full-time US representative.

Addressee	Address on Letter	Salutation / Complimentary Close
Secretary General of the Organization of American States	The Honorable (full name)* Secretary General of the Organization of American States Washington DC 20006	Dear Mr./Madam Secretary General Sincerely

*Address officials as "The Honorable" unless otherwise entitled to "His [or] Her Excellency."

CHAPTER 15
The Personal Letter

Addressee	Address on Letter	Salutation / Complimentary Close
Assistant Secretary General of the Organization of American States	The Honorable (full name) Assistant Secretary General of the Organization of American States Washington DC 20006	Dear Mr./Ms. (last name) Sincerely
United States Representative on the Council of the Organization of American States	The Honorable (full name), US Representative on the Council of the Organization of American States Washington DC 20520	Dear Mr./Ms. (last name) Sincerely

United Nations

Address communications for the United Nations to the US Representative to the United Nations, through the Department of State. Direct communication with the United Nations is inappropriate. Send all notes for the United Nations through the US Representative with a cover note with appropriate instruction. Address officials as "The Honorable" unless otherwise entitled to "His [or] Her Excellency."

Addressee	Address on Letter	Salutation / Complimentary Close
Secretary General of the United Nations	The Honorable (full name) Secretary General of the United Nations New York NY 10017	Dear Mr./Madam Secretary General Sincerely
US Representative to the United Nations	The Honorable (full name) United States Representative to the United Nations New York NY 10017	Dear Mr./Ms. Ambassador (last name) Sincerely
Chairman, US Delegation to the UN Military Staff Committee	The Honorable (full name) Chairman, United States Delegation United Nations Military Staff Committee United States Mission to the United Nations New York NY 10017	Dear Mr./Ms. (last name) Sincerely
US Senior Representative to the UN General Assembly	The Honorable (full name) Senior Representative of the United States to the General Assembly of the United Nations New York NY 10017	Dear Mr./Ms. (last name) Sincerely
Senior Military Adviser to the US Delegation to the UN General Assembly	(Full rank) (full name) Senior Military Adviser to the United States Delegation to the United Nations General Assembly New York NY 10017	Dear (rank) (last name) Sincerely
US Representative on the UN Economic and Social Council	The Honorable (full name) United States Representative to the Economic and Social Council of the United Nations New York NY 10017	Dear Mr./Ms. (last name) Sincerely

Addressee	Address on Letter	Salutation / Complimentary Close
US Representative on the UN Disarmament Commission	The Honorable (full name) United States Representative on the Disarmament Commission of the United Nations New York NY 10017	Dear Mr./Ms. (last name) Sincerely
US Representative to the UN Trusteeship Council	The Honorable (full name) United States Representative on the Trusteeship Council of the United Nations New York NY 10017	Dear Mr./Ms. (last name) Sincerely

State and Local Government

Addressee	Address on Letter	Salutation / Complimentary Close
State Governor	The Honorable (full name) Governor of (State) City ST (ZIP +4 Code)	Dear Governor (last name) Sincerely
Acting State Governor	The Honorable (full name) Acting Governor of (State) City ST (ZIP +4 Code)	Dear Mr./Ms. (last name) Sincerely
State Lieutenant Governor	The Honorable (full name) Lieutenant Governor of (State) City ST (ZIP +4 Code)	Dear Mr./Ms. (last name) Sincerely
State Secretary of State	The Honorable (full name) Secretary of State of (State) City ST (ZIP +4 Code)	Dear Mr./Madam (last name) Sincerely
Chief Justice of a State Supreme Court	The Honorable (full name) Chief Justice Supreme Court of the State of (State) City ST (ZIP +4 Code)	Dear Mr./Madam Chief Justice Sincerely
State Attorney General	The Honorable (full name) Attorney General State of (State) City ST (ZIP +4 Code)	Dear Mr./Madam Attorney General Sincerely
State Treasurer, Comptroller, or Auditor	The Honorable (full name) State (Treasurer, Comptroller, or Auditor) State of (State) City ST (ZIP +4 Code)	Dear Mr./Ms. (last name) Sincerely
President, State Senate	The Honorable (full name) President of the Senate of the State of (State) City ST (ZIP +4 Code)	Dear Mr./Ms. (last name) Sincerely
State Senator	The Honorable (full name) (State) Senate City ST (ZIP +4 Code)	Dear Mr./Ms. (last name) Sincerely

CHAPTER 15
The Personal Letter

Addressee	Address on Letter	Salutation / Complimentary Close
Speaker, State House of Representatives, Assembly or House of Delegates*	The Honorable (full name) Speaker of the (Legislature's name*) of the State of (State) City ST (ZIP +4 Code)	Dear Mr./Ms. (last name) Sincerely
State Representative, Assemblyman, or Delegate*	The Honorable (full name) (State) (Legislature's name*) City ST (ZIP +4 Code)	Dear Mr./Ms. (last name) Sincerely

*In most States, the lower branch of the legislature is the House of Representatives. In some States, such as California and New York, the lower house is known as the Assembly. In others, such as Maryland, Virginia, and West Virginia, it is known as the House of Delegates. Nebraska has a one-house legislature; its members are classed as senators.

Addressee	Address on Letter	Salutation / Complimentary Close
Mayor	The Honorable (full name) Mayor of (city) City ST (ZIP +4 Code)	Dear Mayor (last name) Sincerely
President of a Board of Commissioners	The Honorable (full name) President, Board of Commissioners of (city) City ST (ZIP +4 Code)	Dear Mr./Ms. (last name) Sincerely

Ecclesiastical Organizations

Addressee	Address on Letter	Salutation / Complimentary Close
Catholic Cardinal	His Eminence (first name) Cardinal (last name) (address)	Dear Cardinal (last name) Sincerely
Catholic Archbishop	The Most Reverend (full name) Archbishop of (archdiocese) (address)	Dear Archbishop (last name) Sincerely
Catholic Bishop	The Most Reverend (full name) Bishop of (place) (address)	Dear Bishop (last name) Sincerely
Catholic Monsignor	The Reverend Monsignor (full name) (address)	Dear Monsignor (last name) Sincerely
Catholic Priest	The Reverend (full name), (initials of order) (address)	Dear Father (last name) (informal) Sincerely
Catholic Mother Superior of an Institution	Reverend Mother (full name), (initials of order) (name of institution) (address)	Dear Reverend Mother Sincerely
Catholic Sister	Sister (full name), (initials of order) (name of organization) (address)	Dear Sister (first name) Sincerely
Catholic Brother	Brother (full name), (initials of order) (organization) (address)	Dear Brother (first name) Sincerely
Episcopal Archdeacon	The Venerable (full name) Archdeacon of (place) (address)	Dear Archdeacon (last name) Sincerely

Addressee	Address on Letter	Salutation / Complimentary Close
Episcopal Dean	The Very Reverend (full name), (initials of degree) Dean of (place) (address)	Dear Dean (last name) Sincerely
Methodist Bishop	The Reverend (full name) Bishop of (place) (address)	Dear Bishop (last name) Sincerely
Mormon Bishop	Mr. (full name) The Church of Jesus Christ of Latter-Day Saints (address)	Dear Mr. (last name) Sincerely
Army Chaplain	Chaplain (rank in parenthesis) (full name), USA (address)	Dear Chaplain (last name) Sincerely
Navy Chaplain	Rank (full name) CHC, USN (address)	Dear Chaplain (last name) Sincerely
Air Force Chaplain	Chaplain (rank) (full name), USAF (address)	Dear Chaplain (last name) Sincerely
Marine Corps Chaplain	Chaplain (rank) (full name), USMC (address)	Dear Chaplain (last name) Sincerely
Minister, Pastor, or Rector (with doctoral degree)	The Reverend Dr. (full name) (address)	Dear Dr. (last name) Sincerely
Minster, Pastor, or Rector (without doctoral degree)	The Reverend (full name) (address)	Dear Reverend (last name) Sincerely
Rabbi (with doctoral degree)	Rabbi (full name), (initials of degree) (address)	Dear Dr. (last name) Sincerely
Rabbi (without doctoral degree)	Rabbi (full name) (address)	Dear Rabbi (last name) Sincerely

Private Citizens

Addressee	Address on Letter	Salutation / Complimentary Close
University or college president (with doctoral degree)	Dr. (full name) President, (name of institution) (address)	Dear Dr. (last name) Sincerely
University or college president (without a doctoral degree)	Mr. (full name) President, (name of institution) (address)	Dear Mr./Ms. (last name) Sincerely
Dean of a school (with doctoral degree)	Dr. (full name) Dean, School of (name) (name of institution) (address)	Dear Dr. (last name) Sincerely

CHAPTER 15
The Personal Letter

Addressee	Address on Letter	Salutation / Complimentary Close
Dean of a school (without doctoral degree)	Dean (full name), School of (name) (name of institution) (address)	Dear Dean (last name) Sincerely
Professor* (with doctoral degree)	Dr. (or Professor) (full name) Department of (name) (name of institution) (address)	Dear Dr. (last name) Sincerely
Professor* (without doctoral degree)	Professor (full name) Department of (name) (name of institution) (address)	Dear Professor (last name) Sincerely
Associate Professor* or Assistant Professor* (with doctoral degree)	Dr. (or Professor) (full name) Associate (or Assistant) Professor Department of (name) (name of institution) (address)	Dear Professor (last name) Sincerely
Associate Professor* or Assistant Professor* (without doctoral degree)	Mr./Ms. (full name) Associate (or Assistant) Professor Department of (name) (name of institution) (address)	Dear Professor (last name) Sincerely

*Professor, Associate Professor, and Assistant Professor are academic ranks that may be held with or without a doctoral degree, depending on the position and university policies. "Dr." denotes the award of a doctoral degree and is usually the preferred title by those holding a doctoral degree.

Addressee	Address on Letter	Salutation / Complimentary Close
Physician	(Full name), MD (address)	Dear Dr. (last name) Sincerely
Lawyer	Mr./Ms. (full name) Attorney at Law (address)	Dear Mr./Ms. (last name) Sincerely
One individual	Mr. (full name) Mrs. (full name) Miss (full name) Ms. (full name) (address)	Dear Mr. (last name) Dear Mrs. (last name) Dear Miss (last name) Dear Ms. (last name) Sincerely
Two individuals: Married, no special title	Mr. and Mrs. (full name) (address)	Dear Mr. and Mrs. (last name) Sincerely
Two individuals (men): No relationship specified	Mr. (full name) and Mr. (full name) (address)	Dear Mr. (last name) and Mr. (last name) Sincerely
Two individuals (women) No relationship specified	Mrs. (full name) and Miss (full name) (address)	Dear Mrs. (last name) and Miss (last name) Sincerely

Addressee	Address on Letter	Salutation / Complimentary Close
Two individuals: Marital status and relationship not specified	Ms. (full name) and Mr. (full name) (address)	Dear Ms. (last name) and Mr. (last name) Sincerely
Two individuals (women): Marital status and relationship not specified	Ms. (full name) and Ms. (full name) (address)	Dear Ms. (last name) and Ms. (last name) Sincerely
Three or more individuals: Men	Messieurs (full name) and (full name) and (full name) (address)	Gentlemen ---or--- Sirs ---or--- Dear Messieurs (last name) and (last name) and (last name) Sincerely
Three or more individuals: Married Women	Mesdames (full name) and (full name) and (full name) (address)	Dear Mesdames (last name) and (last name) and (last name) Sincerely
Three or more individuals: Unmarried Women	Misses (full name) and (full name) and (full name) ---or--- The Misses (last name), (last name), and (last name) (address)	Dear Misses (last name) and (last name) and (last name) Sincerely
Three or more individuals: Same last name	Messieurs (given names), Mesdames (given names), and Misses (given names) (last name) (address)	Dear Messieurs, Mesdames, and Misses (last name) Sincerely
Married couple, same last name: husband has special title	Dr. and Mrs. (husband's full name) (address)	Dear Dr. and Mrs. (husband's last name) Sincerely
Married couple, same last name: wife has special title	Senator (wife's full name) Mr. (husband's full name) (address)	Dear Senator and Mr. (last name) Sincerely
Married couple, same last name: both have special titles	Captain (husband's full name) Professor (wife's full name) (address)	Dear Captain and Professor (last name) Sincerely
Married couple, different last names	Ms. (wife's full name) Mr. (husband's full name) (address)	Dear Ms. (wife's last name) and Mr. (husband's last name) Sincerely
Married couple, hyphenated last name	Mr. and Mrs. (husband's first name and middle initial, plus wife's original last name followed by hyphen and husband's last name) (address)	Dear Mr. and Mrs. (wife's original last name followed by hyphen and husband's last name) Sincerely
Organizations	Members (organization name) (address)	Dear Members Sincerely

CHAPTER 15
The Personal Letter

Addressee	Address on Letter	Salutation / Complimentary Close
Informal Groups	Mr. (full name) First Grade Jefferson Elementary School (address)	Dear Students Sincerely

Former Government Officials

Addressee	Address on Letter	Salutation / Complimentary Close
Former President (no title used in address)	The Honorable (full name) (address)	Dear Mr./Ms. (last name) Respectfully yours,
Former Vice President (no title used in address)	The Honorable (full name) (address)	Dear Mr. (last name) Sincerely
Former Member of the Cabinet addressed as "Secretary"	The Honorable (full name) (address)	Dear Mr./Madam Secretary Sincerely
Former Attorney General	The Honorable (full name) (address)	Dear Mr./Madam Attorney General Sincerely
Former Secretary of a Military Department	The Honorable (full name) (address)	Dear Mr./Ms. (last name) Sincerely
Former Postmaster General	The Honorable (full name) (address)	Dear Mr./Madam Postmaster General Sincerely
Former Senator	The Honorable (full name) (address)	Dear Senator (last name) Sincerely
Former Representative	The Honorable (full name) (address)	Dear Representative (last name) Sincerely
Former Justice	The Honorable (full name) (address)	Dear Mr./Madam Justice Sincerely
Former Judge	The Honorable (full name) (address)	Dear Judge (last name) Sincerely

Military Ranks and Abbreviations

Do you know the differences in the ranks of the Services? The *DoD Manual for Written Material* also provides tables that present the pay grade, rank and rank abbreviations for all pay grades in all the Services. These tables have been extracted and included in this handbook (reformatted for conformity) for your ready reference. Take the time to learn the ranks of the other Services ... and the proper abbreviations for them as well. Using the proper rank in your communications with others demonstrates your professional attitude and commands respect from others.

Military Ranks and Abbreviations, Officers

Pay Grade	Army		Navy		Marine Corps		Air Force	
O-10	General	GEN	Admiral	ADM	General	Gen	General	Gen
O-9	Lieutenant General	LTG	Vice Admiral	VADM	Lieutenant General	LtGen	Lieutenant General	Lt Gen
O-8	Major General	MG	Rear Admiral	RADM	Major General	MajGen	Major General	Maj Gen
O-7	Brigadier General	BG	Rear Admiral	RDML[2]	Brigadier General	BGen	Brigadier General	Brig Gen
O-6	Colonel	COL	Captain	CAPT	Colonel	Col	Colonel	Col
O-5	Lieutenant Colonel	LTC	Commander	CDR	Lieutenant Colonel	LtCol	Lieutenant Colonel	Lt Col
O-4	Major	MAJ	Lieutenant Commander	LCDR	Major	Maj	Major	Maj
O-3	Captain	CPT	Lieutenant	LT	Captain	Capt	Captain	Capt
O-2	First Lieutenant	1LT	Lieutenant Junior Grade	LTJG	First Lieutenant	1st Lt	First Lieutenant	1st Lt
O-1	Second Lieutenant	2LT	Ensign	ENS	Second Lieutenant	2nd Lt	Second Lieutenant	2d Lt
W-5	Chief Warrant Officer	CW5[1]			Chief Warrant Officer 5	CWO-5		
W-4	Chief Warrant Officer 4	CW4	Chief Warrant Officer 4	CWO4	Chief Warrant Officer 4	CWO-4		
W-3	Chief Warrant Officer 3	CW3	Chief Warrant Officer 3	CWO3	Chief Warrant Officer 3	CWO-3		
W-2	Chief Warrant Officer 2	CW2	Chief Warrant Officer 2	CWO2	Chief Warrant Officer 2	CWO-2		
W-1	Warrant Officer 1	WO1	Warrant Officer	WO1	Chief Warrant Officer 1	CWO-1		

[1] The Army used Master Warrant Officer at one time; "Master" now indicates a transitional rank; all Army Warrant Officers are Chief Warrant Officers.
[2] The Navy Rear Admiral rank contains two levels: upper half, equal to a two-star flag officer, and lower half, equal to a one-star flag officer. The rank of Commodore was a commissioned one-star rank during time of war. The commander of a fleet of ships is sometimes referred to as "Commodore" as a courtesy title. The rank no longer exists and the title is never officially used.

CHAPTER 15
The Personal Letter

Military Ranks and Abbreviations, Enlisted

Pay Grade	Army		Navy		Marine Corps		Air Force	
E-9	Sergeant Major of the Army	SMA	Master Chief Petty Officer of the Navy	MCPON	Sergeant Major of the Marine Corps	SgtMajMC	Chief Master Sergeant of the Air Force	CMSAF
	Command Sergeant Major	CSM	Master Chief Petty Officer	MCPO	Sergeant Major	Sgt Maj	Chief Master Sergeant	CMSgt
	Sergeant Major	SGM			Master Gunnery Sergeant	MGySgt		
E-8	First Sergeant	1SG	Senior Chief Petty Officer	SCPO	First Sergeant	1stSgt	Senior Master Sergeant	SMSgt
	Master Sergeant	MSG			Master Sergeant	MSgt		
E-7	Sergeant First Class	SFC	Chief Petty Officer	CPO	Gunnery Sergeant	GySgt	Master Sergeant	MSgt
E-6	Staff Sergeant	SSG	Petty Officer 1	PO1	Staff Sergeant	SSgt	Technical Sergeant	TSgt
E-5	Sergeant	SGT	Petty Officer 2	PO2	Sergeant	Sgt	Staff Sergeant	SSgt
E-4	Corporal	CPL	Petty Officer 3	PO3	Corporal	Cpl	Senior Airman	SrA
	Specialist	SPC						
E-3	Private First Class	PFC	Seaman	SN	Lance Corporal	LCpl	Airman First Class	A1C
E-2	Private	PV2	Seaman Apprentice	SA	Private First Class	PFC	Airman	Amn
E-1	Private	PVT	Seaman Recruit	SR	Private	Pvt	Airman Basic	AB

The Personal Letter: Examples

The following personal letters are examples only. Due to the nearly infinite possible combinations of sender and receiver—not to mention the countless types of messages—it is essential to follow the guidance in the previous pages and to consult with your executive staff for tips and techniques specific to your work setting. The first example is a personal letter written in response to a notional inquiry about the format and purpose of the personal letter. This is followed by several "thank you" letters—one with formatting shown; one with an attachment and courtesy copy; and two finished product samples.

- 213 -

A Personal Letter on the Format for a Personal Letter

DEPARTMENT OF THE AIR FORCE
[APPROVED ORGANIZATIONAL LETTERHEAD]

¶ [1.75 inches from top of page; flush with the right margin] 31 July 2014
¶

Colonel Author A. Tome, USAF ¶ [Sender: Second line below the date]
Duty Title ¶
Organization
Street Address ¶
City ST 12345-6789 ¶ [No punctuation between city and state; two spaces between ST and ZIP]
¶
¶

Master Sergeant Getty A. Letter, USAF ¶ [Receiver: Third line below the Sender's address]
Duty Title ¶
Organization
Street Address ¶
City ST 12345-6789 ¶ [No punctuation between city and state; two spaces between ST and ZIP]
¶

Dear Sergeant Letter ¶ [Second line below receiver's address; no punctuation]
¶

  Thank you for inquiring about the Air Force format and purpose for personal letters. First, the format for a personal letter is detailed in Air Force Manual (AFM) 33-337, *The Tongue and Quill*, and begins by using only approved organizational letterhead. Second, the purpose of a personal letter is to convey official information in a personal manner to a limited number of people. Thus, the personal letter is useful for personal responses to inquiries (such as this letter), welcome letters, letters of appreciation, letters of condolence, etc. ¶
¶

  In addition to using only approved letterhead, the standard font style is Times New Roman and the standard point size is 12 points. The standard margins are 1.75 inches on the top for the first page and 1 inch on the left, right, and bottom. If the letter is longer than a single page, use 1 inch margins for the top, left, right, and bottom for the second and subsequent pages. ¶

  The formats for the heading elements (date, return address, receiver's address, and salutation) are important: they convey attention to detail and professionalism. Place the date on the first line in the upper-right hand corner so that the date is flush with the right margin. Next, place the full rank and full name of the sender on the second line below the date followed by the sender's duty title and mailing address. On the third line below the sender's mailing address, place the full rank and full name of the receiver followed by the receiver's duty title and mailing address. Do not use a comma to separate the city from the state abbreviation. The salutation is placed on the second line below the receiver's address with the appropriate form for the rank (refer to the "Forms of Address, Salutation, and Close" in *The Tongue and Quill*) followed by the receiver' last name. Finally, punctuation is not used after the receiver's last name. ¶
¶

  For the body of the personal letter, the paragraphs are indented 0.5 inches from the left margin but they are not numbered. Following the body, include a complimentary close on the ¶

[Page numbers are placed 0.5 inches from the top and flush with right margin] 2

second line below the last line of text as shown in *The Tongue and Quill*, "Forms of Address, Salutation, and Complimentary Close" tables. These tables are drawn from formats used by the Department of Defense for everyone from the President of the United States to your neighbor down the street.

  The final paragraph of a personal letter may include the sender's contact information. Contact information is optional and depends on the purpose of the letter. Contact information, if shown, customarily includes the digital switched network (DSN) telephone number, commercial telephone number, and official email address.

  The signature block for the personal letter is placed on the fifth line below the complimentary close, 4.5 inches from the left edge (another means to place the signature block is to go to the center of the page and then space three times: either method is acceptable). The four blank lines provide ample space for the actual signature. For a personal letter, the duty title of the sender is not used and, although it is rare for a personal letter to extend beyond a single page, letters of 3 or more pages include page numbers on the second page onwards: the first page is never numbered. A two-page letter may include a page number on the second page or it may be omitted since the order of the pages is self-explanatory. When used, page numbers are placed in the upper right-hand corner of the page, 0.5 inches from the top. Finally, the attachment and courtesy copy elements for the personal letter, if used, are as shown, below.

  I hope this answers any questions you had about the purpose and format of the personal letter. If I can be of further assistance, please do not hesitate to contact me by phone at DSN 999-9999 or commercial (999) 999-9999, or via email at author.tome@us.af.mil.

[Second line below text; 4.5 inches from left edge]   Sincerely [No punctuation]

[Fifth line below close; 4.5 inches from left edge]   AUTHOR A. TOME, Colonel, USAF
                  [Duty title *optional* for personal letters]

Attachment: [Third line below signature block] [If none, delete entire element]
[Attachment description, date]

cc: [Second line below last line of attachment element or third line below signature block]
[Rank and name, office symbol, or both] [If none, delete entire element]

[Use 1-inch left, right, top, and bottom margins for page 2 onwards]

Personal Letter: Single Paragraph, Formatting Shown

DEPARTMENT OF THE AIR FORCE
[APPROVED ORGANIZATIONAL LETTERHEAD]

[1.75 inches from top of page; flush with the right margin] 6 June 2014

Chief Master Sergeant Tina B. Green, USAF [Sender: Second line below the date]
Duty Title
Organization
Street Address
City ST 12345-6789 [No punctuation between city and state; two spaces between ST and ZIP]

Master Sergeant Martin O. Grace, USAF [Receiver: Third line below the Sender's address]
Duty Title
Organization
Street Address
City ST 12345-6789 [No punctuation between city and state; two spaces between ST and ZIP]

Dear Sergeant Grace [Second line below receiver's address; no punctuation]

    Thank you for your presentation at our squadron's recent Commander's Call on the local services available to our wounded warriors. The sons and daughters of our community have given so much in the defense of our great nation and now the local community has a chance to give back to them in their time of need due, in large part, to your efforts. Your initiative has opened many doors for our returning heroes to get not only the services they need but to find employment in the community they love. Many of our Airmen, motivated by your presentation, are reaching out to help other local veterans through volunteer work. Your dedication and professionalism are inspirational examples for others to follow. Again, thank you.

[Second line below text; 4.5 inches from left edge]   Sincerely [No punctuation]

[Fifth line below close; 4.5 inches from left edge]   *Tina B. Green*
   TINA B. GREEN, CMSgt, USAF
   [Duty title *optional* for personal letters]

Attachment: [Third line below signature block] [If none, delete entire element]
Chamber of Commerce Letter of Appreciation, 30 May 14

cc: [Second line below last line of attachment element] [If none, delete entire element]
19 AW/CCC

[1-inch left, right, and bottom margins]

Personal Letter: Short Text, Formatting Shown

DEPARTMENT OF THE AIR FORCE
[APPROVED ORGANIZATIONAL LETTERHEAD]

[1.75 inches from top of page; flush with the right margin] 6 June 2014

Chief Master Sergeant Thomas D. Booker, USAF ¶ [Sender: Second line below the date]
Duty Title ¶
Organization ¶
Street Address ¶
City ST 12345-6789 ¶ [No punctuation between city and state; two spaces between ST and ZIP]

Master Sergeant Joan C. Persons, USAF ¶ [Receiver: Third line below the Sender's address]
Duty Title ¶
Organization ¶
Street Address ¶
City ST 12345-6789 ¶ [No punctuation between city and state; two spaces between ST and ZIP]

Dear Sergeant Persons ¶ [Second line below receiver's address; no punctuation]

　　　　I just confirmed some additional information on the format for personal letters with the *Tongue and Quill* editor. The text of personal letters is normally single-paced; however, you may double-space the text of a one-paragraph letter with less than eight lines of text to visually balance the page. Similarly, including the duty title in the signature block adds balance to short letters or closure in lengthy letters; omitting the duty title may keep the letter on a single page. The choice is yours. ¶

¶ [Second line below text; 4.5 inches from left edge]   Sincerely [No punctuation]

¶ [Fifth line below close; 4.5 inches from left edge]   *Thomas D. Booker*
　　　　　　　　　　　　　　　　　　　　　　　　　　THOMAS D. BOOKER, CMSgt, USAF
　　　　　　　　　　　　　　　　　　　　　　　　　　Superintendent, Information Management
　　　　　　　　　　　　　　　　　　　　　　　　　　　and Publications Policy

[1-inch left, right, and bottom margins]

Personal Letter: Final Form

DEPARTMENT OF THE AIR FORCE
AIR UNIVERSITY (AETC)

16 January 2014

Colonel Charles A. Peters
Commander, Squadron Officer College
125 Chennault Circle
Maxwell AFB AL 36112-6430

Mr. Alan R. Humphrey
Program Executive Officer, Business and Enterprise Systems Directorate
490 East Moore Drive
Maxwell AFB Gunter Annex AL 36114

Dear Mr. Humphrey

    Thank you for taking time out of your schedule to speak with Squadron Officer School (SOS) on the importance of personal and professional development. Your insight as a former Active Duty officer for almost 30 years, combined with experience as an Air Force civilian, provided clear and lasting lessons for SOS students to emulate. The words you shared on embracing the opportunities provided by every new assignment are timeless. The students especially appreciated your thoughts on integrating uniformed personnel with the civilian force. Sharing your experience with SOS students provided them a shining example of what it truly means to be a leader and warrior both in and out of uniform for today's Total Force.

    Again, thank you for your superb contribution to and support for SOS. It is great having you on the Squadron Officer College team as we provide company grade officers with premier leadership development opportunities.

                                            Sincerely

                                        CHARLES A. PETERS, Colonel, USAF

CHAPTER 16:

Air Force "Papers"

> *This chapter covers:*
> - Form and Function
> - Point Paper
> - Talking Paper (TP)
> - Bullet Background Paper (BBP)
> - Background Paper
> - Position Paper

The Air Force uses written products ("papers") in many forms for everyday staff work to serve a variety of functions. The functions they serve are not unique to the Air Force, but the format of a talking paper from one Air Force unit to the next should be the same. The goal of this chapter is to clarify and set the Air Force standards for these papers. These standards apply to the young and old alike: check your work to ensure your papers meet the format standard while also answering the mail for the task requiring the paper in the first place. The sample papers in this chapter contain the guidance for how to build each paper, respectively. For example, the point paper sample is about writing a point paper. It contains guidance in the narrative on how to write a point paper as well as a visual example of a finished point paper.

Form and Function

Where possible, the papers use the same or similar formats; however, there are key differences since these papers all serve different functions, much like traffic signs can have similar characteristics but serve different functions. For example, "STOP" and "YIELD" signs are both red to alert us to an intersection but the shape and the text are different: drivers are *expected* to act differently at a STOP sign then they are at a YIELD sign. The same concept holds true for Air Force documents: the format supports the function. Know the different functions of Air Force documents and use the right paper for the task.

Plan your work

The text of your written products will be better if you build it with a plan, such as the seven steps to effective communication presented in chapters 2 through 7. With good source materials you can build your content as either bullet statements (bullets) for the point paper, talking paper and bullet background paper; or as narrative for the other papers. Building better bullets (or sentences) requires discipline and following a few fundamental rules (see chapter 19 for details).

The ABS of bullets

First, all bullet statements must be accurate, brief and specific (ABS). Because there is very little text in a bullet, the text used must be unequivocal (accurate) while being as short as possible (brief) to convey a tightly-focused (specific) point. Second, use the correct type of bullet for the desired purpose–the single idea bullet or the accomplishment-impact bullet.

Single Idea Bullets

A single idea bullet is a concisely written statement of a single idea or concept. Single idea bullets have exactly one idea in the bullet and the bullet serves a specific purpose. Single idea bullets are commonly used in Point Papers and Talking Papers. They may also be used in Bullet Background Papers; however, the bullets in Bullet Background Papers frequently have more content within the bullet to support the single idea. See the example papers later in this chapter.

Accomplishment-Impact Bullets

An accomplishment-impact bullet is a concisely written statement of a person's single accomplishment and its impact on the unit's mission, operations or other related tasks. Accomplishment-impact bullets are typically used in performance reports, recommendations and award submissions to describe someone's work performance or noteworthy off-duty pursuits. However, an accomplishment-impact bullet may be appropriate for the written products described in chapter 16, depending on the purpose and audience. As the name implies, accomplishment-impact bullets contain a clear statement of a single accomplishment that had an impact on the mission, operations or other related tasks. The impact can be implied or specified and should be clear to all readers. Specific impacts should place the accomplishment into perspective (large or small).

1. The Accomplishment Element: Briefly describes the person's actions or behavior.
    a. What did the person (or group) do?
    b. What was the success (or, less often, the failure)?
2. The Impact Element: Describes the results of the accomplishment and it may be either expressly stated or implied. The impact element is vital to describing the relative importance of the action.
    a. What is the impact on the mission (squadron, group, wing, command, Air Force)?
    b. Is this impact statement accurate in scope and strength?
    c. Does it put things into perspective?

Form and Function Quick Reference Table

Form	Function
Point Paper • Single issue • Single page • *Bullets* or phrases • Minimal data	Memory jogger: minimal text outline of a single issue to quickly inform others extemporaneously (no-notice) • Conveys a single, narrow message in a very short time, such as with an "elevator speech" • Give the same short message many times • Requires prior research and content memorization
Talking Paper (TP) • Single issue • Single page • *Bullets* or phrases • Key reference data	Speaking notes: outlines and narrates a single issue to inform others during planned/scheduled oral presentations • Serves as a quick reference on key points, facts, positions • Addresses frequently asked questions • Can stand alone for basic understanding of the issue
Bullet Background Paper (BBP) • Single issue or several related issues and impact • Single or multi-page • *Bullet* statements	Background of a program, policy, problem or procedure; may be a single issue or combination of several related issues • Concise chronology of program, policy, problem, etc. • Summarizes an attached staff package • Explains or details an attached talking paper
Background Paper • Single issue or several related issues and impact • Multi-page • Full sentences, details • Numbered paragraphs	Multipurpose staff communications instrument to express ideas or describe conditions that require a particular staff action • Detailed chronology of program, policy, problem, etc. • Condenses and summarizes complex issues • Provides background research for oral presentations or staff discussions; informs decision makers with details
Position Paper • Single issue or several related issues and impact • Multi-page • Full sentences, details • Numbered paragraphs	Working with proposals for new program, policy, or procedure, or plan for working a problem • Circulate a proposal to generate interest (initiate the idea) • Evaluate a proposal (respond to another's idea) • Advocate a position on a proposal to decision makers
Staff Study • Single issue or several related issues and impact • Multi-page research paper • Detailed discussion with conclusion & recommendations • Format varies to meet need	Analyze a clearly defined problem, identify conclusions, and make recommendations • Assist decision makers and leaders in leading • Research to inform and recommend change • A problem-solving thought process in written form

Point Paper

POINT PAPER

ON

WRITING POINT PAPERS

- Function: Minimal text outline of a single issue to quickly inform others

  -- Short: supports extemporaneous speaking opportunities (e.g. "elevator speech")

  -- Subject matter: requires prior preparation/immersion in background and details

- Format: Baseline standards below are flexible to save space and/or conform to user's needs

  -- Overall: single page with short telegraphic bullets

  -- Page setup

    --- Title: centered; all capital letters; long titles wrap single-spaced under third line (FYI: Use manual line breaks for long title readability or to visually balance the lines.)

    --- Margins: One (1) inch all around

    --- Headings (e.g. PURPOSE, DISCUSSION) are optional

    --- Dashes: single before major thoughts; multiple for subordinate thoughts

    --- Line spacing and text wrapping: single-space within bullets and double-space between bullets; wrap bullets as in this example (wrapped bullets are rare in Point Papers)

    --- Punctuation: open punctuation style—ending punctuation not required

    --- Identification line: One (1) inch from bottom, flush left; *alternatively placed in the footer, one half (1/2) inch from the bottom, flush left as in this example*

      ---- Rank/Title and last name of the point of contact (POC)

      ---- Organization/office symbol

      ---- Telephone: Full DSN or 10-digit commercial

      ---- Typist's initials ("ahd" in the example) (may be the POC or someone else)

      ---- Date in "DD Mmm YY" format

  -- Classified content: See DOD 5200.1-R/AFI 31-401 to prepare classified papers

- Recommendations or conclusion: Give your point a solid sense of the way ahead or closure

SSgt Hines-Davis/SOC/ES/DSN 493-9999/ahd/22 Jul 14

Talking Paper

TALKING PAPER

ON

WRITING TALKING PAPERS

- Function: Speaking notes that outline and narrate a single issue to inform others during planned/scheduled oral presentations

  -- Provides both the outline of a single issue and quick-reference content on key points, facts, data, positions, or frequently asked questions

  -- Can stand alone for basic understanding; better with knowledge topic and related issues

- Format: Baseline standards below are flexible to save space and/or conform to user's needs

  -- Normally a single page (FYI: avoid lengthy chronologies and excessive detail)

  -- Headings (e.g. PURPOSE, DISCUSSION) are optional; save space by eliminating headings, by using run-in headings (e.g. Format, Flow), or both, as in this example

  -- Bullets are short phrases or statements; telegraphic wording saves space

  -- Format the title, margins, dashes, line spacing, and text wrapping as in the Point Paper

  -- Punctuation: Normal rules apply for complete sentences and paragraphs; bullets may have internal punctuation but do not require closing punctuation

  -- Identification line: Format the same as for the Point Paper and place only on the first page, one (1) inch from bottom, flush left; *alternatively placed in the footer, one half (1/2) inch from the bottom, flush left*

  -- Page numbering (if longer than one page): Place the page number for page 2 onwards at the top of page, one-half inch from the top and flush with the right margin

  -- Classified content: See DOD 5200.1-R/AFI 31-401 to prepare classified papers

- Flow: Clear statement, logical support, and closure

  -- Make it memorable with a literary device and solid sense of closure

  -- Include additional information as a for your information (FYI) note at the appropriate place in the text/attached background paper (FYI: This is an example FYI note.)

- Recommendations or conclusion: Give your talk a solid sense of the way ahead or closure

Ms. Kenney/Holm Center/CCS/334-953-9999/jjk/4 Apr 14

Bullet Background Paper

BULLET BACKGROUND PAPER

ON

WRITING BULLET BACKGROUND PAPERS

PURPOSE

Discuss the functions, format, and tips for building a Bullet Background Paper (BBP). The purpose statement informs readers on both the purpose and main points of the paper. It may be a single sentence, as in this example, or a short paragraph in length.

FUNCTIONS

- Concise background information on a single idea

- Summary of a staff package

- Accomplishment summary

- Chronological of a problem

- Support for an attached paper

- Program information

- Information to provide a response to just about any task

FORMAT

- Flexible to save space and/or conform to user's needs

- Main ideas may be presented as headings (e.g. FUNCTION, FORMAT, TIPS) or as subordinate ideas to broader generic headings (e.g. PURPOSE, DISCUSSION, FINDINGS, RECOMMENDATIONS) using dashes and indentation.

- Secondary items follow with a single dash; tertiary and further subordinate items follow with multiple indented dashes. Any item can be as short as a word or as long as several sentences.

- Page setup

  -- Title: centered; all capital letters; long titles wrap single-spaced under third line
     (FYI: Use manual line breaks for long title readability or to visually balance the lines.)

  -- Margins: One (1) inch all around

  -- Dashes: single before major thoughts; multiple for subordinate thoughts

Ms. McKitt/SAASS/AS/334-953-9999/cdb/20 Jun 14

-- Line spacing and text wrapping: single-space within bullets and double-space between bullets; wrap bullets as in this example

-- Punctuation: Normal rules apply for complete sentences and paragraphs; bullets may have internal punctuation but do not require closing punctuation

-- Identification line: Format the same as for the Point Paper and place only on the first page, one (1) inch from bottom, flush left; *alternatively placed in the footer, one half (1/2) inch from the bottom, flush left*

-- Page numbering (if longer than one page): Place the page number for page 2 onwards at the top of page, one-half inch from the top and flush with the right margin

-- Classified content: See DOD 5200.1-R/AFI 31-401 to prepare classified papers

TIPS

-- Write the BBP according to the knowledge level of the expected readers

-- Emphasize main points by using them as headings or short bullets. If additional information is needed, refer to it in the text of the BBP and attach the referenced documents.

-- Strive to minimize the length to communicate quickly with impact

CONCLUSION

The BBP servers many purposes and is no longer than it needs to be to convey the message. The formats for many of the BBP elements are the same as they are for other Air Force papers. End with recommendations or conclusions that bring the discussion to a close.

Background Paper

BACKGROUND PAPER

ON

WRITING BACKGROUND PAPERS

1. The background paper is a multi-purpose communications instrument to transmit ideas or concepts from one office to another. It is an excellent way to express ideas on specific topics and to describe conditions that require a particular staff action. This background paper outlines the basic function and format of a background paper.

2. The primary function of the background paper is to present the background (chronological, problem-solution, etc.) underlying an issue or subject, but it also has other purposes. The background paper has been used to summarize important content into a single, short document or to prepare officials for a speaking engagement by providing them with historical, technical, or statistical background data. There are many other uses as well but all good background papers share some common format attributes for organization, style, and presentation.

3. The organization of a good background paper is no different than that of a point paper, talking paper, or bullet background paper. All these papers open with a purpose that leads to an outline of the main points and ends with a summary, conclusion, or recommendation. The first paragraph of the background paper provides the reader with a clear statement of purpose and an outline or "road map" for the paper. This is followed by the discussion (cohesive, single-idea paragraphs) which leads the reader logically to the conclusion.

4. The style of writing should be professional and in the third person, although writing in first person, active voice will sometimes be more appropriate. Even though the background paper is written in paragraphs, the concise, telegraphic style of the talking paper or bullet background paper is sometimes used (while following the rules of grammar and punctuation for complete sentences and paragraphs). By intent, the background paper is more narrative in style and form; if a shorter format (e.g. bullet background paper or talking paper) will suffice, use it!

5. The format of the background paper varies to meet the needs of both the author and intended readers. By design, the background paper is intended for stand-alone use and it is usually several pages in length (and may include references and attachments). However, brevity is still valued: make the paper as short or as long as necessary to answer the mail, complete the task, or cover the topic adequately. Paragraphs may use bullets; however, the number and letter format of this example is common in many organizations. Of note, the numbering and lettering of paragraphs in this example is identical the format used for the Official Memorandum. Some additional general guidelines for formatting your background paper are as follows:

Mr. Seawright/AU/ES/DSN 493-9999/jcb/18 Jun 14

a. Title: The title for the background paper resembles the title for other Air Force papers. The first title line, "BACKGROUND PAPER," is centered one (1) inch from the top of the first page. The second line, the word "ON," is centered below the first line with one blank line between them. The third line is the title line that conveys the topic of the background paper and it is centered below the second line with one blank line between them. If the third line is long, it wraps to be centered under the third line with no blank lines between them. Manual line breaks may be used to format long titles for readability or appearance (e.g. to visually balance the lines).

b. Margins: All pages use a one (1) inch margin all around.

c. Line spacing, and text wrapping: Single-space within paragraphs and double-space between paragraphs; wrap all paragraphs to align flush with the left margin.

d. Identification line: Format the identification line in accordance with the guidance for the identification line for a Point Paper, placing the identification line only on the first page, one (1) inch from bottom, flush left. *Alternatively, the identification line may be placed in the footer, one half (1/2) inch from the bottom, flush left.*

e. Page numbering: Place the page number for page 2 onwards at the top of page, one-half (1/2) inch from the top and flush with the right margin. *This is a change from previous guidance for background papers; however, this is the same location for page numbering as used for the Official Memorandum and reduces the unique format requirements for different documents.*

f. For classified content, refer to DOD 5200.1-R/AFI 31-401 to prepare classified papers.

5. The key to an effective background paper, like any well-written document, is to get to the point quickly, cover all aspects of the issue in sufficient detail to meet your objective, and close the paper with a sense of finality.

Position Paper

POSITION PAPER

ON

WRITING POSITION PAPERS

1. Position papers are essential tools for Airmen who are tasked to evaluate a proposal, raise a new idea for consideration, advocate a current situation or proposal, or take a stand on an issue. This paper advocates the use of the position paper for these and other functions where Airmen must advocate a position based on the background information and courses of action available.

2. The format of the position paper is identical to a background paper for page setup (margins, title, paragraph numbering, line spacing, text wrapping, page numbering, and identification line). Position papers may be a single page but are typically several pages or more in length. Also, the paragraphs of the position paper, like background papers, are narrative sentences that fully comply with the rules of good grammar and punctuation.

3. The flow of the position paper is similar to other Air Force papers: introduce the topic with a clear statement of purpose; outline the paper; present background information; conclude with recommendations. However, the position paper stands out from other papers by the clear statement of the position taken and actions required.

4. In many ways, a position paper is a written debate. The author must present a clear claim, provide evidence (background information) to support the claim, and demonstrate the logic (the warrant) that ties the evidence to the claim. In addition, the author must also consider counter-arguments from readers and provide evidence and logic why counter-arguments are unwarranted.

   a. The opening statement or introductory paragraph must contain a "clear statement" of your purpose in presenting the issue and "your position" on that issue.

   b. The remainder of the paper should consist of integrated paragraphs or statements that logically support or defend that position.

   c. Adequate, accurate, and relevant support material is a must for the position paper. For classified content, see DOD 5200.1-R/AFI 31-401 to prepare classified papers.

   d. The concluding paragraph must contain a specific recommendation or a clear restatement of your position. This is where you reemphasize your bottom line.

5. The position paper is a valuable tool for Airmen to use to advocate a position. The flow of the paper presents a clear argument and background information while also presenting the logic that ties the background to the position being advocated and the action recommended.

Ms. Skinner/Spaatz/XT/334-953-9999/ks/15 May 14

CHAPTER 17:

The Staff Study

> *This chapter covers:*
> - Purpose
> - Process: Critical Thinking and Problem Solving
> - Writing the Report
> - Complete the Study

Staff Studies are commonly written as official memorandums, but they are specialized in their purpose and presentation. The narrative of this chapter is especially useful for those drafting these types of reports for the first time, but they are also useful for experienced writers to check their work and ensure their reports are answering the mail.

Purpose

The purpose of the staff study report is to analyze a problem, draw conclusions, and make recommendations. Not all organizations routinely use the staff study, but it is an accepted format for a problem-solution report for both the Air Force and Joint Staff. You may never write up a problem-solution in the staff study format; however, if you understand and apply the essential elements of problem analysis, you'll be better prepared for any staff communication. The staff study, as a thought process, is far more important as a process than what you call it or the format used to communicate findings.

Process: Critical Thinking and Problem Solving

1. **Analyze the Audience.** The study may be driven by higher headquarters or your own observations on areas for improvement. In either case, there will be political and operational constraints: do some reflective thinking about the operating environment.

2. **Limit the problem.** Manage the size of the task by setting the who, what, when, why and how of the situation. Narrow the problem statement: do not include unnecessary concerns. Vague or fuzzy problem statements lead to unacceptable reports.

   For example, if the problem is the use of amphetamines and barbiturates among junior Airmen, the problem statement "To reduce the crime rate on base" would be too broad. So would "How to detect and limit the use of dangerous drugs on base." More to the point would be "To detect and end the causes of amphetamine and barbiturate use among the junior Airmen at Wright-Patterson AFB." The problem should eventually be stated in one of three ways:

   a. As a **question** (What should we do to …?)

   b. As a **statement of need** or purpose (The base needs to be able to detect …)

   c. As an **infinitive phrase** (To detect and end the causes of ground mishaps …)

3. **Analyze the Whole Problem.** Do the parts suggest other problems that need separate handling or do the parts relate so closely to the whole that you need only one approach?

4. **Gather Data.** Collect all information pertinent to the problem. (Tips on how and where to conduct staff research can be found in chapter 4).

5. **Evaluate Your Information.** Is the information from reliable witnesses? Is it from qualified authorities? Does it qualify as solid support?

6. **Organize Your Information.** One way to organize information is to place it under headings titled "Facts," "Assumptions" and "Criteria."

   a. **Facts** should be facts, not opinions or assertions. Identify only those facts that directly bear on the problem.

   b. **Assumptions** are important because they are always necessary. To reduce a research project to manageable size, it is usually necessary to accept certain things as being true, even if you are not absolutely sure. The validity of your assumptions usually has a great deal to do with the validity of your conclusions. Sometimes desired conclusions can be supported with certain unrealistic assumptions. In evaluating research, seek out the assumptions and make some judgment as to how reasonable they are. If you feel they are unrealistic, make whatever assumptions you feel are correct and try to judge their effect on the conclusions of the study. Sometimes a perfectly logical study explodes in your face because your assumptions were incredibly weak or simply not supportable.

   c. **Criteria** are those standards, requirements or limitations used to test possible solutions. The criteria for a problem-solution are sometimes provided in complete form by your boss when you are assigned the problem. Sometimes criteria are inherent in the nature of the obstacle causing the problem. The obstacle can only be overcome within certain physical limits, and these limits will establish the criteria for the problem-solution. In most cases, however, criteria are usually inherent in your own frame of reference and in the goal you are trying to attain. This goal and frame of reference will tolerate only certain problem-solutions, and the limits of this tolerance will establish the criteria for the problem-solution.

Any criteria will not be very useful if you cannot clearly test the possible solutions against them! Since weak or irrelevant criteria are often seen in problem-solution reports, let's examine three examples of criteria and assess their value.

- "The total solution must not cost more than $6,000 annually."
- "The solution must result in a 75 percent operationally ready (OR) rate."
- "The solution must be consistent with the boss' philosophy on personnel management."

Criterion one is fine; you could easily "bump" your proposed solutions against a specific cost. Criterion two looks good on the surface, but OR rates result from numerous, complex variables. You probably could not guarantee the decision maker your "solution" would lead to a 75 percent OR rate. It might improve the OR rate or actually lead to a rate higher than 75 percent, but before your boss actually implements your solution, how would you know that? If a criterion cannot be used to test solutions before implementation, it is not an acceptable criterion. Criterion three isn't bad, but it's fuzzy. Perhaps it could be written more precisely or left off the formal report altogether. You could still use it intuitively to check your solutions, but realize when you use "hidden" criteria, your report will be less objective.

7. **List Possible Solutions**. Approach the task of creating solutions with an open mind. Develop as many solutions as possible. The "brainstorming" technique using several knowledgeable people is a popular approach to generating possible solutions.

8. **Test Possible Solutions**. Test each solution by using criteria formed while gathering data. Weigh one solution against another after testing each. Be sensitive to your personal biases and prejudices. Strive for professional objectivity.

9. **Select Final Solution**. Select the best possible solution—or a combination of the best solutions—to fit the mission. Most Air Force problem-solutions fall into one of the three patterns listed below. Do not force your report into a pattern where it does not fit.

   a. Single best possible solution. This one is basic and the most commonly used. You select the best solution from several possible ones.

   b. Combination of possible solutions. You may need to combine two or more possible solutions for your best possibilities.

   c. Single possible solution. Rare; stand ready to defend why there are no alternatives.

10. **Act**. Capture the actions required for the final solution. Your comments here may lead to the specific action(s) your boss should take to implement the solution (written into the "Action Recommended" portion of the report). If there is no implementing document for the decision maker to sign, specify what other action the boss must take to implement the proposal. No solution is complete until action has been planned *and* executed.

In actual practice, the steps of problem solving do not always follow a definite and orderly sequence. The steps may overlap, more than one step may be considered at one time, or developments at one step may require reconsideration of a previous step. For example, the data you collect may force you to redefine the problem. Similarly, while testing solutions, you may think of a new solution or, in the process of selecting a final solution, you may discover you need additional information. In short, problem-solving may not be linear but all the steps should be considered and investigated.

Writing the Report

The sections below present the suggested format for a staff study report. Use only those portions of this format necessary for your particular report. If you omit certain paragraphs, renumber subsequent paragraphs accordingly.

By now you probably realize the staff study is a problem-solution report that presents data collected, discusses possible solutions to the problem, and indicates the best solution. It is not a style to solve a problem. You should mentally solve your problem, and then report the solution in writing. The format of the staff study report includes a heading, a body, an ending and, when necessary, the attachments.

Heading

Leave the MEMORANDUM FOR element blank; this allows the report to seek its own level. After FROM, enter your complete office address. After SUBJECT, briefly state the report's subject; however, use a few extra words if this will add meaning to your subject.

Body

The body contains five parts: **(1) Problem, (2) Factors Bearing on the Problem, (3) Discussion, (4) Conclusion and (5) Action Recommended**. The parts of the body align with the steps of problem solving, as shown below. *No matter how you organize your report, stive to: make it brief, maintain a sequence of thought throughout, show the reader how you reasoned the problem through, and include enough information in the body of the report to make sense without referring to the attachments (but do use attachments for support, as needed).*

Steps of problem solving	Body of staff study
1. Recognize the problem	1. Problem
2. Gather data	2. Factors Bearing on the Problem
3. List possible solutions	3. Discussion
4. Test possible solutions	
5. Select final solution	4. Conclusion (a brief restatement of final solution)
6. Act	5. Action Recommended

CHAPTER 17
The Staff Study

1. **Problem:** The statement of the problem tells the reader what you are trying to solve. No discussion is necessary at this point; a simple statement of the problem is sufficient. You have ample opportunity to discuss all aspects of the problem later in the report.

2. **Factors Bearing on the Problem:** This part contains the facts, assumptions, criteria and definitions you used to build possible solutions to your problem. Devote separate paragraphs to facts, assumptions, criteria and definitions as shown in the sample study report. Obviously, if you write a report in which you have no assumptions or definitions, omit either or both. Include only those important factors you used to solve your problem. Briefly state whatever you include. Put lengthy support material in attachments. Write each sentence completely so you don't force the reader to refer to the attachments to understand what you've written.

3. **Discussion:** This part of the report is crucial; it shows the logic used to solve the problem. Generally, some background information is necessary to properly introduce your problem. The introduction may be one or several paragraphs, depending on the detail required. Once the intro is complete, use one of the following outlines to discuss your thought process.

    a. *When using the single best possible solution*:

       (1) List all possible solutions you think will interest the decision maker.

       (2) Show how you tested each possible solution against the criteria, listing both the advantages and disadvantages. Use the same criteria to test each possible solution.

       (3) Show how you weighed each possible solution against the others to select the best possible solution.

       (4) Clearly indicate the best possible solution.

    b. *When using a combination of possible solutions*:

       (1) List all the possible solutions you think will interest the decision maker.

       (2) Show how you tested each possible solution against the criteria, listing both the advantages and disadvantages. Use the same criteria to test each possible solution.

       (3) Show how you weighed each possible solution against the other possible solutions and why you retained certain ones as a partial solution to the problem.

       (4) Show how and why you combined the retained possible solutions.

    c. *When using the single possible solution*:

       (1) List your single solution.

       (2) Test it against the criteria.

       (3) Show how and why this solution will solve the problem.

4. **Conclusion:** The conclusion must provide a complete, workable solution to the problem. The conclusion is nothing more than a brief restatement of the best possible solution or solutions. The conclusion must not continue the discussion. It should completely satisfy the requirements of the problem; it should never introduce new material.

5. **Action Recommended:** Word the recommendations so your boss need only sign for action. Do not recommend alternatives. This does not mean you cannot consider alternative solutions in the "Discussion." It means you commit yourself to the line of action you judge best. You must relieve the decision maker of the research and study necessary to decide from several alternatives. Give precise guidance on what you want the decision maker to do; i.e., "Sign the implementing letter at attachment 1." (Normally, implementing documents should be the first attachment.) Recommendations like "Recommend further study" or "Either solution A or B should be implemented" indicate the decision maker picked the wrong person to do the study.

Ending

The ending contains the name, rank and duty title of the person or persons responsible for the report and a listing of attachments. Use the official memorandum format for the signature block and attachments.

Attachments

Since the body of the staff study report must be brief, relegate as much of the detail as possible to the attachments. Although seldom required, identify material needed to support an attachment as an appendix to the attachment. Include, as attachments, the directives necessary to support the recommended actions. Here is some addition guidance for attachments:

- The body may reference the authority directing the study. An attachment may contain an actual copy of the directive.

- The body may contain an extract or a condensed version of a quotation. An attachment may contain a copy of the complete quotation.

- The body may contain a statement that requires support. An attachment may state the source and include the material that verifies that statement.

- The body may refer to a chart or information in a chart. An attachment may include the complete chart (designed to fit the format of the report or folded to fit inside the report.)

- If directives or detailed instructions are required to implement the recommended action, include the drafts as attachments.

Tabs

Number tabs to help the reader locate attachments or appendices. Affix each tab to a blank sheet of paper immediately preceding the attachment. If it is not practical to extract the supporting material from a long or complex document used as an attachment, affix the tab to that page within the attachment or appendix where the supporting material is located. Position the tab for attachments as you would for an official memorandum (bottom right on tab cover page for attachment 1 and then slightly higher for each succeeding attachment so all tabs can be seen).

Complete the Study

A good staff study report should represent completed staff work. This means the staff member has completed the analysis and presented a complete solution—a complete study—to the boss. The solution should be complete enough that the decision maker has only to approve or disapprove. Inexperienced staff members may succumb to the impulse to ask the chief what to do when the problem is difficult. However, your job is to advise your boss what should be done—provide answers, not questions. Of course, it's okay to inquire at any point in the problem-solving procedure if you need to find out whether you are on the right track. This coordination often saves untold hours.

Tips

Consider the following tips for problem-solving and preparing a staff study:

- Be creative! Completed staff work provides the opportunity to be heard.

- Schedule time to work the problem. Most problems worthy of analysis require considerable study and reflection.

- Do not assume there is a "school solution" and avoid reductionist "solutions" that assume obstacles do not exist. Conversely, a complex study with a thick report is not necessarily better. Good decision makers focus on the relevance and accuracy of the material and the logic of the argument: be relevant, accurate, and logical in the study.

- Do not work a study in isolation. If you point your finger at someone or some unit, or if the solution requires a change in someone's operation, you'd better get their reaction before you drop the bomb. You can look mighty foolish if you find out later they were operating under a constraint of which you were unaware.

- Does the study answer the mail? If you were the boss, would you be willing to stake your professional reputation on the study? If the answer is "no," it is time to start over.

Format

The format of the final staff study report will certainly be less important than the content; but a poor format will distract readers. Start with the format for the official memorandum: all the elements of the official memorandum may be used (i.e., references, attachments, courtesy copies, and distribution lists). For long studies, an official memorandum as a cover letter followed by the study (as an attachment) may be in order. Your work environment may drive the need for a different format or additional information; but, in the end, these reports are simply specialized applications of the official memorandum.

The Staff Study Report Outline

DEPARTMENT OF THE AIR FORCE
[APPROVED ORGANIZATIONAL LETTERHEAD]

6 June 2014

MEMORANDUM FOR ORG/SYMBOL
                Street Address
                Away AFB ST 12345-6789

FROM: ORG/SYMBOL
       Street Address
       Home AFB ST 12345-6789

SUBJECT: Preparing a Staff Study Report

1. PROBLEM: Clearly and concisely state the problem you are trying to solve.

2. FACTORS BEARING ON THE PROBLEM

    a. Facts. Limit your facts to only those directly relating to the problem.

    b. Assumptions. Should be realistic and support your study.

    c. Criteria. Give standards, requirements, or limitations you will use to test possible solutions. Ensure you can use standards to measure or test solutions.

    d. Definitions. Describe or define terms that may confuse your audience.

3. DISCUSSION: This section shows the logic used in solving the problem. Introduce the problem and give some background, if necessary, then explain your solution or possible solution. Two or three levels of paragraphs may be needed, depending on the study.

4. CONCLUSION: State your conclusion as a workable, complete solution to the problem you described previously in "Discussion."

5. ACTION RECOMMENDED: Tell the reader the action necessary to implement the solution. This should be worked so the boss only needs to sign to make the solution happen.

                                            ERIC A. SCHAFER, Major, USAF
                                            Staff Study Compliance Manager

CHAPTER 18:

The Staff Package

> *This chapter covers:*
> - SSS Fundamentals
> - Completing the SSS Form
> - Assembling the Package
> - Coordinating the Package
> - Sample SSS and eSSS

When you have a staff package that must be coordinated, whether the package is a single page or several volumes, you need something to pull the package together and guide it through the staffing process. Some commands use a software application, such as Task Management Tool, for the staffing process. However, Air Force Form 1768, *Staff Summary Sheet*, is still used throughout the Air Force. The Staff Summary Sheet (known as "SSS" or "triple-S") is the first page of a staff package or the body of the e-mail for the electronic SSS (eSSS).

This discussion here applies to all staff packages where Air Force Form 1768 or its e-mail cousin, the eSSS, is used. Air Force Form 1768 is currently generated by a software application (AF IMT 1768, 19840901, V5 as of this writing) which may be printed for paper packages or sent as an attachment to an e-mail and signed digitally by coordinating officials. Regardless of the method used, paper or electronic, SSS fundamentals, arrangement, and coordination remain the same.

SSS Fundamentals

The SSS is a versatile tool that introduces, summarizes and coordinates the package through appropriate staff offices and officials using the chain of command. Frequently, the SSS is used to coordinate a package so that the last official is fully informed on an issue and can approve the package and/or sign an attachment to implement action associated with the package.

The versatility of the SSS is clear when used in printed form. Printed SSS forms often contain handwritten notes before reaching the approval authority. These notes capture essential thoughts of coordinating officials as it moves through the staff. As a hands-on tool, the SSS form does not require the same level of perfection, such as error-free typing, as the correspondence it covers. In addition to the notes of coordinating officials, the SSS may be corrected neatly and legibly in ink if the content and meaning are still intelligible and clear.

In addition, consider the following fundamentals and guidelines for completing the SSS form:

- Use: Use Air Force Form 1768 only with the staff package it summarizes; *do not* use the form in place of a memorandum or handwritten note.

- Placement: The SSS is attached to the front of the package since it introduces and summarizes the relevant portions of all attached documents. You should not attach a document if it is not relevant to the package or if it is not mentioned on the SSS.

- Length: The SSS is usually limited to a single page since the form is a single page. If additional coordination or summary space is needed, follow these guidelines:
  - Coordination Overflow: If more than ten offices need coordinate on the package, the first ten offices are listed on the original SSS. Beneath the original SSS, add a second AF Form 1768 that has the "TO" blocks renumbered from 11 to 20 and is completed through the subject. The second SSS is attached behind the original SSS.
  - Summary Overflow: Use plain bond paper if additional "Summary" space is needed.

Completing the SSS Form

The software application for AF IMT 1768 sets the format for page setup, font, point size and margins, so users can focus on the content of the form. The coordination section vectors the package through the staff and documents coordination. The action officer and subject tell readers who generated the SSS and the subject of the package. The summary captures the essence of the package and all attached documents to inform the final official to act or to be ready to act. These sections are broken into blocks that should be completed as follows:

Coordination, Action Officer, Subject and Date

- TO: List offices in the order that they should coordinate, approve or sign.
- ACTION: Show the action desired in this column
  - "Coord" for Coordination
  - "Appr" for Approval (normally only one "Appr" and/or one "Sig" entry per SSS).
  - "Sig" for Signature (normally only one "Appr" and/or one "Sig" entry per SSS).
  - "Info" for Information (when the SSS is submitted for information only)

- SIGNATURE (Surname), GRADE AND DATE: This block is broken into two parts. If you are the addressee and you agree with the proposed action, sign your surname, rank or grade, and date on the bottom SIGNATURE line aligned with your office symbol. If you are not the addressee, sign on the top SIGNATURE line aligned with your office symbol.
- SURNAME OF ACTION OFFICER AND GRADE: Rank and last name of action officer.
- SYMBOL: Enter action officer's organization and office symbol (e.g., AF/A1).
- PHONE: The action officer's telephone number (DSN or full 10-digit commercial).
- TYPIST'S INITIALS: Enter the initials of the typist who completed the form.
- SUSPENSE DATE: Enter the suspense date, if any, as appropriate.
- SUBJECT: Enter subject; use the same subject as for the attached correspondence.
- DATE: Type or stamp date at time of dispatch from the signing official's office.

Summary Section

The summary section is heart of the SSS and is adaptable to the purpose or function the package. There are many ways to use the limited space of the summary block efficiently. A common technique is the use of headings. With or without headings, the paragraphs in the summary section are numbered and lettered in the same manner as in an official memorandum.

The guidance here merges the common elements from examples, instructions and experience for completing the summary section with five headings: Purpose, Background, Discussion, Views of Others and Recommendation. These five headings provide a common baseline for all Air Force personnel in completing the SSS, but they can be adapted for local needs, recurring tasks and command preferences. Check with your command for local guidance.

Purpose

The purpose statement tells readers what the SSS is trying to accomplish. The purpose statement may simply be a restatement of the subject. If the purpose is more complex, provide readers a clear statement of the issue and what action is being requested. Another technique is to use the purpose to provide the bottom line up front (BLUF) in the form of a purpose statement.

Background

The background section provides readers (the chain of command) with pertinent historical or contextual factors that shape the issue. Background information should be presented in a logical order (chronologically, geographically, functionally, etc.) appropriate for the issue to answer key questions (what happened, so what and why) as the narrative builds. Finally, save space by using a writing style with run-in headings and telegraphic statements/bullets.

Discussion

This is the meat of the analysis. Discuss the primary point or outline the main points first. Next, link the background information to the discussion with logical analysis. Lead readers to be able to see the way ahead proposed. Follow the logic and organization as used for the background (chronologically, geographically, functionally, etc.) appropriate to the issue. Also, if there are several options or courses of action available, they should be covered in the discussion. Finally, save space by using a writing style with run-in headings and telegraphic statements/bullets.

Views of Others

The views of others highlight opposing views, how they were considered but not recommended, and why. They are essential for a complete analysis, thorough discussion, and proper staffing of the package. This section requires pre-work to engage other offices impacted by the SSS before formal coordination, but when properly socialized early, the package will have broad support during formal coordination. If there are known disagreements or alternatives, present them here so that there are no secrets and the SSS can move forward rather than back to you for more work. In some cases, the views of others will not be needed, such as when there are no disagreements or when the SSS is used for a routine task. In these situations, the views of others may be marked as either "N/A" or deleted, as preferred by your chain of command.

Recommendation

State the recommendation for the senior official, including any action necessary to implement it, in such a way that the official need only sign an attached document to coordinate, approve or disapprove the recommended action. Use this heading only when SSS is routed for action; do not use the recommendation heading when the SSS is submitted for information only.

Signature block

The signature blocks for AF Form 1768 and the eSSS are the same; however, you must take care when sending the staff package so that the signature and the signature block match.

- **AF Form 1768:** Use the signature block for the action officer or the official designated as the office of primary responsibility (OPR) for the SSS package. The signature block is placed flush with the left margin with "//SIGNED//" (to indicate official Air Force information) above the official's name, rank, service affiliation, duty title, organization, and contact information (telephone and/or e-mail). **The signature must match the signature block**: do not sign "for" another official; and do not use an authority line.

- **eSSS as an e-mail:** Use the signature block for the action officer or the official designated as the office of primary responsibility (OPR) for the SSS package. The signature block is placed flush with the left margin with "//SIGNED//" (to indicate official Air Force information) above the official's name, rank, service affiliation, duty title, organization, and contact information (telephone and/or e-mail). **The signature block and the system-generated "From" information must match**: do not sign "for" another official; do not use an authority line; do not add slogans, quotes, or other personalization to an official e-mail signature block.

Tabs

For AF Form 1768, list Tabs aligned at the center in line with the signature block. For the eSSS (e-mail), list Tabs flush with the left margin below the signature block with one blank line between the signature block and the Tabs list.

CHAPTER 18
The Staff Package

Assembling the Package

SSS packages are assembled using the same basic logic and process used to assemble and attach tabs to official memorandums (see chapter 14). The primary difference for SSS packages is that some documents may already have attachments so the entire package must be clearly marked. Clear marking requires differentiating "tabs" from "Tabs." When "tabs" is written in all lower case letters, it refers to the physical dividers attached to each document or divider page, whereas "Tabs," with a capital T, refers to the major groups of information attached to the primary SSS. *The Tongue and Quill* recommends using blank pages with tabs to separate the major groups of information (e.g., outgoing, incoming and background). Likewise, attachments to Tabs may be separated by blank pages with the tab attached to serve as a divider between attachments. With this in mind, list attachments to the SSS as Tabs or attachments as follows:

- Tab 1: Mark the primary document for action, signature, or approval as Tab 1.
    - Attachments to Tab 1: Mark any attachments to the primary document at Tab 1 as attachments (Atch 1, Atch 2, etc.).
    - If you have more than one document for action, mark the second document as Tab 2; the third as Tab 3; and so forth.
- Tab 2: List the incoming letter, directive, or other paper that prompted the SSS as Tab 2 (or sequentially after the last action document). Attachments to Tabs are sequentially numbered from "1" for each Tab (Atch 1, Atch 2, etc.).
- Tab 3: List supplemental documents as additional tabs followed by the record or coordination copy and information copies. Attachments are marked as in Tab 2, above.
- If non-concurrence is involved, list it and the letter or rebuttal as the last tab.

General Order of SSS Documents

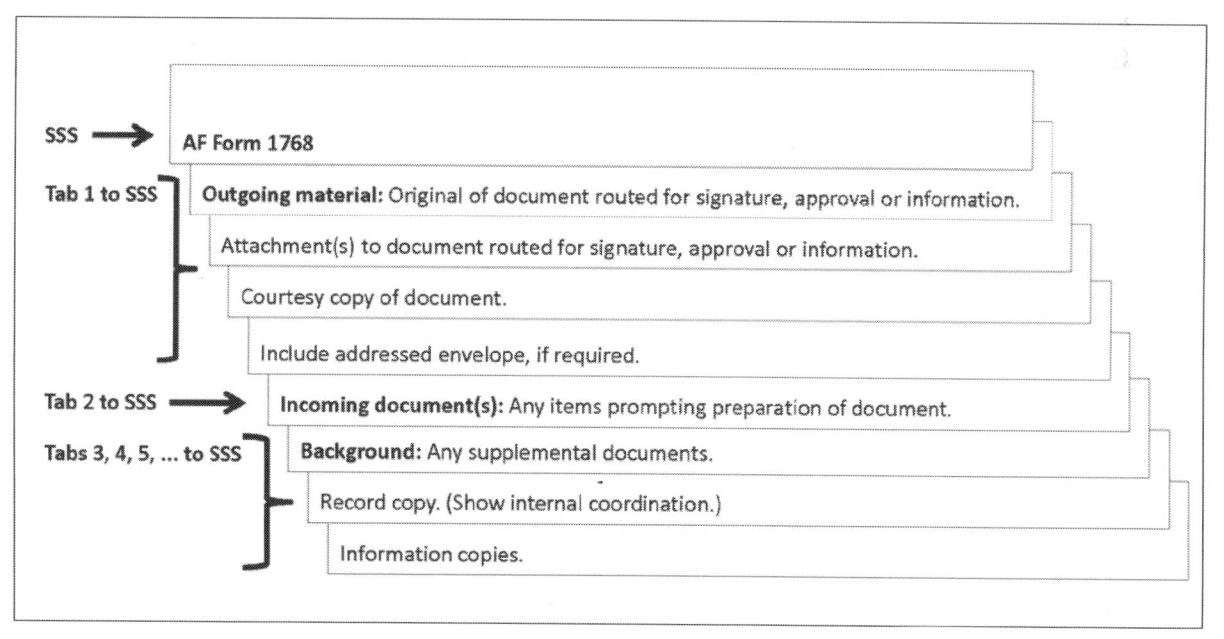

SSS →	AF Form 1768
Tab 1 to SSS	**Outgoing material:** Original of document routed for signature, approval or information.
	Attachment(s) to document routed for signature, approval or information.
	Courtesy copy of document.
	Include addressed envelope, if required.
Tab 2 to SSS →	**Incoming document(s):** Any items prompting preparation of document.
Tabs 3, 4, 5, ... to SSS	**Background:** Any supplemental documents.
	Record copy. (Show internal coordination.)
	Information copies.

Tab Placement on SSS Package Documents

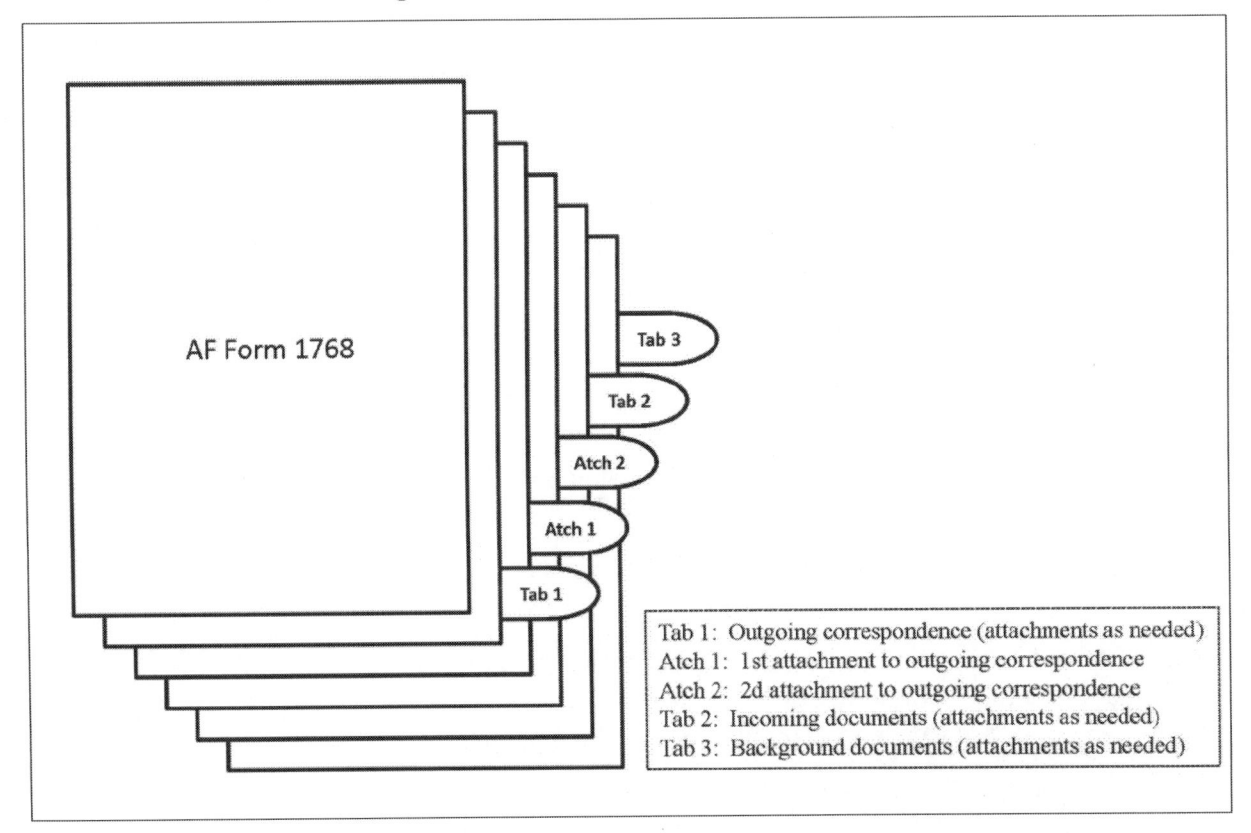

```
AF Form 1768
                    Tab 3
                    Tab 2
                    Atch 2
                    Atch 1
                    Tab 1
```

Tab 1: Outgoing correspondence (attachments as needed)
Atch 1: 1st attachment to outgoing correspondence
Atch 2: 2d attachment to outgoing correspondence
Tab 2: Incoming documents (attachments as needed)
Tab 3: Background documents (attachments as needed)

Coordinating the Package

- **Agreement:** If you are the addressee and you agree with the proposed action, sign your surname, rank or grade, and date on the *bottom* SIGNATURE line aligned with your office symbol. If you are not the addressee (i.e., you work in the office but are not the head of the office), sign on the *top* SIGNATURE line aligned with the office symbol.

- **Disagreement:** When you do not agree with the proposed action, write a memorandum to the action office stating your reasons and write in ink "See Memorandum" in the signature column. Attach your memorandum and return it to the action office.

- **Resolving differences:** As the action officer, try to resolve all differences when you receive a non-concurrence on a SSS.

    o If you cannot resolve the differences, the action officer must write a rebuttal memorandum to the approval authority which states differences discussed with the non-concurring official and explains why you cannot change the proposed action. Attach the rebuttal memorandum and the non-concurrence memorandum as the last tab to the original AF Form 1768, and annotate in pen the additional tab under the list of tabs. Send it to the next addressee shown on the AF Form 1768.

    o If you resolve differences and no changes are made to the AF Form 1768 or to any attachments, the previously non-concurring official shows concurrence by marking through the statement "See Memorandum" and signing surname, rank or grade, and date. The action officer writes "Differences resolved and no changes needed" on the

non-concurrence memorandum, initials the statement, and attaches this memorandum to the record or coordination copy. Then, send the package to the next addressee.
  - If you resolve differences and changes are made to the AF Form 1768 or to any attachments, the action officer must prepare a new AF Form 1768 and coordinate it as a new package with all offices.
- **Closure:** The final reviewer, approval official or signature official sends the package back to the OPR to close the task. One technique is to include the OPR's office symbol as the final block in the coordination section with "File" as the action to ensure the package is vectored to the source for closure.

Sample SSS and eSSS

The guidance and examples that follow are derived from multiple sources and experience; however, check with your command officials for guidance or supplements to AFMAN 33-326.

SSS Format Standards (AF IMT 1768)

- **Format:**
  - Page setup, margins, font, point size and text wrapping: Set by the application for AF IMT 1768; cannot be changed by users.
  - Tabs: Center aligned in line with the signature block lines (see sample SSS, below).
  - Line spacing: Single space within paragraphs (no blank lines); double space between first-level paragraphs (one blank line) and before "//SIGNED//."
  - Paragraph numbering: Number or letter all paragraphs at the left margin. Paragraphs may be sub-divided using the same outline structure as for the official memorandum.
- **Content:** The form-generating software limits the SSS to a single page. If additional coordination or summary space is needed, follow the "SSS Fundamentals" guidance repeated below:
  - Coordination Overflow: If more than ten offices need coordinate on the package, the first ten offices are listed on the original SSS form. Beneath the original SSS form, add a second AF Form 1768 that has the "TO" blocks renumbered from 11 to 20 and is completed through the subject. The second SSS is attached behind the original SSS.
  - Summary Overflow: Use plain bond paper if additional "Summary" space is needed.
- **Signature block:** Use the signature block for the action officer or the official designated as the office of primary responsibility (OPR) for the SSS package. The signature block is placed flush with the left margin with "//SIGNED//" (to indicate official Air Force information) above the official's name, rank, service affiliation, duty title, organization, and contact information (telephone and/or e-mail). **The signature must match the signature block**: do not sign "for" another official; and do not use an authority line. .

SSS Sample (AF IMT 1768)

STAFF SUMMARY SHEET

	TO	ACTION	SIGNATURE (Surname), GRADE AND DATE		TO	ACTION	SIGNATURE (Surname), GRADE AND DATE
1	Org/Sym	Coord	*First, Capt, DDMmmYY*	6			
2	Org/Sym	Coord	*Second, Maj, DDMmmYY*	7			
3	Org/Sym	Appr	*Third, Lt Col, DDMmmYY*	8			
4	Org/Sym	Sig	*Fourth, Col, DDMmmYY*	9			
5				10			

SURNAME OF ACTION OFFICER AND GRADE	SYMBOL	PHONE	TYPIST'S INITIALS	SUSPENSE DATE
MSgt Last	Org/Symbol	DSN 888-9990	abc	YYYYMMDD

SUBJECT	DATE
Staff summary sheet on completing a staff summary sheet	YYYYMMDD

SUMMARY

1. PURPOSE: Provide a sample staff summary sheet (SSS) for use as a baseline/template.

2. BACKGROUND: The SSS introduces and summarizes the issue then coordinates the package through the staff with the goal of obtaining approval for action or signature on an attached document.
   a. The "Org/Sym" flows up the chain of command and through appropriate staff offices for coordination/approval.
   b. Actions include "Coord" (Coordination), "Appr" (Approval), "Sig" (Signature), and "Info" (Information); normally, there is only one "Appr" entry and/or one "Sig" entry on the SSS.
   c. The standard summary section headings (purpose, background, discussion, views of others, and recommendation) provide officials a short purpose statement, pertinent background information, a logical discussion of the information and rationale for any action proposed, the views of other officials impacted by the action, and a recommendation for the senior official (headings can be adapted for local needs, recurring tasks, and command preferences).

3. DISCUSSION: The SSS should be a concise (preferably one page) summary of the package.
   a. Organize the discussion chronologically, geographically, functionally, or as appropriate to the issue or action.
   b. If there are several options or courses of action available, they should be covered in the discussion.
   c. Save space with run-in headings and telegraphic statements/bullets.
   d. For additional guidance on the summary section, see the sample SSS and eSSS in AFH 33-327.

4. VIEWS OF OTHERS:
   a. Good staff work engages other offices impacted by the SSS before formal coordination.
   b. Make revisions or note disagreements so that the SSS moves forward rather than back to you for more work.

5. RECOMMENDATION: State the recommendation for the senior official, including any action necessary to implement it, in such a way that the official need only sign an attached document to coordinate, approve, or disapprove the recommended action. Use this heading only when SSS is routed for action; do not use RECOMMENDATION heading when the SSS is submitted for information only.

//SIGNED//
FIRST M. LAST, MSgt, USAF
Duty Title
Organization
DSN 888-9990 / (334) 953-9990
first.last@us.af.mil

2 Tabs
1. Memorandum for signature
2. AFH 33-327, The Tongue and Quill

Tabs are aligned at the center, in line with the signature block.

AF IMT 1768, 19840901, V5   PREVIOUS EDITION WILL BE USED

eSSS Format (Body of an e-mail)

The eSSS as the body of an e-mail serves the same purposes and has the same elements as the Air Force Form 1768. The primary difference is that you do not use a form to fill in the required coordination, identification and summary elements. If the eSSS format is chosen, the action officer or official designated as the office of primary responsibility (OPR) transmits package electronically (e-mail or other electronic staffing software) to the first reviewer to coordinate/comment. The first reviewer *forwards* the package, with any comments and all the attachments, to the next reviewer. This procedure is repeated until last reviewer listed in the eSSS coordination section has coordinated on the package. The last reviewer forwards the entire package back to the OPR for final action and/or to close the task. With this in mind, consider the following sample SSS and eSSS.

- **Format:**
    - Page setup and margins: Typically set by the e-mail application.
    - Font/point size: Times New Roman font, 12 points.
    - Text wrapping: Text for all paragraphs wraps to the left margin.
    - Tabs: List Tabs flush with the left margin below the signature block with one blank line between the signature block and the Tabs list.
    - Line spacing: Single space within paragraphs (no blank lines); double space between first-level paragraphs (one blank line) and between elements (AO line to SUSPENSE line; RECOMMENDATION to "//SIGNED//," signature block to Tabs, etc.)
    - Paragraph numbering: Number or letter all paragraphs at the left margin. Paragraphs may be sub-divided using the same outline structure as for the official memorandum.

- **Content:** All the sections of the SSS are combined in the body of the e-mail. The first section in the e-mail is the coordination section. The second section combines the staff summary with action officer contact information and the suspense date. While there are no page limits with the eSSS per se, action officers should strive to keep the eSSS summary concise—no longer than two pages when printed. Check with your local command section for further guidance.

- **Signature block:** Use the signature block for the action officer or the official designated as the office of primary responsibility (OPR) for the SSS package. The signature block is placed flush with the left margin with "//SIGNED//" (to indicate official Air Force information) above the official's name, rank, service affiliation, duty title, organization and contact information (telephone and/or e-mail). **The signature block and the system-generated "From" information must match**: do not sign "for" another official; do not use an authority line; do not add slogans, quotes, or other personalization to an official e-mail signature block.

The Tongue and Quill
AFH 33-337, 27 MAY 2015

eSSS Sample (Body of an e-mail)

From: [system-generated user information]
To: [appropriate organizational account, individuals, or distribution list for ACTION]
Cc: [as required for INFORMATION]
Subject: SIGN: Suspense 19 Jun 14; eSSS Format
Date: [system-generated date-time group]

---------------------COORDINATION---------------------
Office	Action	Last Name/Rank/Date
Org/Sym	Coord	Heinz, Lt Col, 17 Jun 14
Org/Sym	Appr/Sig	Smith, Col, 19 Jun 14

---------------------STAFF SUMMARY---------------------

AO: MSgt First M. Last, Org/Sym, DSN 888-9990

SUSPENSE: 25 Jun 14

1. PURPOSE: Present perspective and analysis of an issue (answer the "what" question).

2. BACKGROUND:
a. Pertinent historical or contextual factors that shape the issue; answers "so what?" and "why?"
b. Presented in logical order (chronologically, geographically, functionally, etc.) that supports movement through the package from PURPOSE to RECOMMENDATION.

3. DISCUSSION:
a. The meat of the analysis with the primary point or outline of main points first.
b. Links background with logical analysis; indicates the way ahead; answers "now what?"
c. For additional guidance, see the sample SSS and eSSS in AFH 33-327.

4. VIEWS OF OTHERS: ["N/A" or delete, if none, as preferred by your chain of command]
a. Highlight opposing views and how they were considered but not recommended and why.
b. Complete the thoughts of the discussion (demonstrates proper staffing and analysis).

5. RECOMMENDATION: [Official] approve/sign letter at Tab 1.

//SIGNED//
FIRST M. LAST, MSgt, USAF
Duty Title
Organization
DSN 888-9990 / (334) 953-9990
first.last@us.af.mil

2 Tabs
1. Memorandum for signature
2. AFH 33-337, *The Tongue and Quill*

> Tabs are aligned at the left margin for the eSSS.

CHAPTER 19:

Writing Better Bullet Statements

> *This chapter covers:*
> - Getting started
> - Drafting Accomplishment-Impact Bullet Statements
> - Polishing Accomplishment-Impact Bullet Statements
> - Bullet Statement Mechanics

Bullet statements are used in many Air Force documents, from the Air Force papers discussed in chapter 16 to the official personnel records of Airmen. While this chapter focuses on writing better bullet statements for use in personnel records, the principles here can be used to improve any written product wherever bullet statements are used.

Performance reports/appraisals (officer, enlisted and civilian), awards and decorations are part of everyone's permanent personnel records. These records are used by commanders, managers and supervisors to document an individual's performance over a specific period of time. If you supervise just one person, you play a vital role in his/her career. You provide the opportunities for success and you have the obligation to document employee performance.

Through leadership, mentoring and effective writing, you can ensure the employees you supervise are afforded opportunities for success and increased responsibilities by documenting their success on performance reports/appraisals, awards and decorations. The guidance here is general in nature; you must ensure all performance reports/appraisals, awards and decorations you prepare follow appropriate instructions/regulations and applicable command guidance. Of course, the most important part of documenting performance is getting started.

Getting Started

- **Get Organized:** Keep records of all the accomplishments, awards, and recommendations for all those you supervise. Create a file folder—paper, electronic or both—for each employee and make regular entries to everyone's folder. This will drive you to keep in touch with your subordinates and involved in their professional development.

- **Know the Format:** Most evaluation forms are written using bullet statements. Use the font and point size specified by the governing instruction or software used to produce the report.

- **Editing:** *The Tongue and Quill* includes a section on "The Mechanics of Writing" with guidance for grammar, punctuation, abbreviations, capitalization, hyphens and numbers to help you avoid misspelled words, typographical errors and other mistakes that reflect poorly on you and distract officials reading the report.

- **Write Effectively:** Get the reader's attention. Positive words and phrases leave a lasting impression with readers. Neutral or negative words and phrases give the impression that the person you are writing about is average or below average.

Drafting Accomplishment-Impact Bullet Statements

The heart of effective writing involves writing effective accomplishment-impact statements. If you are like many supervisors, you've likely stared at a blank report and wondered, "How in the world do I even *start* to write effective bullet statements?" Whether you are in that situation for the first or 100th time, here are some steps that will help you write effective accomplishment-impact bullets.

Step 1: Extract the Facts

The first step is the hardest part of bullet statement writing—getting started! Supervisors often get in trouble early because they do not capture information on their employees regularly or completely. Without a good file of accomplishments for each employee, it is hard to write about what each has accomplished.

Gather the Information

Begin by getting organized and creating a file for each employee. Collect all of the information you can find that is relevant to each accomplishment and file this information in the file you have created for that employee. Capture everything you can—direct information and support that may be remotely related to the accomplishment—on paper or electronically. What looks unimportant today may be a key piece of information later. As you gather information and make annotations, consider the following tips for what to look for and how to mark what you find:

- **Isolate the action:** Isolate and record the specific action the person performed.

- **Annotate the record:** Mark the action with a power verb that best describes the action (e.g., repaired, installed, designed, etc.).

- **Measure the action:** Document related numerical information (number of items fixed, dollars saved, man-hours expended, people served, pages written, etc.).

CHAPTER 19
Writing Better Bullet Statements

- **Connect the dots:** Document how this accomplishment impacted the bigger picture and broader mission of the unit, group, wing, installation, command or Air Force.

- **Ask the member:** Facts and figures do not always present themselves easily. Talk to the people you supervise. They are in the best position to clarify information on the tasks they perform, provide details about what they have accomplished, and inform you on how the task was done (e.g., saving time, treasure or talent).

- **Ask others and check the tech:** Ask coworkers and other supervisors who may have seen this person in action. Also, consult Technical Orders, customers served, letters of appreciation, automated work production documents or other sources to get all the information you need.

- **Capture from the start:** Track your subordinate's accomplishments as they happen. Keep a record of significant work performance (both good and bad). This habit will help you be prepared when it's time for a performance report, feedback, award or decoration.

Gathering information does not take as much time if it is performed regularly. Be prepared to schedule ample time with your people and make notes on what you need to include (or verify) in an employee's record. If you think gathering information as a routine takes too much time, consider how long it will take to write a good performance report, award or decoration request without the information—and how much you will spend tracking it down in the face of deadlines and irate superiors. Without documented information on performance, you are forced to rely upon loose generalizations and vague statements rather than convincing facts.

Sort the Information

With the information you have gathered, the next task is to sort the useful items from the items that are not useful. Test each item to see if it is truly associated with the accomplishment you identified earlier or if the item is unrelated to the accomplishment. The test is to ask, "Is this bit of information solidly connected to this single accomplishment?" If the answer is yes, flag the information as useful. If the answer is no, line through or flag the information as not useful—but never throw it away or delete it! Although it may not be useful now, it may be just what you need for another bullet later. Continue applying this question to all of the items you've collected for this bullet statement. Once the bits of information are sorted, you will have a stack of information that pertains precisely to the accomplishment and the bullet statement to be written.

Step 2: Build the Bullet's Structure

The next step is to take the sorted information and organize it into an accomplishment-impact bullet. Group the sorted items for each accomplishment as either the accomplishment (the what) or the impact (who, when, how, why).

The Accomplishment Element

The accomplishment element begins with an action. Action is best expressed with strong action verbs. The table, below, contains a short list of action verbs that can be used to start bullet statements. These are not all the action verbs that can be used, but it should get you started in writing that next evaluation, appraisal, award or decoration package.

Action Verbs for the Accomplishment Element

Accomplished	Achieved	Acquired	Acted	Activated
Actuated	Adapts	Adhered	Adjusted	Administered
Advised	Agitated	Analyzed	Anticipated	Applied
Appraised	Approved	Aroused	Arranged	Articulated
Assembled	Asserted	Assessed	Assigned	Assisted
Assured	Attained	Attend	Authorized	Averted
Bolstered	Brought	Build	Calculated	Capitalized
Catalyzed	Chaired	Challenged	Clarified	Collaborate
Collected	Commanded	Communicated	Compared	Compelled
Competed	Compiled	Completed	Composed	Comprehend
Computed	Conceived	Concentrated	Conducted	Conformed
Confronted	Considered	Consolidated	Consulted	Contacted
Continued	Contracted	Contributed	Controlled	Cooperate
Coordinated	Created	Cultivated	Delegated	Demonstrated
Deterred	Developed	Devised	Displayed	Dominated
Drove	Elicited	Embodied	Emerged	Emulated
Encouraged	Endeavored	Energized	Enforced	Enhanced
Enriched	Ensured	Escalated	Established	Exceeded
Excelled	Expanded	Expedited	Exploited	Explored
Fabricated	Facilitated	Focused	Forced	Formulated
Generated	Grasped	Helped	Honed	Identified
Ignited	Impassioned	Implemented	Improved	Initiated
Inspired	Insured	Invigorated	Kindled	Launched
Maintained	Manipulated	Motivated	Organized	Originated
Overcame	Oversaw	Performed	Perpetuated	Persevered
Persuaded	Planned	Practiced	Prepared	Produced
Projected	Promoted	Prompted	Propagated	Propelled
Quantified	Rallied	Recognized	Rectified	Refined
Reformed	Regenerated	Rehabilitated	Rejuvenated	Renewed
Renovated	Reorganized	Required	Resolved	Revived
Sacrificed	Scrutinized	Sought	Solved	Sparked
Spearheaded	Stimulated	Strengthened	Strove	Supervised
Supported	Surpassed	Sustained	Transformed	Utilized

In some cases, action verbs alone just cannot fully stress the strength or depth of someone's accomplishment. If you need to give action verbs an added boost, use an adverb to modify the verb. Most adverbs are really easy to pick out ... they end with the letters "ly." Try connecting some of the adverbs listed below to the verbs listed above to get a feel for how the adverb-verb combination can intensify the accomplishment element.

Adverbs for the Accomplishment Element:

Actively	Aggressively	Anxiously	Ardently	Articulately
Assertively	Avidly	Boldly	Competitively	Compulsively
Creatively	Decisively	Eagerly	Energetically	Enterprisingly
Enthusiastically	Expeditiously	Exuberantly	Feverishly	Fiercely
Forcefully	Frantically	Impulsively	Incisively	Innovatively
Intensely	Powerfully	Promptly	Prosperously	Provocatively
Quickly	Relentlessly	Restlessly	Spiritedly	Spontaneously
Swiftly	Tenaciously	Vigorously	Vigilant	

Now that you get the general idea about how to begin the accomplishment element, let's look at the rest of this critical part of the bullet statement. Broadly speaking, the accomplishment element contains all the words that describe a single action performed by a person. While this sounds simple, this rule is violated frequently. If two or more actions are combined together in the same bullet, each of the actions is forced to share the strength of that entire statement. So rather than combining two or more actions to strengthen a single bullet, writers must ensure bullets focus on only *one* accomplishment. Two examples of an accomplishment element are below: one uses simply an action verb; the second uses a modifier (adverb) for added emphasis.

> - **Processed** over 300 records with no errors as part of the 42 ABW Mobility Exercise
> - **Tenaciously processed** over 300 records with no errors as part of the 42 ABW Mobility Exercise

In summary, the accomplishment element begins with some form of action (action verb only or a modifier plus action verb) and contains a factual, focused description of one single action or accomplishment. With that established, let's look at the impact element.

The Impact Element (Impact and Results)

The impact element explains how the person's actions had an effect on the organization and the level of impact (e.g., work center, unit, wing, Air Force or Department of Defense). However, the scope of the impact should be consistent with the person's accomplishment. For example, if the accomplishment explains how a person processed a large number of records during a base exercise, the impact should not be stretched to show how the Air Force will save millions of dollars. The impact must be accurate (more on that later); be careful not to stretch the truth when rendering full credit for someone's accomplishment. For the accomplishment element above, the impact element could be as follows:

> - ... all wing personnel met their scheduled clock times

Connecting the Accomplishment and Impact Elements

"ing": Connecting the accomplishment and impact elements together can be done several ways. One of the ways is to use the "ing" form of words. See how the word "ensuring" connects our two elements in the example below:

> - Processed over 300 records with no errors as part of the 42 ABW Mobility Exercise **ensuring** all wing personnel met their scheduled clock times

Punctuation: Another way to connect these two elements together is to use punctuation that joins phrases together (conjunctive punctuation). The most common form of conjunctive punctuation in bullet statements is the semicolon. Let's set off our previous example with a semicolon to see this approach in action:

> - Processed over 300 records with no errors as part of the 42 ABW Mobility Exercise; all wing personnel met their scheduled clock times

Multiple impacts: If you have a situation where a single accomplishment has more than one significant impact, you may show each impact element separately but using sub-bullets. The bullet statement format for a multiple impact accomplishment separates the accomplishment element as the single dash (-) bullet statement followed by impact element sub-bullets with a double dash (--). Start each impact element sub-bullet with an action verb.

> - Processed over 300 records with no errors as part of the 42 ABW Mobility Exercise
> -- Ensured all wing personnel met their scheduled clock times
> -- Helped the wing garner an overall "OUTSTANDING" rating from the IG team

CAUTION: The multiple impacts method of writing bullets for a single accomplishment takes a great deal of space where space is limited (evaluation forms). Some commands do not allow the use of multiple impact lines under a single accomplishment. Check with your local command for guidance. Similarly, familiarize yourself with the appropriate MAJCOM/Base/Wing/unit level guidance for commonly used acronyms, abbreviations, etc. to ensure your documents are complete and well written.

Step 3: Streamline the Final Product

Review: After extracting the facts we built the structure of the performance bullet by separating the information into two elements: the accomplishment element and the impact element. Then we connected the two elements and applied standards to make the bullets strong and meaningful. Now we need to streamline the final product and make the bullet statements accurate, brief and specific (ABS).

Accuracy

Accurate bullets are a must. To be accurate, they must also be correct. If the facts are stretched, exaggerated or embellished, then accuracy is lost. Exaggeration or embellishment, no matter how minor, is not the truth. Evaluations, appraisals, awards and decorations are permanent official records—let them be full of facts and truth that reflects our core values.

CHAPTER 19
Writing Better Bullet Statements

Brevity

Editing for brevity accomplishes two tasks. First, select words that are shortest and clearest, yet most descriptive to the readers. This means that long, confusing words or phrases are replaced with short, clear, common terms. Second, eliminate or reduce unnecessary words. Some of the words that all bullet writers should be looking to eliminate (or at least sharply reduce) are:

- Articles: a, an, the
- Helping verbs: can, could, may, might, must, ought, shall, should, will, would
- Also forms of *be*, *have*, and *do*
  - Forms of *be*: be, am, is, are, was, were, been, being
  - Forms of *have*: have, has, had, having
  - Forms of *do*: do, does, did
- Linking verbs: forms of verbs associated with five senses: look, sound, smell, feel, taste
- Name of the person when their name is printed elsewhere on the document
- Personal pronouns
- Prepositions (use them sparingly): over, under, in, during, within, etc.

Specificity

Specific bullet statements contain detailed facts. To write them, you'll need to be familiar with the people and systems involved. Resist the urge to estimate or generalize. Don't be satisfied with a range (10-20 units), or round numbers (approximately $1000; nearly 3500 customers). Get the exact numbers and use them. With the first round of drafting complete your bullets are ready to be polished.

Polishing Accomplishment-Impact Bullet Statements

ABS stands not only for accuracy, brevity and specificity, but also for the critical "attributes of bullet statements." After the first draft bullets are complete, keep ABS in mind as you prepare to polish your draft statements to clean them up, trim them down and give them the scrubbing they need before they become a permanent part of someone's official record. Consider the following bullet: how could it be sculpted to support both the accomplishment and the impact?

> - Repaired 17 seriously corroded broken or missing Log Periodic (LP) antenna elements in the Atlantic Gateway Antenna System within 3 days by using elements from decommissioned antenna parts saving an estimated $3500 in procurement cost and 4 weeks of expected delivery time

Accuracy

To make the bullet statement *accurate* you need to ensure the facts are correct. Verify the facts by simply asking a few questions. For this example, a few questions revealed a more detailed picture of the actual accomplishment.

- How many antenna elements were actually repaired? How many were replaced? In this example, 17 elements were salvaged from decommissioned equipment and repaired to replace the seriously damaged and corroded elements; an additional 23 elements were repaired (sanded, repainted or recovered).

- How long does delivery really take and why? Four weeks of delivery time seems like a long time; why does it take so long to receive antenna parts? The antenna elements come from only one vendor and the estimated delivery time is based on the relatively low priority of the work order.

Specificity

The content for this example has a close relationship between accuracy and specificity. Details about your work may be likewise connected. The point is that sculpting your ABS does not require them to be done in A-B-S order. Here, we consider the specificity and will close with brevity. In order to make the facts in the bullet statement as specific as possible, follow the same question and answer method used to guarantee accuracy.

- Exactly how many antennas were fixed? A total of 40 antenna elements were repaired or replaced from all six LP antennas in the system.

- How much cost was actually saved? The exact cost charged to the unit for purchasing the 17 replacement antenna elements would have been $3479.

- How would the cost savings be spent? The $3500 cost savings estimate is based on various antenna elements from an AN/GRA-4(V)4 Log Periodic antenna system that do not need to be purchased due to the repair of elements from decommissioned antennas.

- What is the Atlantic Gateway Antenna System? The Atlantic Gateway Antenna System connects Air Force and other DoD users from the eastern seaboard of the US to military personnel in Western Europe.

- How has the repair of the antennas improved service to their customers? Transmit and receive signal strength was improved; static and cross-talk was reduced.

Revised bullet: With the information gathered we can edit the bullet for accuracy and specificity. While not every item of information could be added, the items that are included (shown in BOLD, below) contribute significantly to the message being sent.

> - **Restored 40** seriously corroded, broken, or missing elements **on 6 AN/GRA-4 Log Periodic Antenna Systems** in the Atlantic Gateway Antenna System within 3 days by using elements from decommissioned antenna parts
> -- **Saved** an estimated **$3.4K** in procurement cost and four weeks of expected delivery time
> -- **Sharply improved clarity of voice signal for operators in US and Europe**

The added information enabled us to build an additional impact element and sharpen the details of the draft bullet. The bullet has also grown in length: now we need to sculpt for brevity.

CHAPTER 19
Writing Better Bullet Statements

Brevity

Recall that editing for brevity includes editing for shorter words and the reduction of unnecessary words. Keeping these dual tasks separate may be difficult, so do both at the same time! Changes made to improve one aspect often promote the other. The three sections that follow track the changes before, during and after editing for brevity: bold or underlined items are added; lined through items are deleted.

Before Editing for Brevity

> - **Restored 40** seriously corroded, broken, or missing elements **on 6 AN/GRA-4 Log Periodic Antenna Systems** in the Atlantic Gateway Antenna System within 3 days by using elements from decommissioned antenna parts
>   -- **Saved** an estimated **$3.4K** in procurement cost and four weeks of expected delivery time
>   -- **Sharply improved clarity of voice signal for operators in US and Europe**

Editing for Brevity

> - **Restored 40** ~~seriously corroded, broken, or missing~~ **damaged** elements **on** ~~6~~ **six AN/GRA-4 Log Periodic Antenna<u>s</u>** ~~Systems in the Atlantic Gateway Antenna System~~ **within** 3 days ~~by~~ using ~~elements from~~ decommissioned antenna parts
>   -- **Saved** ~~an estimated~~ **$3.4K** ~~in procurement cost~~ and 4weeks of expected delivery time
>   -- **Sharply improved <u>voice</u> clarity** ~~of voice signal~~ **for** <u>Atlantic Gateway Antenna System</u> **operators in US and Europe**

After Editing for Brevity

> - Restored 40 damaged elements on six AN/GRA-4 Log Periodic Antennas in 3 days using decommissioned antenna parts
>   -- Saved $3.4K and4 weeks of expected delivery time
>   -- Sharply improved voice clarity for Atlantic Gateway Antenna System operators in US and Europe

You've just successfully completed the process of drafting, streamlining and polishing effective accomplishment-impact bullet statements. While the system in the example is dated, the process for drafting, streamlining and polishing bullets is timeless and applies to the accomplishments of all who serve in the Air Force today and tomorrow. With a little more practice, you can Extract the Facts, Build the Structure and Streamline the Final Product with ease. Writing convincing and truthful accomplishment-impact bullets will become almost second nature to you.

Bullet Statement Mechanics

Chapter 16 presented the initial discussion on bullet statement mechanics for the preparation of point papers, talking papers and bullet background papers. The bullets for most evaluations, appraisals, awards and decorations are built in the same way as discussed in chapter 16, but check for specific guidance for the form used by the evaluation, appraisal, award or decoration you are preparing. The guidance that follows reinforces the bullet statement drafting, polishing and formatting of previous discussions with the focus on evaluations, appraisals, awards and decorations. The following outline presents bullet statement mechanics as bullets to give you both written and visual guidance.

Bullet/text format and alignment

- Start main bullets with a single dash (-)
  -- This is a secondary level bullet and it uses two dashes (--)
  -- Text within a bullet wraps so that the first character of the second and any subsequent lines aligns directly under the first character, not the dash, of the line above
- Indent subordinate bullets so that the first dash of the subordinate bullet aligns directly under the first character, not the dash, of the parent bullet one level above
  -- This secondary bullet is subordinate to the "indent subordinate bullets" bullet
    --- This is a tertiary bullet and it uses three dashes (---)
    --- This tertiary bullet is subordinate to "This secondary bullet" above
  -- If bullets are divided, there must be at least two subordinate bullets
    --- The cardinal rule of outlining (chapter 6) states that any topic (or bullet) that is divided must have at least two parts
    --- Though often violated, the cardinal rule applies to bullets

Punctuation

- Use internal punctuation as required for accomplishment-impact bullet statements
- Never use ending punctuation in accomplishment-impact bullet statements

Grammar

- Always start an accomplishment-impact bullet with action (action verb or modified verb)
- Never start an accomplishment-impact bullet with a proper noun or pronoun
- Minimize the use of the individual's name in bullets when it is elsewhere on the document
- Avoid using personal pronouns (he, she, his, her, etc.) in accomplishment-impact bullet statements; these devices typically serve to form complete sentences

CHAPTER 20:

The Official Biography

This chapter covers:

- The Official Biography: Fundamentals
- Getting Started
- Associated Press (AP) Guidance for Official Biographies
- Official Biography Elements

No matter your status (officer, enlisted or civilian) or how long you have served, you have accomplished many things to get you to your current duty location. Capturing and maintaining your accomplishments in a standard biography format is a powerful tool for making personal and professional connections—just as powerful as any modern social media application—and it can help build cohesion at the unit level. When unit members read the biographies of their leaders, they see more than an official Air Force photograph and a list of facts—they see the service that shaped their leaders and the excellence they obtained.

The Official Biography: Fundamentals

Did you know the Air Force maintains the official biographies for all Air Force senior leaders, past and present, for use by anyone with access to the Internet? This fact alone challenges us all in at least two ways. First, all official Air Force biographies should have the same corporate Air Force look—the public expects the military to be standardized. Second, the need to disclose personal accomplishments and facts must be balanced with the need to protect private and sensitive information. The guidance of this chapter compiles information provided by the experts in the Air Force Production (AFPRO) office at the Defense Media Activity (DMA) who publish the official biographies for Air Force senior leaders. The guidance here follows the same protocols used by AFPRO to help all Air Force personnel create a biography with the same corporate Air Force look while also protecting personal or sensitive information.

Getting Started

The official biography is unique among all the written products discussed in *The Tongue and Quill*—the official biography is a public affairs communication tool similar to a news release. As such, it follows the style guidance for a news release developed by the Associated Press (AP) and adopted by the Air Force (see below). The official biography has multiple sections—some are required while a few are optional. For some, the requirement depends on your status (officer, enlisted or civilian), flight rating, and joint experience. Special considerations are annotated where applicable. In addition, the following general guidance applies:

- Format: use [Arial font, size 9] for all text and entries; bold the headings (e.g., **EDUCATION**); use [**Arial font, size 13.5 BOLD**] for the identification line; all line spacing is 1.15.
- Length: Final drafts should be no more than two pages in length when printed.
- Use a *single* space after a period or punctuation mark in the narrative.

NOTE: The official biographies available on the Air Force Portal may be different from the standards presented in this chapter—customs and standards have changed over time. Check with your chain of command for command-specific guidance in preparing an official biography.

Associated Press (AP) Style Guidance for Official Biographies

- Acronyms: Spell out acronyms on first use; minimize the use of military jargon.
- Adjectives: For brevity, minimize the use of adjectives (e.g., "*successfully* led…").
- Months and Dates:
    - Jan., Feb., Aug., Sept., Oct., Nov., and Dec. *are abbreviated when used with a day (e.g. Jan. 1, 2015), and spelled out when used only with year (e.g. January 2015)*
    - March, April, May, June, and July *are always spelled out*.
    - Use commas to separate the day from the year in the "Month Day, Year" format (March 3, 2014) but not when the day is omitted (March 2014).
    - If frocked, say only "Frocked" and do not include a date of promotion.
- Rank: Follows Air Force journalistic style.
    - Spelled out fully in the identification line using all capital letters.
    - Abbreviated rank is used in the narrative with the name of the member.
    - Generic rank (e.g., "the colonel" or "the general") is used when the name is omitted.
- State names
    - All states are spelled out completely when they stand alone without a city.
    - Alaska, Hawaii, Idaho, Iowa, Maine, Ohio, Texas, and Utah *are always spelled out*.
    - Ala., Ariz., Ark., Calif., Colo., Conn., Del., Fla., Ga., Ill., Ind., Kan., Ky., La., Md., Mass., Mich., Minn., Miss., Mo., Mont., Neb., Nev., N.H., N.J., N.M., N.Y., N.C., N.D., Okla., Ore., Pa., R.I., S.C., S.D., Tenn., Vt., Va., Wash., W.Va., Wis., and Wyo. *may be abbreviated when used* **with** *a city*.

Official Biography Elements

The guidance below is presented to help all Air Force personnel draft their own biography using the standards for an official biography used by the AFPRO. All personnel must balance the need for disclosure with the need to protect personal or sensitive information in preparing a biography.

- The preparation of an official biography is covered by the Privacy Act; however, the finished product is public domain and must be in agreement with official records.

- **Follow Public Affairs' guidance for the disclosure of contingency operations locations.** In general, forward operating bases are not normally used on an official biography while some main operating bases, such as Manas Air Base, Kyrgyzstan; Joint Base Balad, Iraq; or Joint Base Bagram, Afghanistan, may be used. If in doubt, use a general term (e.g., Southwest Asia) for the location of a contingency operation.

- **Do not include the names of family members anywhere on the biography.**

Identification Line ("FULL RANK FIRST M. LAST" or "FIRST M. LAST")

- Officer and enlisted. Spell out the full rank and signature block name using bold font and all capital letters (e.g., "**FULL RANK FIRST M. LAST**").

- Civilian. Spell out the signature block name using bold font and all capital letters (e.g., "**FIRST M. LAST**"). Rank is not used for civilian biographies.

Narrative

The narrative has both text and the official photograph. Officer and enlisted biographies typically have only two or three paragraphs; civilian biographies may have up to five or six. Spell out all office symbols, acronyms and organizational names; do not provide details that compromise unit-level operational security (e.g., numbers of people, aircraft or equipment).

- First paragraph.
  - Officer and enlisted. Begins with the abbreviated rank and full name followed by position title (from official records), organization, base and location. Next, provide a brief description of the member's responsibilities in this position.
  - Civilian. Begins with the full name followed by position title (from official records), organization, base and location. Next, provide a brief description of the member's responsibilities in this position. Civilian rank is not used on the official biography.

- Official photograph. The official photograph is placed in the upper right corner of the biography, below the banner, aligned with the top of the first paragraph, and flush with the right margin. The source photograph file should be of high resolution in a standard 8" x 10" or 5" x 7" format. Resize the source file to roughly 3.2" wide x 4" high using a locked aspect ratio and cropping, as required (~ 40% of an 8" x 10" original).

- Second paragraph.
  - Officer and enlisted. Briefly describe the member's career: when the member entered the Air Force (enlisted: month and year of enlistment followed by technical training course attended and the month/year of graduation from technical training;

officer: college attended and commissioning source), years of service (active /guard/reserve), experience (technical/leadership), assignment locations (states/countries) and a summary of the most *significant* assignments (not a "laundry list" of assignments). The final sentence of the narrative, as part of this paragraph or the third paragraph, reads, "Prior to his/her current position, the (rank) was the (position title, organization, base, and location)."

- Civilian. Briefly describe the member's previous significant assignments (e.g., "Prior to his current position, Mrs. Smith was the *position title, organization, base, and location*"). The organization, base and location may be omitted for where the position title inherently describes the organization, base and location (e.g., "Deputy Undersecretary of Defense for Acquisition, Technology, and Logistics" is clearly a Pentagon assignment working for the Secretary of Defense). Follow this with a brief description of the member's responsibilities in the position(s) listed.

- Third paragraph.

  - Officer and Enlisted [*Optional*]. Provide information on the member's other noteworthy assignments, contingency operations experience, deployments and flight information, as applicable. For guard and reserve personnel, this paragraph may include information on the member's civilian profession; however, do not use the names of companies—be generic (e.g., "In her civilian capacity, the general is a pilot with a major airline"). If not included in the second paragraph, the third paragraph may simply be "Prior to his/her current position, the (rank) was the (position title, organization, base and location)."

  - Civilian. Provide information on the member's significant professional experience prior to entering public service (e.g., "Before entering public service, Mrs. Smith was the Chief Executive Officer for *company name*, an industry-leading technology firm specializing in cyber security for advanced logistics systems"). Company names may be used since they are integral to the credentials of civilians.

- Fourth paragraph [*Civilian only*].

  - Describe the member's earlier experience, both public and private, prior to the position(s) described in the third paragraph. May include military service and a summary of publications, as applicable.

  - Fifth and sixth paragraphs may be added to provide logical breaks in the narrative while tracing the member's significant and relevant experience to the member's entry into the workforce following the completion of formal education. Frequently, the narrative concludes with a statement of the college(s) attended and degree(s) earned.

"EDUCATION"

Use bold font and all capital letters for the heading; do not use a colon after the heading. List completed education programs chronologically (first to most recent) by year, type of degree, title of degree/program, institution, city, and state. Include all academic degrees and all professional military education (PME), professional developmental education (PDE), professional continuing education (PCE), and executive courses. For academic programs that merge the type and title of the degree (e.g., "Master of Business Administration" or "Master of Military Operational Art and

| CHAPTER 20
| The Official Biography

Science"), use the merged type and title for the entry. When the institution name includes the state (e.g., "University of Iowa"), do not include the state at the end of the entry. For non-degree PME, PDE, PCE, and executive courses, list only the year, course, school, location and state. For PME only, add "by correspondence", if appropriate, as shown below.

> 2002 Bachelor of Science, Aeronautical Engineering, Auburn University, Auburn, Ala.
>
> 2003 Air and Space Basic Course, Maxwell Air Force Base, Ala.
> ["Air Force Base" is spelled out on first use.]
>
> 2006 Master of Science, Logistics Management, Air Force Institute of Technology, Wright-Patterson AFB, Ohio
>
> 2007 Squadron Officer School, Maxwell AFB, Ala., by correspondence
>
> 2008 Squadron Officer School, Maxwell AFB, Ala.
>
> 2012 Air Command and Staff College, Maxwell AFB, Ala., by correspondence
>
> 2013 Master of Military Operational Art and Science, Air Command and Staff College, Maxwell AFB, Ala.
>
> 2017 Air War College, Maxwell AFB, Ala., by correspondence
>
> 2020 Doctor of Philosophy, Military History, University of Alabama, Tuscaloosa

Work History ("ASSIGNMENTS" or "CAREER CHRONOLOGY")

Use bold font and all capital letters for the heading; *do not* use a colon after the heading. List the member's work history chronologically by month and year entered to month and year departed. *Follow Public Affairs' guidance for disclosure of contingency operations locations.*

- Officer and enlisted personnel use "ASSIGNMENTS" as the heading.
    - Include the official duty title, unit, base and state. (The squadron of assignment is not always necessary, such as while in student status or when the duty title and base sufficiently identify the assignment. If in doubt, include the squadron.)
    - Spell out Air Base (AB), Air Force Base (AFB) and Joint Base (JB) on first use.
    - Do not use a period at the end of an assignment entry unless needed to abbreviate a state (or Washington, D.C.).
    - Spell out the names of all months (*do not follow the AP abbreviation guidance for the names of months in this section*).
    - Capitalize all duty titles (as of October 2011 for all new official biographies).
    - Deployment/contingency experience is placed in parentheses in the same line as the assignment during which the member deployed.
- Civilian personnel use "CAREER CHRONOLOGY" as the heading. If previous military service is listed, include the year you left the service and the reason (e.g., retired, service in the Reserve or Guard, or civilian employment).
    - Include the official position title and the organization/company name.
    - Spell out Air Base (AB), Air Force Base (AFB) and Joint Base (JB) on first use.

- o Do not use a period at the end of an assignment entry unless needed to abbreviate a state (or Washington, D.C.) or as part of a company name (e.g., "Inc.").
- o Spell out the names of all months (*do not follow the AP abbreviation guidance for the names of months in this section*).
- o Capitalize all duty titles (as of October 2011 for all new official biographies).
- o Deployment/contingency experience is placed in parentheses in the same line as the position during which the member deployed.

- Assignment entry format and examples

    1. Month Year–Month Year, Duty Title, Unit, Installation, State

    2. March 2005–February 2008, Duty Title, Unit, Randolph AFB, Texas

    3. February 2008–July 2010, Duty Title, Unit, Maxwell AFB, Ala. (August 2008–January 2009, Duty Title, Unit, Balad Air Base, Iraq)

    4. July 2010–June 2011, Student, Air Command and Staff College, Maxwell AFB, Ala.

"SUMMARY OF JOINT ASSIGNMENTS" [*Officer only*]

This section applies to officer personnel only; delete entire section if no joint assignments. Use bold font and all capital letters for the heading; *do not* use a colon after the heading. The format is the same as for "**ASSIGNMENTS**" with the addition of rank at the end of each entry. List all joint assignments chronologically (first to most recent) by month and year entered to month and year departed. Include the official duty title, unit, base and state. *Follow Public Affairs' guidance for disclosure of contingency operations locations.*

- Do not use a period at the end of an assignment entry unless needed to abbreviate a state (or Washington, D.C.).

- Each entry ends with a statement of the rank held for the joint assignment (e.g., "…, as a colonel").

- Example joint assignment entries

    1. June 2006–June 2008, Assistant Deputy Directorate for Special Operations, Operations Directorate, the Joint Staff, Washington D.C., as a colonel

    2. May 2008–May 2010, Commander, Combined Joint Special Operations Air Component, Joint Base Balad, Iraq, as a brigadier general

    3. August 2012–September 2014, Director, Command, Control, Communications and Cyber (J6), US Pacific Command, Camp H. M. Smith, Hawaii, as a major general

"FLIGHT INFORMATION" [*Officer and enlisted flight rated only*]

This section applies to flight rated personnel only; delete entire section if not flight rated. Use bold font and all capital letters for the heading; *do not* use a colon after the heading. List the member's rating, flight hours and aircraft flown. Use a colon with two spaces after the colon for rating, flight hours and aircraft flown.

- Rating: Level (none, senior, master, command) and type (pilot, navigator, air battle manager, flight surgeon, flight nurse, astronaut, aircrew member).
- Flight hours: Total is approximate (e.g., "More than 2,100") and may include combat time (e.g., "including more than 60 combat hours"). *Do not round up—the hours listed should be slightly less than the actual hours.*
- Aircraft flown: Listed chronologically with the most recent being listed last.
- Example flight information entries

  Rating: command pilot

  Flight hours: more than 2,900 (Use "more than" not "over")

  Aircraft flown: T-37, T-38, OV-10, B-52G, B-1B and B-2

"MAJOR AWARDS AND DECORATIONS"

Use bold font and all capital letters for the heading; *do not* use a colon after the heading. Capitalize (Title Case) the names of all medals and ribbons listed. Accoutrements (devices) are not capitalized (e.g., with bronze star, with two oak leaf clusters, with "V" device). Never use "one" for a single award.

- Officer and enlisted. List the member's major military awards and decorations in descending order of precedence (highest to lowest). It is customary for officers and senior enlisted members to list only Achievement Medals and higher honors. Lower precedent honors are listed only if significant (e.g., Prisoner of War Medal, Outstanding Airman of the Year Ribbon).

- Civilian. List the member's major civilian awards of state, regional or national interest in descending order of precedence (highest to lowest). Former military members should list their major military awards and decorations first, then list civilian awards. If military awards are listed, it is customary for officers and senior enlisted members to show only Achievement Medals and higher honors. Lower precedent honors are listed only if significant (e.g., Prisoner of War Medal, Outstanding Airman of the Year Ribbon).

- Example major awards and decorations entries

  Distinguished Service Medal

  Defense Superior Service Medal with two bronze stars

  Legion of Merit with oak leaf cluster

  Distinguished Flying Cross

  Meritorious Service Medal with four oak leaf clusters

  Air Medal with nine oak leaf clusters

  Air Force Commendation Medal with oak leaf cluster

"OTHER ACHIEVEMENTS" [*Optional for all*]

Use bold font and all capital letters for the heading; *do not* use a colon after the heading. List significant other achievements chronologically (first to most recent) by year, followed by a space, and the title or brief description of the achievement.

"PUBLICATIONS" [*Optional for all*]

Use bold font and all capital letters for the heading; *do not* use a colon after the heading. List the publications chronologically (first to most recent) by title and publication data.

"PROFESSIONAL MEMBERSHIPS AND ASSOCIATIONS" [*Optional for all*]

Use bold font and all capital letters for the heading; *do not* use a colon after the heading. List current and relevant professional memberships and associations by name only.

"EFFECTIVE DATES OF PROMOTION" [*Military only*]

Use bold font and all capital letters for the heading; *do not* use a colon after the heading. List the rank and effective date of promotion using the full rank, month, day and year in AP style.

- Officer. List all ranks from commissioning to the current rank held, such as follows:

    Second Lieutenant June 1, 2000

    First Lieutenant June 1, 2002

    Captain June 2, 2004

- Enlisted. List all ranks from enlistment to the current rank held as shown below.

    Airman Basic Sept. 28, 2003

    Airman March 28, 2004

    Airman First Class Jan. 28, 2005

    Senior Airman Sept. 28, 2006

    Staff Sergeant July 1, 2008

    Technical Sergeant July 1, 2011

    NOTE: *The custom for the official biography for the Chief Master Sergeant of the Air Force is to list only the promotion to Chief Master Sergeant of the Air Force with the heading changed to the singular form* (**"EFFECTIVE DATE OF PROMOTION"**).

- Civilian. Rank is not used on civilian biographies; civilians do not use this section.

" (Current as of Month Year) "

The current as of date (month and year) are written in sentence case and enclosed in parentheses one blank line below the effective dates of promotion section. An example current as of date is as follows: **(Current as of August 2014)**

CHAPTER 21:

The Résumé

> ***This chapter covers:***
> - Function and Organization
> - Seven Steps to an Effective Résumé
> - Things to Include
> - Things to Omit
> - The Résumé Cover Letter
> - Examples

An up-to-date biography is an invaluable tool to help you build a résumé. Although the résumé is not an official Air Force document, it is discussed here to help you when you begin your transition to the private sector work force.

The résumé serves at least two functions: the individual components of the résumé convey important information about your knowledge, skills and abilities to perform the job while the résumé as a whole presents a picture of you and your experience to create a positive first impression. With a good first impression, you can rise above the competition and get to the interview stage where you will need to employ all the skills of effective speaking discussed earlier in this volume. The challenge is to produce a résumé that gets noticed.

Getting noticed is even more difficult today with the advent resumé search engines, online resumé sites, and software applications that make job applications easier to complete. While these advances make applying for a job easier they also increase the size of the applicant pool. However, with a good resumé at the ready you can master just about any online job application or resumé-building software. One advantage of the resumé-building software used by the Office of Personnel Management (OPM) website is the format standardization of all resumés—you cannot set the format and neither can anyone else—so make your resumé shine by building your resumé to accomplish a specific function and organizing your content to achieve that function. With a few simple steps you can create focus within the resumé and clearly link your knowledge, skills, abilities and experience to the qualities the employer is seeking.

Function and Organization

The old expression "form follows function" is especially true with resumés. Organize your resumé for the function it serves. For example, are you using the resumé as a "feeler" to look for opportunities with multiple companies simultaneously; a response to a particular announcement; or a specific request from a person or company? Once you know the function, organize your resumé to accomplish that function and use the key terms used by the employer to get noticed.

1. **The chronological resumé** is an outline of your work experience and periods of employment (in reverse chronological order—most recent information first) that shows steady employment. Titles and organizations are emphasized as are duties and accomplishments. This format is used most often by those with steady employment and/or who want to remain in a current career field. It's also excellent for those who have shown advancement within a specific career field. Detail the most recent 10-year period and summarize earlier experience that is relevant to the position you are seeking.

2. **The functional resumé** emphasizes your qualifications (skills, knowledge, abilities and achievements) as opposed to specific dates and places of employment, and allows you to group them into functional areas such as training, sales, procurement and accounting. List the functional areas in the order of importance as related to the job objective and stress your accomplishments within these functional areas. This format is used most often by people who are reentering the work force or those seeking a career change.

3. **The combination resumé** combines the best of the chronological and functional resumés because you can group relevant skills and abilities into functional areas and then provide your work history, dates and places of employment, and education. This format allows you to cover a wider variety of subjects and qualifications, thereby showing skills that are transferable from one career to another. It works well for those "special" assignment requirements, for military retirees (those who have frequently switched career fields), and is ideal for people whose career paths have been somewhat erratic.

4. **The targeted resumé** focuses on your skills, knowledge, abilities, achievements, experience and education that relate to a specific position. It features a series of bullet statements regarding your capabilities and achievements related to the targeted job. Experience is listed to support statements and education is listed after achievements. This format is probably the easiest to write, but keep in mind it must be re-accomplished ("targeted") for each position you are seeking.

5. **The federal résumé** is most commonly built by the OPM website for federal government jobs. This résumé is commonly five pages by the time all your information is included so it does not follow the "keep it to two pages max" rule. Once you submit your résumé, there may be further forms to complete. When in doubt as to what to include, read the job announcement carefully. If you still have questions, call the point of contact on the job announcement. The OPM website allows users to register and then create and store several résumés within the user's account. When applying for a specific job, users can then attach the most applicable stored résumé or build a new one to target a specific job.

6. **The military résumé** is used to apply for highly selective military assignments, such as an aide or member of an executive staff. The military résumé summarizes your qualifications for the position that may not be apparent in your biography or duty titles. Use the format that best showcases your abilities and include the following information:

   a. Security clearance and date of investigation. This is critical for some jobs; in some cases, you'll need a higher level clearance just to get in the building!

   b. Date of rank. This helps potential supervisors know how your seniority relates to the incumbents in the office ... and helps them know when you'll be up for promotion.

   c. Professional Military Education. Make sure you identify any schools completed while in residence and any distinguished graduate (DG) recognition.

   d. Service Status. Regular Air Force, Air Force Reserve, or National Guard.

   e. Availability. When will you be available for reassignment?

   f. Special Qualifications. Identify special qualifications such as foreign language skills, Acquisition Professional Development Program (APDP), or Joint Officer credentials.

   g. Flying Data. Even if the position is not a flying billet, rated officers may want to include flying data.

Seven Steps to an Effective Résumé

The seven steps to effective communication (chapters 2-9) provide an excellent checklist for building an effective résumé. When writing your résumé, remember, the best qualified person doesn't always get the job—sometimes it's the person with the most effective résumé.

1. Analyze Purpose and Audience. Your purpose is to get hired—which usually occurs after a successful interview—which requires you to get noticed first—which requires you to know a good deal about the job, the company and the employer and have that knowledge reflected in your résumé. Begin by asking yourself questions that need to be answered and then move to step 2.

2. Conduct the Research. Know yourself: your needs and wants (type and level of the position), what you can offer and what you can do for them. Now take time to list your skills and accomplishments. And research the prospective company to learn about the job as well as to "speak their language."

3. Support Your Ideas. Your "ideas" in this context are your qualifications for the job. Likewise, the "support" for your qualifications is your knowledge, skills, abilities, experience and education that support those qualifications.

4. Get Organized. Gather your documents: job descriptions, certificates, licenses and academic transcripts. If you worked for the Department of Defense, "civilianize" those job titles and descriptions to those used in the private sector ... consult the *Dictionary of Occupational Titles*, published by the US Department of Labor. Learning the company's terminology could mean the difference between a 20-second scan and an interview.

5. Draft. Type your draft and prepare to edit.

6. Edit. Read your draft and edit: edit for typos, extraneous information, action words, plain language (businesses typically write on an 8th grade level), neatness, accuracy and consistency in format. It must be long enough to cover relevant information but brief enough not to bore a potential employer (two pages max). Use only key phrases and words appropriate to the job you're seeking. To help you develop your accomplishment statements, review the advice on writing accomplishment-impact bullet statements.

7. Fight for Feedback. Have someone you trust read the résumé and suggest changes and recommendations. Are all the t's crossed and i's dotted? Does it look professional? Visually appealing? Is it easy to read with the strongest points quickly apparent? Is there good use of spacing, margins, indentions, capitalization and underlining?

Things to Include

As a minimum, *definitely include* the following on all résumés:

- Name, mailing address, e-mail address and telephone number (with area code) centered at the top of the first page. [*Balance your privacy with the need for potential employers to reach you easily; limit contact data to what you feel comfortable with providing.*]

- Job objective and/or summary statement.

- Qualifications and work experience relevant to the job you are seeking.

- Education and training (military courses or other conferences, workshops, seminars and continuing education classes) emphasizing those relevant to the position you're seeking.

The following items *may be included* on your résumé if pertinent to the position you are seeking.

- Leadership activities
- Special skills or capabilities
- Professional experience and memberships
- Credentials, licenses
- Career accomplishments
- Languages studied
- Honors and awards
- Military service
- Papers, presentations, published works
- Security clearance

CHAPTER 21
The Résumé

Things to Omit

Omit the following types of information unless they are specifically requested by the employer.

- Personal data (age, marital status, number and ages of children)
- Photograph
- Salary history or requirement
- Religious affiliation
- Specific security information
- Reason for leaving a job and names of bosses
- References
- Hobbies or personal interests
- Months, days—use "years" only
- Irrelevant information

The Résumé Cover Letter

A cover letter is a personal communication written to a specific person in an organization. The cover letter speaks for you to garner the interest of the employer—write the cover letter so that the employer will want to read your résumé and offer you an interview.

- Format: Use white or off-white 8½ x 11-inch high-quality paper following the format for a personal letter (chapter 15). Do not use Air Force letterhead.

- Address the letter, if possible, to a specific person such as the hiring official, work center manager or human resources executive. If addressing the letter to an official position without the name, use gender-neutral terms in the salutation (e.g., "Dear Manager").

- Use a positive tone that is genuine and natural to stress how your association with the firm will benefit you both.

- Use action verbs, personal pronouns, life, conviction, humor, assurance and confidence to sell them on hiring you. Delete irrelevant and negative information.

- Limit the letter to one page; limit the body to two or three paragraphs.
    - First sentence: Grab the reader's attention and use the name of a mutual contact.
    - Highlight your relevant experience, skills and accomplishments that make you unique for the job and entices the reader to call you. Consider using bullets to create eye appeal and place the most relevant information first/at the top.
    - Close with a bid for a brief meeting (don't use interview) and write as though you expect it to occur. Indicate you will follow up with a call to arrange a time.

- Make it professional—edit, edit, edit—then keep the file to draft future cover letters.

Examples

The following pages display an example cover letter and several example résumés with complete contact data to get you started. *You should limit the contact data to what you feel comfortable with providing.* Also, many bases host résumé-building classes; find out what services are available at your base to help you build a content rich and professional résumé that make your knowledge, skills and abilities rise above the rest to get you noticed and hired!

Résumé Cover Letter

July 7, 2014

Mary M. Middleton
PO Box 8765
Seattle WA 54321-1234

Ms. Rena Mitchell
Government Contracts Advisor
Bowe and Burke International Corporation
1472 South 303d Street
Seattle WA 54300-1472

Dear Ms. Mitchell

  I recently read about Bowe and Burke in the newspaper and spoke with Nancy Herron. She mentioned you need a project manager/team leader—I am interested in this position and believe you will find these particular aspects of my background relevant to this position:

- As project manager for a statewide fund-raising campaign, I recruited and supervised personnel, administered the budget, and led the development of promotional materials.
- As manager of 300 volunteers for an organization, I handled diverse management functions—scheduled work, evaluated personnel, organized supply and equipment resources, and controlled cash receipts and other assets.
- I have extensive knowledge of the computer software used by your company and have developed personnel and accounting macro-functions to expedite management actions.
- My bachelor's degree in business administration includes course work in personnel administration and accounting.

  I will telephone you on Wednesday, July 16, to arrange for a meeting where I can learn more about your requirements and tell you more about my background as it relates to you. Thank you for your consideration and I look forward to being in touch.

                       Sincerely

                       Mary M. Middleton
                       MARY M. MIDDLETON

Attachment:
Résumé

Chronological Résumé

KAREN CALLOWAY
123 Center Street
Middletown IA 54321-1234
(515) 333-9999 (Home)
(515) 555-7777 (Cell)
kgalloway@heartland.com

JOB OBJECTIVE   Challenging writer-editor position.

EXPERIENCE

  <u>Writer-Editor</u>, Middletown College, Middletown, Iowa, 2008-Present. Researched and wrote curriculum materials for … Edited curriculum materials written by … Ensured accuracy of facts and figures for … Researched, designed, wrote, and typeset a 55-page administrative handbook … Developed and distributed a 21-page textbook preparation guide for … Supervised three …

  <u>Editorial Assistant</u>, The Middletown Journal, Middletown, Iowa, 1998-2008. Typed, edited, and proofread all articles prepared by reporters and staffers for the weekly newspaper. Produced … Recommended … Prepared …

EDUCATION
   MA, Adult Education, Middleton College, Middletown IA, 2006
   BS, English, Middleton College, Middletown IA, 1998

PROFESSIONAL MEMBERSHIPS
   American Writers Guild
   Association of Professional Editors

AWARDS
   Outstanding Contributor, Middletown College English Faculty, 2009
   Best Book Award, American Council of Teachers of English, 2006

PERSONAL INTERESTS
   Free-lance writing
   Photography
   Publishing

Functional Résumé

CHARLES CATO
1234 High Street
Millbrook AL 36054-0001
(205) 333-4444 (Home)
(205) 555-4400 (Cell)
charlescato@southland.com

JOB OBJECTIVE	Information systems resource manager specializing in microcomputers with emphasis on training and development.
QUALIFICATIONS	<u>Resource Management</u>: Managed $300 million inventory of hardware and software resources for 13 individual computer systems, 5 aircraft simulators, and 40 microcomputers. Reorganized … Identified …, formulated new policies, updated … and revised … Researched and developed … Planned and supervised … Reduced computer supply acquisition costs by $150K through …
	<u>Systems Analysis</u>: Coordinated weekly … Organized, developed, and supervised the … Designed training … and developed self-study course … implemented data base … that resulted in …
	<u>Quality Control</u>: Developed, coordinated, and managed … Assessed contractor … Provided technical analysis of …
	<u>Programming</u>: Developed and maintained …
EDUCATION	MA in Business Administration with emphasis in Information Systems, University of Alabama, Tuscaloosa, Alabama, 2007 (GPA 3.82)
	BS, Mathematics and Computer Science, Tulane University, New Orleans, Louisiana, 2006 (GPA 3.1)

CHAPTER 21
The Résumé

Combination (Chronological and Functional) Résumé

FELICIA VINSON
321 Jefferson Ave
Vienna VA 54321-1234
(703) 555-1234 (Home)
(703) 544-7890 (Cell)
feliciavinson@colonial.com

OBJECTIVE	A career using financial and retail organization skills that offers growth through further education with increasing responsibility.
SUMMARY	Experienced in financial and retail organizations emphasizing office administration, accounting, and supervisory skills.
QUALIFICATIONS	<u>Accounting and Finance</u>. Performed accounting and administrative procedures for large banking institution and retail sales organization. Completed … Balanced … Recorded bank … Calculated daily … resulting in reduction of … and savings of …
	<u>Management and Administration</u>. Administered … Operated computer to verify … Researched monthly … Supervised 3 to 6 employees … Managed retail stores with merchandise worth $300,000, reducing … and saving …
EXPERIENCE	
1992-1997	Manager, Boomers Stores, Washington DC
1991-1992	Assistant Manager, Sun Savings, Wheaton MD
1990-1991	Accountant, Midway Bank, Midway MD
1987-1990	Assistant Contracting Officer, USAF
1980-1990	USAF
EDUCATION	BS, Business Administration, University of Pennsylvania, 1992
	Senior Management Course, University of Northern Virginia, 1993

Targeted Résumé

KEVIN JONES
6953 Oakside Drive
Harris GA 30814-7606
(706) 277-9999 (Home)
(706) 285-8888 (Cell)
kjones@peachtree.com

JOB OBJECTIVE	Senior credit analyst in an engineering department with potential for advancement within the corporation.
CAPABILITIES	- Analyzed credit data to … - Prepared reports of … - Studied, researched, reported … - Evaluated … and prepared reports … - Consulted with … on …
ACHIEVEMENTS	- Responsible for … - Supervised a staff of … responsible for $2 million inventory of … - Maintained … - Acted as … - Saved … work hours and … dollars …
EXPERIENCE	
2007-present	Senior Credit Analyst, Georgia South Corporation, Macon, Georgia
2001-2007	Credit and Collection Manager, General Electric, Clinton, New Jersey
1998-2001	Claims Examiner, Great Western, Billings, New Jersey
EDUCATION	MBA in Finance, Pace University, Monroe, Connecticut, 2002 BS in Accounting, Northeast College, Penham, Massachusetts, 1998 (Honors graduate)

CHAPTER 22:

Envelopes and Mail

> ***This chapter covers:***
> - Envelope Fundamentals
> - Envelope Anatomy
> - Address Format Standards
> - USPS Mail Terminology

We send and receive mail every day with little thought about the technical requirements for addressing the mail. United States Postal Service (USPS) Publication 28, *Postal Addressing Standards*, provides a wealth of information (210 pages) to standardize the address elements of mail items to optimize automated mail handling and decrease the time it takes for an item to arrive at its destination. There are many addressing standards that are beyond the scope of this handbook; however, *The Tongue and Quill* team has extracted essential elements of USPS Publication 28 for ready reference and standardization within the Air Force.

Envelope Fundamentals

Use an envelope appropriate for the size and type of correspondence when prepared for dispatch. The envelope should be rectangular and the correspondence should fit easily, but not too loose, so use an envelope that is only slightly larger than the dispatch-ready correspondence. When choosing an envelope size, be aware that very small and very large envelopes are difficult to process: Normally, use envelopes at least 3.5 by 5 inches and no larger than 6.125 x 11.5 inches. In addition to the size of the envelope, consider the following when selecting an envelope:

- When using window envelopes, be sure that the MEMORANDUM FOR element is visible through the envelope window.

- When several items are to be dispatched together, the largest item that cannot be folded determines the envelope size.

- Do not use envelopes with clasps, staples, string buttons, or similar securing devices for USPS mail—they will jam in the automated mail sorting equipment.

- Limit the thickness of any envelope to 1/4 inch or less when sealed—thicker envelopes will jam the automated mail sorting equipment. Write "NON-MACHINEABLE" above the address on any envelope if it is more than 1/4 inch thick.

Envelope Anatomy

The Post Office designates four areas on the face of an envelope for specific purposes. These areas include the return address area; the postage area; the optical character reader (OCR) read area; and the barcode clear area as shown in the diagram below.

USPS Publication 28, Annex 1, Section A1, Envelope Illustration

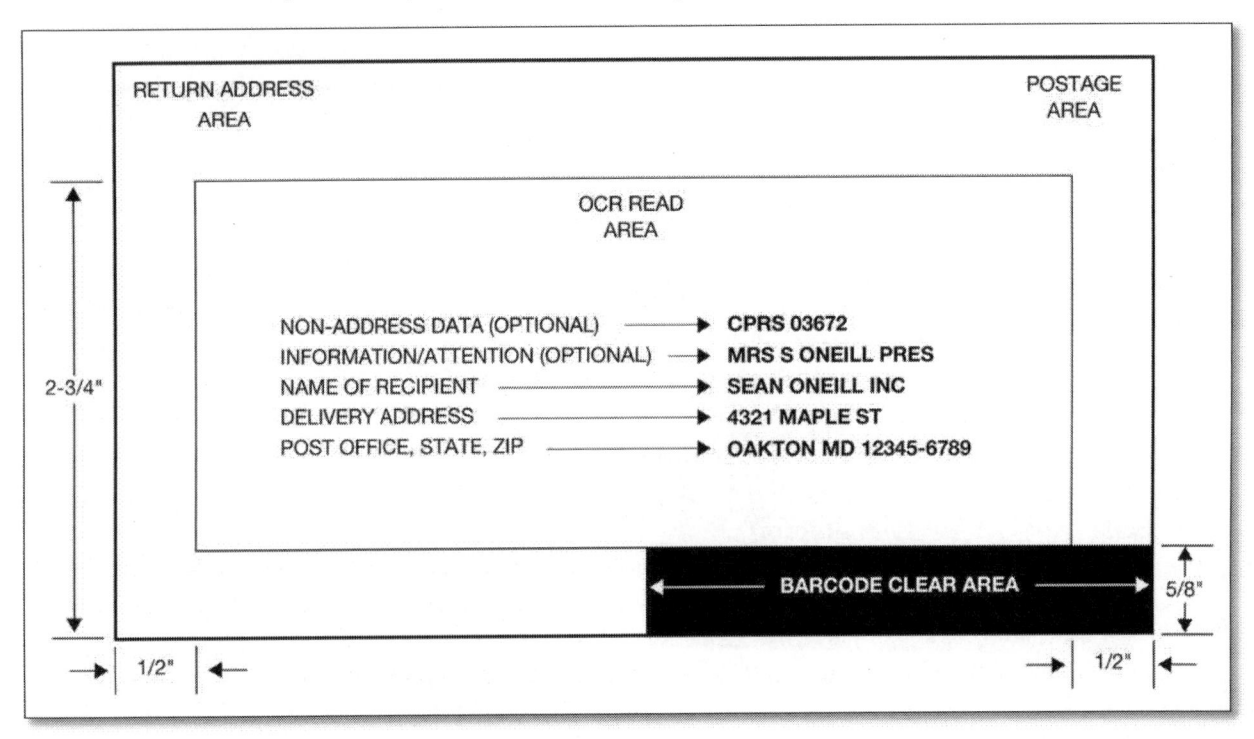

CHAPTER 22
Envelopes and Mail

Envelope Anatomy Details

- The return address area is in the upper left corner of the envelope. The return address is aligned on the left approximately 1/8 inch from the left edge of the envelope and approximately 1/8 inch down from the top of the envelope.

- The postage area is in the upper right corner of the envelope (ensure the correspondence has sufficient postage, if required, before mailing).

- The OCR read area covers the majority of the center of the envelope. The OCR read area is a rectangle with the base 5/8 inch from the bottom of the envelope and extending upwards to 2 3/4 inches from the bottom with 1/2 inch margins from each side. The entire address must be contained within the OCR read area.

- The barcode clear area is in the lower right corner. It extends from the lower right corner of the envelope upwards 5/8 inch with a width of 4 3/4 inches.

The envelope should contain only the information needed in the areas reserved for each purpose without printed or stamped markings of slogans or designs. This also applies to mailing labels, post cards and self-mailers. An example envelope is provided in the diagram below.

Air Force Correspondence Envelope Illustration

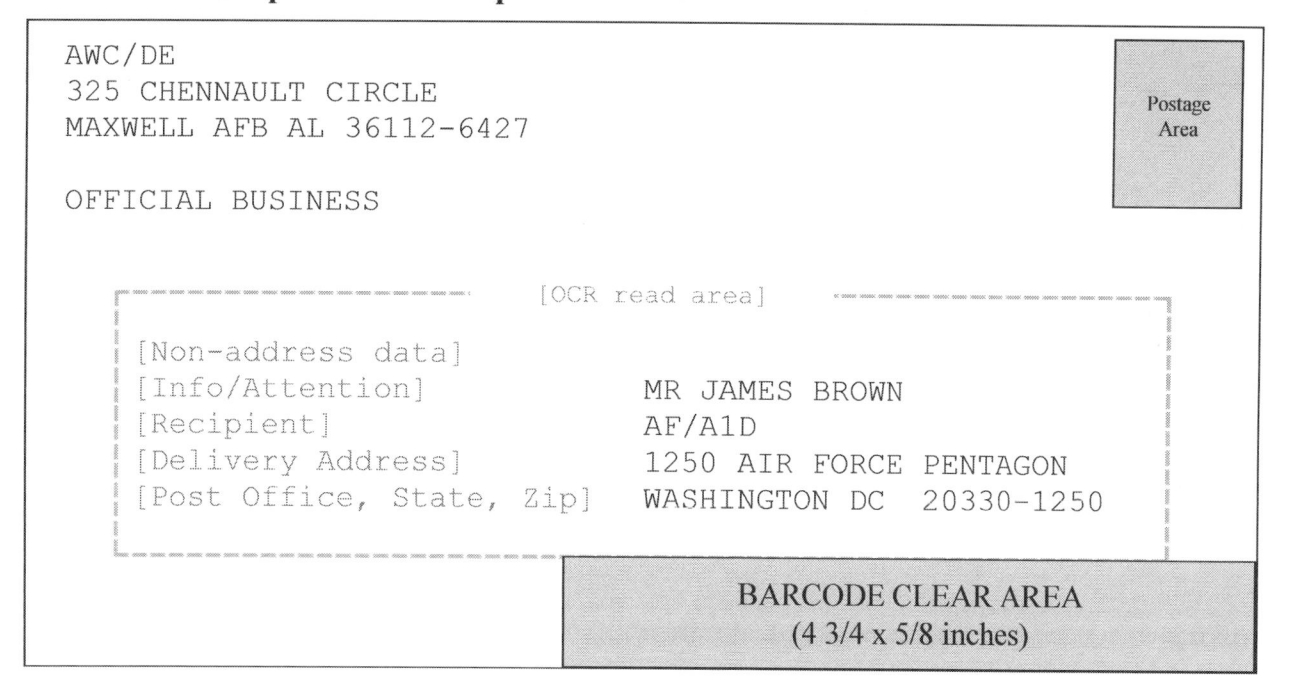

```
AWC/DE
325 CHENNAULT CIRCLE                                          Postage
MAXWELL AFB AL 36112-6427                                      Area

OFFICIAL BUSINESS


                              [OCR read area]

  [Non-address data]
  [Info/Attention]          MR JAMES BROWN
  [Recipient]               AF/A1D
  [Delivery Address]        1250 AIR FORCE PENTAGON
  [Post Office, State, Zip] WASHINGTON DC  20330-1250


                                    BARCODE CLEAR AREA
                                    (4 3/4 x 5/8 inches)
```

Address Format Standards

The USPS provides standards for the address format to make the addresses readable. This helps the USPS identify the correct delivery address the first time that the mail piece is processed. Follow the USPS guidance and additional information in the table on the next page to ensure addresses on your envelopes are readable—by people and automated equipment.

USPS Publication 28 Guidance	The Tongue and Quill Additional Information
Addresses should be typewritten or machine printed in dark ink on a light background using uppercase letters.	Use all uppercase characters whether typed or word-processor printed. Do not use bold, italic, script, artistic or other unusual typefaces. Hand-written addresses or rubber stamps should not be used.
Except for the hyphen in the primary or secondary street number (if needed) or the ZIP+4 Code, all punctuation may be omitted.	Use open punctuation style (omit punctuation), when possible.
All lines of the address should be formatted with a uniform left margin.	Set the left margin for all lines so that the longest line is complete without an overrun to a second line, if possible, and leaves a 1/2 inch margin to the right.
When using a foreign address, always place the country name by itself on the last line.	Self-explanatory.
Address characters must not touch and should be equally spaced.	Use Courier New, Times New Roman, or simple sans serif font with point size of 12.
All lines of the address should be parallel to the bottom of the envelope.	Self-explanatory.
Be sure to include all pertinent information such as the directional code, apartment, floor and suite number.	Include in the delivery address the street designators (e.g., BLVD, DR); directional designators (e.g., NE, SW); the apartment, suite, or room number; and a ZIP+4 code.
The entire address should be contained in an imaginary rectangle known as the OCR read area that extends from 5/8 inch to 2 3/4 inch from the bottom of the mail-piece, with 1/2 inch margins on each side.	See USPS Publication 28 illustration, above.
The barcode clear area, 5/8 inch from the bottom, and 4 3/4 inch from the right edge of the mail piece, is the area where an Intelligent Mail barcode is pre-applied or printed by an OCR.	See USPS Publication 28 illustration, above.
Extraneous (non-address) printing that appears in the OCR read area should be positioned above the delivery address line and as far away from the address block as possible.	Self-explanatory.

The Return Address Area (The Sender's Address)

Place the complete mailing address, without any names, in the upper left corner of the envelope. Use uppercase letters with no punctuation except the hyphen in the zip code. Add "OFFICIAL BUSINESS" at least two line spaces below the return address. Finally, do not use rubber stamps for the return address area of the envelope.

The OCR Read Area (The Recipient's Address)

Overview: Use all uppercase letters in Courier New font (12 points) or similar simple sans serif font. Ensure the characters do not touch or overlap—use one or two spaces between words (be consistent). The address is limited to five lines and all five lines must be within the OCR read area: the first line is no higher than 2 3/4 inches from the bottom and the last line must be no lower than 5/8 inch from the bottom. The address must also leave a margin of at least 1/2 inch from each side of the envelope. The left margin is usually not an issue since the address lines are normally blocked left near the middle of the envelope and run parallel to the long edge. Finally, do not use punctuation in the last two lines of the address except for the dash in the ZIP+4 code (e.g., "12345-6789"). Specific guidance for each line of the address is as follows:

Optional Non-Address Data (Address Line 1)

This line is optional. It appears on the first line in the OCR read area and is followed by the optional attention line. Use this line for any non-address data such as account numbers, presort codes, or mail stop codes. Do not use punctuation for this line.

Optional Information/Attention (ATTN) (Address Line 2)

Use this line to direct mail to a specific person within the office or organization identified in the recipient line. If the letter is sensitive or personal information for the recipient's eyes only, add "PERSONAL FOR MS JANE DOE" on this line. Do not use punctuation on this line.

Recipient (Address Line 3)

Use the organization abbreviation and office symbol for the functional area or office. The organization abbreviation is separated from the office symbol by a virgule (also known as a slash; labeled as the "/" key on standard keyboards). Do not use punctuation on this line.

Delivery Address (Address Line 4)

The delivery address line contains the street or post office (PO) box number (use one or the other, never both), and the room or suite number. Use standard address abbreviations or spell them out fully (e.g., AVE or AVENUE, STE or SUITE) and do not use punctuation on this line.

Post Office (City or Base), State, ZIP Code (Address Line 5)

This line identifies the post office by the city, state, and ZIP code. Use standard USPS two-letter abbreviations for the state and ZIP+4 codes if known. NOTE: the dash in the ZIP+4 code is the only punctuation used on this line. With overseas addresses, do not use the APO/FPO number and geographical location together; doing so enters the mail into international mail channels. Do not type below the last line of the delivery address.

Barcode Clear Area

The barcode clear area is for barcodes only. Most printers have the ability to print barcodes which can help route your letter.

Address Types/Examples (See USPS Publication 28, Appendix A)

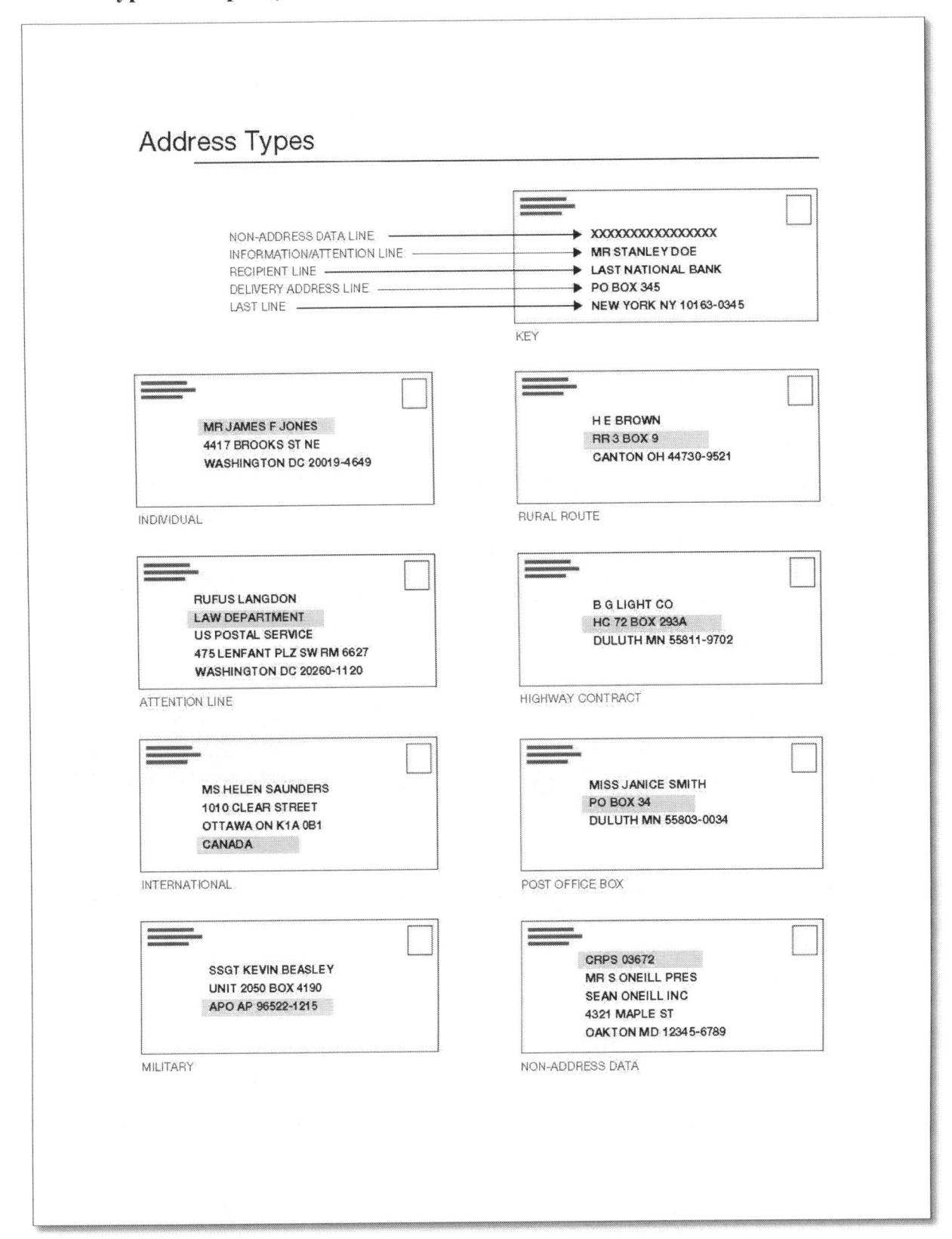

Address Types

KEY
- NON-ADDRESS DATA LINE → XXXXXXXXXXXXXXX
- INFORMATION/ATTENTION LINE → MR STANLEY DOE
- RECIPIENT LINE → LAST NATIONAL BANK
- DELIVERY ADDRESS LINE → PO BOX 345
- LAST LINE → NEW YORK NY 10163-0345

INDIVIDUAL
MR JAMES F JONES
4417 BROOKS ST NE
WASHINGTON DC 20019-4649

RURAL ROUTE
H E BROWN
RR 3 BOX 9
CANTON OH 44730-9521

ATTENTION LINE
RUFUS LANGDON
LAW DEPARTMENT
US POSTAL SERVICE
475 LENFANT PLZ SW RM 6627
WASHINGTON DC 20260-1120

HIGHWAY CONTRACT
B G LIGHT CO
HC 72 BOX 293A
DULUTH MN 55811-9702

INTERNATIONAL
MS HELEN SAUNDERS
1010 CLEAR STREET
OTTAWA ON K1A 0B1
CANADA

POST OFFICE BOX
MISS JANICE SMITH
PO BOX 34
DULUTH MN 55803-0034

MILITARY
SSGT KEVIN BEASLEY
UNIT 2050 BOX 4190
APO AP 96522-1215

NON-ADDRESS DATA
CRPS 03672
MR S ONEILL PRES
SEAN ONEILL INC
4321 MAPLE ST
OAKTON MD 12345-6789

CHAPTER 22
Envelopes and Mail

USPS Mail Terminology

Definitions

- Official Mail. Official matter mailed as penalty mail or on which the postage of fees have been prepaid.

- Official Matter. Official matter is any item belonging to or exclusively pertaining to the business of the US Government.

- Certified. Provides a receipt to sender and a record of delivery at destination. For use with First-Class and Priority Mail.

- Insured. Numbered insured service provides a method to obtain evidence of mailing and a record of delivery.

- Certificate of Mailing. (AF units must not use this service) Provides evidence of mailing.

- Special Handling. (AF units must not use this service) Provides preferential handling to the extent practical in dispatch and transportation, but does not provide special delivery. Applicable to third-and fourth-class mail. Special Services

Types

- Pouch Mail: Used to consolidate mail going to the same location. Contact your local official mail manager or base information transfer center for local pouch listing.

- Holey Joe (Standard Form 65-C): Used to send mail within an organization or base. Address to the organizational designation and office symbol. If more than one person falls under the office symbol, consider using an ATTN line.

- Parcels: Labels should be placed on the top of the box or package. Any container used should be only slightly larger than the mail being sent. Seal boxes and package with paper tape. To help you select the most cost-effective class of mail, review the definition listed on the next page.

Rules

- The United States Postal Service (USPS) shall be used only when it is the least costly transportation method which will meet the required delivery date (RDD), security and accountability requirements. When mailed, official matter shall move at the lowest postage and fees cost to meet the RDD, Security, and accountability requirements.

- Official matter becomes official mail when it is postmarked by a distribution center or is placed under USPS control, whichever occurs first. Official matter ceases to be official mail when control passes from USPS or its representatives to someone else.

- Personal mail (Rules for Employees). Have personal mail sent to your home, not the office. Use personal postage to mail job applications, retirement announcements, greeting cards, personal items, etc.

Classes

- Express Mail. Fastest and most costly. Use only to prevent mission failure or financial loss.
- First-Class. Any mailable item weighting 11 ozs. or less. Certain items must be mailed First-Class such as letters, handwritten or typewritten and post/postal cards.
- Priority. Any mailable First-Class matter weighing over 11 ozs. but less than 70 lbs. Must be marked PRIORITY.
- Second-Class. For magazines and other periodicals issued at regular, stated frequency of no less than four times per year.
- Third-Class. For printed matter and parcels under 1 lb. Four ounces or less-same rate as first-class. Special bulk rates for larger mailings (at least 200 pieces or 50 lbs.)
- Fourth-Class. "Parcel Post" For packages 1 to 70 lbs.

In addition to these classes of mail are two special services—Military Ordinary Mail (MOM) and registered mail. MOM and registered mail are services added to the standard classes of mail.

- MOM goes by surface transportation within CONUS and by air transportation overseas. Add MOM to the second-, third-, or fourth-class endorsement on matter having a RDD not allowing sufficient time for surface transportation. Additional postage is not required.
- Registered. This service provides added protection for a fee. Use only if required by law or a directive. Typically slow and expensive compared to other standard handling. For use only with First-Class and Priority Mail.

Tips

- Make sure mailing address is correct.
- Use of office symbol reduces mail handling time.
- Place city, state and ZIP+4 in the last line of the address.
- Return address is a must. Use your office symbol and ZIP+4.
- Tips for Cost Savings
  - Mailing 7 sheets or less of bond paper: use letter size envelope and limit thickness to 1/4" or less when sealed.
  - Mailing manuals, pamphlets, etc., weighting over 4 ozs: use third-class, special fourth-class, bulk rate or bound printed matter rate.
  - Mailing several items to one address: cheaper to mail everything in one envelope. Check with your mailroom for activities serviced by consolidated mailings.
  - Check with your mailroom for activities/agencies within the local area that are serviced by activities/agencies couriers—no postage required.

CHAPTER 23:

Air Force Publications/Forms

This chapter covers:

- Dual Responsibilities in Developing Publications/Forms
- Publications/Forms Process Overview
- Plain Language Challenge

Official publications/forms serve a vital purpose—they direct and explain the policies and procedures governing Air Force functions. There may be a time in your military career when you are tasked to be the action officer to write, revise or develop an official Air Force publication/form. As the action officer, you are the expert in the various functions, tasks and skills as well as the data gathering and legal requirements needed for the publication/form to be effective. Air Force Instruction (AFI) 33-360, *Publications and Forms Management*, "provides guidance and procedures on creating, managing, and disseminating directive and nondirective publications and forms throughout the Air Force" (p. 1). The guidance here is summarized from AFI 33-360 for the general awareness of all Air Force members.

Dual Responsibilities in Developing Publications/Forms

If you are tasked to create or revise any official Air Force publication or form, you have two important responsibilities to meet. The first responsibility is to provide clear, accurate guidance that others understand and follow. The second responsibility is to get guidance out quickly to those who need it. These responsibilities are equally important, but at times will seem to conflict. A well-prepared publication or form takes less time to publish and reach its users than a poorly prepared one. Said another way, a well-prepared publication or form takes the time it needs to be correct the first time; a poorly prepared publication or form wastes time on the first effort and requires extra time on the second effort to undo the damage caused by the first. Always take the time to prepare a well-written publication or form.

Publications/Forms Process Overview

AFI 33-360, chapter 3, provides an overview of the process for the creation, management, and dissemination of official publications and forms. The Seven Steps to Effective Communication, detailed in chapters 3-9 of this manual, are useful throughout the AFI 33-360 process. Become familiar with the AFI 33-360 process as you prepare and submit a publication or form through the chain of command and staff for approval and publishing.

Process Overview (AFI 33-360, Chapter 3)	Seven Steps to Effective Communication (*The Tongue and Quill*)
Draft and Collaborate Staffing Formal Coordination Certification Approval Publishing	1. Analyze purpose and audience (chapter 3) 2. Research your topic (chapter 4) 3. Support your ideas (chapter 5) 4. Organize and Outline (chapter 6) 5. Draft (chapter 7) 6. Edit (chapter 8) 7. Fight for Feedback and Get Approval (chapter 9)

Plain Language Challenge

Many words may be pronounced in two or more ways to convey different and distinct meanings. For example, the "Publications/Forms Process Overview" section the paragraph closes with a sentence that could have used "publication" twice (once as a noun, once as a verb). For clarity, the verb "dissemination" was used in place of using "publication" as a verb in the same sentence. Consider the following examples where the same word is used twice with two distinct meanings:

Same Spelling, Different Meaning	
• The bandage was wound around the wound. • The farm was used to produce produce. • The dump was so full that it had to refuse more refuse. • We used polish to polish the furniture. • He could lead if he would get the lead out. • The soldier decided to desert his dessert in the desert. • I had to subject the subject to several tests. • How can I intimate this to my most intimate friend? • The wind was too strong to wind the sail. • Upon seeing the tear I shed a tear.	• The right time to present the present is now. • A bass was painted on the bass drum. • Suddenly the dove dove into the bushes. • There was a row among the oarsmen about how to row. • They were too close to the door to close it. • The buck does funny things when the does are present. • A seamstress and a sewer fell down into a sewer line. • To help with planting, the farmer taught his sow to sow. • I did not object to the object.

PART VII:

WRITING MECHANICS

Writing Mechanics

Everything we write is evaluated for writing mechanics. Sometimes the evaluation comes as a grade for a class or sometimes your boss is evaluating you, through your written work, for increased responsibility and other opportunities. Both evaluations are important milestones in professional development: they can both lead to new and interesting personal and professional challenges. The chapters in this final part of *The Tongue and Quill* provide essential guidance on writing mechanics to help you on your way to new challenges and opportunities on the horizon. Consider these "funny signs." What did the author mean and what was actually said? Clearly these authors need some improvement in their writing mechanics.

FUNNY SIGNS

1. IN A LAUNDROMAT:
   Automatic washing machines. Please remove all your clothes when the light goes out.

2. IN A LONDON DEPARTMENT STORE:
   Bargain Basement Upstairs

3. OUTSIDE A SECOND-HAND SHOP: We exchange anything—bicycles, washing machines etc. Why not bring your wife along and get a wonderful bargain.

4. QUICKSAND WARNING:
   Quicksand. Any person passing this point will be drowned. By order of the District Council.

5. NOTICE IN A DRY CLEANER'S WINDOW:
   Anyone leaving their garments here for more than 30 days will be disposed of.

6. IN A HEALTH FOOD SHOP WINDOW:
   Closed due to illness.

7. SPOTTED IN A SAFARI PARK:
   Elephants Please Stay In Your Car

8. SEEN DURING A CONFERENCE:
   For anyone who has children and doesn't know it, there is a day care on the first floor.

9. NOTICE IN A FIELD:
   The farmer allows walkers to cross the field for free, but the bull charges.

10. MESSAGE ON A LEAFLET:
    If you cannot read, this leaflet will tell you how to get lessons.

11. ON A REPAIR SHOP DOOR:
    We can repair anything (Please knock hard on the door—the bell doesn't work).

12. SPOTTED IN A TOILET IN A LONDON OFFICE BLOCK:
    Toilet out of order. Please use floor below.

CHAPTER 24:

Writing Terminology

This chapter covers:

- Common Grammatical and Writing Terms
- Irregular Verbs

The Tongue and Quill is not an all-inclusive style manual. This chapter and those that follow provide Air Force personnel with a quick-reference guide to cure the most common trouble spots and to encourage standardization of Air Force oral presentations and written products. There are many style manuals available and no two are exactly alike. Commonly used style guides include the *MLA Style Guide* from the Modern Language Association, the *Chicago Manual of Style*, the *APA Style Guide* from the American Psychological Association, the *Air University Style Guide for Writers and Editors*, and the *US Government Printing Office Style Manual*, to name a few. The *Air University Style Guide* and *The Tongue and Quill* are based on the *Chicago Manual of Style*, and most of the presentations/papers produced in professional military education courses follow the *Air University Style Guide* or *The Tongue and Quill*.

Common Grammatical and Writing Terms

Grammar terminology is useful to describe problems with writing. The table, below, provides a list of grammatical terms with an explanation and example of each. *The Tongue and Quill* has tried to de-emphasize terminology and teach through examples throughout this book; however, sometimes you need an explanation to go with the example. This table emphasizes areas that are both commonly used and commonly misunderstood, such as the use of modal auxiliaries like can, could, shall, should, etc.

> *People who are experts in grammar don't always write well, and many people who write well no longer think consciously about grammar ... but when something goes wrong in a sentence, a knowledge of grammar helps in recognizing the problem and provides a language for discussing it.*
>
> –H. Ramsey Fowler

Table of Common Grammatical and Writing Terms

Term	Explanation and <Examples>
a/an	Use *a* before *consonant sounds* and *an* before *vowel sounds*. <*a* historical event, *an* emergency.>
Active Voice	Shows the subject as the actor. <The **girl** **sang** a song.>
Adjective	Describes or limits a noun or pronoun. It answers "Which one? What kind? or How many?" <*blue* box, *short* coat, *gregarious* man, *four* stools>
Adverbs	Modifies or limits a verb, adjective or another adverb and answers "When? Where? Why? How much? How far? To what degree?" <*quickly* run, *very* dull, *very* loudly> (also see "Conjunctive or Connective Adverbs" below)
Antecedent	Noun, phrase, or clause to which a pronoun refers or replaces.
Appositive	Word, phrase, or clause preceding or renaming a noun. <*My dog* Maggie.>
Article	Small set of words used with nouns to limit or give definiteness to the application. <*a, an, the*>
Bibliography	A list of books, articles and other works used in preparing a manuscript or other written product.
Bullets	Any punctuation symbol used to emphasize specific items.

Term	Explanation and <Examples>
Case	Forms that nouns and pronouns take when they fit into different functions of the sentence. There are three:
	• **Nominative**—for subjects, predicate nominatives and appositives. <*I*>
	• **Objective**—for objects and their appositives. <*me*>
	• **Possessive**—to show ownership, hence adjectival, functions. <*my*>
Clause	A group of related words containing a subject and a verb.
Conjunctions	Connects words, phrases, clauses or sentences (*and, or, but, nor*).
Conjunctive or Connective Adverbs	Transition words that are often used to connect clauses. <*however, therefore, etc.*>
Consonants	All letters of the alphabet except the **vowels** (*a, e, i, o* and *u*). In some words (*synergy*), the letter *y* acts as a vowel.
Glossary	An alphabetical list of unfamiliar terms and their definitions.
Interjection	Words used to express emotion or surprise (e.g., *ah, alas, great, help*). Strong interjections are punctuated with an exclamation point. <**Wow!** *That's profound.*> Milder interjections are often set off by commas, usually at the beginning of a sentence. <**Oh,** *I guess it wasn't.* **Ouch,** *that hurts.*>
Modifier	Words or groups of words that limit or describe other words. If improperly placed, modifiers can confuse the reader or suggest an illogical relationship.
Modal Auxiliary	Verbs that are used with a principal verb that are characteristically used with a verb of predication and that in English differs formally from other verbs in lacking *-s* or *-ing* forms.
can **could**	Primarily expresses ability; *cannot* is used to deny permission. Sometimes the past tense of *can*. <*We could see the Big Dipper last night.*> Otherwise, *could* expresses possibility, doubt or something dependent on unreal conditions. <*We could see the Big Dipper if it weren't overcast.*>
may	Originally meant "have the power" (compare to the <u>noun</u> *might*). Now it means "permission." Also, *may* is used to indicate possibility. <*You may leave if you are finished with your work.*> *May* is also used in wishes. <*May you recover soon.*>

- 289 -

Term	Explanation and <Examples>
might	Sometimes functions as simple past tense of *may*. <He said he might have time to talk to us.> Often it is used to express a more doubtful possibility than *may* does. <He might return before then.> *Might* is also used after contrary-to-fact conditions. <If I were off today, I might go fishing.>
shall should	*Shall* expresses futurity in the first person; *should* also expresses futurity in the first person, but it adds a slight coloring of doubt that the action will take place. Notice the difference in meaning in these sentences. <I shall be happy to call the VA Medical Center for you.> <I should be happy to call the VA Medical Center for you.> In indirect discourse *should* replaces the *shall* of direct discourse. <I shall call at once. I said that I should call at once.> Many speakers who use *shall* in the first person use *would* in preference to *should*. <I said I would call at once.> *Should* is used to express likelihood. <Sue should be able to finish on time.> *Should* expresses obligation. <We should file these orders more carefully.>
will would	*Will* is the common future auxiliary used in the second and third persons. In addition, it is used with special emphasis to express determination. <You will finish by 4 p.m.> *Would* still indicates past time in expressing determination. <You thought you would finish by 4 p.m.> *Would* expresses customary action in past time. <Our last supervisor would bring us doughnuts every Friday morning.> *Would* points to future time, but adding doubt or uncertainty. <I will if I can. I would if I could.> *Would* replaces *will* in indirect discourse. <He said that he would call.>
must	Expresses necessity or obligation. It is somewhat stronger than *should*. <You must call the director's office immediately.> *Must* also expresses likelihood. <It must have rained last night.>

Term	Explanation and <Examples>
ought	Originally the past tense of *owe*, but now it points to a present or future time. *Ought* is nearly the equivalent of *should*; *ought* expresses necessity or obligation, but with less force than *must*. <We must go. We ought to go.>
dare	Originally a modal only, it is now used primarily in negatives or questions. <He dare not submit the report in that form.> <Dare we submit the report like this?>
need	Not originally a modal auxiliary, *need* is now used to mean *have to*. <He need only fill out the top form. He need not get upset about the delay.> In the meaning "lack," *need* is always a regular verb. <He needs a little help with this project.>
Equivalents of modals:	
be able to	Used instead of *can* or *could* to indicate the ability as a fact rather than a mere potentiality. It is used also to avoid the ambiguity that may result from using *can* to express permission. <He is able to support his mother.>
be to	Indicates future events but hints at uncertainty. <He is to have that report to us tomorrow.>
have to	Commonly substitutes for *must*. It is a stronger expression of necessity. <You have to have that done.>
Other modals are used in speech, but they are inappropriate in writing.	
	had rather instead of *would rather* *had better* instead of *should* or *ought* (In speech, *had better* is emphatic in threats.) *have got to* instead of *have to*
Modals are used with the infinitive of the perfect or progressive.	
	Can be going. *Could have gone.* *Ought to be going.* *Ought to have gone.*
Nouns	Names a person, place, thing, action or abstract idea. <woman, office, pencil, game, Ohio, Maxwell AFB, democracy, freedom>
	• **Abstract Noun**—nouns that name qualities rather than material things. <love, danger>

Term	Explanation and <Examples>
	• **Collective Noun**—nouns that are singular in form but plural in meaning; names a group of persons or things. <audience, army, company, flock, committee, trio>
	• **Concrete Noun**—nouns that can be seen or touched. <table, book>
	• **Proper Noun**—nouns that are capitalized and name specific persons, places or things. <Major Palmer, Ohio, Air War College>
Number	Shows the singular or plural of nouns, pronouns, or verbs.
Object	Noun or pronoun that is affected by the verb. <The man read **the book**.>
Parts of Speech	The basic building blocks of language: nouns, pronouns, verbs, adverbs, adjectives, prepositions, interjections and conjunctions
Passive Voice	Shows the subject as receiver of the action. <A song was sung by **her**.>
Person	Pronouns that denote the speaker (first person; *I, we*), the person spoken to (second person, *you*), or the person spoken of (third person; *she, they*).
Phrases	Groups of words without a subject or predicate that function as a unit (adjective, adverbial, gerund or infinitive phases).
Plagiarism	Using someone else's writing as if it were your own. This serious offense can lead to severe professional and legal consequences. If using another person's material, identify the borrowed passage and credit the author.
Predicate	Tells what the subject does or what is done to the subject, or the state of being the subject is in.
Preposition	Shows the relationship between a noun or pronoun to another word in the sentence. <by, at, up, down, between, among, through>
Pronouns	Substitutes for a noun. Here are three:
	• **Definite:** includes *I, you, he, she, it, we, they*, and all of their forms.
	• **Indefinite:** includes words like *someone, no one, each, anyone* and *anybody*.
	• **Relative:** includes words like *who, whom, which, that*.

CHAPTER 24
Writing Terminology

Term	Explanation and <Examples>
Sentence	Expresses one complete thought with one subject and one verb; either or both may be compound.
	• **Complex Sentence:** contains one main clause and at least one subordinate clause. <*When it rains, it pours.*>
	• **Compound Sentence:** contains two or more main clauses and no subordinate clauses. <*It rains, and it pours.*>
Subject	Tells what the sentence is about; the person, place or thing that performs the action or that has the state of being indicated by the verb.
Tense	Shows the time of the action, condition or state of being expressed. The three tenses—past, present, future—can be expressed in the simple, perfect or progressive.
Verbals	Past and present participle forms of the verbs that act as nouns or adjectives. There are three:
	• **Gerund:** ends in *-ing* and functions as a noun. <*talking, singing*>
	• **Infinitive:** simple verb form used as a noun, adjective, or adverb and usually preceded by *to*. <*to go, to type*>
	• **Participle:** used as an adjective and acts as a modifier in present (*-ing*), past (*-ed, lost*), and perfect (*having lost*) forms.
Verbs	Expresses action or state of being of the sentence. There are six:
	• **Transitive:** transfers action from the subject to the object.
	• **Intransitive:** transfers no action and is followed by an adverb or nothing.
	• **Linking:** acts as an equal sign connecting the subject and the complement.
	• **Auxiliary or Helping Verb:** verb used with another verb to form voice or perfect and progressive tenses. <We *have eaten* there before.>
	• **Principal Verb:** last verb in a verb phrase.
	• **Irregular Verb:** verbs that form past tense and past participle differently (see the table of irregular verbs that follows this table)
Vowel	The *a, e, i, o* and *u*. In some words, the letter *y* acts as a vowel.

Irregular Verbs

Irregular Verbs: Present, Past and Past Participle

Present	Past	Past participle	Present	Past	Past participle
become	became	become	know	knew	known
begin	began	begun	ride	rode	ridden
bet	bet	bet	ring	rang	rung
blow	blew	blown	rise	rose	risen
break	broke	broken	set	set	set
bring	brought	brought	shake	shook	shaken
buy	bought	bought	sing	sang	sung
catch	caught	caught	sink	sank	sunk
choose	chose	chosen	speak	spoke	spoken
come	came	come	spin	spun	spun
cut	cut	cut	steal	stole	stolen
draw	drew	drawn	swear	swore	sworn
drink	drank	drunk	sweep	swept	swept
drive	drove	driven	swim	swam	swum
eat	ate	eaten	swing	swung	swung
fly	flew	flown	take	took	taken
forgive	forgave	forgiven	tear	tore	torn
freeze	froze	frozen	think	thought	thought
give	gave	given	throw	threw	thrown
grow	grew	grown	wear	wore	worn
keep	kept	kept	weep	wept	wept

CHAPTER 25:

Punctuation

This chapter covers:

- Punctuation: Why Do We Need It?
- Open and Closed Punctuation
- Punctuating Terms in a Series
- Punctuation Usage Guide
- Summary

Punctuation: Why Do We Need It?

Why do we need punctuation? Wouldn't writing would be easier without punctuation? No comma faults, no need to worry about open or closed punctuation styles—just words on a page. Dalton Trumbo used such a style in his novel *Johnny Got His Gun*, and it is very difficult to read. Consider the following words:

> **Punctuation marks are a writers road signs they signal to readers the starts stops and pauses that are needed to clearly convey the message**

While this may not be difficult to read by itself, what if this entire handbook were without punctuation? Now consider the same words with punctuation:

> **Punctuation marks are a writer's road signs. They signal to readers the starts, stops and pauses that are needed to clearly convey the message.**

This is much easier to read and understand, isn't it? Punctuation marks are aids writers use to communicate clearly with readers. Improper punctuation can confuse readers, alter the meaning of a sentence, and decrease reading speed. Using punctuation correctly cures these problems.

Open and Closed Punctuation

Though many grammar rules are clear-cut, there are some gray areas where the experts disagree. One area of debate is the use of "open punctuation" versus "closed punctuation." Open punctuation advocates believe that writers should use only what's necessary to prevent misreading, while closed punctuation advocates are more apt to include punctuation whenever the grammatical structure of the material justifies it. For example, the following sentence illustrates how different writers might punctuate a particular sentence:

Open punctuation example—the meaning is clear without using all the punctuation that's needed by the grammatical structure:

> **If used incorrectly they may alter an intended meaning, and if used excessively they can decrease reading speed and make your meaning difficult to determine.**

Closed punctuation example—using all required punctuation does not make meaning clearer and may slow reading speed:

> **If used incorrectly, they may alter an intended meaning, and, if used excessively, they can decrease reading speed and make your meaning difficult to determine.**

In the Air Force, the trend is to towards open punctuation. If you're confused about where to put commas, sometimes the best solution is to restructure the sentence to make the meaning clearer and eliminate the need for extra punctuation.

Modified sentence structure example—a slight change in sentence structure results in fewer words to read and the meaning is clear:

> **If used incorrectly, they may alter an intended meaning; if used excessively, they can decrease reading speed and cause confusion.**

Punctuating Terms in a Series

Punctuating terms in a series is one area where Air Force writers get conflicting guidance: the use of commas to separate three or more parallel words, phrases, or clauses in a series. Here's the rule and its two variants:

The Rule

Use a comma to separate three or more parallel words, phrases or clauses in a series.

Variants

1. **Variant 1—closed punctuation**: Include the comma before the final and, or, or nor.
   - Will you go by car, train, or plane?
   - You will not talk, nor do homework, nor sleep in my class.

2. **Variant 2—open punctuation**: Exclude the comma before the final *and, or* or *nor*.
   - Will you go by car, train or plane?
   - You will not talk, nor do homework nor sleep in my class.

Recommendation

The Tongue and Quill has favored and recommended open punctuation for many years. This recommendation is unchanged, but there are at least **three reasons why you might want to follow the closed punctuation guidelines when punctuating three or more items in a series**:

1. Closed punctuation of series is specified in most commercial grammar guides.

2. Closed punctuation of series is specified in some other Air Force references, including the *Air University Style and Author Guide*.

3. The additional comma specified in closed punctuation may help clarify your meaning, especially when the items in the series are longer phrases and clauses (especially when the clauses include "and" as in "up and down, in and out, and over and under)."

Check to see which approach is preferred for the writing product you're working on. Award packages, performance appraisals, military evaluations and other space-constrained formats typically use open punctuation. Research papers, academic publications and books normally use closed punctuation. Use the approach that best suits your purpose and the needs of the audience.

Punctuation Usage Guide

Regardless of the style, the function of punctuation is to communicate the writer's meaning. The punctuation usage guide that follows covers the most common needs for Air Force writers. Use the guide to help you punctuate your documents and clearly communicate to your readers.

The Tongue and Quill
AFH 33-337, 27 MAY 2015

Apostrophe '

1. **Use an apostrophe to create possessive forms of nouns and abbreviations used as nouns.**

   a. Add *'s* to singular or plural nouns that do not end with an *s*.

   - officer's rank
   - the oxen's tails
   - ROTC's building
   - the children's room

   b. Add *'s* to singular nouns that end with an *s, x* or *z*.

   - A business's contract
   - Mr. Jones's family tree
   - Marx's theories
   - Marine Corps's Ball
   - United States's policy
   - Berlioz's works

   c. Add *'s* to most singular proper nouns, including names that end with *s*.

   - Burns's poems
   - Jefferson Davis's home

   d. Add **only the apostrophe** to plural nouns that end in *s* or with an *s* sound, or to singular nouns ending with an *s* where adding an *'s* would cause difficulty in pronunciation.

   - The two businesses' contracts
   - for righteousness' sake
   - Our bosses' schedule
   - Officers' Club

   e. Add **only the apostrophe** to ancient proper names that end with *s*.

   - Jesus' teaching
   - Moses' law
   - Zeus' temple
   - Aristophanes' play

   f. Add *'s* to the final word of compound nouns to show possession.

   - secretary-treasurer's report
   - eyewitness' comment
   - attorney general's book
   - mother-in-law's car
   - mothers-in-law's cars

   g. Add *'s* to show possession for indefinite pronouns (someone, no one, each, anyone, anybody, etc.), add *'s* to last component of the pronoun.

   - someone's car
   - somebody else's book

   h. To show joint possession for two or more nouns, add the apostrophe or *'s* to the last noun. Add only the apostrophe to plural nouns ending in *s* and *'s* to singular nouns.

   - girls and boys' club
   - aunt and uncle's house
   - Diane and Wayne's daughters

   i. To show separate possession, place the possession indicators on each noun or pronoun identifying a possessor.

   - soldiers' and sailors' uniforms
   - Mrs. Williams's and Mr. Smith's classes
   - king's and queen's jewels
   - son's and daughter's toys

Few men are lacking in capacity, but they fail because they are lacking in application.

–Calvin Coolidge

2. Use an apostrophe to mark omissions or form contractions.

- can't (can not)
- mustn't (must not)
- don't (do not)
- wouldn't (would not)
- I'm (I am)
- won't (will not)
- I've (I have)
- you'll (you will)
- let's (let us)
- it's (it is)
- rock 'n' roll (rock and roll)
- jack-o'-lantern

3. Use an apostrophe to form plurals.

Use an apostrophe to form plurals of certain letters and abbreviations. Make all individual lowercase letters plural by adding 's and make individual capital letters plural by adding *s* alone unless confusion would result. (For example, apostrophes are used with the plurals of A, I, and U because adding an s forms the words As, Is, and Us.) To plural most abbreviations (upper and lowercase), add a lowercase *s*. If the singular form contains an apostrophe, add *s* to form plural.

- dotting the i's
- OPRs, EPRs, TRs
- 1960s
- the three Rs
- S's, A's, I's, U's
- Bs, 1s
- bldgs (buildings)
- B-52s
- six the's
- ain'ts
- ma'ams
- mustn'ts

4. Use an apostrophe to mark a quote within a quote.

"Let's adopt this slogan: 'Quality first.'"

5. Use an apostrophe to represent units of measurement in technical writing (or the accent mark if the apostrophe symbol is not available).

- To specify a length of feet in a measure (The room measures 16' by 29')
- To specify an angle measured in minutes (60' = 1 degree).
- To specify geographical latitude and longitude expressed in degrees, minutes, and seconds. An apostrophe marks the minutes, and seconds are identified with quotation marks. If using the accent mark, a single accent mark identifies the minutes; a double accent mark specifies the seconds.
  Example: The coordinates are 35° 40' 30" N x 60° 20' 30" W.

Format. Be aware that cutting and pasting into word processors from several files or file types can mix two formats for the apostrophe and quotation marks. The normal format is for the apostrophe and quotation marks to be curved; the format in some documents uses "straight quotes." Once the cut-and-paste task is finished, *The Tongue and Quill* recommends a global find and replace for apostrophes and quotation marks to standardize the format to the normal curved style.

Asterisk *

1. **Use the asterisk to refer a reader to footnotes placed at the bottom of a page.**

   - One asterisk* identifies the first footnote
   - Two asterisks** identify a second footnote
   - Three asterisks*** identify a third footnote.
   - Number the footnotes if you have more than three. If it is a literary document, number the footnotes if you need more than one footnote.

2. **Use asterisks to replace words that are considered unprintable.**

   It is a good thing that no cameras or recording devices were present when Smith called Schultz a ***** tonight at the party.

Spacing when using an asterisk

- No space before following a word or punctuation mark within sentence or at the end of a sentence—unless replacing unprintable words, then one space before.
- One space after following a word or punctuation mark within a sentence.
- Two spaces after following a punctuation mark at the end of a sentence—unless manuscript format and using right justified, then one space after. (*The Tongue and Quill* favors two spaces after the end of a sentence. The decision to use one space or two is left up to the individual or organization. Either way is acceptable, but be consistent!)
- No space after an asterisk in a footnote.

Asterisk footnote samples. If the asterisks in the first paragraph of this page were to appear as footnotes, they would appear as follows at the bottom of the footnoted page, separated from the text by a footnote bar (generated automatically in Word) as shown below.

---

*The asterisk can be used as a mark of punctuation to indicate a footnote.

**Use the asterisk with other punctuation as shown here.

***Number the footnotes if you have more than three—unless a literary document.

Brackets [ ]

1. Use brackets to clarify or correct material written by others.

- To clarify: He arrived on the 1st [2d] of June.

- To correct: The statue [*sic*] was added to the book of statutes.

    When [*sic*] appears in the text, as in the example above, it tells the reader something is wrong with the word immediately in front of the first bracket but the word is reproduced exactly as it appeared in the original.

2. Use brackets to insert explanatory words, editorial remarks or phrases independent of the sentence or quoted material.

- Tell them [the students] to report to the auditorium now.

- The tank-versus-tank battles of Villers-Brettoneux is the last significant event for the tank in World War I. [Other accounts of this battle give different versions.]

3. Use brackets to indicate you've added special emphasis (e.g., italics, bold, underline, all capitals) to quoted material when the emphasis was not in the original work. The bracketed material may be placed immediately following the emphasized word(s) or at the end of the quotation.

- *She* [emphasis added] seemed willing to compromise, but his strategy prevailed.

- Tell them to report to the auditorium **now**. [Emphasis added.]

4. Use brackets to enclose an acronym's definition (the acronym written out) or a parenthetical phrase that falls within a parenthetical phrase.

- (All military personnel will wear the UOD [uniform of the day] for the ceremony.)

- (There are three primary theories [or frameworks] for the study of airpower.)

Spacing when using brackets (Opening bracket)

- One space before when parenthetic matter is within a sentence.

- Two spaces before when parenthetic matter follows a sentence (when parenthetic matter starts with a capital and closes with its own sentence punctuation), unless manuscript format and using right justified text, then one space before.

- No space after.

Spacing when using brackets (Closing bracket)

- No space before.

- **One space after** when parenthetic matter is within a sentence or when in manuscript format and using right justified; **two spaces after** when parenthetic matter is itself a complete sentence and another sentence follows.

- No space after if another punctuation mark immediately follows.

Colon :

1. Use a colon to separate an introductory statement from explanatory or summarizing material that follows when there is no coordinating conjunction or transitional expression. (Capitalize the first word of the expression that follows the colon if it is the dominant element and is a complete sentence. For additional details, see the "Capitalization" section.)

- Living in base housing has many advantages: People can walk to work, shopping is convenient, and there are organized activities for the children.
- The board consists of three officials: a director, deputy director and recorder.

2. Use a colon when a sentence contains an expression such as *following* **or** *as follows* **or is followed by a list.** *Notice the capitalization and punctuation in the examples.*

- The new directive achieved the following results: better morale and improved relations.
- Results were as follows: better morale, less work and more pay.
- Consider these advantages when making your decision:
    o You won't have to be somewhere at 0800 every day.
    o You can get more involved in community activities.
    o You can pursue hobbies you haven't had time for in the last year.

3. Use a colon to indicate a full stop before an enumerated or explanatory list.

There are several possibilities for the analyst position: (1) it could remain vacant, (2) it could be converted to a civilian position, or (3) another military member within the organization could be temporarily detailed to the position.

4. Use a colon with a quotation when the word "say" or a substitute for say has been omitted, when the introductory expression is an independent clause, and when the quotation is typed in indented form on separate lines from the introductory clause.

- The general turned [and said]: "Who gave that order?"
- The judge rendered her decision: "Bail is denied."
- The speaker said:

    "The words you will hear from this stage today are the words and opinions of one man—me. I do not come as a representative of my company. I will not answer any question that is in any way related to the company for which I work."

5. Use a colon to express periods of clock time in figures and to represent the word *to* **in ratios and proportions.** *Do not use a colon when expressing time on a 24-hour clock.*

- Time: There is an appointment available at 1430 (2:30 p.m.).
- Ratios: Dilute the concentrate with water using a ratio of 5:1 for a mild cleanser.

6. Use a colon when expressing library references to separate title and subtitle, volume and page number, city of publication and name of publisher in footnotes, and bibliographies.

- Book title: ***Mail Fraud: What You Can Do About It***
- Volume reference: **10:31-34 (Volume 10, pages 31 to 34)**
- Publisher reference: **New York: MacMillan Company**

7. Do NOT use a colon when the enumerated items complete the sentence that introduces them. *Notice the punctuation and capitalization in this example.*

Liaison officers must [Not "Liaison officers must:"]

    a. become familiar with the situation,

    b. know the mission and

    c. arrange for communications.

8. Do NOT use a colon when an explanatory series follows a preposition or a verb (except as in rule 4 for the "Use a colon…" on the previous page).

- [Right] The editorial assistants are Rebecca, Lisa and Yuna.
- [Wrong] The editorial assistants are: Rebecca, Lisa and Yuna.

9. Do NOT use a colon to introduce an enumerated list that is a complement or the object of an element in the introductory statement.

- [Right] Our goals are to (1) learn the basic dance steps, (2) exercise while having fun, and (3) meet new people.
- [Wrong] Our goals are to: (1) learn the basic …

10. Do NOT use a colon when the anticipatory expression is followed by another sentence.

The command section will bring the following foods to the party. The buffet line will be opened at noon with the enlisted personnel being served first.

- Taco Bake
- tossed salad
- chips
- dip

Spacing when using colons

- No space before.
- **Two spaces after within a sentence**—unless manuscript format and using right justified, then one space after.
- No space before or after in expressions of time (8:20 p.m.) or proportions (2:1).

Comma ,

1. Use a comma with the coordinating conjunctions *and*, *but*, *or*, or *nor* when joining two or more independent clauses.

- [Right] The art of war is constantly developing, but twentieth-century technology has so speeded up the change the military strategist now must run to keep pace.

- [Wrong] The rapid expansion of the Air Force ensures a continuing need for qualified college graduates to fill existing vacancies, and also ensures ample opportunities for advancement. [This example contains only one independent clause with a compound verb; therefore, no comma is necessary.]

NOTE: *No comma is needed if the sentence has one subject with a compound predicate connected with a coordinating conjunction because the second half of the sentence is not an independent clause.*

- o Mary Jones received her master's degree last December and is now considering pursuing a doctorate degree in education.
- o I am not only willing to go but also ready to stay a week.

2. Use a comma to separate three or more parallel words, phrases or clauses in a series.

- In open punctuation, exclude the comma before the final and, or or nor.
  "Will you go by car, train or plane?" [open punctuation]

- In closed punctuation, include the comma before the final and, or, or nor.
  "You will not talk, nor do homework, nor sleep in my class." [closed punctuation]

- For longer phrases and clauses in a series, the additional comma specified in closed punctuation may help readability. "Patients are classified as suitable for treatment at the installation, as requiring evacuation to the regional hospital, or as fit for duty."

- The use of *etc.* is discouraged in running text, but when used, it must be set off with commas. Do not use *etc.* when using *e.g., for example,* or *such as*. These terms indicate you are only giving some examples; there is no need to imply there could be more.
  "We will bake cookies, bread, cupcakes, etc., for the party."

3. Use a comma with parallel adjectives that modify the same noun. If the adjectives are independent of each other, if the order can be reversed or if and can stand between the words, the adjectives are parallel and should be separated by a comma. However, if the first adjective modifies the idea expressed by the combination of the second adjective and the noun, do not use a comma.

- a hard, cold winter; a long, hot summer [the summer was long and hot]
- a heavy winter overcoat [winter modifies overcoat; heavy modifies winter overcoat]
- a traditional political institution [political modifies institution; traditional modifies political institution]

4. Use a comma to separate two or more complementary phrases that refer to a single word that follows.

The coldest, if not the most severe, winter Ohio has had was in 1996.

5. Use a comma to set off nonessential or interrupting words and phrases.

   a. **To set off nonessential words, clauses, or phrases not necessary for the meaning or the structural completeness of the sentence.** You can tell whether an expression is nonessential or essential by trying to omit the expression. If you can omit the expression without affecting the meaning or the structural completeness of the sentence, the expression is nonessential and should be set off by commas.

- They want to hire Leigh Iris, who has 10 years of experience, to run the new center.
  [The phrase "who has 10 years of experience" is nonessential information.]

- They want to hire someone who has at least 10 years of experience to run the center.
  [The phrase "who has at least 10 years of experience" is essential information.]

- There is, no doubt, a reasonable explanation.
  [This sentence would be complete without "no doubt."]

- There is no doubt about her integrity.
  [This sentence would be incomplete without "no doubt."]

- This rule includes interrupting words, phrases, or clauses that break the flow of the sentence.

    - The faculty and staff, military, and civilian, are invited.

    - She is a lieutenant colonel, not a major, and will be our new executive officer.

    - The major, a recent promotee, is an experienced pilot.

   b. **With transitional words and phrases, such as** *however, that is (i.e.), namely, therefore, for example (e.g.), moreover, consequently,* **and** *on the other hand,* **when interrupting the flow of the sentence.** A comma is normally used after these expressions, but the punctuation preceding is dictated by the magnitude of the break in continuity. However, when these words or phrases are used to emphasize meaning, do not set off with punctuation.

- It is important, therefore, we leave immediately.

- It is therefore vitally important we don't postpone the trip.

- A. Eaves is highly qualified for the job; i.e., he has 16 years of experience!

- Rebecca and Julie say they will attend—that is, if Robert and Lisa are attending.

- Planes from several bases (e.g., Dover, Lackland and Tyndall) will be in the airshow.

c. **To set off a phrase introduced by *accompanied by, along with, and not, as well as, besides, except, in addition to, including, plus, not even, rather than, such as, together with*, or a similar expression when it falls between the subject and the verb.**

- The faculty and staff, as well as the students, should be prepared for the inspection.
- The fifth and sixth graders, plus their parents, will be transported by bus.
- When the phrase occurs elsewhere in the sentence, commas may be omitted if the phrase is clearly related to the preceding words.
  "We agree, Miss Johnson, our policy was badly processed as well as lost in the mail."

d. **With the adverb *too* (meaning also) when it falls between the subject and verb. Omit the comma before *too* if it occurs at the end of a sentence or clause.**

- You, too, can save money by shopping selectively.
- You should try to improve your typing too.
- If you want to bring the children too, we'll have room.

e. **To set off nonessential appositives. An appositive is a word or phrase appearing next to a noun that identifies it and is equivalent to it. If the appositive is nonessential, set it off by commas. If essential or restrictive in nature, do not set it off by commas.**

- Our cost analyst, Mrs. Sherri Thomas, will handle the details. [In this hypothetical example, we have only one cost analyst, so Mrs. Thomas is "nonessential." If we eliminate her name, the meaning of the sentence would not change.]
- The battleship Pennsylvania was taken out of mothballs today. [Pennsylvania is "essential" to the sentence because there is more than one battleship in mothballs.]
- Their daughter Julie won the contest. The other daughters were really annoyed. [Since they have more than one daughter her name is essential to the sentence.]
- Edward shares a house with his wife Esther in Prattville, Alabama. [Strictly speaking, Esther should be set off by commas because he can have only one wife and giving her name is nonessential information; however, because the words wife and Esther are so closely related and usually spoken as a unit, commas may be omitted.]

f. **To set off the title, position, or organization after a person's name or name equivalent. (Some cases under this rule are appositives; other cases are not.)**

- John Kerry, Secretary of State, will speak at the graduation ceremony.
- The commander, 42d Air Base Wing, is responsible for…

g. **To set off long phrases denote a residence or business connection immediately following a name.**

- Lieutenant Colonel Fernando Ordoñez, of the Peruvian air force in Lima, Peru, will be here tomorrow.
- Lt Col Orlando of Lima, Peru, will be here tomorrow. [The comma is omitted between "Orlando" and "of" to avoid too many breaks in a short phrase.]

6. **Use a comma to set off introductory elements.**

   a. **With introductory elements that begin a sentence and come before the subject and verb of the main clause.** The comma may be omitted if the introductory phrase is five words or less except when numbers occur together. If you choose to use a comma following a short introductory phrase, do so consistently throughout the document.

   - In 1923, 834 cases of measles were reported in that city.
   - In 1913 the concept of total war was unknown.
   - Of all the desserts I love, my favorite is the fruit trifle.
   - Since the school year had already begun, we delayed the curriculum change.

   b. **After introductory words such as yes, no or oh.**

   - Yes, I'll do it.
   - Oh, I see your point.

7. **Use a comma to set off explanatory dates, addresses, and place names.**

   - The change of command, 1 October 2014, was the turning point.
   - The British prime minister lives at 10 Downing Street, London, England.
   - Use two commas to set off the name of a state, county, or country when it directly follows the name of a city without the ZIP code. "The Wright brothers opened a flying school in Montgomery, Alabama, where Maxwell Air Force Base is now located."
   - When the ZIP code follows the name of the state, drop the comma *between* the two, but use one *after* the ZIP code number if there is additional text. "We shipped the package to 325 Chennault Circle, Montgomery AL 36112-6427, but it hasn't been received yet."

8. **Use a comma to set off statements such as *he said, she replied, they answered* and *she announced*.**

   - She said, "Welcome to the Chamber of Commerce. May I help you?"
   - She replied, "I have an appointment with Lt Col Rick Jenkins at 10 a.m."

   NOTE: *If a quotation functions as an integral part of a sentence, commas are unnecessary.*

   They even considered "No guts, no glory!" as their slogan.

9. **Use a comma to set off names and titles used in direct address.**

   - No, sir, I didn't see her.
   - Linda McBeth, you're not changing jobs, are you?

10. **Use a comma with afterthoughts (words, phrases, or clauses added to the end of a sentence).** NOTE: *The word "too" at the end of a sentence does not require a comma—see Rule 5d.*

    - It isn't too late to get tickets, is it?
    - Send them home as soon as possible, please.

11. **Use a comma in the following miscellaneous constructions:**

   a. **To indicate omission of words in repeating a construction.**

   We had a tactical reserve; now, nothing. [The comma replaces "we have."]

   b. **Before for used as a conjunction.**

   She didn't go to the party, for she cannot stand smoke-filled rooms.

   c. **To separate repeated words.**
   - That was a long, long time ago.
   - Well, well, look who's here.

   d. **With titles following personal names.** Jr. and Sr. are set off by commas; 2d, 3d, II, and III are not. In text, "Lee B. Walker, Sr." becomes "Lee B. Walker, Sr., is …" When you must show possession, drop the comma following Jr. and Sr. "Lee Walker, Sr.'s car …"
   - Henry Ford II
   - Lee B. Walker, Sr.
   - James Stokes 3d [or "III"]

   e. **When names are reversed.**
   - Adams, Angie
   - Middleton, Mary
   - Baldwin, Sherwood, Jr.
   - Parks, James, III
   - Brown, Carolyn
   - Price, William, Esq.
   - Ford, Henry, II
   - Walker, Lee B., Sr.
   - First M. Last, IV

   f. **With academic degrees.**
   - James Parks III, MBA
   - Scott H. Brown, PhD
   - In narrative text: "Scott H. Brown, PhD, will …"

   g. **To prevent confusion or misreading.**
   - To John, Smith was an honorable man.
   - For each group of 20, 10 were rejected.
   - Soon after, the meeting was interrupted abruptly.

Spacing when using commas
- No space before.
- One space after, unless a closing quotation mark immediately follows the comma.
- No space after within a number.

CHAPTER 25
Punctuation

Dashes — and –

The em dash (—) (typically three hyphens linked as a single character)

1. Use an em dash to indicate a sudden break or abrupt change in thought.

- He is going—no, he's turning back.
- Our new building should be—will be—completed by June 2004.

2. Use an em dash to give special emphasis to the second independent clause in a compound sentence.

- Our new, but used, pickup truck is great—it's economical too!
- You'll double your money with this plan—and I'll prove it!

3. Use an em dash to emphasize single words.

- Girls—that's all he ever thinks about!
- They're interested in one thing only—profit—nothing else matters.

4. Use an em dash to emphasize or restate a previous thought.

One day last week—Monday, I think—Congress finally voted on the amendment.

5. Use an em dash before summarizing words such as *these, they* and *all* when those words summarize a series of ideas or list of details.

- A tennis racket, swimsuit and shorts—these are all you'll need for the weekend.
- Faculty, staff and students—all are invited.

6. Use an em dash in place of commas to set off a nonessential element requiring special emphasis.

- There's an error in one paragraph—the second one.
- Ensure all students—as well as faculty members—are informed of the briefing.

7. Use an em dash to set off a nonessential element when the nonessential element contains internal commas

Certain subjects—American government, calculus and chemistry—are required courses.

8. Use an em dash instead of parentheses when a nonessential item requires strong emphasis (dashes emphasize; parentheses de-emphasize).

Call Lieutenant Colonels Sims and Forbes—the real experts—and get their opinion.

9. Use an em dash in place of a colon for a strong, but less formal, break in introducing explanatory words, phrases or clauses

Our arrangement with the publisher is simple—we provide the camera-ready copy, and they handle the printing and distribution).

10. **Use an em dash with quotation marks.** Place the dash outside the closing quotation mark when the sentence breaks off after the quotation and inside the closing quotation mark to indicate the speaker's words have broken off abruptly.

- If I hear one more person say, "See what I'm saying!?"—
- Thomas Hardy said, "When I get to 25 Barberry Street, I'll—"

11. **Use an em dash with a question mark or an exclamation mark:**

a. When a sentence contains a question or exclamation that is set off by dashes, put the appropriate punctuation mark before the closing dash.

- I'll attend Friday's meeting—is it being held at the same place?—but I'll have to leave early for another appointment.
- He's busy now, sir—wait, don't go in there!—I'll call you when he's free.

b. When a sentence abruptly breaks off before the end of a question or exclamation, put the end punctuation mark immediately following the dash.

- Shall I do it or—?
- Look out for the—!

The en dash (–) (typically two hyphens linked as a single character)

12. **Before the source of a quotation credit line in printed or typed material.**

The ornaments of a home are the friends who frequent it.

–Anonymous

13. **To indicate inclusive numbers (dates, page numbers, time) when not introduced by the word from or between.**

- The instructions are on pages 15–30 of the text and from pages 3 to 10 in the handout.
- My appointment is 0800–0900. I will be there between 0745 and 0800.
- She worked there from 1979 to 1996 and she said the 1990–1996 period went by quickly.

14. **In a compound adjective when one element has two words or a hyphenated word.**

- New York–London flight
- Air Force–wide changes
- quasi-public–quasi-judicial body

Spacing when using dashes

- No space before or after an em dash (—) or en dash (–) within a sentence.
- Two spaces after the em dash at the end of a sentence that breaks off abruptly (rule 10)—unless manuscript format and using right justified, then one space after.
- When using a typewriter. No space before, between or after the em dash or en dash; the em dash is made using three hyphens (---); the en dash is made using two hyphens (--).

CHAPTER 25
Punctuation

Display Dots/Bullets   ●

1. Use display dots/bullets* to emphasize specific items in either complete or incomplete sentences that are parallel in grammatical structure.

2. Use display dots/bullets when one item is *not* more important than the others and the items do not show a sequence. (If the items show a sequence, use a numbered list.)

3. Capitalize the first word of each item in the display dot/bullet list when a complete sentence introduces them. (The complete sentence may end with either a period or a colon.)

- The prospect for growing drug abuse worldwide can be correlated with the prevalence of the following ingredients:
    - An awareness of drugs
    - Access to them
    - The motivation to use them
- The Coast Guard is a multi-mission agency in the maritime arena.
    - Safety
    - Environmental protection
    - Law enforcement
    - Political-military

4. Use a period (or other appropriate end punctuation) after each item in a display dot/bullet vertical list when at least one of the items is a complete sentence.

- After listening intently to the defense attorney's closing remarks, the jury was convinced of three things:
    - Witnesses lied.
    - False evidence had been presented.
    - The defendant deserved a new trial.
- Two questions continually present themselves to commanders:
    - What is actually happening?
    - What (if anything) can I or should I do about it?

---

*A "bullet" is a generic term for any graphical symbol used to emphasize different items in a list. Display dots, squares, dashes and arrows are the most common symbols used for this purpose, but today's software makes any number of designs possible. Regardless of your choice of bullet graphic, the above guidelines will help readability

5. When the list completes a sentence begun in the introductory element, omit the final period unless the items are separated by other punctuation.

There is a tendency to speak of the commander, but there are, in fact, many interrelated commanders, and each commander uses a separate command and control process to

- o   make information decisions about the situation,
- o   make operational decisions about actions to be taken, and
- o   cause them to be executed within a structure established by prior decisions.

6. A colon can be used to indicate a full stop before a list. A colon is often used with expressions such as *the following items* or *as follows*.

Consider the following advantages when making your decision:

- You won't have to be somewhere at 0800 every day.
- You can get more involved in community activities.
- You can pursue hobbies you haven't had time for in the last year.

7. Do not use a colon when the listed items complete the sentence that introduces them.

- Liaison officers must
  [Not "Liaison officers must:"]
  - o   become familiar with the situation,
  - o   know the mission, and
  - o   arrange for communications.
- The editorial assistants in Production are
  [Not "The editorial assistants in Production are:"]
  - o   Rebecca Bryant,
  - o   Cheryl Cooper,
  - o   Darlene Barnes, and
  - o   Vanessa Clemons.

Spacing when using display dots and bullets

- No space before
- Two spaces after in most cases
- One space after if in manuscript format and using right justified
- Hang indent all remaining lines

Ellipsis ...

The ellipsis in Air Force work is written as three points without a space between them. Most word processors automatically create a single-glyph character for the ellipsis if three periods are typed followed by a stroke on the space bar.

1. Use an ellipsis to indicate a pause or faltering speech within a quoted sentence or at the end of a sentence that is deliberately incomplete.

- "I ... I don't know ... I mean, I don't know if I can go."
- What would you do ...?

2. Use an ellipsis to indicate an omission of a portion of quoted material.

"Four score and seven years ago our fathers brought forth ... a new nation ... dedicated to the proposition that all men are created equal."

3. Use a period followed by an ellipsis to indicate the omission of the end of a sentence.

Work must be measured.... Without such metrics, how can production be assessed?

4. Use an ellipsis *without* a period if the statement is intended to trail off.

He could have easily saved the situation by ... But why talk about it?

5. Use an ellipsis before the ending punctuation to indicate an omission from the end of a question or an exclamation.

What rubric was used to grade the assignment ...? Rubrics are essential for consistency.

6. Use an ellipsis immediately after the terminal punctuation of a sentence to indicate that one or more following sentences or paragraphs have been omitted.

In the last few years, we have witnessed a big change in the age groups of America's violence.... How far and wide these changes extend, we are afraid to say.

7. Do NOT use an ellipsis to signify the omission of words before or after the fragment when a fragment of a sentence is quoted *within another sentence* or to show the omission of text *before* or *after* a quotation, such as an in an epigraph.

Technicians tell us it "requires a steady stream of accurate and reliable reports" to keep the system operating at peak performance.

Spacing with the ellipsis

- No space *between* the three periods within the ellipsis itself.
- One space *before* and *after* the ellipsis within a sentence.
- No space *before* the ellipsis when an opening quotation mark precedes it, and no space *after* the ellipsis when a closing quotation mark follows it.
- No space between the ellipsis and a closing question mark or exclamation point.
- Two spaces *after* ellipsis when it follows a period, question mark or exclamation point unless following manuscript format and using right justified, then one space *after*.

Exclamation Mark !

1. Use an exclamation mark at the end of a sentence or elliptical expression (condensed sentence, key words left out) to express strong emotion (surprise, disbelief, irony, dissent, urgency, amusement, enthusiasm).

- Congratulations on your new son!
- I suppose you consider that another "first"!
- Fantastic show!

2. Use an exclamation mark in parentheses within a sentence to emphasize a particular word.

- He lost 67(!) pounds in 6 months.
- She said what(!)?

3. Use an exclamation mark *along with dashes*: when an exclamation is set off by dashes within a sentence, use an exclamation mark before the closing dash. Most users of *The Tongue and Quill* regularly encounter exclamation points in evaluation reports. When used on evaluation reports, exclamation points should be used sparingly, such as in the following example, to maintain the impact of the exclamation point and not overwhelm the reader:

Our women's club—number 1 in the area!—will host a party for underprivileged children.

4. Use an exclamation mark inside a closing parenthesis of a parenthetical phrase when the phrase requires an exclamation mark and the sentence *does not* end with an exclamation mark.

- Jerry's new car (a 2004 Nissan Maxima!) was easily financed.
- The football game (Alabama versus Auburn) is always a super game!

5. Use an exclamation mark inside a closing quotation mark only when it applies to the quoted material.

- Lt Col Smith said, "Those rumors that I'm going to retire early simply must stop!"
- You're quite mistaken—Jane Palmisano clearly said, "Peachtree Grill at 1215"!
- Mark and Todd have both told him, "You had no right to say, 'Kimberly will be glad to teach Acquisition' without checking with her first!"

Spacing when using the exclamation mark with other punctuation marks

- Two spaces *after* the end of a sentence—unless manuscript format and using right justified, then one space *after*.
- No space *after* when another punctuation mark immediately follows (closing quotation mark, closing parenthesis, closing dash).
- *The Tongue and Quill* favors two spaces after the end of a sentence. Rather to use one space or two is left up to the individual or organization. Either way is acceptable.

CHAPTER 25
Punctuation

Hyphen -

1. **Use a hyphen when dividing a word at the end of a line.**

   Use the "Dividing Words and Paragraphs" tips at the end of this chapter for the continuation of words at the end of a line or paragraphs at the end of a page.

2. **Use a hyphen to join unit modifiers; when you abbreviate the unit of measure, omit the hyphen.**

   - long-term loan
   - 4-hour sortie, 4 hr sortie
   - rust-resistant cover
   - 24-gallon tank, 24 gal. tank

3. **Use a hyphen when expressing the numbers 21 through 99 in words and in adjective compounds with a numerical first element.**

   - Twenty-one people attended with at least 2 that failed to show up.
   - Eighty-nine or ninety miles from here there's an outlet mall.
   - I kept their 3-year-old child while they were away.
   - There will be a 10-minute delay.

4. **Use a hyphen to join single capital letters to nouns or participles.**

   - E-mail
   - T-bone; T-shirt
   - H-bomb
   - U-boat; U-turn

5. **Use a hyphen to indicate two or more related compound words having a common base (suspended hyphen).**

   - It will be a 12- to 15-page document.
   - The cruise line offers 2-, 3- and 7-day cruises at special group rates.
   - Long- and short-term money rates are available.

6. **Use a hyphen to join capital letter(s) and numbers in system designators and numerical identifiers.**

   - F-117
   - B-1B
   - F-16
   - KC-10
   - Su-24
   - T-38

7. **Use a hyphen to form compound words and phrases.** Some compound words are written as two words (post office, air brake, Mother Nature, fellow traveler), some as one (manpower, masterpiece, aircraft), some as a combination of words and joined by hyphens (father-in-law, great-uncle, secretary-treasurer, governor-general, men-of-war, grant-in-aid, mother-of-pearl), and some multiple-word compounds that include a preposition and a description (jack-of-all-trades, but flash in a pan and master of none). There's a growing trend to spell compound words as one word once widely accepted and used. However, sometimes the way you use a compound word or phrase will dictate how you write it—as one word, with a hyphen, or as two separate words. When in doubt, **consult an up-to-date dictionary** or treat as two words if the guidelines on the next pages don't fit.

a. **Use a hyphen with words and phrases that are combined to form a unit modifier immediately preceding the word modified (except with an adverb ending in *ly*). Do not hyphenate these phrases when they follow the noun.**

- an up-to-date report; this report is up to date
- red-faced man; the man with the red face
- a $500-a-week salary; a salary of $500 a week
- decision-making process; the process of decision making
- the X-ray equipment; the X-ray showed
- a well-known author; the author is well known
- a first-come, first-served basis; on the basis of first come, first served

b. **Use a hyphen when two or more proper names are combined to form a one-thought modifier and when two adjectives are joined by the word "and" or "or."**

- Denver-Dallas-Atlanta flight
- black-and-white terms
- yes-or-no answer
- life-and-death situation
- cause-and-effect hypothesis
- go/no-go decision

c. **Use a hyphen when spelling the word without the hyphen creates a homonym.**

- re-cover [cover again]; recover [to regain]
- re-creation [create again]; recreation [play]
- re-count [count again]; recount [to detail]
- re-mark [mark again]; remark [say]
- re-sign [sign again]; resign [quit]
- re-treat [treat again]; retreat [withdraw]
- co-op [cooperative]; coop [to confine]
- multi-ply [as in fabric]; multiply [arithmetic function]

d. **Use a hyphen to avoid doubling a vowel when the last letter of the prefix "anti," "multi," and "semi" is the same as the first letter of the word. Also, use a hyphen when the second element is a capitalized word or a number.**

- anti-inflammatory; anti-Nazi, antiaircraft
- multi-industry; multielement; multimillion
- semi-icing; semi-Americanized; semiofficial
- ultra-German; pre-1914, post-World War II

e. **Use a hyphen to join duplicate prefixes.**

- re-redirect
- sub-subcommittee
- super-superlative

8. Do NOT use a hyphen in these situations:

  a. In compounds formed from unhyphenated proper nouns.

- Southeast Asian country
- Mobile Bay cruise

  b. Between an independent adjective preceding a noun.

- hot water pipe
- big gray cat

  c. In a compound adjective when the first element of a color term modifies the second.

- sea green gown
- grayish blue car

  d. In a compound adjective formed with chemical names.

- carbon dioxide formula
- hydrochloric acid liquid

  e. In a unit modifier with a letter or number as its second element.

- Attachment 3 pages 1-5
- Article 3 procedures

  f. In a unit modifier enclosed in quotation mark unless it is normally a hyphenated term. Quotation marks are not to be used in lieu of a hyphen.

- "blue sky" law
- "tie-in" sale
- right-to-work state

  g. In a unit modifier to set off some prefixes and suffixes (ante, anti, bi, bio, co, counter, extra, infra, inter, intra, like, macro, meta, micro, mid, multi, neo, non, over, post, per, pre, pro, proto, pseudo, sub, re, semi, socio, super, supra, trans, ultra, un, under), *but there are some exceptions*.

    (1) *All* words are hyphenated when used as an adjective compound.

- all-inclusive background
- all-out war

    (2) ***Best, better, full, high, ill, least, lesser, little, low, lower, middle*** and ***upper*** compounds are hyphenated when used as an adjective before a noun; drop the hyphen when used following the noun.

- best-loved book; the book was best loved
- better-prepared man; the man was better prepared
- full-length dress; the dress is full length
- high-level water; water is at the high level
- ill-advised action; action is ill advised
- least-desirable man; the man was least desirable
- lesser-regarded man; he was the lesser regarded
- little-understood man; the man was little understood
- low-level flight; flying at low level
- lower-level position; entry jobs are at a lower level
- middle-class house; he lives with the middle class
- upper-crust society; she is of the upper crust

(3) Some *cross* and *half* words are hyphenated, but some aren't. Check your dictionary and, if not listed, hyphenate.

- crosswalk
- cross-pollination
- cross section
- halfback
- half-dollar
- half sister

(4) *Elect* words are hyphenated, except when they consist of two or more words.

- mayor-elect; president-elect; senator-elect
- county assessor elect

(5) *Ex* (meaning *former*) words are discouraged in formal writing; *former* is preferred. However, when you use *ex* in this context, use a hyphen.

- ex-governor
- ex-commander
- ex-convict

(6) *Fold* words are usually one word, *except* when used with numerals.

- 25-fold
- Tenfold
- Twofold

(7) *Like* words are usually one word *except* when the first element is a proper name, words of three or more syllables, compound words, or to avoid tripling a consonant.

- gridlike
- lifelike
- Grecian-like
- mystery-like
- wall-like
- squeeze-bottle-like

(8) *Mid*, *Post* and *Pre* words are usually one word *except* when the second element begins with a capital letter or is a number.

- midstream
- postgame
- preeminent
- mid-June
- post-Gothic
- pre-Civil War
- mid-1948
- post-1900s
- pre-1700s

(9) *Non* words are usually one word *except* when the second element begins with a capital letter or consists of more than one word.

- noncommissioned officer
- nonattribution
- nonsurgical
- non-Latin-speaking people
- non-European
- non-civil-service position

(10) *Over* and *under* words are usually one word *except* when the compound contains the word *the*.

- overdone steak
- underdone steak
- understaffed office
- over-the-counter drug
- under-the-table kick

(11) *Quasi* words are always hyphenated.

- quasi-judicial
- quasi-public
- quasi-legislative

(12) **Self** as a prefix is joined to the root word by a hyphen. When *self* is the root word or is used as a suffix, do not use a hyphen.

- self-made
- selfish
- selfless
- self-respect
- herself
- itself
- self-explanatory
- himself
- myself

(13) **Vice** compounds are hyphenated except when used to show a single office or title.

- a vice president; vice-presidential candidate
- vice admiral; vice-admiralty
- the vice-consul; vice-consulate's office
- vice-chancellor; vice-chancellorship

(14) **Well** compounds are hyphenated when used as an adjective before a noun; drop the hyphen when used following the noun. *Well* used as a compound noun is always hyphenated.

- well-made suit; suit was well made
- the well-being of the family; consider her well-being
- well-known author; author is well known
- the well-bred dogs; the dogs were well bred

(15) **Wide** words are usually one word *except* when long and cumbersome and when follows the noun.

- worldwide
- university-wide; the virus is university wide

Spacing when using a hyphen

- No space *before* or *after* to combine words, punctuation and/or numbers.
- One space *after* when dividing a word (see rule 1) or using suspended hyphen (rule 5).

Dividing Words

1. Never divide the last word on the first or last lines on a page; do not hyphenate the last words on two consecutive lines; avoid hyphenating more than five lines each page.
2. Never divide monosyllables (one-syllable words). [friend]
3. Never divide words at a vowel that forms a syllable in the middle of the word. [preju-/dice, **not** prej-/udice]
4. Never divide words at a final syllable whose only vowel sound is that of a syllabic "l." [prin-/cipal, **not** princi-/pals]
5. Never divide words of five or fewer letters even when they contain more than one syllable. [**not** i-/deal or ide-/a]
6. Never divide words by putting a single letter on a line. [**not** a-/round nor militar-/y]
7. Never further divide words that contain a hyphen—break these words at the built-in hyphen. [self-/control, **not** self-con/-trol]
8. Divide words containing double consonants between the consonants only when they do not end root words. [permit-/ted; spell-/ing]
9. When possible, divide words after the prefix or before the suffix rather than within the root word or within the prefix or suffix. [applic-/able, **not** applica-/ble; valu-/able, **not** val-/uable; pre-/requisite, **not** prereq-/uisite].
10. Never divide contractions. [**not** can'/t nor won/'t]
11. When necessary to divide a name, carry over only the surname (never separate a first name from a middle initial, an initial from a middle name or initials used in place of a first name). [Annette G./Walker; Ethel/Hall; R. A./Bowe]
12. Divide surnames, abbreviations and numbers only if they already contain a hyphen, and then divide only at the hyphen. [Johnson-/Roberts, **not** John-/son-Roberts; AFL-/CIO, **not** YM/CA; 249-/3513, **not** $55,-/000].
13. A person's rank or title should be on the same line with first name or initials, when possible. [Miss Duncan/Phillips; Dr. Louise/Miller-Knight; Major Larry/Lee]
14. When it is necessary to divide a date, separate the year from month—do not separate the month from the day.

Dividing Paragraphs

1. Never divide a paragraph of four or fewer lines.
2. When dividing a paragraph of five or more lines between two pages, each page must have at least two lines of text.

Italics *Italics*

1. Use italics in printed material to distinguish the titles of whole published works: books, bulletins, pamphlets, periodicals, newspapers, plays, movies, symphonies, poems, operas, essays, lectures, sermons, legal cases and reports. For title plurals, the plural ending is not italicized. (e.g., "There were five *Journal*s on the shelf." The "s" in "*Journal*s" is not italicized.)

- *The Chicago Manual of Style*
- *The Phantom of the Opera*
- AFMAN 33-326, *Preparing Official Communications*
- *Star Trek*
- *The Montgomery Advertiser*
- *Miranda v. Arizona*

2. Use italics in place of the underscore to distinguish or give greater prominence to certain words, phrases, or sentences. Both the underscore and italics are acceptable, but not in the same document. Use sparingly.

- Air Force *doctrine* has been the subject of much debate.
- Air Force doctrine has been the subject of much debate.

3. Use italics in printed material to distinguish the names of ships, submarines, aircraft, and spacecraft. Italicize the name only, not initials or numbers preceding or following the name. (In typed material, the underscore is generally used for this purpose.) Do not italicize the class or make of ships, aircraft and spacecraft; and names of space programs.

- USS *America*
- *Nautilus*
- B-1B *Lancer*
- *Friendship* 7
- *Columbia*
- frigate
- U-boat
- Spruance
- Boeing 707
- Gemini II

4. Use italics in typed material to distinguish foreign words *not* part of the English language. Once an expression has become part of the English language (in the dictionary), italics is unnecessary.

- *vakfiye*
- *poêle*
- *le cheval*
- *Luftwaffe*
- blitzkrieg
- Perestroika
- vis-à-vis
- com d´état

5. Use italics for punctuation (except parentheses and brackets) marks that immediately follow the italicized word, letter character or symbol.

- What is meant by *random selection?*
- *Point:* one-twelfth of a pica

Parentheses ( )

1. Use parentheses to enclose explanatory material (a single word, a phrase or an entire sentence) that is independent of the main thought of the sentence.

- The ACSC students (542 of them) will begin classes the second week of June.
- The results (see figure 3) were surprising.

2. Use parentheses to set off nonessential elements when commas would be inappropriate or confusing and dashes would be too emphatic.

- Mr. Henry Anderson, Jr., is the general manager of the Montgomery (Alabama) branch. [Parentheses are clearer than commas when a city-state expression is used as an adjective.]
- All the classes will meet three days a week (Mondays, Tuesdays and Thursdays). [Parentheses are used in place of commas because the nonessential element contains commas.]
- I suggest you contact Edward Clinton (a true professional) for his recommendation. [Parentheses used in place of dashes to de-emphasize the nonessential element.]
- Contact Ms. Louise Robinson—the manager of the house in Tuscaloosa—and ask her if a room is still available. [Dashes are used in place of parentheses for emphasis.]

3. Use parentheses to enclose enumerating letters or numerals within a sentence.

- Our goals are to (1) reduce the number of curriculum hours, (2) eliminate the 90-minute lunch period, and (3) reduce the number of personnel needed to accomplish the mission.
- Also, include the following when you file your medical costs: (a) hotel charges, (b) meal costs (including gratuities), and (c) transportation costs.

4. Use parentheses to set off or enclose numbers or letters identifying specific levels of an outline. Recall the cardinal rule of outlining: *any topic that is divided must have at least two parts.* Every "1" must have a "2" and every "a" must have a "b" (and so forth) for every level/sublevel. Refer to chapter 6 for detailed outline examples.

5. Use parentheses (or quotation marks) to enclose a nickname or a descriptive expression when it falls between a person's first and last names. When it precedes or replaces a person's first name, simply capitalize it.

- George Herman (Babe) Ruth
- Stonewall Jackson
- Major William F. (Clark) Kent
- the Iron Duke

6. Using parentheses along with other punctuation

a. **If an item in parentheses falls within a sentence, place comma, semicolon, colon, or dash outside (never before) the closing parenthesis.**

- I'll see you later (probably Friday), but remember to collect your money.

- I'll attend the meeting (as I said I would); however, you'll have to go to the next one as I have another commitment.
- She's passionate about two important issues (and strives to support them): homeless children and a clean environment.

b. **Use a period before a closing parenthesis only when the parenthetical sentence stands on its own or when the closing parenthesis is preceded by an abbreviation containing punctuation.**

- The results were surprising. (See the analysis at atch 2.)
- Many flower heights (e.g., 6 in., 12 in., 36 in.) will be featured in the show.

c. **Put a question mark or quotation mark before a closing parenthesis only when it applies to the parenthetical item and the sentence ends in a different punctuation.**

- The Pentagon (you've been there, haven't you?) is a fascinating building.
- Doris Williams said she would go. (In fact, her exact words were, "Go golfing? You bet! Every chance I get!")

d. **When using an exclamation mark or question mark to emphasize or draw attention to a particular word within a sentence.**

- You call this fresh(!) food.
- They said they will buy us four(?) machines.

Spacing when using parentheses (Opening parenthesis)

- One space *before* when parenthetic matter is within a sentence.
- No space *before* when using exclamation or question marks to emphasize or draw attention to a particular word within a sentence.
- Two spaces *before* when parenthetic matter follows a sentence (when parenthetic matter starts with a capital and closes with its own sentence punctuation)—unless manuscript format and using right justified, then one space *before*.
- No space *after*.

Spacing when using parentheses (Closing parenthesis)

- No space *before*.
- One space *after* when parenthetic matter is within a sentence.
- Two spaces *after* when parenthetic matter is itself a complete sentence and another sentence follows—unless manuscript format and using right justified, then one space *after*.
- No space *after* if another punctuation mark immediately follows.
- *The Tongue and Quill* favors two spaces after the end of a sentence. Rather to use one space or two is left up to the individual or organization. Either way is acceptable.

Period .

1. Use a period to end declarative and imperative sentences.

- Declarative: His work is highly satisfactory.
- Imperative: Don't be late.

2. Use a period to end an indirect question or a question intended as a suggestion or otherwise not requiring an answer.

- She wanted to know how to do it.
- He asked what the job would entail.

3. Use a period with certain abbreviations; however, some abbreviations are written without punctuation—check your local command style guide. (NOTE: "Miss" is not an abbreviation.)

- Mr. • Mrs. • Ms. • Dr. • Sr. • Jr. • i.e. • e.g. • etc.
- in. [inch vs. the word *in*]   • no. [number vs. the word *no*]

4. Use a period to form ellipses (three periods that indicate a pause or faltering speech within a sentence, or an omission of a portion of quoted material). *Refer to the ellipsis section of this chapter for more information.*

5. Use a period after each item in a vertical list/outline when at least one of the items is a complete sentence.

- After listening intently to the defense attorney's closing remarks, the jury was convinced of three things:
  - Witnesses lied.
  - False evidence had been presented.
  - The defendant deserved a new trial.
- After listening to the defense attorney's closing remarks, the jury was convinced that
  - several witnesses had perjured themselves,
  - false evidence was presented and
  - the defendant deserved a new trial.

6. Do *not* use a period in a vertical list/outline when the list completes the sentence begun in the introductory element unless the items in the list are separated by other punctuation.

The following fighter aircraft were lined up on the runway for the airshow:

- F-16
- F-35
- F-22

CHAPTER 25
Punctuation

7. Use periods after numbers and letters in an outline when the letters and figures are *not* enclosed in parentheses (such as in the numbered and lettered paragraphs of this chapter). Recall the cardinal rule of outlining: *any topic that is divided must have at least two parts.* Every "1" must have a "2" and every "a" must have a "b" (and so forth) for every level/sublevel. See chapter 6 for detailed outline examples.

> Example
> 1. Main point 1
>   a. First supporting evidence
>   b. Second supporting evidence
>   (1) First detailed support
>   (2) Second detailed support
>   (a) First additional support
>   (b) Second additional support
> 2. Main point 2

6. Using a period with parenthetical phrases. Place a period inside the final parenthesis only when the item in the parentheses is a separate sentence or when the final word in the parenthetical phrase is an abbreviation that is followed by a period.

- I waited in line for 3 hours. (One other time I waited for over 5 hours.)
- One other committee member (namely, Dr. Glen Jones, Sr.) plans to vote against the amendment.

7. Using a period with quotation marks: period placed inside a closing quotation mark.

She said, "I'll go with you."

8. Using a period with a dash only when used with an abbreviation that contains periods.

Tony Lamar's desk is 48 in.—his is the only odd-sized desk.

Spacing when using a period

- Two spaces *after* the end of a sentence.
- No space *before* unless an ellipsis.
- One space *after* an abbreviation with a period within a sentence.
- No space *after* a decimal point or *before* within two numbers.
- No space *after* when another punctuation mark immediately follows (closing quotation mark, closing parenthesis, comma following an "abbreviation" period).
- Two spaces *after* a number or letter that indicates an enumeration (rule 5b).
- *The Tongue and Quill* favors two spaces after the end of a sentence. Rather to use one space or two is left up to the individual or organization. Either way is acceptable.

Question Mark ?

1. Use a question mark to indicate the end of a direct question.

- Did he go with you?
- Will you be able to attend?

2. Use a question mark with elliptical (shortened) questions and to express more than one question within a sentence.

- You rang? For what purpose?
- Was the speaker interesting? Convincing? Well versed?
- Who approved the sale? When? To whom? For what amount?

3. Use a question mark after an independent question within a larger sentence.

- The question "Who will absorb the costs?" went unanswered.
- When will the reorganization take place? will surely be asked.

4. Use a question mark to express doubt.

- They plan to purchase three(?) new Pentium computers with individual scanners for us.
- Jackie Baltzell and Gayle Magill have been associated with her since 1990(?).

5. Use a question mark before a closing parenthesis only when it applies solely to the parenthetical item and the sentence ends in a different punctuation mark.

- At our next meeting (it's on the 16th, isn't it?), we'll elect a new president. As the gun opened fire (was it a .50-caliber gun?), all movement ceased. [Question marks were used within parentheses because sentences require a period at the end.]
- Are tickets still available (and can I get two), or is it too late? [Question mark is omitted within parentheses because sentence ends with a question mark.]

6. A question mark is placed inside the closing quotation mark only when it applies to the quoted material or when the same punctuation is required for both the quotation and the sentence as a whole.

- She asked, "Did you enjoy the trip?" [Question mark belongs with quoted material.]
- Why did he ask, "When does it start?" [Question mark is same as ending punctuation.]
- Did you say, "I'll help out"? [Quoted material is not a question; therefore, question mark applies to the sentence as a whole.]

7. When a question within a sentence is set off by dashes, place the question mark before the closing dash.

The new class—isn't it called Super Seminar?—begins tomorrow.

Spacing when using a question mark...

- Two spaces *after* the end of a sentence—unless manuscript format and using right justified, then one space *after*.

- No space *after* when another punctuation mark immediately follows (closing quotation mark, closing parenthesis, closing dash).

- *The Tongue and Quill* favors two spaces after the end of a sentence. Rather to use one space or two is left up to the individual or organization. Either way is acceptable.

Quotation Marks " "

1. Use quotation marks to enclose the exact words of a speaker or writer. With few exceptions, a quotation must be copied exactly as it appears in the original. If the quotation is woven into the flow of the sentence, do not use punctuation preceding the opening quotation mark. When words interrupt a quotation, close and reopen the quotation.

- Robert Frost said, "The brain is a wonderful organ; it starts working the moment you get up in the morning and doesn't stop until you get to the office."

- Why does she insist on saying "It just won't work"?

- "A pint of sweat" says General George S. Patton, "will save a gallon of blood."

- **NOTE:** Do *not* use quotation marks to set off an indirect quotation. Why does she insist on saying that it just won't work?

2. Use quotation marks to enclose slogans or mottoes, but not signs or notices.

- He had a "do or die" attitude.

- "Live and let live" is a common phrase.

- He has a No Smoking sign in his car.

- There is a Gone Fishing notice on his door.

3. Use quotation marks to enclose words or phrases used to indicate humor, slang, irony or poor grammar.

- They serve "fresh" seafood all right—fresh from the freezer!

- For whatever reason, she just "ain't talkin'."

NOTE: When using quotation marks with other punctuation, the comma and period are always placed inside the closing quotation marks; the semicolon is always placed outside the closing quotation marks; the dash, exclamation mark and question mark are placed according to the structure of the sentence.

4. Use quotation marks with words and phrases that are introduced by such expressions as *cited as, classified, designated, entitled, labeled, marked, named, signed, the term, or the word* **when the exact text is quoted.** Capitalize the first word when it begins a sentence, when it was capitalized in the original, when it represents a complete sentence, or when it is a proper noun.

- The card was signed "Your friend, Diane."
- The article was entitled "How to Write English That is Alive."
- "Fragile" was stamped on the outside of the package.
- The report is classified "secret" and can't be distributed.

NOTE: Do not enclose these expressions: *called, known as, so-called,* etc.

  o The flower was called an American Beauty rose.
  o The boy whose name is "Bill Kent" was known as Clark Kent.
  o The so-called secret report can now be distributed.

5. To enclose the title of any part (chapter, lesson, topic, section, article, heading) of a published work (book, play, speech, symphony, etc.). The title of the published work should be italicized in word processor files and printed materials; titles are underlined only if typed using a manual typewriter.

- Air Force Doctrine Annex 1-1, *Force Development*, has an appendix entitled "Institutional Competency List."
- When you read "Documents Standards" section of *The Tongue and Quill*, recall…

6. Use quotation marks to enclose titles of complete but unpublished works such as manuscripts, dissertations and reports.

- We need to read the "The Evolution of a Revolt" report as soon as possible.
- The title of his dissertation is "Impacts of Banning Smoking from Public Places."

7. Use quotation marks to enclose the titles of songs and radio and television shows.

- They sang "The Star Spangled Banner" before the game began.
- "M.A.S.H." is still being shown on TV.

8. Use quotation marks to denote inches.

6" × 15" [Use inch (") mark and multiplication (×) mark if using typewriter or computer that has these keys.]

9. Use quotation marks (or parentheses) to enclose a nickname or descriptive expression when it falls between a person's first and last names. However, when it precedes or replaces a person's first name, simply capitalize it.

- George Herman "Babe" Ruth
- the Iron Duke
- Major William F. "Clark" Kent
- Stonewall Jackson

10. Use quotation marks to enclose misnomers, slang expressions, nickname, coined words or ordinary words used in an arbitrary way.

- His report was "bunk."
- The "invisible government" is responsible.

Spacing when using quotation marks (Opening mark)

- Two spaces *before* when quoted matter starts a new sentence or follows a colon—unless manuscript format and using right justified, then one space *before*.
- No space *before* when a dash or an opening parenthesis precedes.
- One space *before* in all other cases.
- No space *after*.

Spacing when using quotation marks (Closing mark)

- No space *before*.
- Two spaces *after* when quoted matter ends the sentence—unless manuscript format and using right justified, then one space *after* (see page 302, spacing).
- No space *after* when another punctuation mark immediately follows (semicolon, colon).
- One space *after* in all other cases.

Semicolon ;

1. Use a semicolon to separate independent clauses not connected by a coordinating conjunction (*and, but, for, or, nor* and *so*), and in statements too closely related in meaning to be written as separate sentences.

- The students were ready; it was time to go.
- War is destructive; peace, constructive.

2. Use a semicolon before transitional words/phrases (*accordingly, as a result, besides, consequently, for example, furthermore, hence, however, moreover, namely, nevertheless, on the contrary, otherwise, that is, then, therefore, thus,* and *yet*) when connecting two complete but related thoughts and a coordinating conjunction is not used. Follow these words/phrases with a comma. Do not use a comma after *hence, then, thus, so* and *yet* unless a pause is needed.

- Our expenses have increased; however, we haven't raised our prices.
- Our expenses have increased, however, and we haven't raised our prices.
- The decision has been made; therefore, there's no point in discussing it further.
- The decision has been made so there's no point in discussing it.
- The general had heard the briefing before; thus, he chose not to attend.

3. Use a semicolon to separate items in a series that contain commas (when confusion would otherwise result).

- If you want your writing to be worthwhile, organize it; if you want it to be easy to read, use simple words and phrases; and, if you want it to be interesting, vary your sentence and paragraph lengths.

- Those who attended the meeting were Martha Brown, Dean of Education; Colonels David Jones, Dean of Distance Learning; Samantha White, Chairman of Leadership and Communications Studies; and Todd Walker, Chairman of Joint Warfare Studies.

4. Use a semicolon to precede words or abbreviations that introduce a summary or explanation of what has gone before in the sentence.

- We visited several countries on that trip; i.e., England, Ireland, France, and Germany.

- There are many things you must arrange before leaving on vacation; for example, mail pickup, pet care and yard care.

Spacing when using a semicolon

- No space before.
- One space *after*.

Summary

The punctuation usage guide is a starting point. Using the proper punctuation conveys direction for your readers; it helps your message convey the impact, significance, emotion and even the breaks between thoughts and ideas. It is not difficult to use the proper punctuation; start with the basics and grow your skill as your other communications skills grow.

CHAPTER 26:

Abbreviations

This chapter covers:
- Definition and implications
- Types of abbreviations
- General guidelines
- Common abbreviations
- Researcher's guide to abbreviations

Several prior chapters provided specific tips to improve your prose through better drafting (chapter 6), editing (chapter 7), format choice (chapter 16) and writing better bullet statements (chapter 19). One challenge that persists, especially in written communications, is the tension between the number of words (length) and meaning. Anyone familiar with texting and social media understands this tension between time and space. With more words you can convey more meaning but the time required to read more—and the space required to carry the meaning—are limited. For example, recent changes to the officer and enlisted evaluation forms have reduced the amount of space to record individual accomplishments. As such, the need to convey more meaning in less space is highly important: we need to keep our messages short.

Definition and Implications

What is an abbreviation? The definition and implications may surprise you.

> *Ab-bre-vi-a-tion (noun) \ə-ˌbre-ve-ˈa-shən\: a shortened form of a word or name that is used in place of the full word or name*
>
> –Merriam-Webster's *Online Dictionary* (2014)

This definition is broad and implies the need for further information about the types, forms and appropriate uses for abbreviations in Air Force documents. If you have ever had any of the following questions, you understand the need for more information:

- What are the types of abbreviations?
- What's the appropriate abbreviation for a specific word?
- Can I use abbreviations in this document? If so, what types are allowed?
- How is the abbreviation written—all uppercase, all lowercase or a combination of both?
- Can I use just the abbreviation or must I spell it out?
- How do I make an abbreviation plural—add an *s*, or an *'s*?

Though these questions are insignificant when compared with the issues facing the Air Force and the nation, the ability to communicate clearly—with or without abbreviations—remains an essential skill for all Air Force personnel. Answers to these questions begin by understanding the types of abbreviations. Which type to use is driven by two principles—the formality of the document and clearly conveying meaning. In general, use the shortest form of the word appropriate for the document that clearly conveys the meaning.

Types of Abbreviations

Abbreviations appear in Air Force documents in many forms to include acronyms, brevity codes, contractions and truncations. With the growth of technology there has been an explosive growth in the forms of abbreviations and the number of common abbreviations in use. The sections that follow cover only a few examples for each so that you can recognize the types and know how to apply the general guidelines for their use in the official forms, letters and papers you prepare.

Single Letter/Few Letter Abbreviations

Single letter/few letter abbreviations are exactly what the label suggests: words that are represented by a single or just a few important letters. Examples include "n." for noun, "gov." for government, "ltd." for limited, or "ID" for identification. According to the Encyclopedia Britannica online, "these abbreviations are usually spoken as the whole word they represent."

Acronyms

Acronyms are pronounceable words formed by combining the initial letter(s) of the words that make up the complete term. Most acronyms are written in all caps without punctuation, but some are so commonly used they are now considered words in their own right.

- AAFES (**A**rmy **a**nd **A**ir **F**orce **E**xchange **S**ervice)
- laser (**l**ight **a**mplification by **s**timulated **e**mission of **r**adiation)
- NATO (**N**orth **A**tlantic **T**reaty **O**rganization)
- radar (**ra**dio **d**etection **a**nd **r**anging)
- scuba (**s**elf-**c**ontained **u**nderwater **b**reathing **a**pparatus)
- ZIP code (**Z**one **I**mprovement **P**lan code)

The English language uses acronyms so frequently that the original full term is no longer needed to convey meaning, such as with laser, radar and scuba. This is not the case with brevity codes as they tend to be very specific to life and work experiences.

Brevity Codes (a.k.a. "Initialisms")

A brevity code is a combination of letters—pronounced letter by letter—designed to shorten a phrase, sentence or group of sentences. Outside the military, brevity codes are known as initialisms. While many brevity codes/initialisms are widely known, each working community or military specialty tends to build a language of its own with brevity codes. Fortunately, most official forms have a place dedicated for spelling out brevity codes. When used within the text of documents, brevity codes should be written out fully on first use followed by the brevity code in parentheses as shown, below. Also, when brevity codes begin with b, c, d, g, j, k, p, q, t, u, v, w, y, or z, the indefinite article *a* is used. With a, e, f, h, i, l, m, n, o, r, s, or x, use *an*.

- ABU (Airmen's Battle Uniform)
- BX (Base Exchange)
- CFC (Combined Federal Campaign)
- DoD (Department of Defense)
- NCO (Non-Commissioned Officer)
- PCS (permanent change of station)
- POW (prisoner of war)
- TDY (temporary duty)
- UOD (uniform of the day)

Contractions

Contractions differ from both acronyms and brevity codes in that contractions are shortened forms of words in which an apostrophe indicates the deletion of letters. Contractions are common in informal work but should not be used in formal, professional work unless needed to convey a distinct personal tone, such as in a letter or an e-mail to a specific person or group.

- can't (cannot)
- I'll (I will)
- I've (I have)
- it's (it is)
- mustn't (must not)
- we're (we are)
- wouldn't (would not)
- don't (do not)
- I'm (I am)
- isn't (is not)
- let's (let us)
- they're (they are)
- won't (will not)
- you've (you have)

General Guidelines

Regardless of the form of the abbreviation, the following general guidelines are useful in helping you determine how, when and where to use abbreviations. The guidelines that follow are not comprehensive or directive—but they are a good place to start. In general, use the shortest abbreviation allowable for the document that clearly conveys the desired meaning.

Using Abbreviations

- Use abbreviations in *informal* documents, manuals, reference books, business and legal documents, scholarly footnotes, etc., when needed to save space.

- Use only approved abbreviations for formal/official documents, such as performance evaluations and award nomination forms.

- Spell out the acronym or brevity code the first time it is used. If a large section of text occurs between uses, write it out again to remind readers of its meaning.

- When used, use abbreviations sparingly, correctly and consistently.

Instances to Limit or Avoid Using Abbreviations

- Avoid beginning a sentence with an abbreviation (except Mr., Mrs., Ms., Dr.), acronym or brevity code.

- Avoid using contractions in formal documents when style, elegance and formality are important. Use acronyms and brevity codes sparingly in formal documents or provide a glossary that defines all acronyms and brevity codes used in the document.

- Avoid using abbreviations of all types in main headings.

- Avoid using words that are offensive, profane or repulsive when assigning acronyms, brevity codes and contractions.

- In formal writing "United States" is a noun (The United States is a leading producer of several grains); "US" is an adjective (US policy regarding energy).

- When using an abbreviation, use a figure to express the quantity in a unit of measure (without a hyphen in a unit modifier). [3 mi, 55 mph, 50 lb, 33 mm film]

Specific Abbreviation Forms and Formats

- Write abbreviations "first," "second," "third," "fourth," etc., as 1st, 2d, 3d, 4th, etc.

- Use the shortest form when there's a choice between the abbreviated form and the contraction form. [gov vs gov't]

- Write all abbreviations without punctuation unless confusion would result. [The abbreviation for *inch* (in.) might be confused with the word *in*, the abbreviation for *number* (no.) might be confused with the word *no*, etc.]

- Write abbreviations for single words in lowercase letters. [hospital–hosp; letter–ltr]

- Use the same abbreviation for singular and plural forms after spelling it out. [area of responsibility (AOR)–areas of responsibility (AOR)]

- When ambiguity could result, form the plural with a lowercase *s* and never use an apostrophe to form the plural. [letters–ltrs; travel requests–TRs; area of operations–AO; areas of operations–AOs]

- Do not cap the words just because the acronym or brevity code is capped. Check a source book, the library or the office of responsibility for the correct form. [OJT–on the job training; OPSEC–operations security; JIPC–joint imagery production complex; JCS–Joint Chiefs of Staff]

Bottom Line: If in doubt, *spell it out*.

- Contact the office of primary responsibility for the proper use of abbreviations when writing articles, manuals, handouts, instructions, performance reports, award citations and narratives, and unit histories.

- Find out if your organization has any style preferences regarding abbreviations and use it. Otherwise, consult the latest dictionary or use the Joint Publication 1-02, *Department of Defense Dictionary of Military and Associated Terms*, for terms and definitions.

Common Abbreviations

Days

Sunday	Monday	Tuesday	Wednesday	Thursday	Friday	Saturday
Sun	Mon	Tues	Wed	Thurs	Fri	Sat

Months

Most Air Force writing uses the common abbreviates for the months of the year. However, official biographies use the Associated Press (AP) form (see chapter 20). The difference between the forms is that all months with five or fewer letters are always spelled in AP form. Stated differently, the months of March, April, May, June, and July are always spelled out completely in AP form.

	January	February	March	April	May	June
Common	Jan	Feb	Mar	Apr	May	Jun
AP	Jan	Feb	March	April	May	June
	July	**August**	**September**	**October**	**November**	**December**
Common	Jul	Aug	Sep	Oct	Nov	Dec
AP	July	Aug	Sep	Oct	Nov	Dec

Years

Years are abbreviated by using only the last two digits when used as part of a date or with an apostrophe when used to denote a year group or graduation year. The last two digits of a year may also be combined with an acronym to denote specific annual events such as fiscal or academic years.

- Used as a date: In the date 10 Nov 14 the number 14 is the abbreviation for 2014.
- Used as a year group: The '05 year group for the 2005 year group.
- Used as a graduation year: The Class of '12 for the Class of 2012.
- Used with an acronym: FY14 for fiscal year 2014; AY14 for academic year 2013-2014.

State and Possession Abbreviations

State	*Unites State Postal Service*	*Common*	*AP*
Alabama	AL	Ala.	Ala.
Alaska*	AK	-	Alaska
Arizona	AZ	Ariz.	Ariz.
Arkansas	AR	-	Ark.
California	CA	Calif.	Calif.
Colorado	CO	Colo.	Colo.
Connecticut	CT	Conn.	Conn.
Delaware	DE	Del.	Del.
Florida	FL	Fla.	Fla.
Georgia	GA	Ga.	Ga.
Hawaii*	HI	-	Hawaii
Idaho*	ID	-	Idaho
Illinois	IL	Ill.	Ill.
Indiana	IN	Ind.	Ind.
Iowa*	IA	-	Iowa
Kansas	KS	Kans.	Kan.
Kentucky	KY	Ky.	Ky.
Louisiana	LA	La.	La.
Maine*	ME	-	Maine
Maryland	MD	Md.	Md.
Massachusetts	MA	Mass.	Mass.
Michigan	MI	Mich.	Mich.
Minnesota	MN	Minn.	Minn.
Mississippi	MS	Miss.	Miss.
Missouri	MO	Mo.	Mo.

CHAPTER 26
Abbreviations

State	Unites State Postal Service	Common	AP
Montana	MT	Mont.	Mont.
Nebraska	NE	Nebr.	Neb.
Nevada	NV	Nev.	Nev.
New Hampshire	NH	-	N.H.
New Jersey	NJ	-	N.J.
New Mexico	NM	NMex.	N.M.
New York	NY	-	N.Y.
North Carolina	NC	-	N.C.
North Dakota	ND	NDak.	N.D.
Ohio*	OH	-	Ohio
Oklahoma	OK	Okla.	Okla.
Oregon	OR	Oreg.	Ore.
Pennsylvania	PA	Pa.	Pa.
Rhode Island	RI	-	R.I.
South Carolina	SC	-	S.C.
South Dakota	SD	SDak.	S.D.
Tennessee	TN	Tenn.	Tenn.
Texas*	TX	Tex.	Texas
Utah*	UT	-	Utah
Vermont	VT	Vt.	Vt.
Virginia	VA	Va.	Va.
Washington	WA	Wash.	Wash.
West Virginia	WV	WVa.	W.Va.
Wisconsin	WI	Wis.	Wis.
Wyoming	WY	Wyo.	Wyo.
American Samoa	AS	-	-
District of Columbia	DC	-	-
Federated States of Micronesia	FM	-	-
Guam	GU	-	-
Marshall Islands	MH	-	-
Northern Mariana Islands	MP	-	-
Palau	PW	-	-
Puerto Rico	PR	-	-
Virgin Islands	VI	-	-
* In AP style, Alaska, Hawaii, Idaho, Iowa, Maine, Ohio, Texas and Utah *are always spelled out.*			

Other Air Force Abbreviations

Within the Air Force there are many types of workplaces, and they are organized into one or more major categories. These categories include major command (MAJCOM), numbered air force (NAF), direct reporting unit (DRU), and field operating agency (FOA). For example, Pacific Air Forces (PACAF) and Air Combat Command (ACC) are major commands; Ninth Air Force (9 AF) and 24th Air Force (24 AF) are numbered air forces; the United States Air Force Academy (USAFA) is a direct reporting unit; and the Air Force Personnel Center (AFPC) is a field operating agency. The full list of MAJCOMs, NAFs, DRUs, etc., can be found on the public Air Force website at http://www.af.mil/AFSites.aspx.

Phonetic Alphabet

The military version of the phonetic alphabet is presented here as a tool to help verbalize the spelling of acronyms and other abbreviations verbally.

A	Alpha	H	Hotel	O	Oscar	V	Victor
B	Bravo	I	India	P	Papa	W	Whiskey
C	Charlie	J	Juliet	Q	Quebec	X	X-ray
D	Delta	K	Kilo	R	Romeo	Y	Yankee
E	Echo	L	Lima	S	Sierra	Z	Zulu
F	Foxtrot	M	Mike	T	Tango		
G	Golf	N	November	U	Uniform		

Academic Degrees

There are numerous academic degree titles and each has at least one common abbreviation. With the growth of specialized studies there has been growth in the number of specialized degree titles. The important point regarding academic degrees is to understand the level of study—undergraduate (associates and bachelors) or graduate (masters and doctoral)—and the field of study. For example, you would not want to see a doctor for illness unless the person holds a doctorate degree in the appropriate medical field. Some general examples are listed below.

- Associates Degrees: Associate of Arts (AA); Associate of Science (AS)
- Bachelor's Degrees: Bachelor of Arts (BA); Bachelor of Science (BS)
- Master's Degrees: Master of Arts (MA); Master of Science (MS)
- Doctor of Philosophy (PhD); Juris Doctor (JD); Medical Doctor (MD)

Secondary Address Unit Indicators

Use secondary address unit indicators to save space within the limited area available for the address on envelopes and letters, such as these common secondary address unit indicators:

- Apartment–APT
- Building–BLDG
- Department–DEPT
- Floor–FL
- Room–RM
- Suite–STE

CHAPTER 26
Abbreviations

Latin Abbreviations

Abbreviation	Full Latin Term	Meaning
A.M.	*ante meridiem*	before noon
c. or ca	*circa*	about, approximately
e.g.	*exempli gratia*	for example, for instance
et al.	*et allii, et alia*	and other people/things
etc.	*et cetera*	and so on, and other things
ib, ibid.	*ibidem*	in the same place
i.e.	*id est*	that is to say
loc. cit.	*loco citato*	in the place cited/mentioned
op. cit.	*opere citato*	in the work cited/mentioned before
P.M.	*post meridiem*	after noon
P.S.	*post scriptum*	after writing
Pro tem.	*pro tempore*	for the time, temporarily
Q.E.D.	*quod erat demonstrandum*	which was to be shown
Sc.	*sic*	thus used, spelt, etc.
v.,	*versus*	vs. against
v.v.	*vice versa*	the other way around

Units of Measure

- Degrees Celsius–°C
- Degrees Fahrenheit–°F
- Foot–ft
- Gallon–gal
- Hertz–hz
- Inch–in.
- Kilogram–kg
- Kilometer–km
- Mile–mi
- miles per hour–mph
- Millimeter–mm
- nautical miles–NM
- pounds per square inch–psi
- revolutions per minute–rpm

Researcher's Guide to Abbreviations

app	appendix	l (el)	line (plural: ll) [not recommended because the abbreviation in the singular might be mistaken for "one" and the plural for "eleven"]
art	article (plural: arts)	n	not, footnote (plural: nn)
b	born	nd	no date
bk	book (plural: bks)	no.	number (plural: nos)
c	copyright	np	no place; no publisher
ca	circa, about, approximately	NS	new series
cf	confer, compare [confer is Latin for "compare": *cf* must not be used as the abbreviation for the English "confer," nor should *cf* be use to mean "see")	op cit	*opere citato*, in the work cited
ch	chapter (in legal references only)	OS	old series
chap	chapter (plural: chaps)	p	page (plural: pp) [it always precedes the numbers; when "p" follows a number, it can stand for "pence"]
col	column (plural: cols)	para	Paragraph (plural: pars)
comp	complier (plural: comps); complied by	passim	here and there
d	died	pt	part (plural: pts)
dept	department (plural: depts)	qv	*quod vide*, which see (for use with cross-references
div	division (plural: divs)	sc	scene
e.g.	*exempli gratia*, for example (do not use with "etc.")	sec	section (plural: secs)
ed	edition, edited by editor (plural: eds)	[sic]	so, thus; show erroneous material intentionally kept in text
et al	*et alii*, and others	sup	supplement (plural: sups)
et seq	*et sequens*, and the following	supra	above
etc.	*et cetera*, and so forth	sv	*sub verbo*, *sub voce*, under the word (for use in references to listing in encyclopedias and dictionaries)
fig	figure (plural: figs)	trans	translator, translated by
fl	*flourit* flourished (for use when birth and death dates are not known)	v	verse (plural: vv)
i.e.	*id est*, that is (use with etc.)	viz	videlicet, namely
ibid	*ibidem*, in the same place	vol	volume (plural: vols)
id	idem, the same (refers to persons, except in law citations; not to be confused with ibid)	vs	versus, against (v in law references)
infra	below		

CHAPTER 27:

Capitalization

This chapter covers:

- General Capitalization Guidelines
- Specific Capitalization Guidelines

General Capitalization Guidelines

Air Force writers and reviewers spend an excessive amount of time trying to determine the appropriate use of capital letters (and abbreviations and numbers, as well). The reason for using capital letters is to give distinction or add importance to certain words or phrases, but style guides and command preferences differ. If someone else is signing the document, that person has the last word. The best advice we can give you is to find out what style your organization prefers and use that style consistently.

One thing we can all agree on is that we are Airmen with a capital "A." Our doctrine now defines Airman to include all officers and enlisted personnel, regardless of rank, component (regular, reserve, or guard), or specialty, and all Department of the Air Force civilians.

Although we can't possibly cover every situation, what follows is designed to provide some measure of consistency within the Air Force. You must ensure consistency within everything you write or type. A word of caution: When you're preparing Air Force publications, performance reports, forms/IMTs, awards or other unique packages, consult the appropriate manuals or the office of primary responsibility to determine their unique requirements such as Joint Publication 1-02, *Department of Defense Dictionary of Military and Associated Terms*.

Specific Capitalization Guidelines

The general guidance for capitalization provided in the previous section is intentionally brief to set the stage for the specific capitalization guidance provided below.

First Words

1. **Capitalize the first word…**

   a. of every sentence.
   - Twenty-one people attended the secret presentation given by the chief of staff.
   - Many government employees were furloughed in 2002 and again in 2013.

   b. of every sentence fragment treated as a complete sentence.
   - Really? No! So much for that.
   - More discussion. No agreement. Another hour wasted.

   c. of direct questions and quotations placed within a sentence even if quotation marks are not used.
   - The commander asked this question: How many of you are volunteers?
   - The order read "Attack at dawn."

   d. of items shown in a list (using numbers, letters or display dots) when a complete sentence introduces them.

   The commander listed the following responsibilities of liaison officers:
   - Become familiar with the situation.
   - Know the mission.
   - Arrange for communications.

   e. in the salutation (e.g., "Dear Mrs. Smith") and complimentary closing (e.g., "Sincerely" or "Respectfully yours") of a letter.

   f. after a hyphen when the hyphenated word is followed by a proper noun or adjective (e.g., "non-English speaking people").

   g. after a colon when the

   (1) word is a proper noun (e.g., "Two courses are required: English and Economics.") or the pronoun I (e.g., "Everyone else went shopping: I stayed in the car.").

   (2) word is the first word of a quoted sentence (e.g., "When asked to explain the difference between a sofa and a love seat, the boy said: 'I don't know, ma'am, because you don't put your feet on either one.'").

   (3) expression after the colon is a complete sentence that is the dominant or more general element (e.g., "A key principle: Nonessential elements are set off by commas; essential elements are not set off.").

(4) material following the colon consists of two or more sentences (e.g., "There are several drawbacks to this: First, it ties up our capital for three years. Second, the likelihood of a great return on our investment is questionable.").

(5) material following the colon starts on a new line.

    They gave us two reasons:

      1. They received the order too late.

      2. It was Friday and nothing could be done until Monday.

(6) material preceding the colon is an introductory word such as NOTE, CAUTION, WANTED, HINT or REMEMBER (e.g., WANTED: Three editorial assistants who know computers as well as editing and typesetting.).

h. each line in a poem. (Always follow the style of the poem, however).

> I used to write quite poorly.
>
> My boss said it made him ill.
>
> But now he's feeling better
>
> 'Cuz I use *The Tongue and Quill*!
>
>   –TSgt Keyes

2. Do not capitalize the first word...

a. of a sentence enclosed in parentheses within another sentence unless the first word is a proper noun, the pronoun *I*, the first word of a quoted sentence, or begins a complete parenthetical sentence standing alone.

- The company finally moved (they were to have vacated 2 months ago) to another location.
- One of our secretaries (Jan Smith) will record the minutes of today's meeting.
- This is the only tree in our yard that survived the ice storm. (It's a pecan tree.)

b. when it is part of a quotation slogan or motto if it is not capitalized in the original quotation (e.g., General MacArthur said that old soldiers "just fade away.").

c. shown in enumeration (running text or list format) when completing the sentence that introduces them (running text example–"Liaison officers must 1) become familiar with the situation, 2) know the mission and 3) arrange for communications.")

d. the first word of an independent clause after a colon if the clause explains, illustrates or amplifies the thought expressed in the first part of the sentence (e.g., "Essential and nonessential elements require altogether different punctuation: the latter should be set off by commas, whereas the former should not.").

e. after a colon if the material cannot stand alone as a sentence.

- I must countersign all cash advances, with one exception: when the amount is less than $50.
- Three subjects were discussed: fund raising, membership and bylaws.

Proper Nouns and Common Nouns

1. **Capitalize all proper names (the official name of a person, place or thing).**
   - Person: Joanne Johnson; Cliff Brown; George Washington
   - Place: the Grand Canyon; New Jersey; Squadron Officer College
   - Thing: February; Monday; the Constitution

2. **Capitalize a common noun or adjective that forms an essential part of a proper name, but not a common noun used alone as a substitute for the name of a place or thing.**
   - Statue of Liberty; the statue
   - Washington Monument; the monument
   - Vietnam Veterans Memorial; the memorial
   - Potomac River; the river
   - Air War College; the college
   - Berlin Wall; the wall

3. **If a common noun or adjective forming an essential part of a name becomes removed from the rest of the name by an intervening common noun or adjective, the entire expression is no longer a proper noun and is not capitalized.**
   - Union Station; union passenger station
   - Eastern States; eastern farming states

4. **Capitalize names of exercises, military operations, military concepts, etc.**
   - Exercise ULCHI FOCUS LENS
   - Operation ENDURING FREEDOM
   - Military concepts: Principles of War; Command and Control; Precision Engagement

Titles of Literary and Artistic Works and Headings

1. **Capitalize all words with four or more letters in titles and artistic works and in displayed headings.**

2. **Capitalize words with fewer than four letters *except*...**
   a. Articles: the, a, an
   b. Short conjunctions: and, as, but, if, or, nor
   c. Short prepositions: at, by, for, in, of, off, on, out, to, up

3. **Capitalize short verb forms like *Is* and *Be*, but not *to* when part of an infinitive.**
   - How to Complete a Goal Without Really Trying
   - "Reorganization of Boyd Academy Is Not Expected to Be Approved"

4. **Capitalize all hyphenated words in titles, etc., except articles and short prepositions; coordinating conjunctions; second elements of prefixes (unless proper noun or proper adjective); and *flat*, *sharp* and *natural* after musical key symbols.**

   - Run-of-the-Mill; Twenty-first Century; One-eighth; Self-explanatory
   - English-Speaking; Large-Sized Mat
   - Ex-Governor
   - E-flat Concerto

5. **Capitalize articles, short conjunctions and short prepositions when:**

   a. the first and last word of a title (e.g., "A Son-in-Law to Be Proud Of").

   b. the first word following a dash or colon in a title.

   - *Richard Nixon—The Presidential Years*
   - *Copyright Issues of the Air Force: A Reexamination*

   c. short words like *in*, *out* and *up* in titles when they serve as adverbs rather than as prepositions. These words may occur as adverbs in verb phrases or in hyphenated compounds derived from verb phrases.

   - "IBM Chalks Up Record Earnings for the Year"
   - "Sailing up the Rhein"

   d. short prepositions like *in* and *up* when used together with prepositions having four or more letters.

   - "Driving Up and Down the Interstate"
   - "Events In and Around Town"

Names of Government Bodies, Employees, National and International Regions, Documents

1. **Capitalize these items, *except* when used in a general sense...**

   a. full and shortened names of national and international organizations, movements, and alliances and members of political parties.

   - Republican Party; Republican platform; republican voters
   - Democratic Party; Democratic platform; democratic voters
   - Communist Party; Communist bloc; communism; Bolshevik; Bolshevists
   - Federalist Party; Federalist; Russian Federation; Supreme Soviet

   b. full and shortened names of US national governmental and military bodies.

   - US Government; the Federal Government; government workers
   - US Congress, Congress; House of Representatives, the House; executive branch
   - United States Air Force, Air Force; US Navy, Navy; Marine Corps, the corps

- Department of Defense (DoD), Defense Department; Department of the Air Force
- armed forces, armed services; Joint Chiefs of Staff, the joint chiefs
- Air National Guard, the Guard; Air Force Reserve, reserve officer, reservist

c. titles of government employees.
- US President, the President, Presidential campaign, commander in chief
- Congressman Jones, a congressman; Senator Smith, a senator
- Secretary of State, Russian President, British Prime Minister
- Navy officer; naval officer; service chiefs; chief of staff

d. full titles of departments, directorates and similar organizations.
- Department of Labor, the department
- Directorate of Education, the directorate
- Air War College, the college
- Squadron Officer School, the school

e. full titles of armies, navies, air forces, fleets, regiments, battalions, companies, corps, etc., but lowercase *army*, *navy*, *air force*, etc., when part of a general title for other countries.
- United States Air Force, the Air Force; the Navy's air force
- Continental army; Union army; Fifth Army; the Eighth; the army
- Royal Air Force; British air force; British navy; the navy
- People's Liberation Army; Red China's army; the army

f. full names of judicial bodies.
- Supreme Court, the Court; California Supreme Court, state supreme court
- Fifth Circuit Court, circuit court; Montgomery County Court, the county court

2. **Capitalize *Marine* according to logical fit: If *Army*, *Navy*, or *Air Force* can be used logically for *Marines*, use *M*. If the word *soldier* or *soldiers* logically fits it, use *m*.**
- Michael Johnson enlisted in the Marines; a company of Marines
- three marines led the charge…

Names of State and Local Government Bodies

1. **Capitalize the full names of state and local bodies and organizations, but not the shortened names unless mentioned with the name of the city, county or state.**
- Virginia Assembly; the assembly
- Montgomery County Board of Health; the board of health will …

2. **Capitalize the word *state* only when it follows the name of a state or is part of an imaginative name.**

    - New York State is called the Empire State.
    - The state of Alaska is the largest in the Union.
    - After an assignment overseas, we returned to the States.

3. **Capitalize the word *city* only when it is part of the corporate name of the city or part of an imaginative name.**

    - Kansas City; the city of Cleveland, Ohio, is …
    - Chicago is the Windy City; Philadelphia, the City of Brotherly Love

4. **Capitalize *empire*, *state*, *country*, etc., when they follow words that show political divisions of the world, a county, a state, a city, etc., if they form an accepted part of it; lowercase if it precedes the name or stands alone.**

    - 11th Congressional District, his congressional district
    - Fifth Ward, the ward
    - Roman Empire, the empire
    - Washington State, the state of Washington

Acts, Amendments, Bills, Laws, Publications, Treaties, Wars

Capitalize the titles of official acts, amendments, bills, laws, publications, treaties and wars, but not the common nouns or shortened forms that refer to them.

- National Security Act of 1947; Second Amendment
- Immigration Reform Bill; Sherman Anti-trust Law
- Air Force Manual 33-326; the manual
- Treaty of Versailles; the treaty
- World War II, WWII; the two world wars

Programs, Movements, Concepts

1. **Capitalize the names of programs, movements, or concepts when used as proper nouns, but not when used in a general sense or latter day designations.**

    - Medicare Act; medicare payments
    - Civil Rights Act; a civil rights leader
    - Socialist Labor Party; socialism
    - Veterans Administration; veteran benefits
    - the New Deal, the New Frontier, the Great Society; the War on Poverty

    NOTE: Also capitalize their *imaginative* or common names.

2. **Capitalize terms like *republican, democrat, socialist* and *communist* when they signify formal membership in a political party, but not when they merely signify belief in a certain philosophy.**
   - a lifelong democrat [person who believes in the principles of democracy]
   - a lifelong Democrat [person who consistently votes for the Democratic Party]
   - a lifelong independent [person who believes in examining people/issues on their merits and independent from any other political party alignment]
   - a lifelong Independent [person who aligns with the Independent Party movement]
   - the right wing; the left wing

3. **Do not capitalize nouns and adjectives showing political and economic systems of thought and their proponents, except when derived from a proper noun.**
   - communism, communist; fascism, fascist; socialism, socialist
   - Bolshevism, Marxism-Leninism

Military Rank, Medals, Awards

1. **Capitalize military rank when it is used with a proper name, but not when it stands alone.**
   - Colonel Larry D. Grant and his secretary, Linda Wilson; the colonel
   - We have 30 majors and 26 lieutenant colonels.
   - She's a staff sergeant in the Air Force.

   NOTE: After initially identifying by full grade and name, use only the surname with the short grade title. Do not mix abbreviations with full words (Lt Col, not Lt Colonel).
   - Brigadier General Richard S. Glenn then General, Brig Gen, Gen Glenn
   - Master Sergeant Stephanie Reed then MSgt or Sergeant Reed
   - Chief Master Sergeant Susan Sharp then CMSgt or Chief Sharp

2. **Capitalize specific names of medals and awards.**
   - Medals: Medal of Honor; Legion of Merit; Purple Heart
   - Awards: Nobel Prize; Pulitzer Prize; Oscars and Emmys

Titles

1. **Capitalize official titles of honor and respect when being used with a proper name or in place of a specific proper name.**
   a. national officials such as the President, Vice President, cabinet members, the heads of government agencies, and bureaus.
      - President Adams; Vice President Smith
      - Secretary of State; Secretary of Defense; Attorney General…

- Director of National Intelligence; Director of the Federal Bureau of Investigation
- Chief Justice of the Supreme Court

b. state officials.
- the Governor; the Lieutenant Governor
- the attorney general; the senator

c. foreign dignitaries.
- the Queen (of England); the Prince of Wales
- Prime Minister
- The Chancellor

d. international figures.
- the Pope
- the Secretary General of the United Nations.

2. **Capitalize any title (even if not of high rank) when it is used in direct address, except *madam*, *miss*, or *sir* if it stands alone without a proper name following.**
- Please tell me, Colonel, what risks are involved in this campaign.
- I need to take some leave today, sir.
- I asked the colonel what risks were involved in this campaign.

3. **Also capitalize imaginative names used to refer to specific organizations.**
- Big Blue [IBM]
- Ma Bell [AT&T]
- the Baby Bells [the US regional phone companies]
- the Big Board [the NY Stock Exchange]

4. **Do not capitalize:**

a. organization officials.
- The commander will visit ...
- The committee's meeting minutes were read and approved.

b. job titles when they stand alone (e.g., "Marion Conroy has been promoted to the position of senior accountant.").

c. general terms of classification.
- The Commandant of ACSC; an intermediate service school commandant, ...
- Have your director of research call me.
- Squadron Leader David Jones of the Royal Air Force

- Samuel A. South, USAF, Retired, went …; Samuel A. South retired from …
- The 2d Security Forces Squadron Commander; the squadron commander
- United States senator; a state governor
- every king; any ambassador

d. *former*, *late*, *ex-* or *-elect* when used with titles.

- the late President Truman
- ex-President Clinton
- Mayor-elect Bawley

e. family titles when preceded by *my*, *your*, *his*, *her*, *our* and *their* when used to describe a family relationship.

- Let me ask my mother and dad if that date is open for them.
- Do you think your brother Bobby would like to meet my sister Fern?
- Frank wants us to meet his Uncle John. ["Uncle John" used as a proper noun.]
- Frank wants us to meet his uncle, John Cunningham.

f. *the* at the beginning of a title, except when actually part of the title or when used as part of an official name or title at the Secretariat or Air Staff level (e.g., *The New York Times*; The Adjutant General; The Inspector General).

g. titles that follow a personal name or used in place of a personal name.

(1) departments within an organization.

- The Air War College quarterly award winners are Debbie Baumayr, dean of education secretary, and Joan Parten, human resource advisor.
- I'm applying for a job in your Directorate of Education and Curriculum.
- The vacancy in our directorate has been filled.

(2) local governmental officials and those of lesser federal and state, except in writing intended for a limited readership where the intended reader would consider the official to be of high rank.

- Francis Fahey, mayor of Coventry, Rhode Island, appeared before a House committee today. The mayor spoke forcefully about the national news service release.
- The Mayor promised only last fall to hold the city sales tax at its present level. [editorial in a local newspaper.]
- I would like to request an appointment with the Attorney General. [memo to the state attorney general's office.]

Colleges, Universities, Organizations, Committees, Agencies

Capitalize the proper names of colleges, universities, organizations, committees and agencies, but not the common nouns that refer to them.

- The Air University; the university
- Veterans Administration; the administration
- 42d Air Base Wing; the wing
- the National Security Agency; the agency

NOTE: When using the abbreviated form of a numbered organization (e.g., ABW versus Air Base Wing), do not use *th*, *st*, or *d* with the number. When writing it out in its entirety add the *th*, *st*, or *d* to the number (e.g., either "42d Air Base Wing" or "42 ABW")

NOTE: The *preferred* style is to use the long method in written text and the shortened method in address elements, charts, graphs, notes and bibliography.

- Maxwell Air Force Base, Alabama, has … or Maxwell AFB, Alabama, is …
- Maxwell AFB AL 36112-3648 or HQ USAF CO 80840-6254 [address use only]
- Maxwell AFB, AL (or "Ala.") [notes or bibliography]

Academic Degrees, Course Titles, and Subjects

1. **Capitalize the names of specific course titles, but not areas of study.**

    - American History 201 meets on Tuesdays and Thursdays.
    - Esther is studying psychology and early childhood development.

2. **Capitalize academic degrees following a person's name and when the complete title of the degree is given, but not when they are used as general terms of classification.**

    - H. A. Schwartz, Doctor of Philosophy
    - Bachelor of Arts Degree in Literature; Master of Science Degree in Adult Education
    - BA, MA, PhD, LLD, MD, DDS, EdS
    - master's degree; bachelor's degree; bachelor of arts degree

Nouns with Numbers and Letters

Do not capitalize nouns followed by numbers or letters unless using full titles and then the first word and all-important words are capitalized.

- Not capitalized: annex A; appendix D; attachment 2; exhibit A; paragraph 3; tab 2; table 10; page 269; room 154; building 1403; volume 1; line 4; rule 3; chapter 5; article 2; chart 10; map 1; note 1; verse 3; part II; figure 7…
- Capitalized:
    - Annex A, Institutional Competency List
    - Chapter 14, The Official Memorandum

Compass Directions

1. **Capitalize compass directions when referring to specific regions or when the direction is part of a specific name, but not when merely indicating a general direction or location:**

    a. general direction/location.
    - East Montgomery; Eastern United States; West Alabama
    - travel north on Interstate 65 to exit 179 and go to the west side of town

    b. specific regions or a part of the world.
    - vacation in the Far East; they were raised in the Deep South
    - Northern Ireland; New England; Sun Belt; West Coast; North Pole
    - Central Europe; the Continent [Europe]
    - clouds forming in the south

    c. part of a specific name.
    - Southland Dairy Company
    - Northeast Manufacturing Corporation

2. **Capitalize words such as *northern*, *southern*, *eastern* and *western* when referring to people in a region and to their political, social or cultural activities, but not when merely indicating a general location or region.**
    - Southern hospitality; Midwesterner; Eastern bankers; the Northern vote
    - southern California; northern Maine

Celestial Bodies

Capitalize the names of planets, stars and constellations. However, do not capitalize the words *sun*, *moon* and *earth* unless they are used with the capitalized names of other planets or stars.

- He traveled to the ends of the earth seeking a way climb to the sun.
- The Earth is small compared to Jupiter and Saturn.

Days of the Week, Months, Holidays, Events, Periods, Seasons

Capitalize the days of the week, months, holidays, historic events and periods. Do not capitalize seasons or latter-day designations.

- Sunday; Monday
- January; February
- Veterans Day; New Year's Day
- Battle of the Bulge; Battle of Britain; World War II

- Roaring Twenties; Roaring 20s. *The numerical designation of an era is lowercase if it is not part of a proper noun (e.g., twenty-first century, the nineteen hundreds).*
- Dark Ages; Middle Ages; Ice Age
- spring, summer, fall, winter
- age of steam; nuclear age; space age; rocket age

Races, Peoples, Languages

Capitalize races, peoples and languages.

- Races: the Sioux; African-American; black; Caucasian; white
- Peoples: Hispanic; Latin American; Mexican
- Languages: Mandarin Chinese; English; French; Finnish; German

Commercial Products

Capitalize trade names, variety names and names of market grades and brands, but not the common nouns following such names.

- Trade name with common noun: Elmer's glue; Scotch tape, Ivory soap, Pepsi cola
- Variety names: McIntosh apples; American Beauty rose; USDA Choice beef
- Brand name: Xerox; Pepsi, Coke or Coca-Cola
- Brand name that capitalizes common noun: Krazy Glue

Religious References

1. **Capitalize all references to a supreme being.**
   - God; the Almighty; Yahweh; the Lord; the Holy Spirit; the Messiah
   - the Supreme Being; Allah

2. **Capitalize personal pronouns referring to a supreme being when they stand alone, without an antecedent nearby.**
   - Give praise unto Him; thus said the Lord; into His loving care
   - My Father; grant us Thy mercy; Our Father

3. **Capitalize references to persons revered as divine.**
   - the Apostles; Saint Peter; John the Baptist
   - Buddha
   - the Prophet

4. **Capitalize the names of religions, their members and their buildings.**
   - Names: Christianity, Judaism, Islam, Buddhism (broad religions)
   - Names: Methodist, Baptist, Catholic (denominations) or Sunni, Shia (sects)

- Members: Christians, Jews, Muslims, Buddhists
- Buildings: Saint Mark's Episcopal Church; Temple Beth Shalom
- the Roman Catholic Church [the entire institution]
- the Roman Catholic church on Bell Road [indefinite reference to a specific building]

5. **Capitalize references to religious events.**
   - the Creation; the Flood; the Exodus; the Crucifixion; the Resurrection
   - Birth of Mohammad

6. **Capitalize names of religious holidays.**
   - Christmas; Easter; Yom Kippur; Hanukkah
   - Eid Al-Fitr; Eid Al-Adha

7. **In general, do not capitalize references to specific religious observances and services.**
   - bar mitzvah; seder; baptism; christening
   - Some exceptions: the Eucharist; the Mass; the Hajj

8. **Capitalize (do not quote or underscore) references to works regarded as sacred.**
   - the Bible; the Talmud; the Torah; Kaddish; the Koran
   - the Old Testament; the New Testament
   - the Ten Commandments; the Lord's Prayer; the Apostle's Creed…
   - the Revised Standard Version; the New International Version…
   - the Book of Genesis; Philippians 1:3; Psalms 23; Joshua 9: 1-5
   - Exception: "biblical sources" used to refer to general sources from the Bible

CHAPTER 28:

Numbers

This chapter covers:
- Three General Rules
- Specific Guidance
- Summing things up

It is impossible to establish a single rule for the consistent use of numbers in documents—the editors of *The Tongue and Quill* and other style guides have tried. When expressing numbers, keep in mind the significant difference in the appearance of numbers. Figures will grab your attention immediately because they stand out more clearly from the surrounding words, while numbers expressed in words are unemphatic and look like the rest of the words in the sentence. The bottom line for the numbers is this: **figures emphasize; words de-emphasize.**

Three General Rules

The following guidelines cover the preferred Air Force style of expressing numbers. Remember, however, that personal and organizational preference and appearance may override these guidelines. If your organization has a preferred style—use it. If not, read on for three general rules on the use of numbers.

1. In **general**, numbers 10 and above should be expressed in figures, and numbers one through nine should be expressed in words.

2. In **scientific and statistical material**, all numbers are expressed in figures.

3. In high-level **executive correspondence** and **nontechnical, formal,** or **literary manuscripts, citations, decorations, memorandums to the general, textbooks and articles**, spell out all numbers through one hundred and all round numbers that can be expressed in two words (one hundred, five thousand, forty-five hundred). All other numbers are written in figures (514). For tables, charts, and detailed statistical data, use figures (not words).

Specific Guidance

Numbers Expressed as Figures: Almost always

The following categories are almost always expressed in figures, *unless used in high-level executive correspondence and nontechnical, formal, or literary manuscripts.* The categories with a bold pointer (◄) are to be spelled out if included in high-level executive correspondence and nontechnical, formal, or literary manuscripts. Finally, when you abbreviate a unit of measure in a unit modifier, do not use a hyphen.

Time ◄

- payable in 30 days
- waiting 3 hours
- 15 minutes later

Age ◄

- a 3-year-old horse
- a boy 6 years old
- a 19-year-old woman

Clock Time

- at 9:30 a.m. Eastern Standard Time
- at 3:15 p.m. Greenwich Mean Time (1515 Z).
- no later than 6 o'clock [do not use a.m. or p.m. with o'clock]
- must be completed by 0800 [do not use the word hours when expressing military time]

Money

- a $20 bill; $3 a pound; $5,000 to $10,000 worth; $2 million; $9.00 and $10.54 purchases
- The candy costs 75 cents [If the sentence contains other monetary amounts requiring the dollar sign, use $.75]
- a check for $125 [if sentence contains other monetary amounts requiring the cents, use $125.00]
- US $10,000   10,000 US dollars
- Can $10,000   10,000 Canadian dollars
- DM 10,000   10,000 German deutsche marks
- £10,000   10,000 British pounds
- ¥10,000   10,0000 Japanese yen

Measurements ◄

- 110 meters long
- 5,280 feet
- 23 nautical miles
- 2 feet by 1 foot 8 inches
- 8 1/2- by 11-inch paper
- 200 horsepower

CHAPTER 28
Numbers

Dates

- 5 June 2004 or 5 Jun 04 [when abbreviating the month, also abbreviate the year]
- 21st of July
- Fiscal Year 2004, FY04, the fiscal year
- Academic Year 2003, AY03, the academic year
- from 4 April to 20 June 2005
- Class of 2004 or Class of '04
- July, August and September 2004
- on the 13th send it to

Dimensions, Sizes, Temperatures

- a room 4 by 5 meters
- a 15- by 30-foot room
- size 6 tennis shoes
- thermometer reads 16 degrees

Percentages, Ratios, Proportions, Scores, Voting Results

- a 6 percent discount [use % in technical writing, graphs, charts]
- a 50-50 chance
- Alabama 14, Auburn 17
- a vote of 17 to 6
- a proportion of 5 to 1; a 5-to-1 ratio
- 20/20 or twenty-twenty vision
- an evaluation of 85

Latitude and Longitude

1. In nontechnical text:
   - the polar latitudes
   - from 10°20′ north latitude to 10°20′ south latitude
   - longitude 50° west
2. In technical work and tables:
   - lat 32°25′20″ N, long 85°27′60″ W
   - The map showed the eye of the hurricane to be at 32°25′60″ N, 85°27′60″ W.

Numbers Referred to as Numbers and Mathematical Expressions

- pick a number from 1 to 10
- multiply by 1/4
- number 7 is considered lucky
- No. 1—You're No. 1 in my book.

Abbreviations, Symbols, Serial Numbers, Document Identifiers

- $25
- paragraph 3
- serial number 0958760
- lines 5 and 13
- 46-48 AD
- attachment 2
- Proverbs 3:5-7
- pages 273-278

Unit Modifiers And Hyphenations ◄

- 5-day week
- 110-metric-ton engine
- 1 1/2-inch pipe; 1½-inch pipe; not 1-1/2
- 8-year-old car
- 10-foot pole

Numbers Expressed as Figures: Numbers in a related series

When a sentence contains numbers used in a related series and any number in the series is 10 or more, express all numbers in the series in figures (except the first word of the sentence if it is a number or if included in high-level executive correspondence and nontechnical, formal, or literary manuscripts◄). When a number is always a figure, it doesn't change the other numbers to figures in the same sentence.

- Six children ate 9 hamburgers, 14 hot dogs and 6 Popsicles.
- Our office has five officers, two sergeants and six civilians.
- Our office, which is only 200 square feet, contains five desks, nine chairs, two bookcases and five people.

Numbers Expressed as Figures: Numerical designations of military units

1. Air Force units. Use figures to designate units up to and including wings. Use figures for numbered air forces only if using the abbreviation AF.

   - 19th Logistics Group; 19 LG [but "19TH LOGISTIC GROUP" on address label]
   - 18th Wing; 18 WG
   - Ninth Air Force, 9 AF
   - 79th Fighter Squadron; 79 FS
   - 42d Mission Support, 42 MSS

   NOTE: Keep in mind when you abbreviate the organizational name (CSG, TFW, AD, AF, etc.) do not use *th*, *st*, or *d* with the number.

2. Army units. Use figures to designate all army units except corps and numbered armies. Use Roman numerals for corps and spell out numbered armies.

   - 2d Army Group
   - III Corps
   - 7th AAA Brigade
   - First Army
   - 2d Infantry Division
   - 92d Infantry Regiment

3. Marine Corps units. Apply same rules as army units.
4. Navy units. Use figures to designate all navy units except fleet.
    - Seventh Fleet
    - Carrier Group 8
    - VF31

Numbers Expressed as Figures: Making figures plural

Numbers expressed in figures are made plural by adding *s* alone. To plural a number used as part of a noun, place the *s* on the noun and not the number: DD Forms 282; but "file the 282s."

- in the 1990s
- temperature in the 80s
- four 10s in the deck
- two F-16s at the base

Numbers Expressed in Words

General rule

Spell out numbers from 1 through 9; use figures for numbers 10 and above in ordinary correspondence.

- I need nine copies of this article.
- At the conference, we got over 11 comments to start a new ...

Numbers that introduce sentences

Spell out numbers that introduce sentences. A spelled out number should not be repeated in figures (except in legal documents).

- Twelve people volunteered for the job; not twelve (12) people ...
- Eight children participated in the relay race.

Related numbers close together

Related numbers appearing at the beginning of a sentence, separated by no more than three words, are treated alike.

- Fifty or sixty miles is the nearest gas station.
- Five to ten people will probably respond.

NOTE: Related numbers in the same set are also treated alike.

- The $12,000,000 building had a $500,000 tower.
  [Not written as $12 million because of its relation to $500,000.]
- We mailed 50 invitations and only received 5 RSVPs.

Formal writing

Spell out numbers in formal writing and numbers used in proper names and titles along with serious and dignified subjects such as executive orders and legal proclamations.

- the Thirteen Colonies
- the first Ten Amendments
- The Seventy-eighth Congress
- threescore years and ten

Fractions

Spell out fractions that stand alone except with unit modifier.

- one-half of the vote; but 1/2-inch pipe (unit modifier) or ½-inch pipe
- six-tenths of a mile

NOTE: A mixed number (a whole number plus a fraction) is written in figures except at the beginning of a sentence.

- 1 1/2 miles; 1½ miles; not 1-1/2 miles
- One and a half miles

Compound modifiers

Spell out compound modifiers and numbers of 100 or less that precede hyphenated numbers.

- three 10-foot poles; two 4-hour sorties; 120 1-gallon cans
- one hundred 1-gallon cans; twenty 5-year-old children
- three 1 1/2-inch pipes (preferred); three 1½-inch pipes

Rounded and indefinite numbers

Spell out rounded and indefinite numbers.

- the early nineties; but the early 1990s
- the twentieth century; nineteenth-century business customs
- hundreds of customers; approximately six thousand soldiers; a woman in her fifties

For style and grasp

For typographic appearance and easy grasp of large numbers beginning with million, use words to indicate the amount rather than 0s (unless used with a related number).

- $12 million; 2 1/2 billion (preferred) or 2½ billion; $2.7 trillion
- $6,000,000 and 300,000 troops later… (not $6 million and 300,000 troops later…)
- $300,000 (not $300 thousand)

Forming plurals of numbers as words

Form the plurals of spelled-out numbers as you would the plurals of other nouns—by adding s, es or changing the y to i and adding es.

- ones; twos, sixes
- twenties; fifties; nineties

Numbers: Making sense of the rules for words and figures

Now that you have seen the general and specific rules for using figures or words for numbers you may be asking if there is an easier way to make sense of the rules. The broadest general rule is "always express numbers as figures unless the number starts the sentence, or unless the use of figures would confuse the reader or would look weird." While this notion makes sense, it does not help you when your numbers, words and figures are all running together. Sometimes specific rules are just what you need.

Roman Numerals

Roman numerals are used frequently in modern times. In uppercase form they identify the major sections of an outline; in lowercase italics form they number the front matter (table of contents, forward, preface, dedication, etc.) of research papers and books. The uppercase Roman numerals are presented in the table, below, alongside their Arabic equivalent. A dash above a Roman numeral (e.g., "$\overline{V}$") is 1,000 greater than the numeral without the dash above (e.g., "V").

Roman Numerals and Arabic Equivalents

I	1	XXIX	29	LXXV	75	DC	600
II	2	XXX	30	LXXIX	79	DCC	700
III	3	XXXV	35	LXXX	80	DCCC	800
IV	4	XXXIX	39	LXXXV	85	CM	900
V	5	XL	40	LXXXIX	89	M	1,000
VI	6	XLV	45	XC	90	MD	1,500
VII	7	XLIX	49	XCV	95	MM	2,000
VIII	8	L	50	XCIX	99	M$\overline{V}$	4,000
IX	9	LV	55	C	100	$\overline{V}$	5,000
X	10	LIX	59	CL	150	$\overline{X}$	10,000
XV	15	LX	60	CC	200	$\overline{L}$	50,000
XIX	19	LXV	65	CCC	300	$\overline{C}$	100,000
XX	20	LXIX	69	CD	400	D	500,000
XXV	25	LXX	70	D	500	M	1,000,000

Other Combinations of Roman Numerals

Other Roman numerals are derived by prefixing or annexing letters. Prefixing a letter is subtracts the value of that letter, while annexing adds the value. For example, 40 is L minus X = XL; 45 is L minus X plus V = XLV; and 60 is L plus X = LX.

Roman Numeral as Years

The other combinations of Roman numerals allows you to express complex dates, such as years, with strings of letters that sometimes have fewer characters than their Arabic equivalent, but sometimes there are many more—and performing math functions is difficult compared to the Arabic forms where places have specific values (i.e., ones, tens, hundreds, etc.)

- 1600 = MDC
- 1900 = MCM
- 1947 = MCMXLVII
- 1999 = MCMXCIX
- 2000 = MM
- 2014 = MMXIV
- 2015 = MMXV

Summing Things Up

This chapter has covered many, but not all, uses of numbers in Air Force documents. If you keep your documents focused (recall the FOCUS principles discussed in chapter 1) then the formats for the components of your documents should support your focus. If something is detracting from that focus—fix it. The standards presented here are best practice—use them to be your best!

Made in the USA
Lexington, KY
01 October 2018